THE GUN DIGEST BOOK OF
SPORTING DOGS

By Carl P. Wood

Edited by Jack Lewis

DBI BOOKS, INC.

I would like to dedicate this book to Ivy. I only had to write it, she had to put up with me while I wrote it.

Publisher
Sheldon Factor

Editorial Director
Jack Lewis

Art Director
Sonya Kaiser

Art Assistant
Kathy Ryan

Copy Editor
Shelby Pooler

Production
Yinet Gonzalez

Cover Photo
John R. Falk

Produced by

Arms and Armour Press, London, G.B., exclusive licensees and distributors in Britain and Europe, Australasia, Nigeria, So. Africa and Zimbabwe, India and Pakistan; Singapore, Hong Kong and Japan.

ISBN: 0-910676-72-0

Library of Congress Catalog Card Number: 84-062678

CONTENTS

INTRODUCTION

There are probably as many approaches to dog training as there are dog trainers. Nearly all of us use certain proven techniques in the beginning, copying those of others who have been successful in the field. But, as time goes by, we add to these techniques, incorporating our own tricks of the trade that have been learned through trial and error.

Dogs are like people, I've found. They come in all sorts of temperaments and what might work in training with one dog does not necessarily prove successful with another. Thus, the ideas I have tried to impart in this book are based upon my own experiences. I know there are dog trainers who will not agree. For example, I believe in having my hunting dogs in my house as much as possible. My feeling is that such close association builds a close comradery. But I also can show you trainers who feel that allowing a dog in the home is the cardinal sin following the old military tradition that "familiarity breeds contempt."

All I can say is that I have found the training methods herein work for me. They also work for others to whom I have introduced them. I can only hope they will prove successful for you, too.

I must acknowledge Doug Catlett, Bunny Pease and Dan and Bernice Carter for their help, as well as members of the Potomac Chapter of the NAVHDA and Ed and Pete Bailey who introduced me to the organization. Bodo Winterhelt, who taught me so much, and Jane Popham of the Purina Company also must be thanked for their contributions.

Finally, I owe a debt of gratitude to Jack Lewis, who spent more than two years advising me and wading through parts of this manuscript, and to Sonya Kaiser, who turned it into the form you see here.

Carl P. Wood

Carl P. Wood,
Falling Waters, West Virginia

Chapter 1

EARLY MAN, EARLY DOGS

THE BONES of man and dog are intermingled in middens dating as far back as the Neolithic. This would indicate that dogs had been domesticated this long ago and there is considerable evidence that the association — perhaps I should say unique, almost symbiotic relationship — between the two species goes back much farther. Dog bones are indicated in association with early human remains found in scientific digs on early sites in Africa.

Cynological, or dog, evolution has been traced as far as the Eocene epoch where a wee beastie that somewhat resembled the European polecat (not to be confused with the American skunk often erroneously called a polecat) or the North American fisher lived. This little fellow, known as Miacis, was the ancestor of Cynodictis that in turn was ancestor to both dogs and cats. Being the ancestor to both dogs and cats may possibly have given Cynodictis a split-personality complex. In any event, it appears that Cyno-

Artist's impression of the Neanderthal Man shows what he considered to be dogs of the era, but the likelihood is that these animals were considerably larger, with a heavier muzzle during that beginning period of history.

The Bettmann Archive

The Relationship Has Grown From The Days Of The Caveman

This artist's rendition of male and female Greek greyhounds dates to Second Century A.D.

dictis' descendants — after having branched off into both the bear and cat families as well as hyenas and civets — evolved into Cynodesmus, a somewhat less small beast that in turn fathered the raccoon and weasel families as well as Tomarctus, an even more formidable beastie that developed into the Fennec fox, and African hunting dog families. It also was the progenitor of the true canine genus which is composed of coyotes, jackals, wolves, and our true friend *Canis familiaris,* the modern dog.

When I was studying biology in high school, the dog was *Canis domesticus,* but I suppose the people who are responsible for such things have ample reason for making such changes, if only to keep the layman from having any correct knowledge of such arcane matters.

There is some indication that in the near future the jackal and coyote may be placed in separate genera as was the case with the fox, which suddenly ceased to be *Canis vulpes* and became *Vulpes vulpes*. Further contributing to the need for separate genus classfications is the establishment of many variants in separate localities by the coyote. Taxonomical rules would seem to dictate that the coyote should indeed be considered a separate family.

Another problem — encountered to greater or lesser extent in any species with which man has carried on extensive breeding programs — is the great variations found between the many man-made breeds. Taxonomical classification depends to a great extent on skull formation. The differences in skull shapes among the many different breeds developed by man are much greater than those between, for example, dogs and foxes. A taxonomist who was not

These four dogs, recreated from limestone carvings of Antefaa, Twelfth Dynasty, were from 2000 B.C. era.

aware of the breeding histories of the pit bull and the collie, chow, foxhound, and Pekinese, if suddenly confronted with the skulls of these breeds, would without hesitation identify them as different species and perhaps different genus.

Knowing the histories of these breeds is the only thing that keeps them identified as *Canis familiaris.* Different species are the result of natural breeding patterns. Breeds are the result of man's breeding programs. I am not qualified to say this is correct classification, but it is certainly food for thought.

It is widely believed that the wolf, *Canis lupus,* is the progenitor of all modern breeds of the dog. Recently, however, there has been some considerable thought given to the dingo, *Canis dingo,* with some authorities believing that the dingo was an early dog that was present when Australia was isolated. Others believe the dingo is a regressive, but formerly domesticated, animal that was brought to Australia by the ancestors of the Bushmen in their migration down the islands from Asia. If the dingo was indeed present when Australia was first isolated, it pushes the origin of the true dog back much earlier than presently is believed by current authorities. Perhaps the most famous wild "dogs" are the African wild dogs, sometimes known

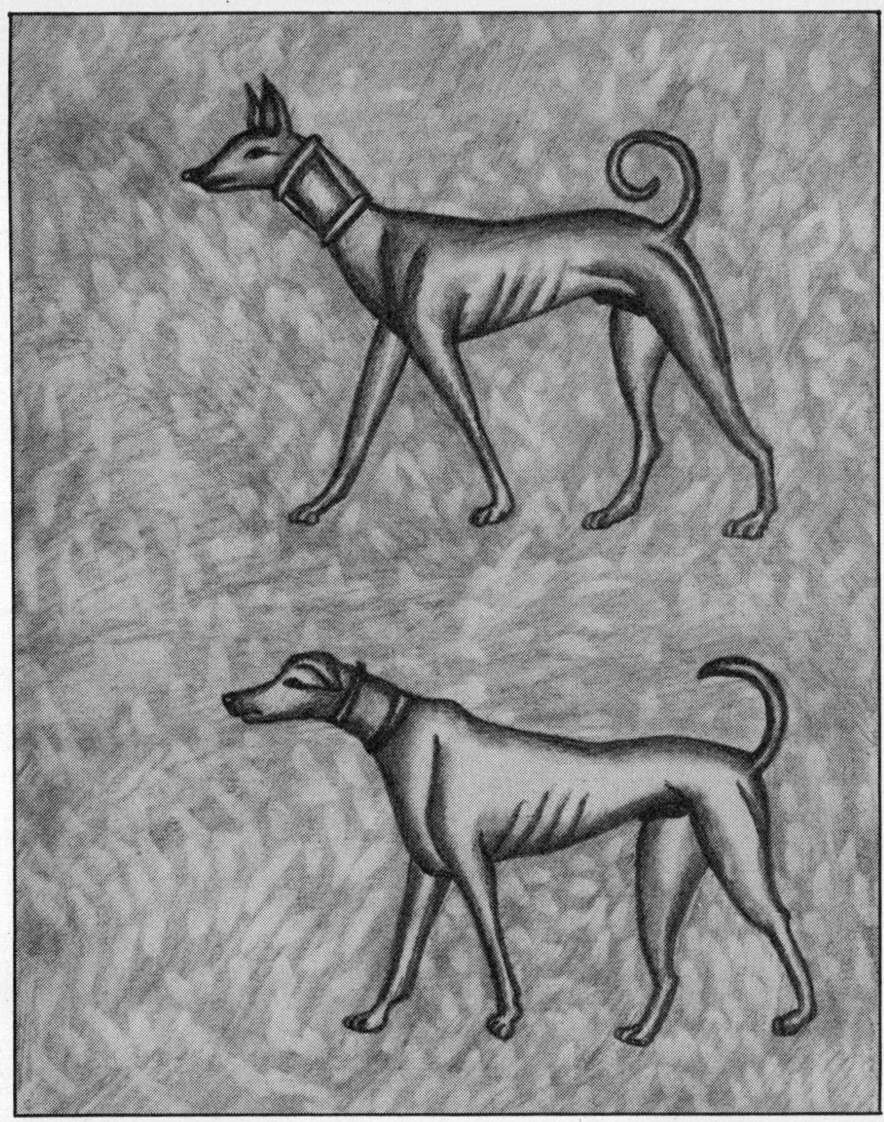

The greyhound at top has pointed ears and a restraining collar. Lower dog is of the same breed, but has floppy ears and a tail similar to today's.

as Cape hunting dogs. These are not true dogs, but closely related to the hyena. There are many species of wild dogs throughout the world, each of these species an interesting story in itself.

We will never know the exact circumstances of the first mutual friendship between man and dog. We can, however, come up with some pretty good estimates. In all likelihood the scenario goes something like this:

Og had been the only survivor of a raid on his tribe by another group of troglodites. He had been banged about a bit in the fight in which all the other adult males in his group had been killed, the women captured. He had managed to hide in the tall grass until the raiders had left, then traveled some distance to a cave with which he was familiar.

On reaching the cave, he found a litter of pups in a rear corner of the cave. He had knocked several on the head and eaten them, but allowed a pair of them to live as he had all he wanted to eat. He put the remaining two in a crevasse and built a rough wall of rocks to keep them from escaping until he was ready to eat them.

The luck of the chase favored Og and he had not found it necessary to use the dogs for food. He gave them scraps of food to keep them alive and a trickle of water furnished them with drink. After a time, the pups began to look forward to his returning from his forays.

Alone and missing the society of his friends, he began to take the pups out of the enclosure to play with them much as he had played with his own children before the raid. Soon the dogs became tame and Og started to take them along on short searches for food. On one such trip, they came unexpectedly upon a young antelope and when Og missed his throw with the spear the young dogs gave chase, bringing the animal to bay at the foot of a cliff. Og had followed the yapping of the dogs and this time he did not miss with the spear.

Realizing the value of the dogs as hunting companions, Og regularly took them along on his hunts and soon learned to place himself where the dogs would drive game to him.

One day, Og may have been surprised by two of the warriors of the tribe that had destroyed the rest of his clan and was nearly killed. He was saved only by the savage attack of the two dogs on his enemies which distracted them long enough for him to make his escape. Knowing he would now be hunted, Og could have ambushed the two enemies on their return to camp. He was successful in killing one of them, but the other escaped and Og knew that he would soon be back with more of his enemies.

Og returned to his cave and gathered up his few tools and weapons, then crossed the mountain into the territory of a tribe with whom his people had sometimes traded good flint for staves of a wood which made fine spear shafts.

Drawings, reproduced from the tombs of Beni Hassan, circa 2200 B.C., reflect the various breeds of Egyptian dogs. History shows that the Egyptians used crosses involving wolves, jackals and foxes in their breeding programs.

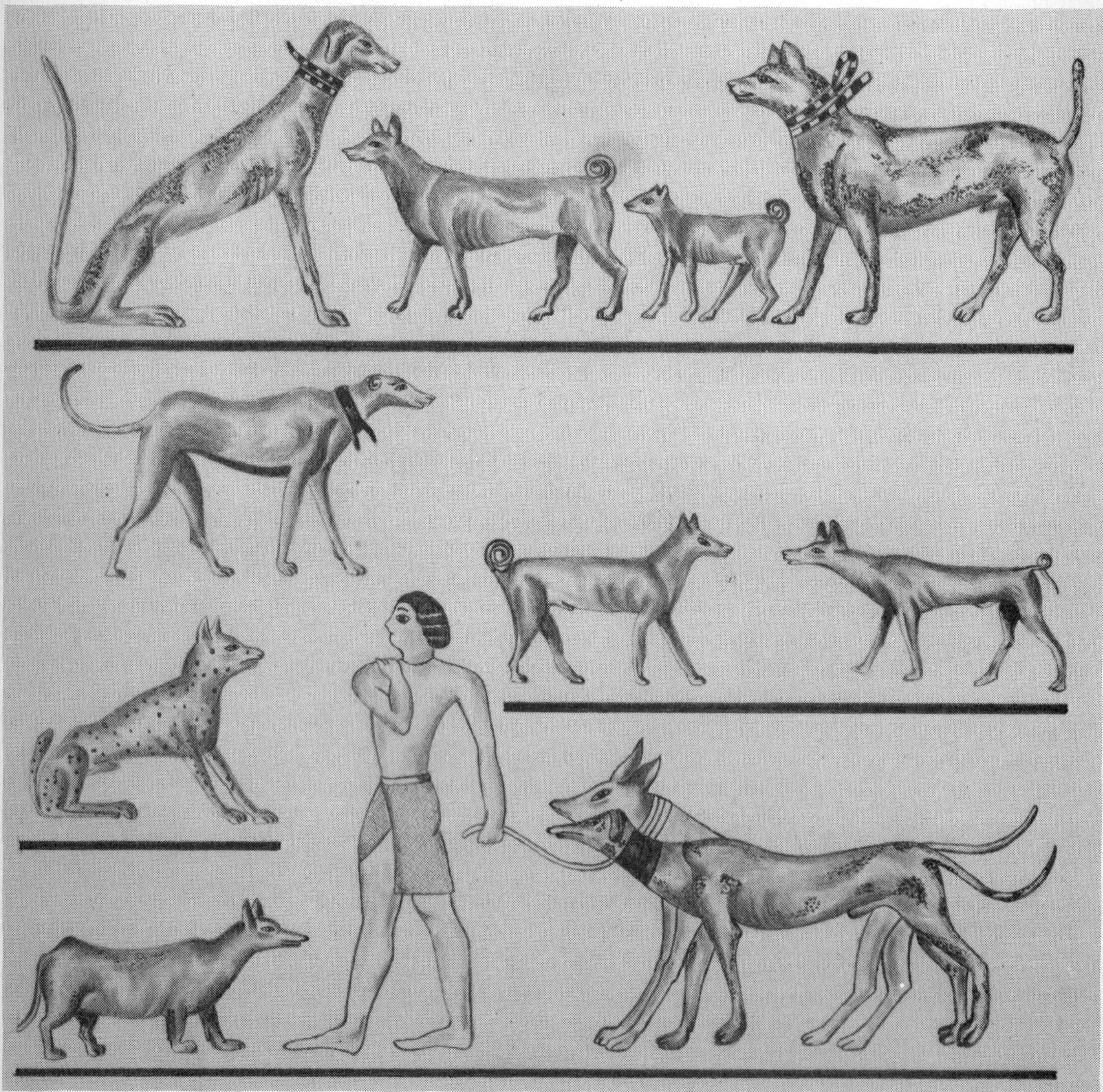

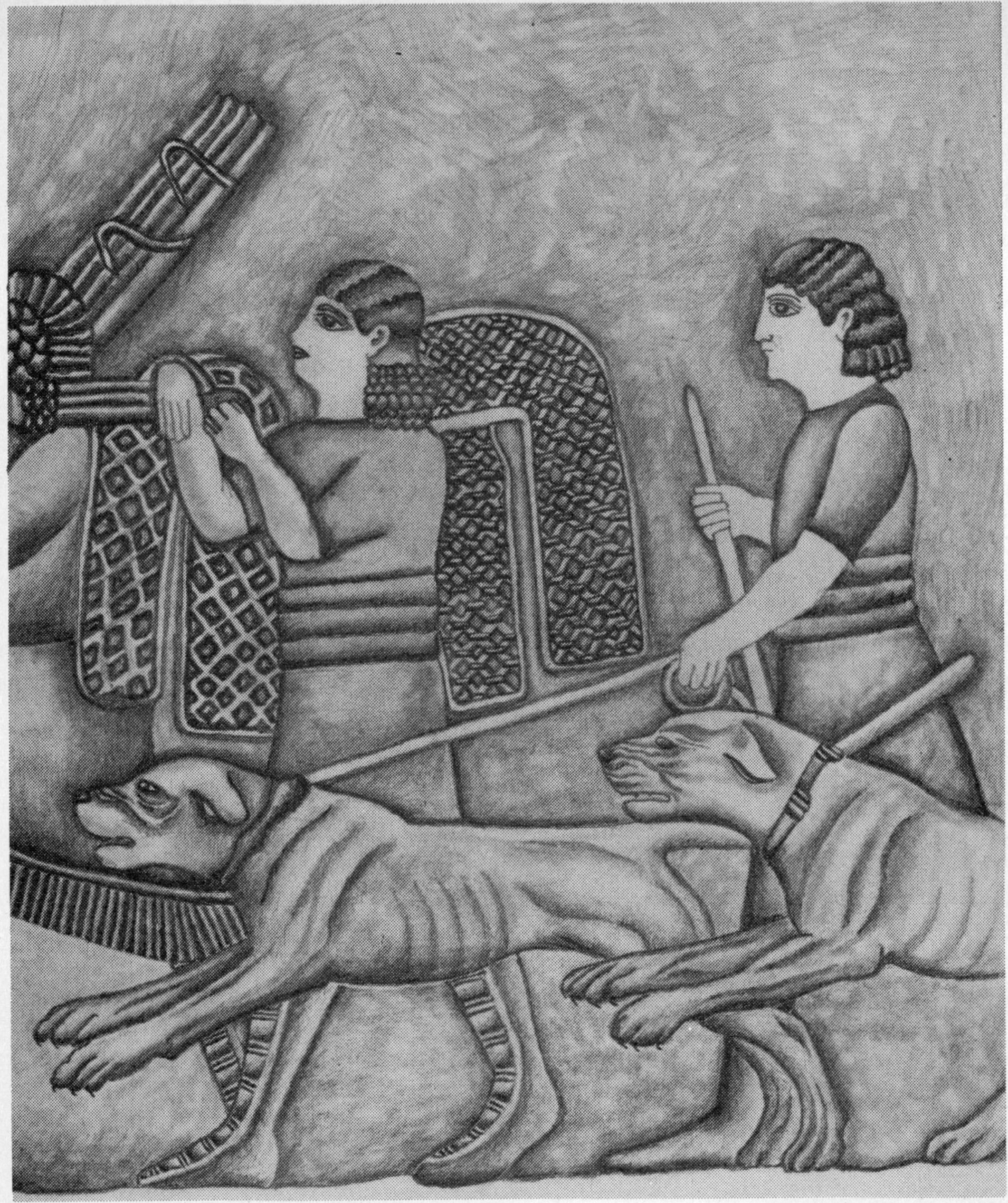

Enormous dogs of the mastiff type were bred by Assyrians in about 600 B.C. They were used for war and hunting lions and other large animals. This drawing has been reproduced from engraving on an uncovered stone frieze.

Though Og was careful in his approach to the strange tribesmen, he had great difficulty in getting them to accept the dogs. They were accepted only after a few of the more adventurous young hunters had accompanied him on a hunt in which they were able to kill several game animals the dogs brought to bay. The dogs also had been able to track a wounded animal over a stony ridge.

Suddenly it seemed everyone wanted dogs and there were many forays to capture live ones. The cavemen soon learned it did no good to capture fully grown dogs and they were successful only in taming a few of the young ones they caught.

Eventually, the female of Og's pair had pups and these were the foundation stock of the domesticated pack that allowed Og's adopted people to surpass the neighboring tribes and eventually control a large territory by virtue of having to spend less effort in hunting due to the use of the dogs. The time the dogs saved in hunting allowed these people to have more time for other activitites which in turn led to their becoming the dominant tribe in the area. Og may never have become a chief among his new people, but he must have been revered. In time, the practice of keeping dogs became widespread and this was the start of the unique relationship between man and dog.

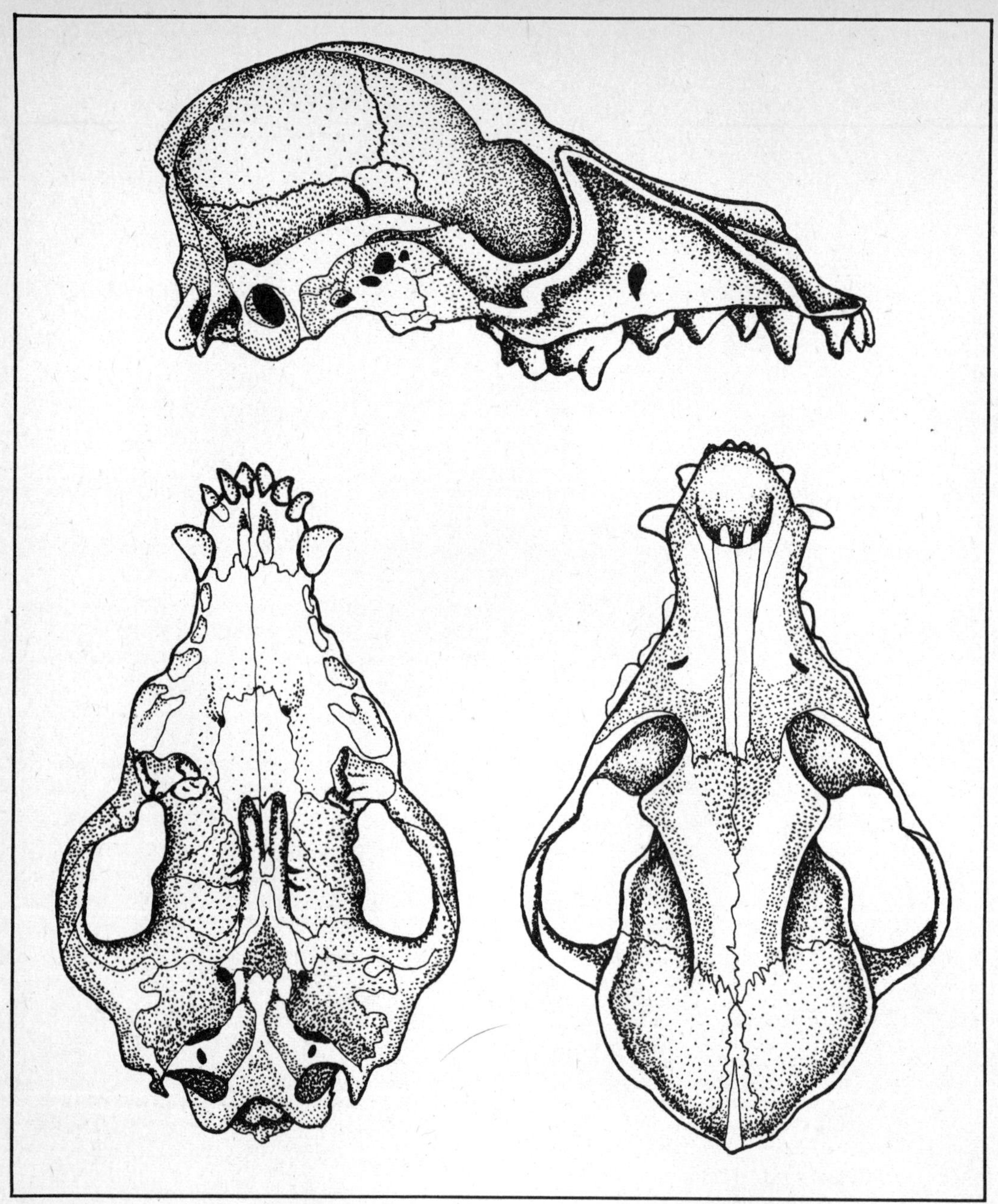

This series of drawings illustrates the skull construction of a domestic dog of more recent centuries. The dog's brain cavity has grown larger with breeding and passage of time.

The preceeding story is purely speculation, but it outlines what well may have happened in many different places and times.

By the time of the Ice Ages, man had tamed many different strains of dogs that could be useful to him. In addition to hunting and tracking, dogs were useful as sentries around the dwellings of early man. They also were considered fine food, especially for ceremonial use. An example of this is the use of the dog by American Indians. The Indians used the dogs as hunters, sentries, beasts of burden and food. Before the introduction of the horse, Indians used dogs to carry their belongings from one campsite to another on travois. Travois are simply poles fastened on each side of an animal by a belt or strap around the body, the other end dragging on the ground behind the animal. A platform or pouch between the two poles served as the cargo carrier.

There is substantial evidence that men were using different types of dogs for different purposes at an early time. Even the Egyptians seem to have stabilized certain breeds for different uses. There are household records of the Pharaohs accomplishing many hunting kills using dogs. We find similar records among the Assyrians. Many leading men in the earliest societies of which we have records kept detailed records of their hunting exploits with frequent mention of exceptional exploits of favorite dogs.

Drawings of Saluk-type hounds were found in the tomb of Rekhma Ra, who died about 1400 B.C. Note refined breed look.

As the early civilizations grew, the more easily trained dogs were trained for specific purposes such as herding, guarding and as burden bearers. A pack dog cannot carry so much weight as other beasts of burden, but it can go where no other such animal can or will go. Hunting dogs were soon divided into types and, although they were not known by the same names, we had the progenitors of setters and pointers, coursing dogs, flushing dogs and hounds.

The spaniel was the ancestor of many of our modern sporting breeds, valued highly in early times. King Howell of Wales established a code of laws in which the value of various breeds of dog, depending on the state of their training, was set forth. Among early hunting records that mention the various breeds then in use was *Livre de la Chasse,* written by Gaston de Foix in 1387. Dame Juliana Berners also mentions some of the early sporting breeds in her writings in the *Boke of Saint Albans* in 1483. Shakespeare writes of Mastiff, Greyhound, Mongrel, Hound, Spaniel, Brach, Lym, Bobtail Tikes and Trundle Tails.

The dog seemingly has been well thought of for most of man's known being and all of his recorded history. It is difficult for us to fully appreciate today just what an important place the dog filled in early societies.

Today we spend less than twenty percent of our time in obtaining enough food to live comfortably, in point of fact we here in the civilized Western world have too much food. Many of us are overweight as a result of too easily available rich foods. Contrast this with primitive societies where roughly eighty percent of an entire group's time was spent in procuring enough food for a bare existence. It is only when we fully understand this compelling daily need to go forth and find food enough for another day that we begin to see what a great help the scenting and tracking ability of the hunting dog was to such societies.

Understanding the above leads one to see why there has been such effort expended in developing the dog to fill the different needs of different peoples. Those living in open plains areas must have a dog that is fleet and able to overtake game, chasing it by sight. This gives rise to the coursing breeds such as the greyhound, wolfhound, afghan, whippet and deerhound. People living in an area of brushy hills or forested country must have a dog capable of following game unerringly from the scent the animal leaves behind, often never sighting the quarry until it catches up to it at the end of the chase. This need has given rise to breeds such as the bloodhound, which was the ancestor of many of the popular scent tracking hound breeds of today such as beagles, bassetts, foxhounds, coonhounds, et al.

Often there is a need for dogs capable of fighting and holding large animals until the hunter can catch up to the action. This has given us such breeds as the Plott and the Norwegian elkhound, to name only two of this type. In other areas, where the quarry is gamebirds there was the need to have a dog to locate and hold birds until the hunter could approach and throw a net over the birds as they huddled on the ground. Many English setters tend to crouch or drop to the ground when they point today to avoid a net that isn't there! Today, this is considered undesirable, but dogs formerly were bred for this trait. It is this inbred behavior that is surfacing when dogs act in this manner.

The dingo, a wild dog found in sections of Australia, is a throwback to the wild breeds of the late Stone Age.

Chapter 2

EARLY BREED DEVELOPMENT

Lack Of Historic Records Leaves A Void As To How Some Sporting Breeds Came To Be

THERE IS a great amount of evidence to show that various breeds of dog had been developed by the dawn of recorded history. The earliest of cuneiform writings that have been discovered and translated contain references to dogs and the hunting exploits of the great men of the time. The same holds true for Egyptian hieroglyphics and, in addition, there are pictorial records of the Pharoahs hunting with dogs. There is every reason to believe that, if we had some form of record from even earlier periods, we would find the same to be

This old print shows a spaniel type working as flush dog for waterfowl. Author contends this presents an enigma, as it shows traits of cocker, clumber and springer. It could be a portrait of a spaniel type that has been lost with time or just poorly drawn. He contends the muzzle is too slender for cocker, body too long for clumber and the legs too short for those of a springer as we think of the breed by the standards of modern-day breeding and conformation.

In English print circa 1686 by Barlow, the dogs appear to be springer spaniels that are only a little different than today's.

true, as the evidence indicates that dogs were being bred for specific purposes far before the earliest records came into being.

There really is little specific information as to the development of more than a few breeds before the medieval period. Prior to this time, the only existing records indicate herd, guard, coursing and hound types without much detail as to the appearance and character of these — with the sole exception of the long-legged coursing types followed by a Pharoah in a chariot. The crude drawings found of these have an appearance not too unlike a modern gazelle hound.

While there is reference to lion dogs and hounds in Greek and Roman literature, we do not find much breed information. Around 1570 A.D., the first serious listing of breeds was compiled. This work is by the founder of Caius College in Cambridge, England, Johannes Caius. There is a good deal of conflicting information written about this man in various recent books on dogs. I have not personally seen the original or even a copy of his work, *De Canibus Britannicis,* and probably couldn't read it if I had, so I will quote Jones and Hamilton in *The World Encyclopedia of Dogs,* a publication I have found to be highly reliable and authentic. Caius lists sixteen breeds as follows: harrier, terrier, bloodhound, gazehound, greyhound, lyemmer, tumbler, stealer, setter, spaniel, comforter (also known as the Spaniel gentle), sheepdog, mastiff, wapp, turnspit and dancer. Caius most likely was familiar only with dogs then known in England. There undoubtedly were other breeds with which he was not familiar in other European countries, to say nothing of the breeds of Asia, Africa and other far cor-

This old English print faithfully reproduces a cocker spaniel in action. Hunter uses flintlock shotgun of era.

This print was done circa 1780. By that time, the cocker spaniel breed had been well established as illustrated.

ners of the world.

There have been many attempts at classification of the various breeds of dogs, some by type or conformation, some by the uses for which the dogs were bred, and various other systems, but none really seem adequate in all respects. Perhaps the most silly classification system was that of Henry Pye. He proposed that all dogs be divided into four basic groups: white, black, gray and yellow. These groups should be divided further by each dog's monetary value and beauty.

Many others have tried their hand at similar groupings based on one characteristic or another, but there have been no really succesful classifications except the one presently in use. It was established by Ferelith Hamilton of London, who divides and groups more then 150 recognized breeds and around 350 varieties. (These figures are only approximate as there are so many different organizations involved.) Hamilton established seven groups as follows: working or herd dogs, working utility dogs, gun or sporting dogs, hounds, terriers, toy dogs, and spitz or Nordic dogs.

We are concerned with only two of these groupings — gun dogs and hounds. I have difficulty in classifying the coursing dogs with the scent-working trail hounds, but can offer no better grouping for such dogs as the Norwegian elkhound, which runs both by scent and sight.

Perhaps the most venerable of all the breeds that fall within the parameters of this book is the bloodhound. Xenophon, a Greek writing about the year 400 B.C., described the use of a hound that sounds very much like the bloodhound for hunting hares. It is generally believed that the original stock of the bloodhound came from ancient Constantinople, spreading first to Greece, then to Rome. The conquering Roman legions took the breed to all parts of the civilized world. Claudius Aelianus spoke most favorably of the bloodhound in his famed *Historia Animalium,* written in the Third Century A.D.

The next significant record of the bloodhound is in the Eighth Century, when the two strains, into which the breed had seemingly split, were bred and kept pure for hundreds of years by the Abbots of Saint Hubert. There was a black line of bloodhound and a white line. It seems as though every monastery kept and bred a pack of one or the other strain of bloodhound. It is impossible to determine at this late date differences between the black and white strains, but they are thought to have been significant.

The various monasteries were quite zealous in keeping their particular strain of hound of pure blood. This gave rise to the term, "blooded" hound, signifying that these dogs were of the finest breeding. In later times, the word "bloodhound" was used to describe these dogs which were

This illustration was done by the noted English artist, Howitt, 1750-1822, and shows cocker spaniel to advantage.

Print by James Ward, circa 1800, shows spaniels being used as jump or starting dogs, while the spotted greyhound is ready for the chase. This technique is still being used in the world of modern dogs and hunting.

This 1810 print from the work of Abram Cooper illustrates the use of a cocker spaniel during woodcock hunting trip.

known more properly as the St. Hubert's hound. Contrary to popular opinion, the word "bloodhound" has nothing to do with the dogs being attracted to blood, but is a synonym for "blooded hound."

It is commonly believed that the Crusaders brought back new strains of hounds from the Near East. These were crossed with the St. Hubert hound to produce types such as the red Schweisshund, the black English bloodhound, and the white and gray French bloodhounds. The English are credited with breeding the bloodhound in the Seventeenth Century to the type and characteristics with which we are familiar today. It is thought that this rather slow-moving hound was developed so that hunters would have a relatively slow-moving deer or other animal at which to shoot and, also, so that the houndsman could follow the hound closely when it was used to track highwaymen and other criminals.

The use of the black English bloodhound in tracking criminals gave rise to the name sleuthhound. The bay of the bloodhound allegedly brought fear to the heart of the criminal and hope to the lost for centuries. The bloodhound was brought to the American colonies early where it was used to track runaway slaves and criminals.

The bloodhound — or perhaps the St. Hubert hound — is thought to have given rise to the modern pointing breeds when it was crossed with the spaniel. Another of the oldest breeds, the spaniel's roots can be traced back into the mists of man's early history. As indicted by the name, the spaniel, as a breed, is thought to have originated in Spain. At this distant time, it is impossible to tell whether the Moorish period of Spain had any marked effect on the breed's development. Some authorities believe the Moors greatly improved the breed, while others contend they just used the same dogs in use by the Spanish at the time of the occupation.

It is known that the Moors used the early spaniels as flushing dogs for their falcons in the sport of falconry. Spaniels were used also as water dogs, both as retrievers and as duck flushers in falconry. The spaniels also were used to put up the game, and greyhounds then would run it to earth. This type of sport was common on both the European Continent and England.

A researcher does not get far into the origins of modern breeds without discovering that the spaniel is the common ancestor to a great many of them. Although the spaniel was used and bred throughout Europe, it was in England that the breed came into its own. English spaniels were developed into many distinct breeds, all of which show their common ancestry, although of many diverse forms.

With the single exception of the Brittany, which was developed in France, all of the recognized spaniel breeds seen today were developed in England. There also is evidence of early English spaniel breeds that have disappeared over the centuries.

All of the modern pointing dogs can trace their ancestry back to the spaniels of early England. In addition to the

This study of a cocker spaniel was done some two centuries back and illustrates how little breed has changed since.

This woodcock shooting scene was done about 1800. It suggests dog conformation of that era.

American cocker, English cocker, American water, Irish water, Brittany, clumber, springer, field, French, German, Picardy, Pont Audemer, Sussex, and Welsh Springer spaniels, there are the Barbet, Braco Italiano, Drentse Partrijhond, pointing Griffon, wire hair Griffon, long coat Griffon, Kooikerhondje, Munsterlander, Auvergne, German longhair, German roughhair, German shorthair, and the German wirehair. Pointers and Spanish pointers are of spaniel ancestry as are the Portuguese Perdiguero and Portuguese water dog; the Chesapeake Bay, curly coated, flat coated and golden Labrador retrievers; the English, Gordon and Irish setters; Spinone, Stabyhoun; Wetterhoun; Weimaraner and, disputedly, the otterhound, as well as the Boykin spaniel.

There can be little argument that the spaniel was the most significant early breed in the procrection into the sporting dogs of modern times.

An older member of the spaniel clan, the setting spaniel, is perhaps the oldest bird hunting dog of which we presently have knowledge; supposedly it was the ancestor of all the breeds previously listed. Unlike the setting dogs of today, the setting spaniel is supposed to have pointed from training rather than by instinct as do today's setting breeds.

Supposedly, the Spanish pointer is the first dog that pointed game from instinct with the tight concentration we expect from pointing dogs today. There has been much conjecture as to the crossbreeding that produced the Spanish pointer, but conjecture is all it ever will be unless someone finds concrete information on the subject.

We call this dog the Spanish pointer, as Spain is where the first records of the breed were found. It could have been developed just as easily in any part of southern Europe. easily in any part of southern Europe.

It may have been in a single dog the tendency to point game was seen and recognized as such a valuable trait that it was developed by linebreeding from this single source. This is entirely possible, as the principles of breeding were well known in Europe at least as far back as the time of the Roman Empire. Regardless of origin, once this line of pointing dogs had been genetically stabilized, they spread rapidly through the civilized world, often being presented as gifts to royalty.

In considering these early breeds and their uses, bear in mind that only the nobility "owned" anything in those

Print by artist George Morland, done about 1790, appears to feature spaniels that are clumber or cocker prototypes.

times. The vast majority of people were not allowed to hunt and if one had a dog, it was the property of the landowner as were the individuals themselves. Thus, breed development had to be by the reigning nobility or their agents. However, few of these noblemen knew how to write; writing was virtually a property of the church. As a result, few breeding records were kept. Most breeding records were word-of-mouth situations, remembered by the gamekeepers of each estate and verbally passed on to their successors. At best, this system was good for precious few generations before memory failed; mistakes in genealogy were made, then compounded. Records often were forgotten or lost in some sudden change or catastrophy. Only in the case of the Saint Hubert hound do we have actual breeding records from this period.

A few centuries later, with writing a public skill, we find the beginning of serious breeding records. Once adequate breeding records had been established, the development of the various breeds proceeded rapidly as many noblemen set up good breeding programs and placed the development of superior dogs high on their list of priorities.

A major contributing factor in the development of good hunting dogs was the beginning use of firearms for hunting small game, but long before the introduction of firearms, a crude invention was used to take waterfowl and small game.

This method called for a crossbow with a shaft or quarrel having a cup on the end which was filled with shot, small stones, chopped bits of iron or whatever was available. This shaft, with its cup of small projectiles, was shot at both birds and ground game with what historians claim was good effect in the hands of a good marksman.

This excellent drawing of a springer spaniel was published in 1802 and was the work of European artist, P. Reinagle.

The Norwegian elkhound is a primary example of the type of sporting dog that has changed little over the centuries.

EMERGENCE OF MODERN BREEDS

The History Of Civilization Parallels The Development Of Dogs Through The Ages

AN UNDERSTANDING of the roots of the different breed types is neccesary in order to appreciate the efforts of those who developed the various breeds to fit their hunting-role dogs we are fortunate enough to have today. Due to the efforts of these early breeders, we can confidently expect a beagle puppy to develop into a pretty fair rabbit chaser; an English setter or pointer to find and hold birds until we are able to come up, flush and shoot at them; and a Labrador or springer to flush and retrieve game for us.

It is important to understand that this did not just happen, and that keeping the various breeds at the degree of ability we routinely expect today is dependent on the constant vigilance of the various breed clubs. With a few generations of breeding dogs that do not come up to the expected field performance of the breed, we will have lost a large part of the breed's capability to perform.

As an example, we need look no further than at what the dog show people did to the Irish setter. The Irish setter was a fine field dog in the 1920s, but this breed with its deep mahogany coat attracted the attention of the show people who bred solely for coat and conformation without respect to the field ability of these dogs; by the 1940s they had produced a breed that was worthless as a gun dog. Fortunately, a few breeders kept some of the field strain and today we are starting to see a few good field dogs due to the efforts of those individuals who worked hard to salvage this fine breed.

Breeds we now use in hunting vary widely as to period of origin. At one end of the scale we have the Norwegian elkhound; remains of this breed have been found in Viking burials dated by archaeologists as old as 5000 years. These skeletal remains indicate that these 5000-year-old dogs were essentialy the same as the elkhound bred today.

We previously mentioned the greyhound-type dogs pictured in the Egyptian pyramids. Dogs that appear to be much like the pointer also are depicted in the pyramids, but we have no way of knowing whether these were actually pointing dogs; not all dogs that look like pointers are point-

The greyhound differs little from the breed that was used by the ancient Egyptians, it resembles drawings in tombs.

ers. To the untrained eye, a dalmation looks much like a pointer; on one occasion, I listened while an elderly lady explained to a small boy, looking at my spotted pointer in the dog box in my Jeep, how these dogs were kept at the fire hall and followed the fire engines to a fire when she was a girl. At the other end of the breed age scale we have the Catoctin Mountain bird dogs presently being developed by Del Seely of River Hill Game Farm at New Columbia, Maryland.

Many of the breeds we now use in hunting have been brought to their present form within the last two hundred years and, in numerous cases, in the last century. The archtypes of these breeds have existed for hundreds of years, but they were not finely bred dogs for a specific job that we have, until the current wave of breed specialization influenced their development. Until recently, hunters desired a more general purpose hunting dog.

The Norwegian elkhound is an almost perfect example. This breed has existed in its present form for thousands of years. There is a good reason for this long breed life. Through circumstances we will never know, this dog reached a zenith of perfection in ancient times. I suspect this breed is only one of many different types of similar characteristics. Although there were likely some differences in conformation and coat — depending upon climate and type of terrain in the area where they were developed — certain references in old writings indicate that there were, at one time, many breeds or strains possessing traits similar to the elkhound. The elkhound is the only one of these breeds that has survived, possibly because the dog is so superbly suited to the job he does.

The Norwegian elkhound is literally a paragon of virtue — I know of no breed that has as many capabilities. Breeds such as some of the versatile breeds and the basenji, approach the elkhound in having so many talents, but none of them is his equal. I haven't owned one yet, because to do justice to one of these dogs, it should be the only dog you own.

The elkhound is a true general purpose dog. Whatever you are hunting that's the kind of dog he is; and he's pretty good at it. The specialist breeds such as the pointer or the greyhound may surpass the elkhound in their specialty, but they are single-purpose dogs. Be it squirrels or moose, ducks or bears, the elkhound will be right in there doing his job. (Perhaps I should mention that, when we say elkhound, we actually are saying moosehound as the European moose is known as an *elg* or elk. So they are really moosehounds.)

The elkhound is best described as a bundle of energy. Standing about twenty inches at the shoulders, short coupled, with medium length of leg, erect perked ears, it has a fairly long, hard coat with an overall gray appearance, although the coat actually is composed of short soft body hair underlying hard gray guard hairs with black tips. The

Popular in dog show circles today, the Samoyed probably can trace ancestry back to the wolves of the Arctic area.

elkhound can live comfortably in below-zero temperatures, yet does not show nearly as much discomfort in hot weather as many less heavily furred dogs. The American Kennel Club does not list weight in the breed standard, but from those I've seen, forty-five to fifty pounds would be the weight of a large male, with females somewhat smaller. Picture this small, energetic dog bringing to bay and holding a full-grown bull moose until hunters arrive to kill the game with spears, and you will begin to understand the concentrated energy and spunk that goes into the making of the elkhound.

Most true hounds depend almost entirely on their noses in the pursuit of game. While the elkhound has as keen a nose as any of the traditional scent-trailing hounds and can follow a trail strictly by scent as well as any hound, it also uses its eyes and ears in the pursuit of its quarry. Possessed of limitless courage, they also use a great amount of intelligence. Whereas many of the hound breeds are prone to rush upon a formidable animal to be killed or badly injured, the elkhound will watch for an opening much as a boxer does, then get in, get his bite and get safely out of harm's way.

The first elkhound with which I came in contact was owned by a high school friend. Labeled with the apt, if unimaginative, name of Lady, she was an "anything" dog. Both Fred and I were blessed with fathers who had trained us in the safe handling of firearms and allowed us to hunt on our own. At that time, the mid-1930s, there were no deer or bear in our part of West Virginia, but we were blessed with a great abundance of both gray and fox squirrels, rabbits, raccoon, opossum, red and gray foxes, plus great flocks of waterfowl and upland game birds.

In addition to our home farm, we had relatives who held large acreages. With such an abundance of hunting available, Lady had her work cut out for her. Squirrel season came in early fall and we always started the season with the bushytails. Lady was one of the best squirrel dogs I've ever seen. She seemed to know just what game we were after

Such dogs as the golden retriever are thought to have originated from a cross of mastiffs with polar dogs. After that came infusions of pointer and spaniel blood that has given them their conformation and enthusiasm for hunting.

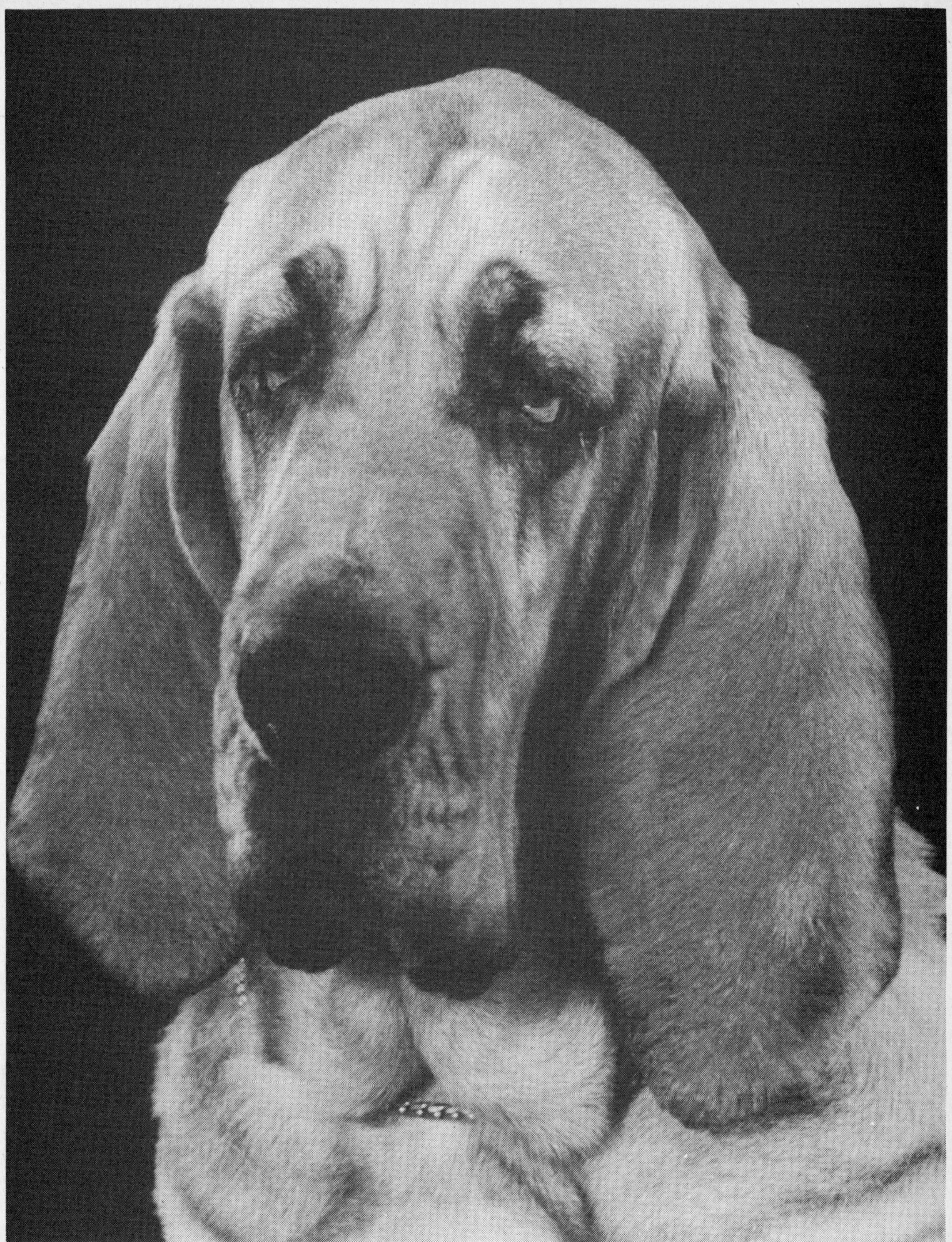

The bloodhound, noted for his trailing abilities, seems to have been descended from mastiff stock with many crosses.

and, as soon as we hit the woods, she would be off with her keen nose searching for the scent of squirrel. It never seemed to be long before we would hear her *Yark! Yark! Yark!,* telling us, "Here's that ol' squirrel we're looking for."

We would approach the tree from opposite sides and soon Fred's bolt-action Mossberg or my Winchester pump would crack and a squirrel would hit the ground. If the squirrel wasn't quite dead, Lady took care of that with a spine-breaking shake and delivered the game to hand. As soon as she had delivered the squirrel, she would be off to find another.

Often, the next we'd see of Lady would be when she would come in quietly carrying a squirrel she had caught and killed herself. This performance was greeted with mixed feelings, as we would much rather have shot our own squirrels. Lady exhibited amazing speed and dexterity. On scenting a squirrel, she would follow the scent upwind, taking advantage of whatever cover was available. If she could get to within twenty yards of a squirrel that was twenty yards from a tree, she had it. With a sudden rush she would be on the hapless squirrel and snap it up and kill it with a shake of the head like a terrier with a rat.

Later in the year, when there had been a few frosts, we would switch from squirrels to rabbits. Lady was an excellent jump dog and would trail the rabbits around to the gun. She would often catch a rabbit and bring it to us. As Fred and I didn't particularly appreciate this ability, we used my beagles more often on rabbits; I suspect this ability of the elkhound to catch small game was highly prized and bred for by the Vikings who did not have .22 rifles and 12-gauge shotguns.

Lady also was deadly on woodchucks, known in the West Virginia vernacular as ground shoats or ground hogs. She would spot a shoat at long range and casually meander in the general direction of the hole. In this manner, she often was able to get to a point where she could rush the shoat and catch it before it could reach the hole. When she caught one she would almost invariably throw it high in the air and pounce on it as it hit the ground, breaking its neck almost instantly.

A full-grown ground shoat will weigh twelve pounds or more and is a very formidable opponent for most dogs. I've seen the ground shoat emerge the victor from many a fracas with ordinary farm dogs, but I never saw Lady have any problem in killing them. Most dogs that have killed ground shoats have plenty of scars to show for it, but Lady never got a mark on her.

If her oblique approach failed to get her within striking range of a ground shoat, she often would settle down on the downwind side of the hole and await the re-emergence of the shoat with seemingly limitless patience. She would stay as still as a stump until the shoat had reached a point far enough from its hole for her purposes, then the quarry would be finished in a sudden rush.

There were two major problems with lady and ground shoats. First, I would much rather have killed them with my .22 Hornet. Secondly, she insisted on bringing them all to the house and dropping them at the kitchen steps.

I remember one summer day when Fred came out from town, bringing Lady, and we left her at the house while we drove over to Opequan Creek to fish.

When we got back from fishing we found four large groundhogs lying at the foot of the kitchen steps. After Fred went back to town I took the shoats out and dropped them down a sinkhole. Fred came out for another fishing trip about a week later and we again left Lady at the farm, as she was forever running up and down the bank while we were fishing. When we returned that evening we found the well ripened ground shoats from last week as well as two fresh ones by the steps.

Fred also used Lady for 'coons and opossum. She would tree and stay there until we shot her game out for her. Lady was also a pretty good flushing dog for quail and grouse, but she worked too far out and most everything she jumped was out of range. She would bring a fox around its circle, but as she was a silent trailer, giving tongue only when in sight of her quarry, it was difficult to anticipate where the fox was in order to head it off for a shot.

Once she came back with a gray fox she had killed. I'll never know for sure just what transpired. I don't feel Lady could have run down a fox, although she could perhaps match its speed for a short distance. I suspect that the fox tried the usual gray fox trick of climbing up a leaning tree in order to let the dog go on by.

For those not familiar with this trick, a gray fox does not run as far or as fast as its red cousin, preferring to weave a twisted trail through the thickets in a circle of only a few hundred yards. The fox will often locate a leaning tree of about forty-five degrees and run three or four circles around it in a circle about seventy-five feet in diameter, passing close by the leaning tree at one point. After making several circles around the same tracks, the fox will leap onto the leaning tree and climb up the trunk from which vantage point it will watch the hounds follow around the circle until they are completely baffled and go off to hunt another fox. This trick is almost a sure thing with most of the traditional trail hounds.

I suspect that Lady, being of a breed that uses its eyes as well as nose, spotted the fox up a tree and, being a pretty fair climber, went up the tree and brought the fox out to kill it in a short burst of speed.

On another occasion, Lady showed the stuff she was made of. We had a big Tamworth boar hog that weighed nearly six hundred pounds. We kept this boar as we liked the leaner type "bacon" hog that this breed represented. The hogs were kept in a heavily fenced lot of about an acre. One day in the fall, this big boar tore a hole in the fence and got into a field of young barley that bordered it. This barley was attractive food to the hogs and soon all of the sows and gilts had gotten out, too, and were feeding on the barley; rooting it up and messing up the field in general. The boar had six-inch tusks and a bad temper. He had routed our English shepherd stock dog and the neighbor's collie. The situation was at a standstill. I'd called dad at his office and he had said the boar was too valuable to shoot, except as a last resort. I was starting to think in terms of a last resort when Fred arrived with Lady for an evening squirrel hunt.

Fred allowed as to how Lady could put the boar back in the hog lot or wear him plumb out so we could. I had put up a couple of long gates to form a vee at the hole where the hogs had gotten out and, sure enough, Lady put all the hogs except the boar back through the hole in the fence. When

The Siberian husky is obviously a descendent of wolves, a fact that is reflected in temperament and its looks.

she started working the other hogs, the boar had run off to a rock break and watched the other hogs being chased.

After all the others were back through the hole, Lady went for the boar. He ran at her, but she was too agile for him to catch; soon she started nipping at him and herding him toward the hole in the fence. When he got close to the gates we'd set up as a funnel, he ran back to the center of the field and took up a stand. Lady kept after him and soon he was covered with froth all over his mouth and jowls. He kept trying to get at her, but was only wearing himself out. His rushes became shorter and slower, until he simply fell over, completely exhausted. Mean and vicious as he was, I felt sorry for him. He was as game as they come, but he simply couldn't catch that dog. Seeing that we weren't going to get him to walk through the hole in the fence, I went and got two heavy ropes and two heavy draft horses. We had a hard time freeing him from the ropes without getting bitten after dragging him back to the hog lot, but finally got it done and repaired the hole in the fence. Needless to say, by this time, it was too late to get any hunting done.

The Norwegian elkhound does have some traits that are often seen as disadvantages. One fault is that they seldom are able to hunt with other dogs. This probably is brought about by their fierce loyalty and jealousy. The two I have known were fierce fighters and simply wouldn't allow another dog to come close to their masters. I saw Lady completely devastate a large German shepherd twice her size. We could not use any of my bird dogs, when we had her along, as she whipped them easily and chased them away. One of these was a big rangy pointer of no little reputation as a fighter in his own right.

Another sometimes troublesome trait is that they are slow to accept people as friends. It took at least three trips afield before I could put a hand on Lady. When Fred's family first moved into our area, we discovered we had the same interests, but I was nearly bitten several times. Once when Fred and I were wrestling in his yard, Lady jumped on my back and stood over me, growling. Once she had accepted me, I could play with her, woolly her around on the ground, or do any of the things we normally do when playing with a dog, but it took time to develop this. In stating that the Norwegian elkhound is seldom able to hunt with other dogs, this means they do not work well with strange dogs. This breed is often used in bear packs and they do get along with the other dogs in the pack reasonably well. Dogs that are used as part of a pack do not usually have as close a rapport with their masters as dogs that are hunted individually and they do not develop the fierce jealousy of which I spoke. Then, too, they usually live in close quarters with the other dogs in the pack and become used to being with these particular dogs. For example, it is common for foxhunters to bring their dogs and meet at some prearranged point and simply turn their dogs loose to hunt. The breeds used are Walker, July, Trigg, black and tan and such. When the dogs are turned loose there will be a round of stiff-legged tail sniffing and perhaps a few growls, but then the dogs will go hunting. When we tried the same thing with elkhounds, there invariably would be a big dogfight.

The above is not to be construed to mean that the elkhound is bad tempered or of poor disposition. On the contrary, it is a loyal watchdog, but not prone to attack people for unknown reasons as do some other breeds. They are great with children and I cannot think of a more alert watchdog or a breed upon which I would rather depend as a guard dog. The elkhound is a breed that will accept you in their own time and terms. A thief won't win the dog's affection by feeding it a few nights, then pat the dog on the head and proceed to break into the owner's house.

The other elkhound I came into contact with was owned by a bear hunter and was used alone to track and tree bears. Its owner was a descendant of the well-known frontier scout Lewis Wetzel and I'm told this man and dog have taken many bear. Think of it: one forty-pound dog treeing a four-hundred-pound bear.

I have discussed the Norwegian elkhound at length, as I feel it is important the reader understand the sort of dogs that our ancestors had five thousand years ago. This is the root stock for the dogs we have developed today. Our ancestors needed a dog that was useful in any situation from tracking and bringing big game to bay, to bringing in small game it caught and guarding the homestead. If one were not too particular what one eats — and believe me, our forebears of one thousand years ago weren't — a small family could live well off what Lady dragged to the foot of the stairs. It must be taken into consideration that Lady's success was in relatively unhunted territory during the most favorable season. Had she hunted the same area over a long period of time, the small game would have been thinned out and the success of her hunting reduced accordingly.

The elkhound is typical of a number of breeds found around the Arctic circle, all showing the appearance of their wolf ancestors. Some of these breeds are chow, husky, malamute, akita, schipperke, and the samoyed. One of the key distinctions between these breeds and the wolf, from which they developed, is that the dog's tail curls up over its back and is carried proudly, almost like a banner; the tail of the wolf hangs limply behind it. Some theories hold that these wolf-like circumpolar breeds were the first breeds domesticated. Others hold that the pariah

The Labrador retriever, as we know him today, is far removed from the mastiffs that formed its ancestory.

The Great Pyrenees came from crossing the short-haired mastiff with the polar breeds that boast longer coats. The St. Bernard is a relative to this particular breed.

dogs of the Asian subcontinent at some early time were genetically manipulated by men to become the first breeds developed for a specific purpose; in this case, use as herd dogs.

The third ancient group of dogs is the sight-hunting gazehound. It is widely believed that these were selected and bred for speed at an early date in civilization.

In addition to being able to run at great speed, these dogs are endowed with the best eyesight of all the canids. These sight hounds run with a gait more like that of a rabbit than the gait of most other breeds of dog. They run with a motion that seems to be a curling up and uncurling, instead of a gallop. The gazehounds have been developed into many breeds by different peoples having diverse needs and uses for a coursing dog. The blood of the basic gazehound runs in such seemingly diverse breeds as the collie and the greyhound, the saluki and the whippet to name a few. Collies are basically gazehound-polar crosses, while some of the wolfhound breeds are of gazehound-pariah ancestry.

The polar, pariah, and gazehound types are thought to be the earliest breeds developed by man as basic prototypes of future breeds. It was not long before a fourth prototype was developed: the mastiff family. It is widely accepted that the mastiff type is the result of acromegaly, a disturbance of the pituitary gland which results in the production of excess growth hormones causing gigantism. This is one of the more frequent mutations and usually is not successful, but in the case of the dog, this characteristic was cherished and they were bred for use as war dogs and sentinels. Acromegaly really means oversize extremities, but in the case of the dog, the term is used to refer to the entire animal.

Giant dogs seem to have originated in northern India or Tibet. They were much sought after and soon had spread throughout the entire civilized world. Mastiff types, similar to those of the present, were used by the Assyrians and were further bred by the Greeks and Romans. The Romans called them *mansuetus,* meaning "tame" in Latin, because of their use as family guard dogs. Later developments gave us such varying types of mastiff as the Great Pyrenees and Saint Bernard by crossing the basic short-haired mastiff with longhaired polar breeds. At the other end of the coat length is the Great Dane.

The development of these four breeds, plus the development of the bloodhound from basic mastiff stock, set the stage for the development of the modern breeds. The bloodhound is thought to have been developed in Tibet from mastiff stock selected and bred solely for their tracking ability over a period of centuries. Once the bloodhound had been developed to a fine-honed scenting and tracking animal, it become the basis of many other breeds of widely differing abilities.

One of the breeds developed from the scenting hound was the pointer. We find portraits of the pointer in ancient Egypt where they were used as spotting dogs. Canid authorities believe the tendency, of many breeds of dog, to freeze on first contacting the scent of prey was seized upon and selectively bred over an early period, resulting in the steady "point" we have today.

Retrievers do just what their name says: They retrieve downed game for the hunter. They are believed to have originated from a cross of the mastiff type with polar dogs and the later infusion of pointer and spaniel blood.

Spaniels are thought to have originated from rather small mastiff breeds used by the French, Spanish, and Basque peoples of Southwestern Europe to catch and retrieve waterfowl. Selective breeding has given them a tight, wavy coat that is easy to shake water from and which does not pick up dirt and weeds.

The poodles make up a race of highly specialized retrievers developed in central Europe as water dogs. Poodles are highly intelligent and once were considered capable hunters. Unfortunately, the poodle's intelligence, ability to accept training and good disposition has resulted in great popularity as pets. This, in turn, brought about the breeding of poodles without regard to field ability and has resulted in the loss of much of this fine breed's hunting traits. It would be a worthwhile project for someone to breed the poodle back to its former abilities as is being done with the Irish setter.

CANINE BODY STRUCTURE

Man's Breeding Programs Have Produced Specialized Characteristics — And Some Damage!

Chapter 4

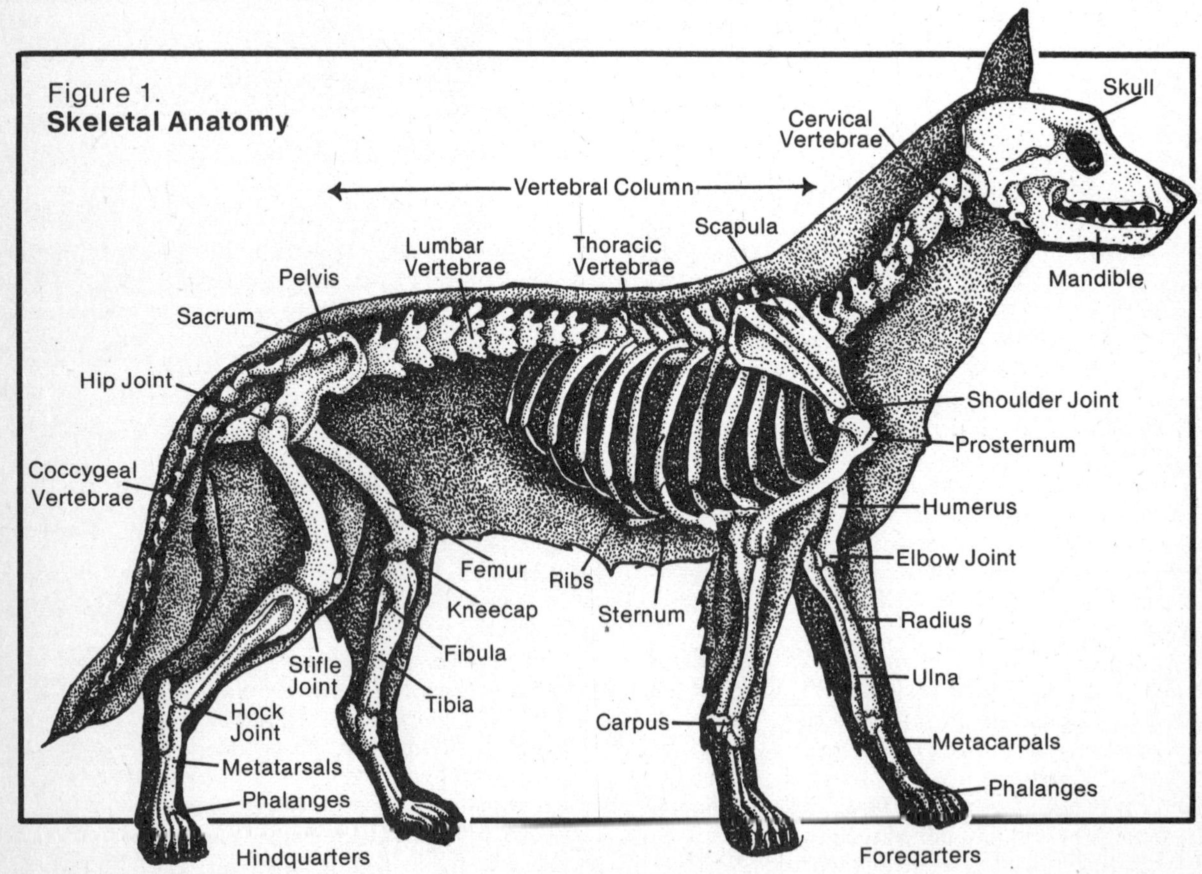

Figure 1.
Skeletal Anatomy

IT IS NECESSARY that we understand a bit about how a dog is put together in order to understand the physical reasons governing dog behavior and capability.

Like all mammals, a dog has a bony skeleton covered with muscles and a skin or hide, articulated by tendons, fasciae and ligaments through which the muscles act to cause movement, this network of tissue also holding the structure together. The major sector of this skeletal structure is the backbone or vertebral column. The vertebral column is divided into four sections. The front end is the neck or *cervical vertebrae.* The second section is known as the *thoracic vertebrae.* The third section is the *lumbar vertebrae,* while the tail vertebrae are known as the *coccygeal vertebrae.*

Next in importance — if one part of a structure in which all parts are truly necessary can be said to be more important than any other — is the skull. There is wide divergence in skull conformation among the many breeds. Long-headed dogs such as the collie are called *dolichocephalic.* Breeds having skulls of moderate length in proportion to length are said to be *mesocephalic;* beagles and fox terriers are good examples. Breeds having short, broad skulls are said to be *brachycephalic.* Bulldogs, pugs, and Boston terriers are examples of brachycephalic dogs.

The skull houses the brain and eyes, while the lower front part is the upper part of the jaws opposing the lower jaw or mandible. The remaining major parts of the skeleton are the limbs. The front or thoracic limbs are attached to the shoulder blade which is known as the *scapula.* First bone in the limb and directly attached to the scapula is the *humerus.* The humerus, in turn, is attached to the *radius* and *ulna.* In dogs the ulna is much longer than the radius, the upper end extending well past the end of the radius and terminating in a heavy section to which the lower end of the shoulder muscle attaches. This projection is known as the *olecranon* process and is responsible for the tremendous leverage exerted by the front shoulder muscles. The radius and ulna terminate at the *carpus,* which serves the same purpose as man's wrist bones, and this is attached to the metacarpus or pastern which in turn is attached to a front foot made up of five "fingers" just as your hand or mine. The difference is that the dog walks on the tips of its fingers.

The rear leg of canids is composed of a femur which hinges on the pelvis. There is a long overhang of the pelvis behind the femoral joint known as the pelvic tuber. The muscles attach to this extension and to the lower end of the femur to give the great driving power of the dog's hind legs. The femur attaches to the tibia and fibular end, in turn, they join a ball socket in the *tarsus* or ankle bone. The ball joint

Dog (Female) showing position of main organs

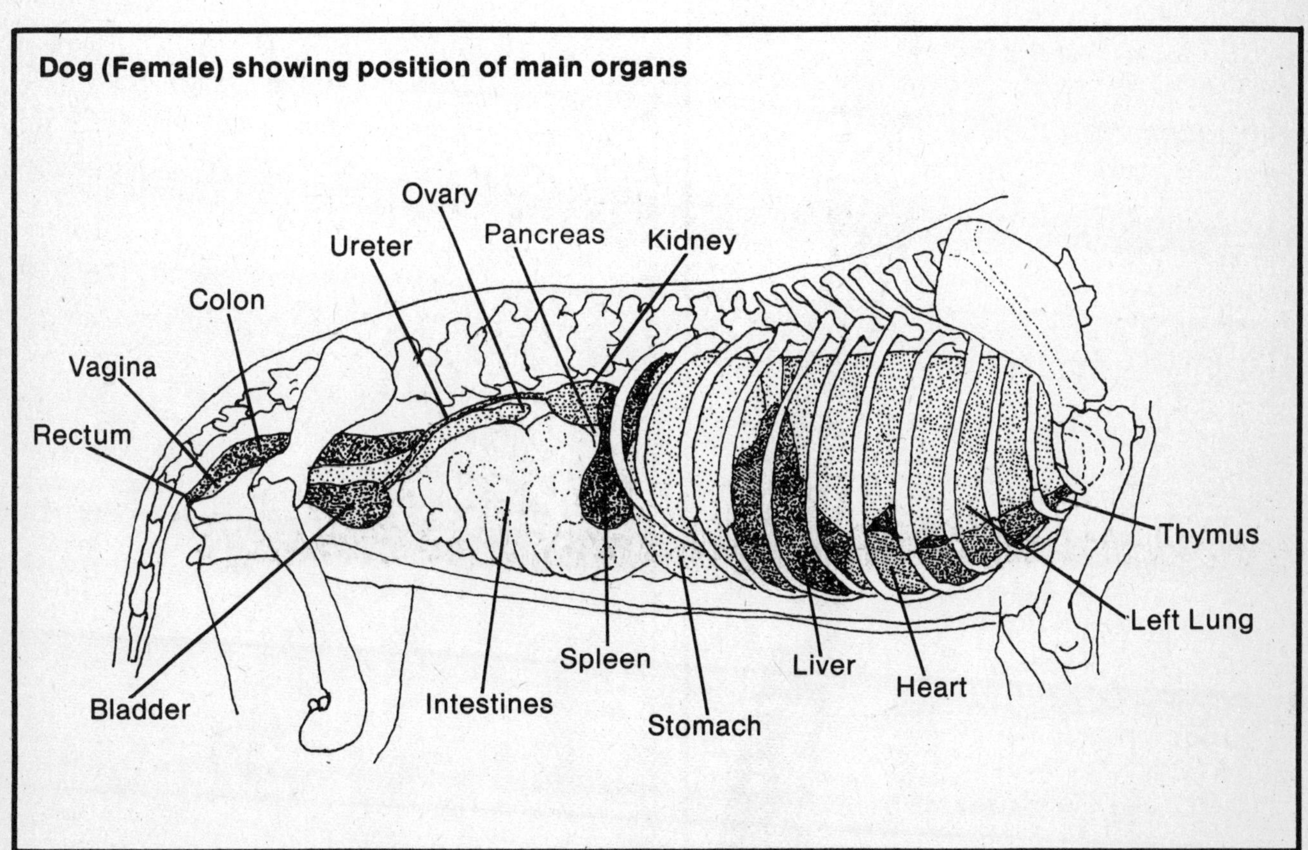

on the tarsus is well below the *calcaneal* process which is an attachment for musculature similar to the olecranon process in the front leg and similarly gives leverage to the muscles. The tarsus leads to the metatarsus which in turn leads to the four toes and a much shortened fifth toe which is useless and is commonly known as a dewclaw. Again, we find the dog walking on the tips of his toes.

In spite of the great difference in size and shape, all canids have the same skeletal structure. The basic difference between the dachshund and the greyhound is in the length of the humerus and radius in proportion to the dog's size. The length of the radius has been greatly exaggerated in the greyhound and minimized in the dachshund. They both have the same skeletal structure.

Again, in common with all mammals, the thorax contains the heart and lungs. The lungs extract oxygen from the air and the heart pumps the blood to carry the oxygen to the muscles so they can burn the food that has been digested by the viscera contained in the lumbar section of the body.

There is a lot more to canine anatomy than this, but the above should be sufficient for the parameters of this book.

If the reader will look at one of the wild canids, such as the wolf, fox or dingo, he will note a finely constructed animal that is well adapted to the efficient use of the ecological niche into which it has evolved to fit. Most breeds of dog also are custom tailored to fit the purpose for

THE HIND LEG

Side View
Front View
wing of Pelvis
Pelvis
Acetabulum
Ilium
Femoral Head
Pubic Symphysis
Pelvic Tuber
Femur
Patella
Tibia
Fibula
Calcaneal Process
Tarsus
Metatarsus
Phalanges

Rawboned conformation of this Irish setter is obvious, as he brings in a partridge shot by his owner/trainer.

which they were bred. A greyhound is a fine-tuned running machine. An English setter is a superbly designed bird-finding and holding instrument that can be depended upon to accomplish its job with grace and aplomb. The English pointer is a similar tool with a bit more speed and range, but less finesse, that goes about the work of finding and pointing birds with no nonsense.

THE FRONT LEG

Front View

Side View

Scapula

Spine of Scapula

Clavicle

Humerus

Olecranon Process

Radius

Ulna

Carpus

Metacarpus

Phalanges

Any of the scenting hounds has a nose made for following a trail and a body designed to allow the dog ample running ability. A well conditioned dog can keep going for great lengths of time. Most breeds are genetically engineered to it their purpose.

Unfortunately, some breeds have been overbred. By

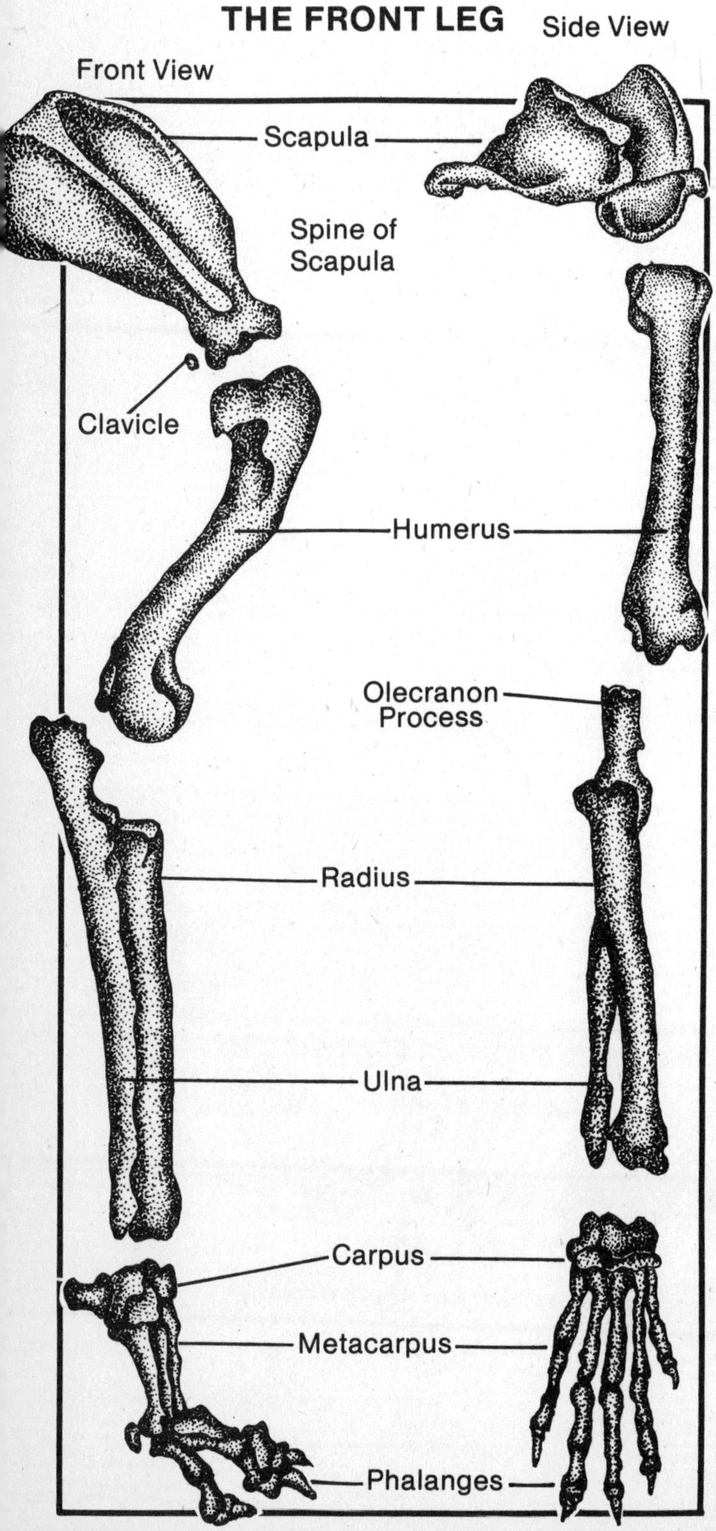

This hard-hunting Brittany takes a well earned break during a hunt. He has been bred for such activities.

this, I mean that, in attempting to enhance certain characteristics, the breeder has caused the breed either to lose some needed characteristics or has overdeveloped some trait to the point that it interferes with the natural functions of the breed.

For example, bulldogs and pugs often have breathing problems due to the distortion of their nasal passages. Some of the coursing breeds are prone to leg breakage due to the extreme length of their leg bones, just as is the case with some racehorses bred for similar purposes.

In the case of bulldogs and pugs an attempt has been made to breed for nasal passages so that the dog can breathe properly and easily while holding a tooth-grip on whatever animal it has attacked. In some instance, this

Figure 11.
Teeth — Side View

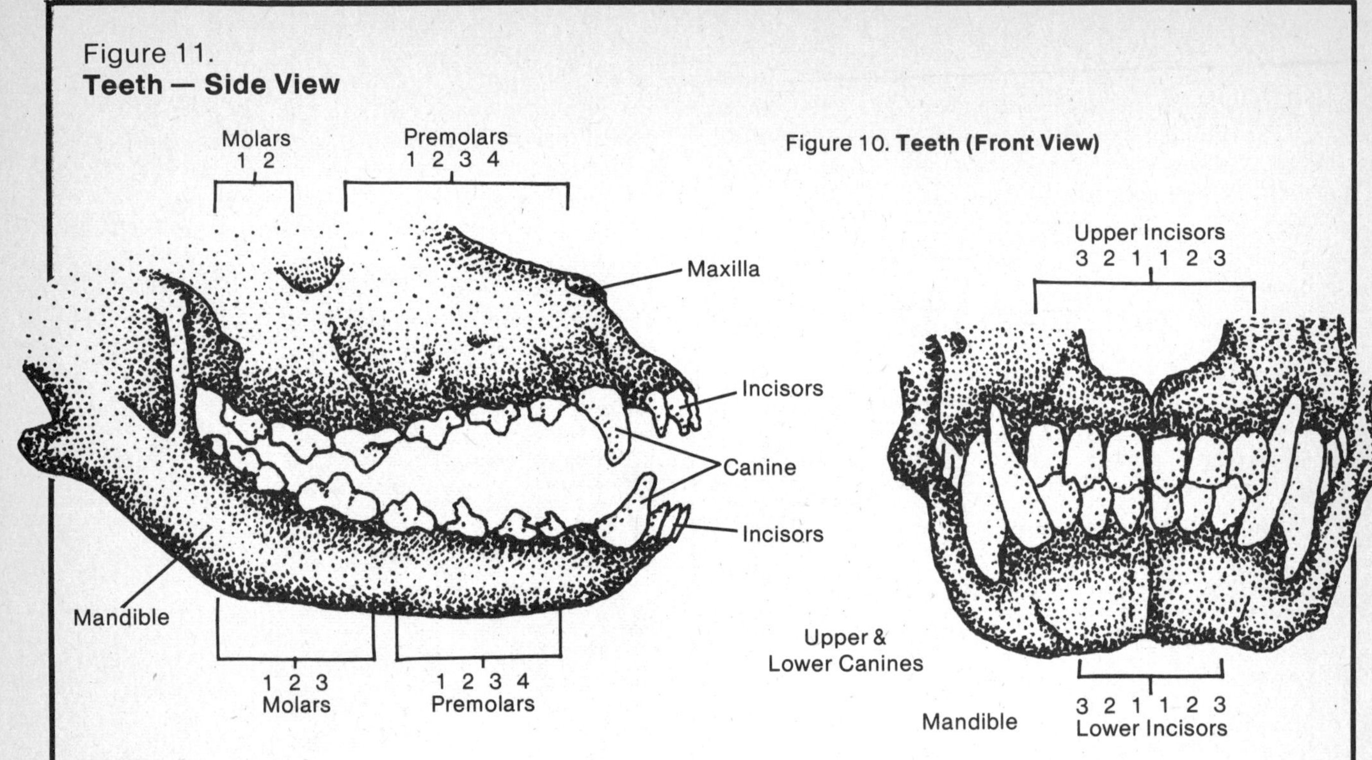

Figure 10. **Teeth (Front View)**

The head is joined to the rest of the body by the spinal column. This is made up of a series of small bones called vertebrae. Each vertebra consists of a central portion or body from which processes arise, both dorsally as well as laterally — it is through holes in the center of the vertebral bodies that the spinal cord runs to transmit nervous impulses to and from the brain. In this way maximum bony protection is afforded the spinal cord. The spinal column itself is divided into five sections. The first of these is termed the cervical or neck portion. It is followed, in turn, by the thoracic, lumbar, sacral and coccygeal sections, as illustrated in Figure 12.

Figure 12.
Vertebral Column

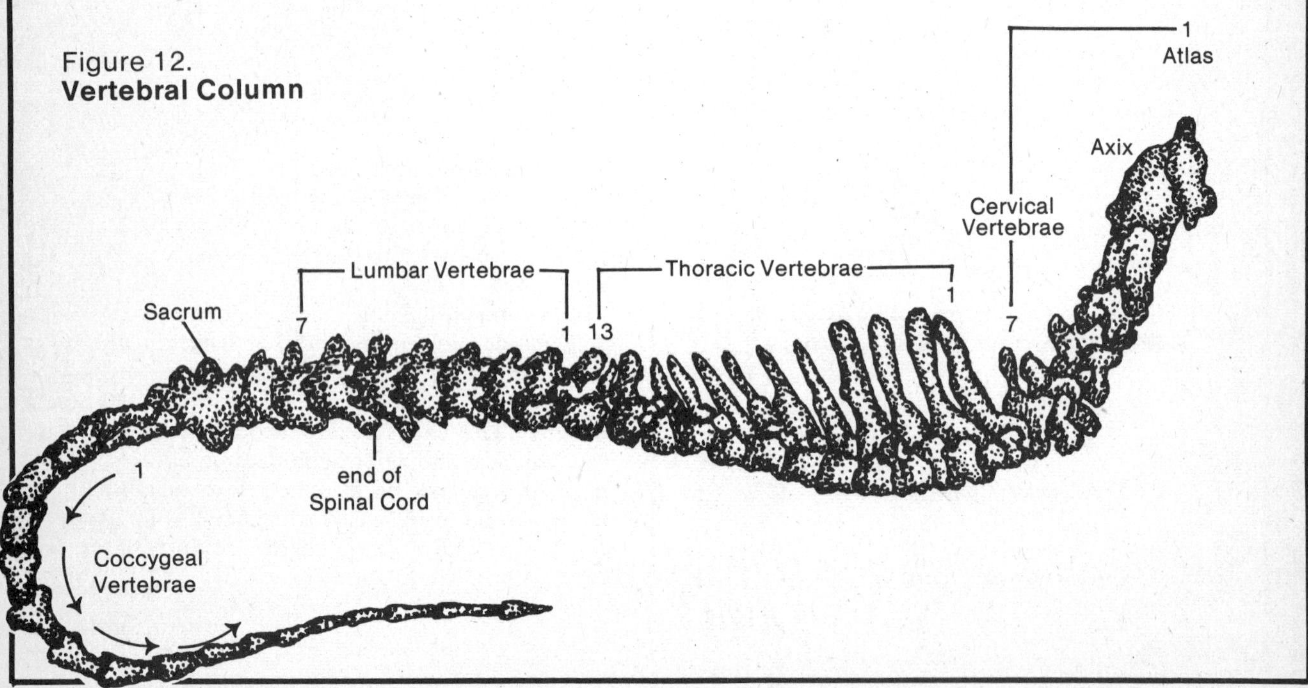

has been accomplished, but in those dogs that have nasals so convoluted as to make normal breathing difficult, it obviously has not been successful.

With coursing dogs, the extreme length of limb has caused much difficulty and discomfort in some breeds in addition to the tendency of the extremely long bones to break. Usually, when such a condition develops, it is soon bred out, but may recur for many generations in isolated instances.

I do not wish to place too much emphasis on overbreeding, but it is one of the many hazards that we encounter when we tamper with an organisim that nature has been adapting for millions of years to fill a particular ecological niche.

The accompanying illustrations of canid anatomy should illustrate just how a dog is constructed and articulated. Take particular note of the pelvic tuber and calcaneal processes in the hindquarters, and the scapula and olecranon process in the forelimb. Here is the driving mechanism of the dog.

Man's breeding programs have modified the structure of the dog in varying degrees. Only in those breeds that are highly specialized is there any great amount of modification. It might also be noted that those breeds showing the most modification are the breeds that require the most care and support from man.

This should tell us something.

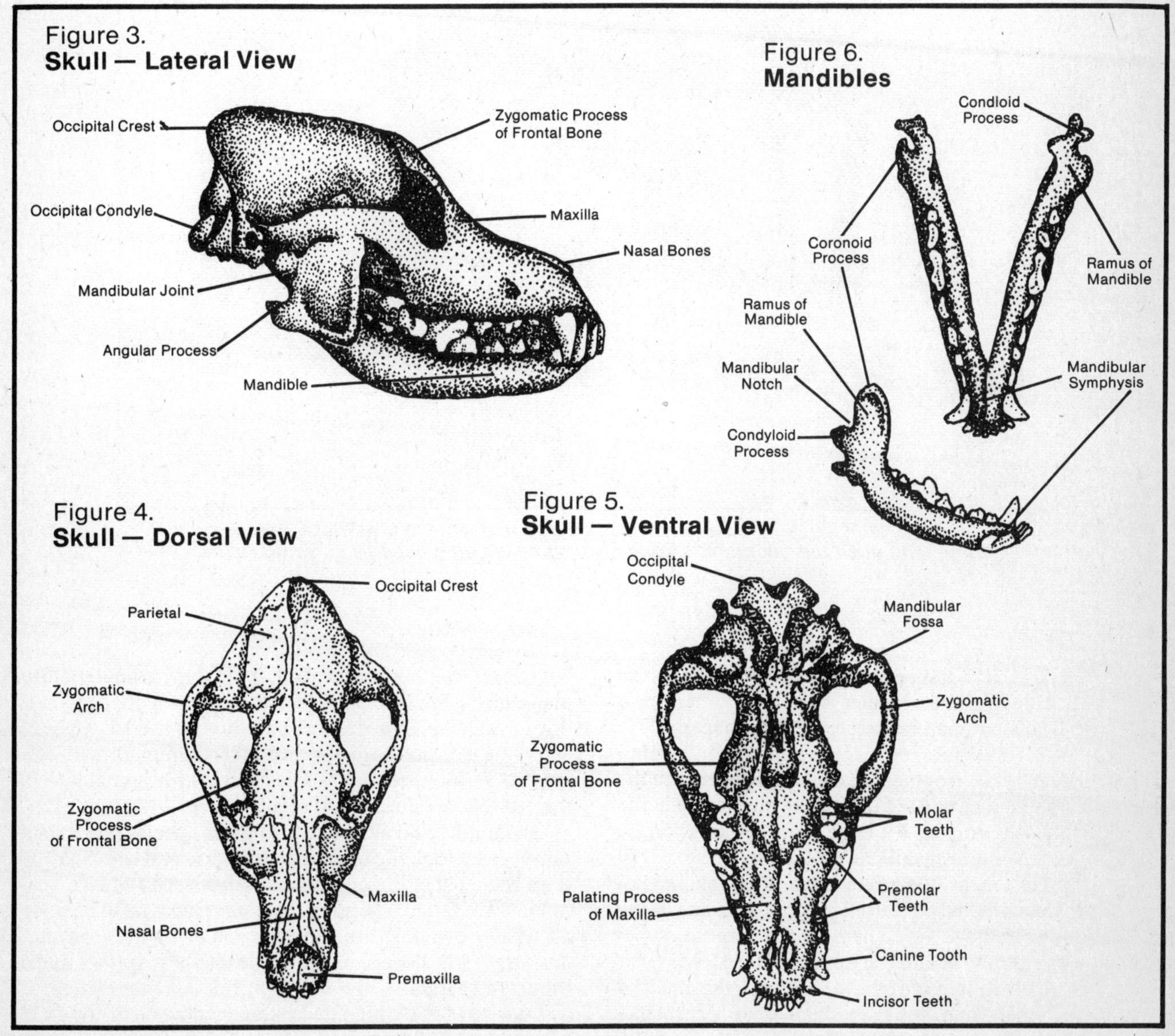

Figure 3.
Skull — Lateral View

Figure 6.
Mandibles

Figure 4.
Skull — Dorsal View

Figure 5.
Skull — Ventral View

Chapter 5

MODERN BREEDS AND THEIR USES

The Labrador retriever is considered a multi-talented dog that is used for different types of hunting, depending upon the geographic area in which he is being used by knowing trainers.

THE HUNTING dogs we are using today are the product of the breeding and development programs outlined in the preceeding chapters.

It is not possible in these pages to fully detail the history of the development of each breed, because the early development of most of the basic types is lost in the mists of time. Of course, we have more information on some archtypes than is available on others.

In several instances, there is no clear dividing line between the breeds as they are used in more than one of the classifications we have set up here for the purpose of discussion. Viz: retrievers and the flushing breeds. Many of the breeds involved are used by one person for flushing and retrieving upland game, while another owner of the same breed may use his dog strictly as a waterfowl dog. Any of the breeds to be discussed may be trained as squirrel dogs, but some have more natural ability in this particular effort than others. In some parts of our country, a good squirrel dog is valued highly and there are breeds used as squirrel dogs that are not used for any other hunting breed designated as "squirrel dog." The squirreler is a vital part of the American hunting dog scene.

Geography and availability of game species makes certain types of dog regional in distribution and use. Squirrel dogs are most common in our southeastern states. Coonhounds are found wherever there are raccoons to be hunted. Waterfowl dogs are concentrated along the seashores and large river systems. The beagle is to be found wherever there are rabbits — and that is just about everywhere.

Their uses in hunting make some members of the same breed seem to be entirely different dogs in different circumstances. In West Virginia where I live, the Labrador is thought of primarily as a waterfowl dog that is sometimes used to flush small game or tree squirrels. I have a friend in Nebraska who owns a Lab; he considers his dog as being strictly a ringneck pheasant and prairie chicken finder and retriever. While I personally would prefer a pointing breed for use on the Nebraska birds, the black Lab does a fine job for my friend and he is quite happy with the dog's performance. So we must look at all of the abilities of each breed before deciding which specific dog is best for our use.

Climate also has a lot to do with the breeds one finds in use in different localities. Along the southern coasts we find Boykin spaniels, cockers, clumber spaniels, golden retrievers and Brittany spaniels in use as waterfowl retrievers. Moving up the coast to the North, we find more Labradors and Chesapeake Bay retrievers are doing the same job. The reason for this is obvious. The chessie can stand weather conditions that would kill any other breed. The Labrador retriever is a hardy dog, capable of withstanding pretty rough conditions also, but he is no match for the chessie when conditions are really bad.

Across the Northern border of the United States, these hardy breeds may be found in use as waterfowl dogs, with the Lab doing service as a flush dog in addition to his waterfowl work. This is not to be taken to mean that there are no goldens, flat-coated, or curly-coated retrievers in the Northern tier states, but the heavier coated breeds are more popular and certainly better suited to cold weather work.

Moving over into the Mississippi Flyway we come across more goldens and flat coateds, as we move south from the coldest states. By the time we reach St. Louis, we are in golden retriever country. And when we reach the great waterfowling grounds around Stuttgart, Arkansas, we are once again in the Southern breed range, although the black Labrador is much in evidence here. Indeed, the Lab's personality makes him a popular dog wherever one goes.

The West Coast, with its warm climate, is an area where all breeds are in use. These include such European breeds as the Irish water spaniel, Welsh springer spaniel, Sussex spaniel, wire-haired griffon, wetterhound and most of the versatile breeds.

Wherever local game laws allow the use of hounds to hunt black bear we find the Plott hound, Airedale-hound crosses, Norwegian elkhounds and other locally devloped dogs that are used along with cold-nosed trail hounds such as Walker, Trigg, July, black-and-tan and blueticks

This pair of Plott hounds has been bred and trained to take on a bear, putting it in position for a shot by the hunter. This particular breed is used primarily in hunting larger game such as bears, mountain lions and similar angry types.

to make up packs of bear hounds. From the maple forests of Vermont to the Great Smokies and from blue ridge mountains of the Southeast to the rain forests of the Northwest coastal states such dogs are bringing bears to bay and tree, keeping them there for taking by the hunter. These are brave, bold dogs that often are injured or even killed in the pursuit of their quarry. Following a pack of bear dogs is work for young men in good condition who can stand the rigors.

In a small town in Massachusetts horses and riders may gather. The Noanet pack of beagles is to run today. The riders are in full panoply just as if this were to be a formal foxhunt. The rules will be much the same, but the game will be rabbits and the dogs will make up a fine pack of almost identically matched beagles. Soon all is in readiness. A rabbit is started and the pack moves out in perfect unison. The riders follow close on and it is a beautiful display of dog work and horsemanship as the bunny is run to earth.

On a hilltop near Warrenton, Virginia, others are gathering; riders are faultlessly atttired in red jackets, black riding breeches, black ties and spotless boots. They step from their Mercedes Benzs, Rolls Royces, Lancias, Cadillacs and Bentleys and gather in groups, talking discreetly, while their lackeys drive horse vans and trailers to a location nearby.

Soon a truck loaded with hounds arrives. The hounds making a great noise of barking and baying in anticipation of the hunt they have come to know will follow such preparations. The huntmaster gently tootles on his bugle and the riders representing old money, mount up and the hunt moves out. The fox that has been released ahead of the hounds is started and the hunt is off on a great chase. The huntmaster tootles "Gone Away" and the riders stream over the first low hedge jump. The local farmers hear the hunt and hope the riders don't damage their crops of newly sprouted barley and wheat too badly.

Thirty miles to the west, near Strasburg in the foothills of the Blue Ridge Mountains, a car and a pickup pull off the road into a farm lane and park. The pickup has dog crates in it from which occasional baying of hounds is heard. Two men dismount from the pickup and four more get out of the car. They talk for a bit, then one man stays with the truck, while the rest pile into the car. They drive along the side of the ridge and around a bend in the dusty road. The man left at the truck hears the car stop and the door shut twice before it moves out of hearing. He waits another half-hour, then starts letting foxhounds out of the crates. Usually there are six dogs, three in each crate. The dogs mill around for a bit, stretching and sniffing tails, then they follow the man as he moves toward a series of rock breaks in the nearby field.

After about twenty minutes and a few hundred yards, one of the older dogs breaks into an eager whimper. Two more dogs scurry to join this hound and one of them offers a full-throated bay. This brings the rest of the dogs and soon the whole pack is hesitantly sniffing and whimpering with an occasional yelp. While the hounds are sorting out the track, the hunter hears a sudden sharp yapping from what sounds like a small dog in the woods on the hill above him. Soon the noise is interrupted by the "spang" of a .22 rifle and the shrill yelping on the hill stops. A squirrel has just met its maker at the hands of another hunter.

Soon the hounds get the trail straightened out and work it along at a fairly good pace for several hundred yards. Suddenly, they all seem to be trying to bark and bawl faster than they can get the sounds out of their throats as they dash off across the ridge. The hounds have struck hot and are now running a strong scent that is hours fresher than the one they had been following up to the point when the fox had been roused from its bed. Having gotten the dogs onto a good hot track, the hunter knows it's time to find a stand from which to await developments. He realizes that to return to the area from which it was jumped, the fox probably will pass through a small meadow at his rear near the foot of the hill.

As he walks down toward the small meadow he hears the hounds veer to the east and thinks the fox might pass by the willow crossing where Ed Wright is supposed to be posted. He hopes Ed is where he is supposed to be and is alert. It would be nice to be able to make a kill earlier than usual, then he could take the hounds over to Ruble's place. He had been debating just where to go this morning all last evening. Here at LeMaster's Farm, there were more foxes but not many really good crossings, as the land is too broken up by small, wooded ridges for the foxes to be forced into many narrow routes of travel. Ruble's is open farm country with just enough wooded limestone outcrops to make it attractive to foxes.

The foxes tended to run the fence rows there by necessity, as there was not much other cover and it was easy to find a good crossing. Then, too, Bo Ruble was an old hunting partner and would likely want to go along on the hunt. It is not by chance that Ruble's fence rows are overgrown and he has much more game than his neighbors.

As he sits down on a fallen locust tree overlooking the small meadow, this dog man hears the hounds bear a bit more to the east There is little doubt that the fox is heading up the brushy gully Ed Wright is covering. It should be just about time for the fox to be getting there. Then he hears the distant boom of Ed's shotgun and waits for the dogs to come up with the dead fox and offer a few barks before they fall silent.

It does not happen. The dogs give tongue right on through the spot where Ed shot and one can hear them going up the far side of the ridge beyond the gully. Wright had missed his shot. Our dog men can tell just when the dogs cross the top of the ridge and start down the far side, as their sounds fade abruptly. A stung fox is going to be a long runner that might well go straight out of the county and over the next mountain. It would be a rough job gathering up the hounds then. No way to tell until he hears the hounds again. Should be able to hear them as they go over the mountain; if they do.

Chuck LeMaster is walking along a small ridge on his dad's farm with his .22 rifle and his dog, Tizzy. He hopes Tizzy will soon find a squirrel track and chase the squirrel up a tree so he can get a shot. It wasn't many Saturday mornings that his dad would let him off the barn work to go hunting and he wants to make the most of it.

He hears the sound of vehicles on the ridge below him and wonders who is going back the old road up to Back Branch Furnace. Then he decides he'd better have a look, because his father doesn't want too many people messing around there this close to deer season. He walks to the edge

Large hounds such as those of bluetick or redbone breeding are favored for large game, but they also do a fine job of bringing big snowshoe rabbits to the gun.

of the timber and downslope he can see the old road. A pickup truck followed by an auto come around the bend. He recognizes the truck and dog boxes of Mr. Barney. That's okay, his dad likes Mr. Barney to kill some of the foxes and last winter he'd taken him along one day. It's tempting to go down and ask to go along now but that wouldn't be good manners. Besides he would need a shotgun and he wouldn't know what to do with Tizzy while fox dogs were around.

Thinking of Tizzy, he takes the strap he uses for a lead out of his pocket and catches her and ties it to her collar. Tizzy is a "mostly cocker spaniel" dog and, in spite of her small size, is feisty enough to start a fight with one of the big foxhounds and get hurt.

Chuck watches as the vehicles stop a few hundred yards down the road. The Barney truck stays there and the car moves on around the hill to let out standers. He watches as the dogs search and hears them make a strike. As soon as the foxhounds start to bawl, he knows they will not be interested in anything else and lets Tizzy go. Soon Tizzy hits a squirrel track and trees the rodent. Easing around the tree, young LeMaster spots the big fox squirrel and pots it with an easy shot.

All of the above happenings take place on the first Saturday in November. There is a lot of hunting with dogs each weekend every fall throughout the United States. Without dogs, it wouldn't be nearly as much fun. Without dogs, a lot of game would be lost. Hunting dogs are an inherent part of hunting today This chapter attempts to show how the dogs are used and the abilities of the various breeds.

Pointers, Setters And How To Tell The Good Ones From The Others

I PULLED off the gravel farm lane and let my Llewellin setter, Kate, out of the box in the back of the Jeep wagon. Then I loaded up the little twenty-two-inch barreled 12-gauge Franchi over-and-under and walked toward a grassy swale that bordered a small brook. This was one of the best woodcock covers in the area and I'd hurried home from work as I had been doing each morning for the last week to see if there were any flight birds in yet.

Kate swung around to the east to be downwind of the patch of cover and immediately locked into point. I moved into good shooting position and put my thumb on the safety, making sure it was all the way over to the left so it would fire the cylinder-bored barrel first. Then I spoke to the solidly pointing young setter.

"Get 'em," I said. Kate made one jump, coming down almost on top of a woodcock which flushed from under her feet. As the bird rose, I picked out the point where it would make that customary pause before leveling off into flight. Correcting a bit to catch up with the bird as it hung at the top of its rise, I pulled the trigger and the bird crumpled. At the shot, four more birds flushed and I quickly swung on another and folded it. I broke the gun to reload and again spoke to the little lady setter standing just where she had landed when she jumped the bird and told her, "Fetch!"

As the tan and white setter went off to pick up the first bird, I slipped in a couple more rounds of number 9s with 1-1/8-ounce loads. Kate picked up the dead bird and started toward me. About half way, she froze into a point. It was a scene bird dog men dream about: that little setter locked up on a bird with one in her mouth. But I'd had the pleasure of watching this trick before.

I started to move toward the pointing dog and as I went by a four-foot high bog willow, another woodcock burst from under it. I let the bird go, as Kate wasn't pointing it, and moved into shooting position and had her flush another bird. This one zagged when I zigged and the shot charge and the bird went separate ways.

I took the downed bird Kate delivered and sent her to find the other one, which she soon retrieved to hand. Moving along the little brook, the dog soon was on point again. My question had been answered. The flight birds were in and in full force. The banks of this little stream, only two feet wide, hosted myriad of woodcock. I soon had a limit of birds.

Later that day, my teenage son, John, arrived home from school and I took him to another cover where he soon shot his limit. It was one of those red letter days in the heart of a bird dog man. After John had filled his limit we went to still another covert and, leaving the guns in the car, let the dog point seventeen woodcock, one after another. This would have been a perfect opportunity for some dog training but, the dog was performing as well as anyone has a right to even hope. We had as much pleasure in watching the dog work as when we had been shooting. It was just a bit trying, though, when Kate pointed a grouse that flew straight away across an open field and neither of us had a gun.

The Llewellin setter is one of the finest bird dogs of the present time. At one time, the Llewellin strain had almost disappeared, but thanks to the efforts of such dedicated men as the late Harold Shaw of La Grande, Oregon; Judge Claude Miller of Yuba City, California; Dr. Harold Ersig of Toledo, Ohio and Henry P. Davis, the Llewellin strain was saved. Davis was public relations director for Rem-

Left: Well-trained pointer brings a quail to hand. (Right) Author's pointer, Woodie's Big Jim looks up on a covey of quail. Wood says this is one of the few dogs that could do well in field trials and in the hunting fields as well.

This dog has come to point in an off-balance position to avoid bumping the bird that is near patch of snow in front of the dog's nose.

ington Arms, considered the dean of gun dog men, and also was dog editor of *Sports Afield* for many years.

I have several letters from Henry P. Davis regarding the Llewellins. The breed's future was helped greatly by an article written by Frank Dufresne in the November, 1964 *Field & Stream* in which he called Grande Ronde Blizzard the greatest dog he had ever seen in the field. This proclamation was made after a hunt with Harold Shaw and Blizzard. Such praise from one so widely known and respected may have been the push needed to get people interested in the Llewellin. Grande Ronde Blizzard was the sire of the dog, Kate, mentioned earlier.

This dog, called Doc, runs all out in covering the field. Photo illustrates speed, desire of pointers.

Along about here, some readers no doubt are going to protest that there is no such breed as the Llewellin setter, adding that there is only one breed of English setter. There has long been controversy on this matter and quite likely there will continue to be. My answer is that my Kate dog is registered in the American Field Stud Book as a *Llewellin Setter.* The pure strain of Llewellin is as different from the "grade" or Laverack setter as a setter differs from a Brittany. To shed light on this controversy, let's look at the history of English setters. I can write with confidence here as I have the breed records and breeding lines all the way back to R. Purcell Llewellin's Laverack setter, Countess. Countess was the first dual champion and the base from which the Llewellin was developed. Harold Shaw passed along a great mass of records on the Llewellins and asked me to be the breed warden for Llewellin setters shortly before he died.

The English setter is one of the oldest breeds of gun dogs existing today. The breed was defined and standardized by the London Kennel Club in 1873, although the breed had been in existence long before that date. The first recorded breeder was Edward Laverack, whose records go back to around 1860. However these "setting dogs" are mentioned as far back as the 1300s.

Llewellin purchased his original brood stock from Laverack, but the two men had entirely different approaches to the goal of improving their dogs. Laverack believed in line breeding to intensify those characteristics he wanted in his dogs. (Line breeding is commonly accepted practice in breeding for certain qualities.) Llewellin had different ideas about how to achieve his goals. He believed in outcrossing carefully to certain breeds that had desired traits, main-

Doc flash-points a dead quail before picking it up. Many dogs will point a dead bird in this manner for a moment before pick-up. (Right) Quail crouches before a dog on point. Usually, a quail is not so visible.

taining that while line breeding could intensify a characteristic, it could not bring in a characteristic that was not already present. It does not take a discerning eye to tell a Llewellin from a Laverack.The Laverack is the classic show-type setter with a deep muzzle and long, heavily feathered coat. The Llewellin is a lighter, more dainty dog with a more sharply pointed muzzle and is generally smaller. Most colors are permitted in these breeds by the registry and there are those that are spotted, ticked or of solid color. Then there are the Beltons.

Belton is a village in Northumberland, England, where Laverack hunted. Belton-colored dogs have small spots larger than the type of spots called "ticking." Some of these spots may be fairly large, especially around the ears, and often one or both ears may be of the darker color. In any event, the background color is mostly white among Beltons while the spots may be black, tan, lemon or liver. Occasionally, one is found that shows some fine ticking, but this is not a prominent characteristic of Beltons. Perhaps it may be more descriptive to call the speckling on Beltons as "patches of spots." The American Kennel Club breed standard describes Belton as, "...an intermingling of colored and white hairs." This is true, of course, but a lot of combinations of colored and white hairs do not add up to Belton coloring. When we come to something like this, we realize why judging schools are necessary.

All of this concentration on Llewellins is not to infer that there are not truly great dogs among the Laverack setters. Some of the finest pointing dogs to be found anywhere in the world come from the "Old Hemlock" Laverack Beltons bred by George Bird Evans of Bruceton Mills, West Virginia, one of the foremost breeders of English setters in the world today. Evans also is a leading dog writer. I have derived many hours of pleasure from his many books about bird dogs and hunting.

The Old Hemlock dogs are grouse specialists, being far more careful in their approach to game than the ordinary English setter. A grouse dog must be especially cautious in its approach to game. A startled grouse almost invariably will flush and a dog that goes crashing about through the brush is going to startle it. Perhaps, this is the main reason that we find few pointers used as grouse dogs. Pointers generally run faster than setters and are less careful in their approach to game; they create much more commotion in heavy cover than setters.

Now, before everyone jumps to tell me about how great

their pointers are on grouse, let me state that I know there are some pointers that are excellent grouse dogs; I have hunted with a few. I am speaking of the majority of the breed. And I do realize that the colder temperatures of most grouse country makes the long coat of the setter more practical throughout most of the grouse range.

To speak strictly without prejudice to any breed is difficult. Everyone is at least partially "kennel blind;" this is a phrase used by dog people to note the all too human tendency to overlook the faults of one's own dogs and breeds while often exaggerating the faults of other dogs and breeds. Having admitted to being somewhat kennel blind — more than can be said for some self-proclaimed authorities — I still tend to evaluate the many breeds of pointing dogs used in this country at present in a fair light.

That I am partial to the Llewellin setter may result from the fact that the most outstanding dogs I've owned have been Llewellins; or it may be that the Llewellin is the best pointing breed for the kind of hunting I do here in the eastern panhandle of West Virginia. I hunt quail, grouse, woodcock and ringneck pheasants. I also hunt doves, geese and ducks, none of which call for a pointing dog. Much of my hunting is done in heavy cover where a big running dog does not offer an advantage. I've owned most of the pointing breeds but have not had much satisfaction. I once had a big English pointer named Woody's Big Jim. He was on the field trial circuit with a professional handler for a time and did better than I expected. For open country, where a big running dog is in demand, the pointer has no equal. There are so many different breeds of pointers that it was customary until a few years back to identify the entire breed range simply as English pointer. This practice has been dropped, so for the purpose of this book, when I speak of a pointer, I mean the dog formerly known as English pointer. Any other will be designated by whatever breed of pointer it is, such as German shorthaired pointer.

As hunting breeds go, the pointer is relatively new; these dogs have existed in their present conformation for only about eighty years. The first recorder of this breed was William Arkwright of Sutton Scarsdale, England. Arkwright was instrumental in the development of the modern pointer from around 1890 to 1920 and wrote a book which is the accepted definitive work on the breed.

Prior to Arkwright's work, the history of the pointer is sketchy and seems to run back only about two hundred years. Generally thought to be of European origin, one authority states that the present-day pointer was developed from the setter, Italian pointer, bull terrier, greyhound, foxhound, bulldog and Newfoundland. This is a mixture that could have produced anything and I offer it here only because it is an accepted theory. Whatever its origins, the pointer can be one of the great gun dogs of all time. Almost all of the champions in recent national field trials have been pointers with the exception of one setter of Crockett breeding. Most setter fanciers are happy that their breed is not too heavily used in field trials, as this

The author considers this a classic example of a proper point. It comes from natural ability with good training.

would tend to make breeders try for more speed and wider range, the last thing one needs in a grouse and woodcock dog.

Field trial breeding is the greatest problem with pointer dogs today. They have been bred to run big for the field trial circuit and, because of such breeding, it is difficult to find a good gun-dog pup. When the owner of a good hunting bitch decides to breed her, he thinks he will be able to sell the pups only if he can show that the sire of the pups was a field champion. This causes our prospective breeder to take his bitch to a field champion and spend big money on a stud fee. He might be much wiser to find a nearby dogowner who has a good male gun dog and watch the dog work in the field to be sure this dog has the traits to compliment the characteristics of his bitch. In all likelihood, such breeding will produce pups with the abilities needed for the local conditions encountered in hunting.

If you are hunting quail in small hilly fields with briar and honeysuckle patches interspersed with grain fields, you do not need or want a big running dog that you are going to chase all over creation or run to keep up with. You need a reasonably close-working pointer with good nose and high pointing and biddability instincts. In the Plains states and on the big plantations in the Deep South, one can use a bigger running dog, especially if quail hunting from horseback as is the custom in the South.

Common sense can tell a lot about breeding if we only think a bit, instead of being swept off our feet by the glamour of the big time field champions. I'm not a geneticist, but I have studied breeding enough to have a pretty good idea of how to breed the characteristics I am looking for in a pup. I also have had the benefit of lengthy correspondence with master breeder Harold Shaw and there is much breeding information in the Llewellin breed book. The hunter who owns a good pointer bitch first should know her traits. Let us assume the bitch is a bit on the small size, has a real choke-bored nose, runs close to the hunter, has a tendency to creep a bit when she has to hold her point for a long time and is a bit hard-mouthed.

The ideal dog to breed this bitch to would be a rather large dog that has a reasonably good nose, runs just a bit too wide for the local cover, is staunch on point and is tender-mouthed. In such a cross, the characteristics of one dog tend to balance the opposite traits in the other. If the bitch is small and is bred to a large dog, this should result in normal-sized puppies. Since the bitch has such an excellent nose, you don't absolutely require a male with an exceptional nose. As the bitch hunts rather close in, she is bred to a dog that runs a bit far out, hopefully, this should result in a medium-range offspring. The bitch needs staunch-

This Brittany has broken point at the flush. This is a bad habit that can endanger the dog's safety and can be avoided by proper training.

Bodo Winterhelt shows off a fine-looking pointer that is of German shorthair breeding. As expressed in text, some dogs do well in field trials, but fail in field.

ing up a bit so the dog should be very staunch to give the needed steadiness to the puppies. And finally the hard-mouthed bitch needs a soft-mouthed mate to balance the tendency to chew the game on retrieve.

So we find that rather than being a mysterious and difficult subject, the basics of breeding are a matter of common sense. It would be simple, indeed, if it always worked out like this, but there are several flies in the proverbial ointment. It is highly unlikely that you can find a male whose characteristics so perfectly balance those of the female. We are going to have to trade off one or more points.

For example, the prospective breeder may be faced with a choice between a dog that is staunch but hard-mouthed or one having a tender delivery that is even smaller than the bitch. You have to decide which of the undesirable characteristics to eliminate and which you can live with.

To further complicate the matter, we must remember that dogs are individuals. No two pups in the litter are going to be exactly the same in temperament and have the same traits. In breeding, we can only hope to shift the average of the dog's characteristics in the direction we want them to go. We have barely skimmed the surface of the rules of genetics, but the idea here is to get the prospective breeder started in the right general direction; to keep someone from breeding a pair of dogs that have the same faults. There are many dog breeders who really believe the only requirement for a good litter of pups is to find a dog that is registered as the same breed.

The pointer is a rather large dog. The breed standard calls for a height of twenty-two to twenty-four inches, and a weight of forty-four to sixty-six pounds. Many of the pointers in field use today are much larger. My Big Jim weighed about seventy-five pounds, and my present pointer, Doc, weighed eighty-seven pounds the last time he was weighed to determine the proper dosage of worm medicine. There is a reason for this increase in size; bigger dogs are better able to get through heavy cover.

The pointer has been bred for and is at its best as a covey dog. Finding a covey, waiting for us to shoot birds on the covey rise, then moving on to find another covey. My Jim dog could be made to work the singles, if one kept an eye on him and called him in as soon as he tried to drift away. But as soon as he could slide out of sight, he was off to find another covey. This is fine when birds are plentiful, but frustrating when birds are scarce. One advantage of this behavior is that the coveys didn't get overshot. A covey never should be shot down to less than eight birds, if they are to come through the winter to breed another covey the following summer.

Though he won field trials, Jim was never much for grouse or woodcock. He moved too fast and made too much noise in heavy cover. He would point woodcock, but absolutely refused to pick one up. The best I could get out of him with downed woodcock was to get him to make a halfhearted point on the dead bird. If he wasn't watched closely, he would cock his leg and thoroughly dampen them. He just plain didn't like woodcock. This is not uncommon, as many pointers and some setters do not like to retrieve woodcock. Many of those I have spoken with on this subject feel it has to do with the odor of the woodcock caused by its diet of earthworms.

In contrast with the behavior of Jim in heavy cover and on woodcock, my Llewellin, Kate, glided through heavy cover like a cat. Whenever she approached birdy-looking cover, she would always circle to approach the cover from downwind. She would instinctively close in her search pattern in thick brush so I could keep visual contact with her or at least hear her bell.

When she picked up bird scent, she would glide forward into pointing range and creep up on the bird. Then her tail

Philip Swain offers praise to his dog which bears the unlikely name of Mogollon Rufus O'Shaunessy. If there is any doubt, this dog is of Irish setter breeding.

This Brittany spaniel proves his worth and ability as a water retriever, illustrating that water is no problem.

would go up and there was the bird, be it quail, grouse, pheasant or woodcock.

Like George Evans' Old Hemlock setters, Kate was the end result of many generations of breeding by a master breeder and geneticist who was ruthless in his culling of dogs that did not quite measure up to his standards. Harold Shaw was in his nineties when he passed on to the Big Cover in the Sky and had devoted most of his life to developing Kate's family of Llewellins. In just a few short years, due to the refusal of some to breed as he had outlined, this particular strain of Llewellin is nearly lost.

The short, hard coat of the pointer allows it to work in warmer weather. A more heavily-coated dog would be unable to work due to heat exhaustion, one of the hazards of running dogs in hot weather. Its short, hard coat also makes the pointer almost burr proof. Cockleburrs, dock, Spanish needles and similar plant seeds are the bane of long-haired dogs. They get caught in the feathering on the dog's coat and are hard to remove. It is often necessary to spend an hour or more with curry comb to remove burrs.

I have been saying that breeders who want hunting dogs should not breed to field champions, but I have no malice toward the big-time professional handler field trial, per se. As stated before, I once put a dog on circuit, but the more I saw of field trials, the more I realized how little this completely artificial situation had to do with hunting. I am primarily a hunter and, although I have a deep interest and love of hunting dogs, they are still primarily a means to further my pleasure and success in the field, as well as companions in my home. Neither of these purposes is abetted in any way by the big circuit field trial. At the risk of offending those in the field trial business — and it is a business — let me explain what I feel is wrong with the major circuit field trial:

There is a drawing for running order and the dogs are drawn two at a time. The two dogs drawn together will be run together as bracemates. The judges, dog handler, field marshal and many others, known as the gallery, mount horses and ride out into the field. The dogs are cast loose to find game with the judges and handlers following close to the dogs, while the field marshal keeps the gallery at a distance not to interfere with the dogs' work.

If the dogs split, one judge will follow each dog. When one of the dogs points, the handler goes in to flush the birds. No shooting is done and the dog is expected to remain steady to flush. The dogs are expected to run to the horizon and find as many coveys as possible.

A brace of dogs will often cover several miles while under judgment. This does not mean that they will travel this far in one direction, but their meanderings will add up to a lot of miles and they sometimes will end up a couple of miles from where they were put down. In this sort of trial, a dog can become a champion without ever having had a bird killed over it or retrieving a bird. To me, this is not a test of dogs. This approach certainly does not encourage the breeding of the kind of dogs we need in the hunting we

The author poses with Kate, his Llewellin setter that is mentioned often in text. He considers this dog to be one of the best woodcock dogs in the United States.

encounter today. We often are restricted to a small area surrounded by posted land and often highways where a wide-running dog is likely to be killed in traffic. Further, one of these field champions may have no retrieving instinct at all. This is not what we look for in a hunting dog.

I wrote an article stating these views for *Sports Afield* magazine and engendered a lot of complaint and argument from field-trial devotees and those who breed dogs from field-trial stock and to field-trial standards. The most common argument is that it is hard to get dogs to reach out for the long sweeps of bird country the trial judge is looking for and easy to get a dog to stay in close. There was a pro handler who took one outstanding field trial champion and got it to work nicely to the gun. However, such dogs are the exception rather than the rule.

When I decided to work my Jim as a gun dog, I had difficulty hacking him down to gun-dog range and he never really was happy in such work, until he became old and slowed down.

However, there is hope on the horizon. Recently two organizations devoted to hunting-type pointing dogs have been organized. The National Birdhunters Association, and the National-Shoot-To-Retrieve Association (NSTRA) are foot hunting and handling field-trial associations which are awarding field-trial wins for dogs over which birds are shot and retrieved. If the judges do not put too much emphasis on range, dogs that attain championships under these organizations should make excellent breeders.

Probably third in popularity among pointing breeds is the Brittany spaniel. The Britt, as it is commonly called, is a splendid pointer and retriever. Standing nineteen to twenty inches tall and weighing thirty-five to forty pounds, the Britt is considerably smaller than most of the other pointing breeds. Don't let this size fool you; this is a strong, elegant one hundred percent hunting dog that need make no apology because of his size. He can stand up to rough conditions and come through. He is a strong swimmer and will retrieve geese from rough water that look to be half as big as he is. Having good pointing instincts, the Britt is right at home in the bird fields on quail and the wooded thickets for grouse and woodcock; and pheasants are no problem either.

The small size of this breed has made it a favorite of those who do not have much room for a dog. Pleasantly playful and happy, they fit in well in the home where there are children. They don't need to be coddled and can be kenneled outside in all but the most severe weather.

Origin of the Brittany spaniel is one of the most controversial of the popular pointing breeds. About the only thing authorities will agree upon is that they came from

Kate, author's Llewellin, is on point in the woods that she loves to hunt in season.

Tool of the trade in teaching dogs is the author's 12-gauge Franchi over/under. Note woodcock.

Brittany in France as the name indicates. The most common story is that the Britt was developed by the peasants of France in the Middle Ages as a poacher's dog. Being small in size, they were hidden easily and were bred to be an all-purpose dog for use in taking the nobility's game. They did not breed true to type until around 1910 and lack of conformity makes it difficult to trace the origin. At any rate, in the beginning of the Nineteenth Century, a Breton count living at Pontou kept small English-bred setters for woodcock hunting. One of these setters was bred to a local hunting breed and this litter produced two short-tailed puppies that are supposed to be the beginning of the Brittany we know today.

Gaston Pouchain, president of the the Brittany Spaniel Club of France, has called the breed, "maximum of quality in a minimum size." Introduced into the United States in 1931, the Britt obtained AKC recognition in 1934. Numbers increased slowly until the end of World War II. Then the number of Brittanies increased rapidly until, by 1969, there were 20,000 in AKC registries. There is good reason for this rapid increase in popularity: A relatively small pointing breed that has a strong pointing instinct, the dogs can be trained easily by anyone willing to devote time and effort.

In the field the Britt moves at a gallop. When one comes into heavy cover, he moves with a bouncy gait that allows him to be seen bobbing up and down in the weeds and brush by the hunter; such movement also allows the dog to see over surrounding growth. One of the best breeds for use on ringneck pheasant, as they soon learn to circle ahead of a running bird to hold it for the gunner, they also have a strong desire to hunt to the gun and thus are not likely to become self-hunters.

Over the years I've owned three Brittanies. The first, named Bruno, was the best of the three; a great gun dog. He was given to me as a puppy and about four months of age before I did much with him other than training him to come when called, to stop, sit and stay. As a training effort, this was the minimum I could reasonably expect to get by with until hunting season opened and he would be six months old. I was living on a farm at the time, raising and training beagles for sale, so I didn't have all that much time for a bird dog.

A cold snap came in September and I took Bruno along one evening when I went to check the corn crop. As I walked down a lane bordering an alfalfa field, Bruno suddenly came into a classic point. As I came up to the dog, I could hear squealers on the ground in front of him. (Squealers are immature quail that do not yet fly well and make a lot of chirping, chirring and squealing noises.) I steadied the pup on his point by gently pushing him toward the birds while petting him and telling him what a good dog he was. When you push a young dog that is on point toward the birds, the dog instinctively resists the pressure and this causes it to become more firmly established on its point.

After I had firmed Bruno up on his point and let him hold for about four minutes, I walked up and put the birds up with some difficulty. As the pup tried to run past me to chase the birds, I caught him and stopped him from chasing. I was making a great to-do over him while restraining him from following the birds. On the return from the cornfield, I took Bruno into the area where the same birds had settled in from their flight. Bruno was soon locked up tight on them again. This time, to see what he would do, I did not steady the pup up any. I simply walked in and put the birds

This photo illustrates well how close quail will lie for good dog.

up. When the birds rose, the pup took a couple of tentative steps and I "whoahed" him sharply. He stopped and I made over him a lot. This was about the only training Bruno ever got. I took him out a few more times before the season opened and he performed well. I expected to teach him to hunt dead and retrieve, so I threw a scented dummy for him a few times and hid it a few times. He found the dummy and retrieved it with aplomb. When the season opened, Bruno performed well, both finding and pointing birds and retrieving. This first experience with the breed made me a Brittany fan.

My second Britt was a female pup which I got as my son's first pointing dog. Although well bred, Una never showed the sort of things the experienced pointing-dog owner looks for in a pup. She would not point a quail skin on the end of a pole and string, nor did she act birdy in cover as a puppy. We yard broke her to whoah and heel and come and tried to get her to point live birds or scented dummies and whatever else might appeal to her. All I got was a noteworthy lack of success.

Bird season came in when she was about 14 months old and we took her out with the older dogs. She wouldn't point and showed little interest in working cover until I shot a quail over one of the other dogs. The quail fell near her and she grabbed it as it fluttered a bit and ate it before we realized what was happening.

This seemed to determine her main interest in life: eating birds. I tried all the standard methods such as putting nails sharpened on both ends in dead birds for her to bite into and filling a dead bird with cayenne pepper. None of it worked. She got to the point where she would hide when one of the other dogs she had been working with would start to make game. Then when a bird was shot, she would make a mad dash to grab the bird and run off to eat it before we could catch her.

One day she got her just desserts. I shot a ringneck over one of Big Jim's points and, as he was going in to retrieve the bird, she snatched it out from under him. Jim was getting along in years and not inclined to put up with much nonsense from a young bitch. He ran her down, soundly thrashed her and came back carrying the bird with his head held high.

Such behavior cannot be tolerated in a dog so we finally had to dispose of her. There are some dogs in any breed which do not live up to their breed expectations, displaying bad traits which are uncharacteristic of the breed. Usually such bad traits can be corrected, but individual dogs are so recalcitrant that they cannot be made to perform. I tried everything I knew to break Una of eating birds. I was unable to correct the fault even through the most stringent corrective measures, including a shock collar. Such dogs never should be bred, since we do not want to perpetuate such bad behavior.

My third Britt was owned by a good friend who used the dog as a versatile dog in both hunting and North American Versatile Hunting Dog Association's trials. This dog had done well in the versatile trials; a good pointer, tracker and retriever on both land and water. His one bad fault was in chasing birds when they flushed. By repeatedly upsetting him at the end of a check rope, I was able to get him pretty well out of this bad habit, but he never became totally broken of this fault. He might point and hold solidly all day, then on the tenth point, he would break at the flush and chase. While not desirable, I could live with this fault. You could kill a lot of birds over this dog in a day's hunting. An occasional lapse into chasing was a small price to pay for all the things this dog did right. Actually, all dogs have some fault or other, just as do people. If no man is perfect, is it logical to expect our dogs to be? Some dogs have worse and more faults than others. If a dog's faults are outweighed by his good points, you have a good dog.

The German shorthaired pointer is one of the more popular hunting dogs in the United States at present. A breed that has much to offer the hunter, the GSP is the end product of a long breeding program which resulted in crossing the Spanish pointer with both Italian and English pointers. Over the years, various outcrosses to other pointing breeds and retrievers have resulted in a dog of distinguished appearance and abilities. Standing twenty-four to twenty-five inches and weighing fifty-five to seventy pounds, these are rather large dogs, whose dense coat is short and coarse. Although many colors are acceptable, chestnut roan with dark chestnut head and ear-markings seem the most popular.

High spirited, but very trainable is perhaps the best description of the GSP. They are tireless all-day hunters, dependable retrievers, excellent guard dogs, tops as trackers and highly capable in the water. The GSP is classed among the versatile dogs and, as such, is capable of pointing a covey of quail, bringing a rabbit around to the gun after seeking it out in the thickets, tracking down a wounded deer and retrieving ducks and geese from large bodies of rough water all in the same day if given the opportunity. Much of what was said about the English setter is applicable to this breed in so far as field work is concerned. Most GSPs are quite careful in their approaches to game and, while not the equal of the setter as a grouse dog, they are popular in the grouse coverts of New England where their owners often use them also as retrievers for waterfowling. Highly adaptable to a wide variety of climates and living conditions, the GSP is as at home in the house as in an outside kennel on a snowy winter day. Solid and dependable, this is a working breed that is not easily confused or discouraged by adverse conditions. Hunting in Pennsylvania with a friend, his GSP came to a solid point near a rock outcrop of large stones with many groundhog holes in and around them. In spite of our best efforts to put up a bird we could find nothing, so my friend decided the bird had gone into one of the goundhog holes.

As the bitch insisted on pointing the spot, Frankie put the dog on leash and led her away for some distance. When she was released, she went right back to the spot and established point. Again we both looked carefully around the area, but could find no evidence of a bird. This time the bitch was led a long distance before she was released. When she was turned loose, the bitch again started for the rock break which was well over a hundred yards away.

This was too much and my friend lost his cool and began shouting and chasing the dog. She got to the rock break ahead of Frank and, just before he ran up to catch her, she made a dive for the rocks and extracted a live hen pheasant from the rocks. The dog's owner realized that he had made a mistake and called her in to him. She came, bringing the pheasant.

The Irish setter is now on the road to recovery as a hunting breed after having been almost ruined as a gun dog by the bench breeders. Until the 1930s, the big Irishman was one of the more popular hunting breeds in America, but suddenly we started getting Irish setters that had little hunting or pointing instinct and were so silly-headed as to be almost untrainable.

The breed fell rapidly from popularity among hunters and was seldom seen in the field. These dogs were absolutely beautiful, having little in common with the dogs we had known. The old Irish setters had quite a bit of white in them and almost always had at least a white blaze on the chest. Most were rather cobby of build. Then the dog suddenly being bred for show was tall, graceful, had a beautiful mahogany coat with little, if any, white in it. The new breed was beautiful, but useless. This seemed to happen almost overnight.

Many of the gun dogs in our area were Irish setters and were fine dogs. Then there seemed to come a time when the old dogs died and were replaced with new dogs that just wouldn't hunt. It could be said that the breed "crashed." This was actually the second such crash, as the breed had been largely destroyed by bench breeders in the 1860 era, according to the breed histories. In about 1870, a few breeders who still had good field-type Irish setters started rebuilding the breed and, by 1910, they had a fine gun-dog breed that again had become popular. This field strain had a lot of dogs with white chest markings and white bellies. The second wave of show breeding for conformation and color left these dogs in poor repute as hunters.

As had happened before, those few who had good field-bred dogs started over again. The second "crash" seems to have been more regional throughout the United States, some geographic areas having fine hunting Irish setters

This photo, taken in an Illinois cornfield, illustrates soft-mouth technique that good pointer uses for pick-up.

while other sections had little left but show dogs.

At present, there are many Irish setters of both show and field breeding. The breed is becoming more popular, but in spite of the interest, there appears an excellent chance of now maintaining two definite strains: field-bred and show-bred. A look in any magazine carrying kennel advertisng will show both field-bred and show-bred Irish setters advertised. There is room for both so long as they are kept separate. Personally I would like to see a separate registry for each strain. This would ensure there would be no repeat of the aforementioned "crash." There seems to be something about the beautiful mahogany coat of this breed that demands of show dog people that they experiment for even more beauty.

Standing twenty-one to twenty-four inches, and weighing thirty-three to fifty-five pounds, with that long, silky mahogany coat, these graceful, streamlined dogs are a beautiful sight in the field as they make bird-finding sweeps at great speed. A lot of them, though, still retain some of the mule-headedness they got from show breeding. I've only owned one of these big red Irishmen and had poor success in training, even though the dog was well bred. It seemed necessary to take drastic steps to "get his attention." As I was used to having good, biddable dogs, I did not keep this one long. A close friend, Doug Catlett, had one of these red setters some twenty-five years ago that he trained into a pretty fair gun dog. There are a lot of good Irish setters around and I am aware that my experience with the breed is not necessarily typical.

The finest Irish setter I've seen is Mogollon Rufus O'Shaunessy, owned by Philip and Susan Swain of Woodbridge, Virginia. In 1977, at the Potomac Chapter Utility Trial held near Tuckahoe, New Jersey, Rufus earned a prize II in qualifying for the second time as a NAVHDA Utility dog. This was high attainment, indeed, for a dog from a breed that is supposed to be straight upland pointer. But if you knew Rufus, it would be no surpise. The dog is a gentleman, not to mention trustworthy, loyal, helpful, friendly, courteous, kind, obedient, et al.

Phil and Susan Swain have invested a lot of training time and effort in Rufus, but it has paid off handsomely. To qualify for Utility dog in a NAVHDA test, Rufus had to: track a duck through a swamp in a high wind, then swim a quarter mile to catch the duck before the wind blew it away. He also had to walk at heel through a maze without undue tugging at the leash, then remain by the blind while his handler went off into the brush out of sight of the dog and fired two shots. He must show good manners by the blind while several shots were fired and a duck was thrown into the water; he was required not to move from the blind until told to do so, then retrieve the duck when sent to do so.

In another segment of the test, he was called upon to demonstrate a good search pattern in upland hunting; find and point quail and pheasants in the game field; remain

The Gordon setter is not especially popular in the U.S., but is gaining stature. The breed originated in Scotland.

With a good working pointer, there never is doubt when he is on game. This classic stance is the type to win points in any major field trial.

steady to wing and shot when the birds were flushed; retrieve the shot bird to hand. This Irish setter was required to follow the scent left by a dead bird being dragged for a hundred yards and hidden. He had to retrieve the hidden bird, demonstrate good nose, desire to hunt and work, show stamina and cooperation, handle well and exhibit obedience and, in the overall opinion of the judges, be qualified as a finished gun dog in all respects. That's a mighty tall order. To the best of my knowledge, Rufus is the only Irish setter to qualify thus far as a Versatile Utility dog and he may well be the only one to ever do so

Big Red, as the Irish setter is commonly known, is here to stay. Every year more of them become fine field dogs. In addition, they make good companion and guard dogs.

The Gordon setter is not especially popular in America today, but has a small, devoted following that is growing at a steady rate as the sterling character of these black and tan setters becomes known.

The Gordon is the only Scottish gun dog, development of this breed generally being credited to Duke Alexander of Gordon. A breeding program which started in the early 1770s resulted in a really fine working dog by the early 1800s. The breed passed to the Duke of Richmond in 1835 and he continued building the breed at Gordon Castle. The breed became known as Gordon Castle setters and the first pair was exported to America in 1842.

Then disaster struck. Show breeders succeeded in destroying the original breed almost completely. By 1875, Robert Chapman of Heather Kennels was working to try to save the breed and was largely successful. The Gordon of today is the result of Chapman's efforts; it is a somewhat more heavy and cobby dog than was the original Gordon developed by Duke Alexander.

Standing twenty-four to twenty-seven inches and weighing up to eighty pounds, the distinctively marked Gordon is a striking example of the hunting dog. The color is black with chestnut-colored markings. There usually is a chestnut spot over each eye, a stripe around the end of the muzzle and down onto the throat and chest, the insides of the front and hind legs and the same coloring on the outer sides under the legs. These markings are not found on any other breed to so great an extent. If you see a large dog with a silky black coat set off with distinctive red chestnut markings, it is safe to assume you are looking at a dog of mostly Gordon ancestry.

A controversy over the Gordon in America has been going on for at least forty years and shows little sign of dying down. Incidentally, the Gordon setter inspires strong passions which lead to impassioned differences of opinion among pointing-dog men. The dispute allegedly resulted in the editor of a major dog magazine resigning his position a few years ago.

The dispute involves the nature and appearance of the Gordon setter. This breed admittedly is neither as agile nor fast, nor does it have the snappy actions and appearance of other pointing breeds. This is said to be largely the result of the damage done by show breeders.

At any rate, the Gordon is a sort of easy-going dog that gets the job done with a minimum of fuss and bother. The Gordon does a workmanlike job instead of the dashing, often flashy performance of the other popular American pointing breeds against which the Gordon is compared most often. The Gordon also has a rather loose-fitting hide and carries his tail at trail arms rather than at attention; this is true even when pointing. These factors, along with the Gordon's rather laid-back style, grate on some dog men's sense of perfection.

In spite of its seemingly easy-going approach, the Gordon gets the job done in fine form with less apparent bother. My limited experience with the breed has been that the

The late Harold Shaw (left) was a top breeder of the Llewellin strain. He is shown with his dog, Grande Ronde Blizzard, and Bill Brown, Oregon Game Commission. The author considers this dog one of the finest seen. (Below) In Southern quail country, two rangy pointers are put down to work area beside hunting-rigged jeep.

workmanlike approach taken by the Gordon results in as many or more birds brought to the gun as any of the other breeds, unless one is hunting grouse. The Gordon's size and seeming clumsiness prevent it from doing a really great job on grouse. But the pointer is no great shakes as a grouse dog either.

The Gordon gives the appearance of being a great oaf when he really isn't. His status from an individual viewpoint seems to depend upon whether you are interested in shooting birds or watching flashy dog performance. If it's birds that interest you, the Gordon will find them for you and deliver them nicely to hand.

The Gordon setter has many characteristics that make one like him. While not a fawning lap dog-type, it makes an excellent companion and, in spite of its size, does well in the home. The Gordon setter is among the most loyal dog breeds and does not take up easily with strangers. These dogs are excellent with children, unusually healthy and free of the twitches, jumpiness, and restlessness that makes some breeds a pain in the neck as companion dogs. They are diligent in their every move and a field that has been hunted by a Gordon has been thoroughly hunted. It is

highly unlikely that another dog is going to come along and find birds they have missed. Above all, they are highly intelligent.

Dr. R.E. Gale of Hagerstown, Maryland, had a Gordon named Gordon Macbeth, but it answered to "Gordo." This was the first Gordon setter I hunted over and it happened more years ago than are comfortable to contemplate. We went to a farm in Jefferson County, West Virginia, where there were always lots of quail. I had an English setter along, but Doc Gale wanted to hunt Gordo alone first so I could see how he performed.

Gordo had just been returned from a couple months with a professional trainer. He had been shaped up for the opening of quail season and supposedly was raring to go. We took him on leash past the farm buildings and released him in a large stubble field that had a lot of the ragweed seeds that quail love. Gordo moved off at a slow trot when given the "Hie on" command. This was surprising to me, as I had never seen a young bird dog put down fresh that didn't seem to try to be everywhere at once. They would take off in a blaze of speed until they had worn the first edge off their exhuberance at being out of the kennel and afield. None of this for Gordo. He just started hunting as if he had been down for hours and was starting to tire. Of course, I had heard all the bad stories about Gordons; that they were lazy, slow, clumsy and sloppy, had little desire to hunt, as well as all the other stories told by their detractors. And I also was familiar with the feelings of the Gordon fanciers.

This German shorthair seems a trifle bored by it all after he has helped this young hunter take a pheasant.

Watching Gordo run, I was starting to agree with those who claim Gordon setters are lazy and lack desire. Then, near a fencerow where I'd shot many a quail over the years, he stopped. I don't mean that this dog went on point. He simply stopped and stood still. There was none of the eager, intense, almost vibrant attention which seems to fairly shout when a dog goes on point. He was just standing there relaxed as if he had gotten tired of running and stopped.

"There they are" Doc said.

"You mean he's pointing?" I asked.

"That's it." Doc replied. We moved in behind Gordo and each of us went slowly by the dog, one on either side. The birds came up with a roar and we each dropped at least one. Gordo stood the shooting without visible emotion. At Doc's, "fetch!" Gordo moved to where he had marked down the dead birds and made a smooth pickup of a dead bird. He walked back and delivered it to Doc with that slow, ponderous wagging of his tal that I was to learn meant he was happy. After delivering the bird he took off again without any command and searched about a bit until a crippled bird fluttered out in front of him. With a surprising burst of speed, Gordo easily caught the bird and returned it to hand.

We sat down and rested a bit to give the birds time to spread a bit of scent. Flight tends to dissipate the scent from game birds and makes it almost impossible for a dog to find and point them immediately. When Gordo saw that we had stopped, he came over without command, going first to Doc to let him know that a pat on the head would be appreciated. After a bit of praise from Doc, he came over and checked me out. After what he evidently considered his due pat and ear rub, he lay down, quite content to wait until we moved on.

With most pointing dogs this early in the hunt, it would have required at least a firm put down to get them to stay with us and many would have required a leash to hold them. Sitting there, I decided that Gordo was a sort of "comfortable" dog to have around since it didn't require any hassle to get him to do what was necessary. I also wondered how long it would be before he ran out of steam and just quit hunting. I firmly believed a dog that hunted this slowly when starting out had to be out of condition and low on desire.

We continued to hunt at a comfortable walking pace (Doc was getting on in years a bit even then, while I was in my late twenties) for the rest of the day. We sat down and ate a sandwich after a couple of hours. Gordo came over and let each of us know it was all right with him if either of us decided to give him a bit to eat, but he didn't pester us, even after we'd given him a taste. When it came on to evening, I realized that Gordo was still moving at the same pace he'd started out at and was still covering every birdy-looking place as well as when we had started. Although my English setter would have hunted much more rapidly, she couldn't have found any more birds or covered the ground any better than Gordo had.

The Breeding Of Foxhounds Depends Upon The Type Of Fox Hunter Involved!

Foxhunting and riding to the hounds is a popular type of recreation in many sections of the Eastern United States.

MENTION FOXHUNTING to different persons and you will bring totally different visions to their minds. To one person, fox hunting brings the picture of a group of of nobs attired in red coats and formal hats mounted on fine horses in hot pursuit of a large pack of matched hounds that are pursuing the wily Renyard across hill and dale; the entire operation directed — perhaps, one would say orchestrated — by the Hunt Master with his horn.

To another, it brings the vision of a group of Good Ole Boys sitting around a campfire, sipping corn squeezins and toasting strips of venison over the fire, while they listen to their dogs run a fox around and around his territory. From time to time, someone may comment on the vocal performance of a particular dog. These men all recognize the voice of each dog and determine a great amount of just what the dog is doing, as well as its position in the pack. When the dogs come to a check in the trail, there will be bets made as to which dog will be first to move the line forward.

These dogs will likely run all night and, toward dawn, the men will place some old coats on the ground and get into their vehicles to return home after scrupulously paying off all bets. Those who have to go to work early will be the first to leave.

The next day, the backwoods foxhunters will return to the spot and their dogs probably will be lying on the coats they left for them. Often a man may pick up the dogs of a friend, but only if he has been specifically asked to do so. The man who steals one of these dogs from the spot where they are waiting for their masters has a very short life expectancy. It has been said that it is safer to steal one of these fellow's wife than to mess with his dog. This sounds pretty wild, but I'd not be the one to question it. These men spend years developing exactly the dog they want and they are dead serious about their foxhunting.

Still another scene is called up on the mental screen by thoughts of foxhunting. When they think of foxhunting, they think of a cold clear day in late Fall when they have driven to a good fox area with one or more good dependable foxhounds. One of the group will act as the leader. He will undoubtedly be one who knows the area and the fox crossings. The leader will assign a hunter to a particular crossing and that hunter is expected to cover that area and not leave until the hunt is over.

Foxes living in a particular area seem to establish certain routes of travel that they use in traversing their territory. A fox pursued by hounds generally will travel these routes. Usually they will keep pretty much to cover, but there usually are places where they are forced to cross openings and where they may be forced into a narrow track by the natural lay of the land or man-made boundaries and obstacles. These points where a fox may reasonably be expected to cross an opening are known as crossings. Most of these crossings are given names by the foxhunters who regularly hunt the area, thus the leader of a group may say, "Chub, you go up to Martin's Corner. Dave, I think you might do well down along the narrows at the creek. Lee, you ought to cover the little field gap with that cannon of yours. I want Mike up on the old sawmill pile, and if it sounds like they're going down towards Ed Miller's lane, slip across the hill and cover that. I'm going to put the dogs down in the big bottom and ease up onto the hill down by the meadow."

The dogs probably will strike a hot fox track near the rocky breaks above the meadow. Foxes like to lie up in a spot where they can see all around them in the daytime, and if the houndsmen know where they lie up, it generally is pretty easy to get a chase going. Then it is up to the dogs to push the fox past one of the crossings where the hunters are waiting.

Most of the hunters will be carrying 3-inch 12-gallon magnums loaded with number 2 or BB shot. Occasionally there will be someone with a 3½-inch 10-gauge magnum. The guns will all be tightly choked and the loads will be the longest range loads available, either handloads or factory premium long range loads.

As you can see, foxhunting is comprised of three separate and distinct sports: the formal chase with horses and hounds, the nighthunter who just wants to hear some good hound music and the fellows who are out to reduce the fox population. These groups do not intermingle. In

Horsemen are spread out across the hills as they follow the dogs that are on scent of a fox in the shallow ditch.

Little has changed in formal foxhunting since the first hounds were introduced in Maryland by Robert Brooks in 1650.

fact, there is some enmity between the fox-shooting hunters and the other two groups. The nighthunters and horsemen feel they need all the foxes the area will support and resent it when foxes are killed. However, the fox shooters are popular with farmers and game departments. Actually, there is little danger that the foxes will be overshot, as they do well at surviving hunters, trappers and farmers.

Almost all of the scent-trailing hound breeds are used in foxhunting, the most popular being the American foxhound. Today's American foxhounds are descended from hounds that were brought to Maryland by Robert Brooks in 1650.

There has been much development from the original dogs imported from England. Among the men who have left their mark on foxhounds are Dr. Thomas Walker of Virginia, who started breeding in 1742 and Lord Fairfax, who began his breeding program in 1746. George Washington was introduced to foxhunting by Fairfax and established a pack in 1759, when he was only 14. The list of foxhound breeders then expanded explosively and only a few of the most famous are listed here. T.Y. Henry, G.W. Mauphin, George Birdsong, Hayden C. Trigg, Willis Goodman and Nimrod Gosnell are a few of the outstanding men who left their mark on foxhound breeding. Many of these men have a strain of hound that carries their name today.

There is a National Foxhunters Association that conducts field trials and many activities for foxhound men. In addition to the American foxhound, there is the English foxhound from which the American strain was partly bred. The English foxhounds are less rangy than the American breed and they are of more uniform conformation.

The nighthunters are constantly crossing different strains of foxhound and other breeds such as black and tan, bloodhound, bluetick, Plott, redbone, beagle, basset and other dogs of mixed hound ancestry in an effort to develop the ultimate foxhound. They breed for trailing ability, stamina, voice, intelligence and whatever other characterstic they desire in their hounds. These are sociable men, ready to share their sport with all who are truly interested. If you are interested in hearing some good hound music, go to the barbershop in most any small town in Appalachia and ask where you might find some of the local foxhunters. If it is in the fall, winter or early spring, when they are running the dogs, and you seem to be the sort that meets their approval, you may be invited to travel to the hunt area with them where the dogs will be put down and a fire built. Do not expect to go hunting in the summer; they do not run the dogs then for several reasons. The first reason lies in the fact that snakes such as rattlers, copperheads and water moccassins are active in warm weather and a dog is apt to get bitten. In the Deep South, where snakes are active all year, there are many dogs lost to snakes. Those that survive learn to be wary of the scent of snakes. Another reason for not running during summer months is that the fox vixens are busy feeding their kits and vulnerable to the hounds. Incidentally, many states have established fox seasons, while others class them as vermin to be hunted at any time.

If invited to go night hunting with a foxhound group or individual, you will be well advised to do a lot of listening and little talking. If you will listen carefully to both the baying of the hounds and the comments of the men, most of your questions will be answered. Soon you will learn to recognize from their voices which dog is in the lead, when they come to a check, when the fox has gone to ground or the dogs come to a loss. This is a great sport, especially for those who have reached the age where they are either physically unable, or too smart to go thrashing around behind a pack of hounds in the daytime much less at night.

The various strains of the American foxhound are widely used to hunt game other than the fox. The Walker strain, descended from the dogs of Dr. Thomas C. Walker, is popular as deer hounds in areas where hunting deer with hounds is permitted, as are the Trigg, July and Gosnell lines. Some of the packs used by the horse-riding foxhunters are English foxhounds, but most of them are made up predominantly of Walkers. These horseback hunters go to great lengths to obtain conformity of size, color and type within a particular pack. Puppies are culled for no other reason than the presence of a brown spot in the black saddle marking preferred by the houndsman of the pack. To see one of these hound packs that have been established for a period of fifty or more years is to see a pack of nearly identical dogs. I have often wondered how the houndsman tell the individual dogs apart. The conformity that can be obtained by determined breeding is almost total. Another

The favored hound among foxhunters — whether the society types or the Good Ole Boys — is the Walker-bred strain.

Note that the hounds are less than fat. If carrying too much weight, they cannot maintain the fast pace of hunt.

breed used in foxhunting that is not bred from the English foxhound is the black and tan hound. These dogs are thought to be direct decendants of the Talbot hound of the Eleventh Century.

The black and tan hound is a highly adaptable hound. One of the most popular breeds for coonhunting, it often is found in bear packs for its sure nose and far-reaching voice. The immediate ancestor of the black-and-tan is the black and tan Virginia foxhound. A separate and distinct breed from the American foxhound, it was formerly popular throughout the Southeast. Although less of the extreme megacephaly of the bloodhound is evident in the black-and-tan, they generally resemble the bloodhound and have many of the same characteristics.

The black and tan hound, Bugle, mentioned in the chapter on coonhounds, was an excellent example of the versatility and intelligence of this breed. When hunted at night, he was a straight cooner and a good one. If I took him out in the daytime, he could be put on any track we came across and he would run it until I either killed the game or it went to ground. Only rarely did he come to a loss.

Bugle would run a rabbit around in a circle like a beagle or chase a fox into the next county and back. I think this was due to the rapport I established with this dog as I raised him from a puppy. If he took a trail that seemed to be a fox track and I didn't have time or inclination for a long chase, it was easy to call him off. On the other hand, if a cow strayed from the herd, I could put him on her track and he would bay her trail until he came up with her and then bark treed until she ran back to the rest of the herd.

Bugle lived to be 16 years old and ran and treed several 'coons and brought a fox around to the gun the winter before he died. This dog was an excellent example of the value of good breeding, being out of the finest bloodline of his day. It has been a long time and his registry papers are buried somewhere in a mass of other old papers, but I believe he was out of Ten Oaks Dixie Belle by Grand Honor of Ten Oaks.

Another such versatile hound breed is the Plott hound. Developed as bear dogs, these hounds serve well at just about any hound job one puts them to. The Plott will turn in a nice performance on any game from rabbits to moose and bear although using a Plott as a rabbit dog would seem akin to using a .458 magnum elephant rifle for squirrel shooting.

Another breed sometimes used for foxhunting is the basset hound. The basset has been described as a short-legged bloodhound; indeed, the analogy is apt as both breeds are megacephalic and similar in many ways. The basset was developed by the nobility in France primarily for use as a badger hound. After the French Revolution put royalty out of business, their bassetts fell into the hands of the commoners who put them to work as rabbit and hare hounds. In the United States, the basset is used primarily as a rabbit hound, but some also work out well on deer and are used by fox shooters who want a slow-moving hound that will not cause the fox to run so far they can't get a shot at it.

The name, "basset," comes from the french word *bas,* meaning something low to the ground and it is quite descriptive of this breed.

The basenji or African barkless dog is another of those breeds that are sometimes used to hunt foxes. This breed is a recent import from Africa and there is not too much experience with them. People who own them have found they will hunt literally anything they are trained to hunt and do a creditable job of it too. A friend in Martinsburg, West Virginia, has a basenji that he used to chase and hunt foxes. I have heard that they make excellent squirrel dogs, but as they are unable to bark to let the hunter know where they are, they must be trained to hunt close. One note of caution: if you own cats, do not let a basenji near your home. They will kill every cat in the neighborhood.

Many other breeds and crossbreeds are used to hunt foxes. Many of these are regional breeds generally used only in one area They were developed by persons living in that particular area to meet the specific needs of local hunters. These local breeds are not recognized by any official registry, but this does not mean that they are any less efficient or capable at the job for which they were bred. There are yellow tics, fices, an old breed known as the cur dog, boomers, mountain hounds and many breeds with which I am not at all familiar. In some parts of the country the coursing breeds are used as fox and coyote dogs.

A book could be written about each breed of hound and, in most instances, the various breed clubs have such books. For those who want more information on any particular breed, the best bet is to contact the breed club.

Following a pack of dogs through heavy underbrush can be a chore whether you are mounted on a horse or are afoot.

With The Talent To Tree Its Quarry, The Coonhound Can Be From Many Breeds

There are those outdoorsmen who feel there is nothing more exciting than following a pack of hounds behind a bobcat, a fox or a raccoon. Once the game has been run up a tree, dogs are excited; it's an anticlimax for hunters.

"PULL INTO the tracks on the left just this side of the bridge," Alex Cunningham said, "if you can get past the first two mudholes and around the bend. That way, the spooners won't be messing around your vehicle."

We spun and slithered our way through the first two mudholes, not an easy thing in the days of two-wheel-drive only, and came to a stop. As I turned off the engine, I could hear the rushing of Opequon Creek which was about twenty feet to the left. As I opened the door to get out, my big black and tan, Bugle let out a deep bawl of excitement and shattered the still of the night. That bawl also sent a shiver up the spine of every 'coon within 1½ miles.

"I checked this place out yesterday morning. 'Coon

tracks all over the place. We oughta put up a bunch tonight. Hope so. A 'coon hide is worth six to seven bucks, what with most of the hunters off fightin' the Japanese or Krauts." Cunningham ran his sentences all together, as he put down the tailgate of my truck and reached for the latch on his dog box. It was the fall of 1943, and we were planning to put a dent in the local raccoon supply. Alex put down the two blueticks and his big redbone, Drum, all of which promptly disappeared into the night.

"How about leaving that meat grinder of yours in the box for a while? I'd like the pups to get a chance to do something before they get run over by that beast," Alex suggested.

"Okay, but only for an hour or so," was my answer. The young blueticks were coming on strong and did need a chance to do it on their own. Alex's redbone was old and slow, but like the mill of the gods, extremely sure. The pups soon should outrun him and be on their own.

It was only minutes before Drum opened on a fairly hot track, sounding his cry. The pups joined in and they were off, down the creek with the two pups drawing ahead of the older, deeper-voiced dog, sounding good. It was easy to tell when they struck hot. (The term, "struck hot" denotes the moment, the dogs hit the spot where the 'coon had been when it first heard the dogs and took off to escape them.) The sudden surge of fear tends to release adrenaline, making the track scent much stronger as the dogs reached the spot where their game had been less than five minutes ago.

The dogs ran for about three hundred yards and came treed right on the bank of the creek. The "tree" barks had a sort of muffled sound and Alex Cunningham voiced my own thought: "They ain't barkin' up."

We soon came upon the scene to find that the dogs all were barking into a cavity under the roots of a giant willow.

"Tarnation! Gone to ground," Alex said. The raccoon had indeed gone into the hole and was beyond our reach.

This smooth-running cross of bluetick and Walker blood knows it's time to hunt when her master removes chain.

There is no fooling this big redbone hound. He knows that he has a 'coon up a tree and it's waiting to be taken.

This is not an unusual situation when 'coon hunting and is the reason 'coon hunters who are interested only in catching a lot of fur for financial, rather than sporting, reasons will go to a silent trailing dog. A silent trailer does not give voice on the track and thus comes upon the game suddenly without giving it time to find a hole or den tree.

We continued down the creek and soon the dogs struck a hot track which the pups ran, with old Drum conspicuously silent.

"Bet it's a possum," Alex said.

"No argument there," was my reply.

Soon the bluetick pups were barking treed again and we came upon a small sycamore against which the pups were jumping and barking. I had been looking high in the tree, but when I turned the light into the lower branches, there at the base of a limb were two eyes shining at me. They weren't the right color for an opossum and were too small for a 'coon. Moving around so the light would shine more fully on the spot, I saw that we had treed a fine yellow house cat!

We caught the dogs and put them on leashes to lead them away from the kitty cat. We had barely gotten away from the tree when old Drum cut loose with a deep bellow. He sounded to be about a hundred yards away across a small bottomland cornfield beyond which was a timbered ridge.

As we started across the field, the dogs kept getting entangled in the corn and we soon realized that we were going to break down a lot of the farmer's crop if we tried to take them through on the leashes. We decided to take a chance on letting the pups loose, hoping they would go to the sound of Drum's voice instead of returning to the treed cat. Fortunately, they did so and we soon arrived at a big limestone outcrop which was covered by timber.

This treeing Walker is a patient and a dependable 'coon dog.

The Walker and redbone (in background) are busily keeping the 'coon up the tree, while the young Trigg (right) isn't just certain what all the fuss is about. But whatever comes along, he will be ready through his own heredity.

The pups had joined Drum and all three dogs were running hot and sweet. They came to a check and milled around at a low spot in the limestone ridge where a small stream cut through. After a short wait, while the dogs nosed about in ever-widening circles, the female bluetick let out a few tentative yips a short distance up the small branch creek. Those first few yipping sounds became stronger, then she broke into a full bay and soon was joined by the other two dogs.

"Hey! Hey!" Alex chortled. "Listen to the little bitch. She's figured that one out for herself and is coming right along."

Dog people commonly refer to females as bitches and males as dogs. Alex's reference to the female pup as a bitch was not an epithet or slur on the dog, but a simple statement of gender and a way of indicating that he was aware and pleased that it was the female pup that had worked out the difficult spot in the raccoon's trail. For him to have referred to the female pup as a dog would have been incorrect. Many uninitiated people today have difficulty understanding this, seemingly regarding the use of the term as a slur on the animal involved, because "bitch" is often used as a slang word of defamation in the English of today.

The dogs ran another hundred yards up the small stream branch and again came to a check. After a few moments of silence, we heard Drum's sharp, "*yark yark,*" that indicated a treed animal. Soon the pups joined in and, when we arrived at the big gum tree, they all were barking up and trying to climb the tree.

Looking the tree over with my big 'coon hunter's spotlight, I spotted the telltale gleam of eyes about three-quarters of the way to the top of the tree. Moving around, trying to get a better look, I saw that it was a mature male with good fur. Drawing my .22 rimfire revolver, I moved around until I could get a good shot at the animal's head. I dispatched it neatly and the pups were on it as soon as it hit the ground. After allowing them to get a good mouthful of dead raccoon, Alex and I put them on the leashes and

What it is all about: Treed 'coon looks down upon the dogs while hunters try to catch up.

Well trained 'coon hounds boast a special type of cry to announce that the raccoon had been treed.

gathered the animal up before they damaged the hide. We circled back to the truck where we picked up my big black and tan, Bugle, and went upstream where we succeeded in collecting a few more 'coons.

The long-ago account can be considered as a fairly representative description of a night of 'coon hunting as it is done in the East and South. It is a popular sport that seems to have a steady growth pattern over the years, the number of 'coons taken in any given season directly proportional to the price of their hides.

The same people usually hunt each year, but in those years that the prices for hides are low, they tend to leave more 'coons for breeding stock. The resulting increase will be taken in a year when the price is better. Following hounds through the woods in the dark of night requires that one be in good physical condition so as to be able to get to the site where the 'coon trees.

Although the money derived from the sale of hides is often substantial, one has to do a lot of 'coon hunting in order to break even on the cost of keeping a pack of hounds for a year. Far more 'coon hunters keep dogs for the sport involved than for dubious profits on fur sales.

The black and tan, redbone and bluetick are the most popular dog breeds for 'coon hunting. There is a strain of treeing Walkers that is often used and there are people who have crosses of the various 'coon dog breeds that believe they are the better dogs.

The most important requirement for a good coonhound is that the dog "tree." This means that the dog will stay at the tree, hole or other location where the 'coon is brought to bay and give tongue until the hunters arrive on the scene. The "tree" bark should sound different from the trail bark so the hunters can determine when the game has treed. The tree bark is generally a short chop or yelp, while the trail bark is a long, drawn out sound.

There are many different breeds that are used, one way or another, as coonhounds. Most any breed that will follow a trail and bark "treed" can be and most likely has been used as a 'coon dog. An example of this is the Plott hound. This breed was developed by the Plott family as bear dogs.

The dogs have been put on leashes. This will prevent them from damaging the fur when the animal is brought down.

'Cooner noses the downed game animal with seeming curiosity. Hunters allow them to test the animal after it is taken as a reward for their efforts.

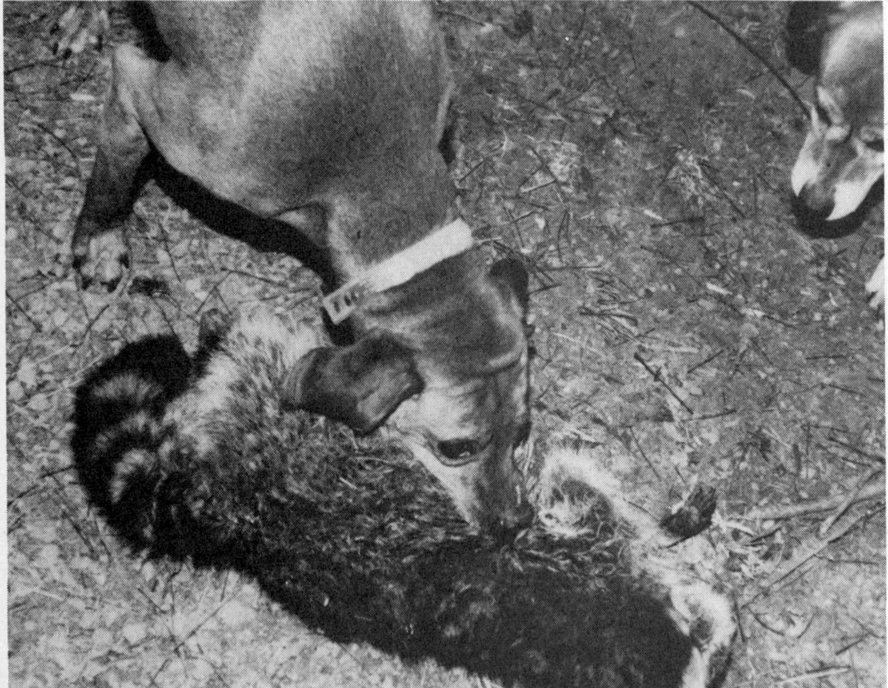

Redbone gets a good mouthful of the 'coon, but this is discouraged by the use of hunter's leashes.

They were known widely both for their tracking ability and their fighting prowess when a bear had been brought to bay. They were, perhaps, the finest bear dogs in the world before someone started using them on raccoons and they were found to be both sure on the trail and solid at the tree. Today, many 'coon hunters use Plotts as straight 'cooners.

"Straight cooner" is an important phrase to 'coon hunters. It is used to describe a dog that will run only raccoons, and will not be distracted by such "trash" game as opossums, skunks, weasels, mink, foxes, wild and domestic cats, rabbits or any game other than the raccoon. Such dogs are extremely valuable and bring high prices. Some hunters demand that their dogs be straight 'cooners, while others do not mind the dogs chasing other game as long as the dogs stay away from skunks and rabbits.

The so-called "silent trailer" is favored by many 'coon hunters. This type of dog will put up more game that can be collected by the hunter than will the open trailer. The silent trailing dogs do not furnish the "music" of the chase; instead, they tend to drift silently through the hunting area until they strike a track. Still silent, they will follow the track until they come upon the game. Coming suddenly on the game, the dogs rush upon it and the game, not having time to pick a defensive position of its choice, is forced to tree in whatever is immediately available.

There is no question that the silent hunting dog is the more efficient game getter but, as mentioned earlier, they do not arouse the excitement of the chase. The first the hunter hears from these dogs is their barking as they suddenly rush upon the game. The silent dogs are expected to remain at the tree and give tongue until the arrival of the hunter just as do the open trailers.

The silent trailing dog is usually of mixed breeding. Generally they are three parts hound breed and one part terrier or fice. Often, Airedales are bred into silent trailing 'coon hounds to add a bit of fighting spirit. Another breed that one often hears of being bred into silent trailing hounds is the yellow fice.

Although this is not a breed accepted by any of the various dog registry books, the yellow fice has been found throughout the hill country of West Virginia, North Carolina, Virginia, Kentucky, Tennesee and southern Ohio for generation upon generation. Many of the hill families jealously guard their fice dogs and will not sell them or allow strangers to breed to them. These dogs vary somewhat in conformation in the different localities, but most are medium in size. Such a dog will weigh thirty pounds or so; it is short-haired; is either pointed- or lop-eared; muscular; and offers a somewhat snipe-nosed appearance. Though generally yellowish, they can vary in color from dark brown to light blond. A majority of those I have seen are of about the color of the Vizsla. Indeed, they resemble the Vizsla to a great extent, except that they carry their tails curled over the back in a manner reminiscent of the Nordic breeds.

There are many breeds of 'coon hound and many ways of hunting them. One 'coon hunter may prefer to hunt with a single open trailer, reeling in the hound music without too great an interest in collecting a lot of 'coons. Another may work with a mixed breed silent trailer if he is interested primarily in hides; still another may use several of his own dogs in cooperation with one or more friends and their dogs. However you go at it, the end result should be a 'coon looking down at you from the branches, with the dogs jumping against the base of the tree.

The 'coon that has been taken by the hunter after being treed by the dogs has prime pelt, is worth goodly sum. Some hunters do run dogs for the sake of the profits, but the majority tend to do it primarily for the sport.

MODERN BREEDS & USES:

The Beagle Is America's Most Popular Hunting Dog Today

THE BEAGLE has often been described as a "merry little fellow." Certainly, there are few if any breeds more aptly suited to what they do; neither have I seen any that take more obvious pleasure in doing their thing. Give a beagle a snootful of fresh, intoxicating rabbit scent and a chance to pursue the source of the scent and his happiness is complete.

As breeds are reckoned, the beagle is a relative newcomer to the hunting scene. Beagles are basically small editions of the English foxhound, bred small to decrease their running speed as well as to suit the size of the dog to the quarry pursued. We really don't need a dog the size of the foxhound to effectively pursue a rabbit.

By the late Eighteenth Century, there were several different sizes and conformations of beagle hounds. The larger soon were bred down until 1880, when several beagles were imported from the Royal Rock pack. By that time, the size had been pretty well stabilized. This importation had a great influence on American beagles and most of the breed in this country at present can number one or more of this Royal Rock pack in their ancestry. The National Beagle Club was formed in America in 1888 and has been instrumental in establishing the size and other characteristics of American beagles.

The beagle is the most popular hunting dog in America today. More hunters go afield in the company of beagles than most other breeds combined. There is good reason for this. The beagle is easily kept, clean, friendly and makes a good house pet, as it is tolerant of cats, children, close quarters and most other banes of a dog's life.

The beagle requires little training to become an efficient rabbit hound. Simply running with older dogs that are chasing rabbits is usually all that is required to get a pup started. Once started, the young beagle will pretty much train itself insofar as chasing rabbits is concerned. If a truly satisfactory hunting companion is desired, the beagle should be trained by yard breaking, as described in another chapter; many also are trained to respond to hand and whistle signals in the field.

As with other hound breeds, unless carefully trained to hunt to and for the gun, the beagle tends to become a "self-hunter." This term means that the dog is simply interested in pursuing the game without reference to the hunter. When hunting with the self-hunter dog, the hunter is obliged to follow the dog instead of the dog hunting with and following the hunter. This is a poor hunting relationship that should not be tolerated.

There is a way to prevent a young dog from becoming a self-hunter. When first starting the dog on game, the dog must be made to return frequently to the hunter while in the field. One of the best methods to encourage this is to kill a few rabbits over the dog so that the beagle learns to associate being allowed to catch and actually get his mouth on the rabbit with proximity to the hunter and the sound of the gun.

This is a critical point in the training of the young beagle. You must allow the dog to get hold of the rabbit where it fell at the end of the track, but the dog should not be allowed to chew the rabbit enough to impair its table use. It is important that the gunner not approach too close to the dead rabbit when he has killed it. Simply move close enough to make sure the game is dead, then hold position to allow the dog to come upon the dead rabbit as he follows the track.

The reaction of a young dog upon coming onto his first dead rabbit often is amusing. A good hound is interested primarily in the track and scent of the game, following each intricate twist and turn of the track. When a dog puts his head down for another sniff and his nose suddenly contracts the rabbit, the reaction is often rather violent and may take one of two forms. The most common is a sudden yelp and a jump backwards from this strange creature that smells so good and had been trying so hard to escape. I have seen good beagles run back to their master from this first raw contact showing every evidence of being scared to

A proud little beagle shows off her hunters and the rabbits she chased for them during the hunt.

death of it. The other reaction is the exact opposite. In this instance, the dog violently attacks the dead rabbit, often ripping it to shreds and eating much of it.

The second reaction is the harder one with which to deal. The pup that was frightened by the rabbit carcass will in all likelihood take the next fresh rabbit trail that it comes upon with its usual enthusiasm. It seems to have forgotten the fright it was given by the last similarly scented monster it suddenly came upon. Having had several bunnies shot over it, such a dog often simply goes in search of another bunny to chase. In the case of a wounded rabbit, it is well to note where it was that the dog last gave tongue and search there; it is likely that the rabbit was able to run only this far before collapsing.

In the case of the dog that attacks the dead rabbit, the trainer is in for a bit of a hassle. It is imperative that the dog not be punished severely for attacking the game. I know of no surer way to ruin a young dog than to severely reprimand it for grabbing the game it is supposed to chase.

I have seen promising dogs ruined by severe treatment from their owners for "hard mouthing" a rabbit. Any dog, after being clobbered a couple times for grabbing the rabbit it had been chasing, will get the idea: "Hey, the boss man jest don't want me messin' with them things. They smell awful good, an' I sure like to follow their track, but boss man gives me a whuppin' when he catches me at it. Best thing this ol' hound can do is stay strictly away from them."

The most common approach to the above problem is to take the rabbit gently from the dog, while petting and lavishing praise. You must get the idea across to the dog that the rabbit is yours, his responsibility was fulfilled when he found the rabbit at the end of the trail and had given it a couple of shakes. With most dogs, this is much

Arnold Napier and Jim Shirley of Tomahawk, W. Virginia, with former's beagle and the rabbits she brought to the gun. Both men are dedicated hound men who also own packs of 'coon dogs in addition to the favored beagle.

easier than it sounds. Some beagles can be trained to retrieve rabbits, but this is not common and requires a lot of training with a fifty percent success ratio at best.

Another problem frequently encountered is that some beagles seem to be driven to bury every rabbit they can. This trait is thought to rise from the natural instinct to hide food for later use. Regardless of the reason for this trait, it can be a troublesome problem for which the only solution seems to be to quickly get to the spot where the dog was last heard.

As mentioned, the most simple way to get a young beagle started in the rabbit chasing game is to allow the pup to run with older dogs that are proven rabbit trailers. If trained dogs are not available, the next option is to take the untrained beagle to a location where it is likely to encounter rabbits, then keep the dog in close as you systematically beat the brush until a rabbit is jumped in a place where the dog can see it.

Usually the dog will give chase by sight and often will simply start trailing and baying naturally as though it had been doing this for years. This isn't surprising, as this is what the beagle and hundreds of generations of its hound ancestors have been bred for. It is a genetic trait that the beagle should follow and bay a rabbit track. But, not all beagles exhibit this trait, so it is necessary to "start" some of them. If your pup doesn't self-start on the first few rabbits with which it comes in contact, don't be discouraged; it probably will just take a bit more work to get the dog started trailing and baying rabbits. "Baying," incidentally, is the act of a dog in barking on the trail of the game it is following.

Usually it is only necessary to jump a few more rabbits and allow the dog the opportunity to chase them. In the event this does not start your beagle pup chasing rabbits, try setting a box trap in a rabbit path to catch a live rabbit. With someone to help, take both the dog and trapped rabbit to the center of a large open area where there is no cover for fifty or more yards in any direction. Take a firm grip on the dog's collar and have your assistant hold the rabbit close enough that the dog can get a good snootful of rabbit scent. Then release the rabbit on the ground just in front of the dog; a half-second later, let the dog go. This should result in a chase. If not, you may have a problem.

If the foregoing methods do not get your beagle started,

This pair of rabbit hunters check that all is right before they venture into the field to hunt behind eager beagle.

This experienced beagle is working out a rabbit trail before taking to the track.

the next step is to get the pup in with one or more good beagles while they are chasing rabbits. This usually is a sure-fire method.

Almost all purebred beagles will chase a rabbit, although some are more proficient than others. Some work a bit differently, but most will get the job done. There are, however, a few that simply will not give chase. In the event you are unlucky enough to come up with one of the rare beagles in this category, you have two options: If you desire to keep the dog simply as a pet, have it neutered and keep it as a pet. The other option is to get rid of it.

If you bought the pup from a reputable kennelman, he usually will give you another pup of approximately the same age. Under no circumstances should you give the dog away unneutered, as the person to whom you give the dog may breed it and the last thing desired is more pups from a dog that won't chase rabbits. It may seem harsh, but for the good of the breed and to decrease the chances of someone else getting a dud, it is better to neuter the dog.

I have always liked to hunt with two or more beagles, as they make fine music when in full cry on a hot track, but one good beagle is more than adequate for the hunter who simply wishes to hunt rabbits.

After you have trained your beagle to your desires, you may wish to test it against others in a field trial, but don't be unduly dismayed if your good gun dog beagle does not do well in field trials. Beagle field trials are a whole different world from the hunting field. Most of the dogs that win these trials are specialists, bred and trained for this specific purpose. In general, the field trial beagle is a much slower and more vocal dog than those used for hunting. For many years, I was a judge at the Hagerstown Beagle Club and attended and qualified in the AKC judging clinic and school. The last one I attended was held at The National Beagle Club near Falls Church, Virginia, one of the most prestigious beagle clubs in the nation.

A beagle field trial generally is run along the following lines: When the entries close, usually at 9 a.m., the dogs will be measured to determine whether they will run in the twelve- or fifteen-inch class. (Dogs over fifteen inches are not eligible to run in sanctioned or licensed trials.) When filling out the entry form for an AKC trial, it is necessary to give the dog's registration number. This eliminates the unregistered dog from competition.

After the class in which the entered dogs will run has been established, the name of each dog running in that class is put in a narrow-necked opaque bottle and an impartial person withdraws two name cards at a time. The two dogs drawn together will be run together as brace mates. In the event there is an uneven number of dogs entered, the single name left in the container will be known as the "bye dog" and will be paired with the remaining dog of any brace that has one withdrawn from the competition. The order in which the braces were drawn also establishes the order in which they will be run. The first brace drawn will be the first brace run, with the bye dog, if any, being the last to run.

Both the running order and the brace mate drawn are important. It is difficult for even the best of dogs to run well with a wild brace mate that scurries about in all directions and confuses the track. The running order is important in that the earlier braces generally have better scent-holding conditions than those run after the sun has thoroughly dried the dew of the night before.

On cloudy or overcast days the running order is not as important and, in the event of rain, the later braces may have better running conditions provided it does not rain too hard. Ideal running conditions call for a damp, cool day when it has rained several hours earlier with little, if any, wind. Dogs are expected to run in anything less than a downpour and I have judged dogs in a gale. A good judge has to make allowance for the changing conditions in evaluating a dog's ability. If there is no dog needing a brace mate when the time comes for the bye dog to be put down, a volunteer dog may be asked for from among the entered dogs that already have run. This dog will not be under judgment while running with the bye dog, as it is simply to meet the rule that no dog may be run without a brace mate.

The trial is started with the first brace of dogs being taken into the field and kept on leash until they are put down on a hot track. Persons other than the judge, marshal and owners or handlers of the braces currently running are

It often is necessary to cover a lot of ground in order to get up a rabbit for the beagles to chase. Many will head straight for a groundhog hole when they are jumped.

called the "gallery." The gallery is composed of those whose dogs are scheduled to run in the next several braces, as well as interested persons and spectators. The gallery will spread out in a line under the direction of the marshal and beat the brush until they jump a rabbit. Seeing the rabbit, the spotter will call, "Tallyho!"

In the event a sitting rabbit is spotted, the spotter will call out, "Tallyho in a squat." The judges will ask those who saw the rabbit exactly where it ran and the dogs will be put down on the track. Should the dogs not readily take the track, the handlers have the option of refusing the track and requesting another rabbit. If either dog readily takes the track, then both dogs are committed to that track. If "tallyho in a squat" is called, the person who has spotted the bunny will keep an eye on it until the judges arrive to jump the rabbit out of sight of the dogs in the current brace. Then the dogs are brought in and put down on the track. As the dogs take the track, the judges will run near the dogs so they can keep them in sight while they work the track.

The dogs should run the rabbit track with a smooth, calm action, keeping to the track or slightly downwind of it without dashing to and fro; they should frequently give tongue when they have a good snootful of rabbit scent. In the event the dogs come to a discontinuity in the track — known as a "check" — they should circle in ever-widening circles around the spot where they last had the scent rather than dashing wildly about in several directions. When either of the dogs picks up the scent and bays it, the other dog should go immediately to it and if it smells the track, should give tongue. A dog should not bay when it does not have the scent. A dog that gives tongue when not actually smelling the scent is known as a "babbler" and is demerited severely by the judges.

We now come to a highly controversial subject that I would prefer to avoid, but which is a part of any honest discussion of beagle trials. The controversy lies in the speed at which a dog must pursue the rabbit in an energetic manner. Many beagle trial judges disagree as to what constitutes energy.

The beagles that win the field trials today are, for the most part, what we call "walkie talkies." Loosely interpreted, this means that the dogs follow slowly on the track of the rabbit, baying at almost every step. Many beaglers feel dogs such as these are too slow to be useful as hunting dogs. This feeling is illustrated by the reaction of an old West Virginia hillbilly who had kept hunting beagles for most of his sixty-plus years; I took him to the first beagle trial he had ever seen. After watching a few braces run, he remarked, "Shex, these dang lazy mutts'd run all day in the shade of a poplar leaf."

While overstated, his comment exemplifies the sentiments of many. I have often been at odds with other judges on the subject of the speed and industry of some of the dogs we were judging.

The reason many judges give for placing such slow dogs is that a fast dog will push too many rabbits in the hole. I agree that too close a chase will put some rabbits to ground, but I feel there are many dogs being awarded championships today that are too slow to be good hunting dogs. At one time I owned a champion, Ben's Golden Freckles. A smooth-running bitch, she produced many winning pups. I also hunted over her. She eventually would bring a rabbit around to the gun, but it generally took the better part of an hour with farm country rabbits and she was almost hopeless on hard-running mountain rabbits. I should interject here that the whole idea of a dog running a rabbit is that a rabbit almost invariably runs in a circle back to the point from which it started. Farm and brush country rabbits generally run in a circle of less than two hundred yards in diameter, while mountain rabbits that live in more open country often run as much as a mile circle. Both are the same species of cottontail rabbit and the difference in running characteristics is believed to be caused by habitat.

At the time I owned Freckles I also owned a young bitch named Jubie. She was a real smoker; i.e., she ran a fast,

Hunter beats the brush with his beagles, trying to jump a rabbit that the dogs will bring back to his shotgun.

Wayne Lanzendorfer allows his beagles to get a good smell of the rabbit he has just shot. This allows the dogs to know the rabbit has been taken and they will take up a new trail.

tight track and any rabbit whose track she had was required to move fast if it didn't want to become dog food. (Actually she caught several young rabbits and brought them to me almost unhurt.) Jubie wouldn't have a chance as a field trial dog, but I could kill three of four rabbits over her, while a champion brought one around.

After many years of judging beagle trials, I have come to the opinion that the real reason many judges place slower dogs is that they are easier to keep up with and in sight while judging. Most beagle judges work on foot and, after following several braces over a long course, one does tend to appreciate the dog that is easier for the judges to keep in sight. Also many in the gallery like to watch the dogs work and they too have difficulty following a fast dog.

The judges will be looking for the dog that follows close on the track without unnecessary searching from side to side, not reaching too far from where it last had the track when it encounters a check. The dog should exhibit good nose in finding the track. It should not stop and go back over the last part of the track it has just run, unless there is real difficulty in moving farther along the track.

It is amazing what a rabbit will do to put a dog off the track. It is common for a rabbit to stop and lick all of its feet, then make a long leap at right angles to the direction it had been traveling. I have seen them run up the trunk of a leaning tree and jump twenty feet into a thick clump of brush to remain perfectly still until practically stepped on. One day, while judging at the Hagerstown Beagle Club with Russ Snyder, we were standing in a small depression in a field where there had been recent timbering. The dogs were working a rabbit on a steep bank about forty yards away. We saw the rabbit sneak down the bank and come toward us. It stopped about twenty yards away, not having seen us. After looking about in all directions, it made a leap of about seven feet to the top of a big stump that had been cut about 3½ feet above the ground. After jumping to the top of the stump, the rabbit saw us, but sat quite still as the dogs worked the track right up to the point from the leap that had been made. After casting about for a time, the dogs returned to their handlers and were faulted for a loss.

Judges carry a notebook with which they note the score and any other pertinent information regarding each dog. After all of the dogs have been run, the outstanding dogs will be run in a second and third series until each dog has had a chance to run against the dog placed immediately above it. This applies only to the four high-scored dogs. These dogs are awarded first, second, third places and best dog, with no placing for the fourth dog.

In areas where rabbits are scarce, the dogs running in the brace under judgment may be "cast." This simply means that they are let off the leash in order to help find and jump rabbits. In this event, the trial is conducted in the same fashion, except that the dog making the strike is caught up. The other dog of the brace is brought in and put on the track in the event it was at some distance from the dog making the strike and did not come into the baying.

MODERN BREEDS & USES:

Retrievers and Waterfowling Dogs Have Been Developed Over Centuries Of Trial And Error

"KEEP YOUR hat brim below the edge of the pit Woody. They're turning now," Buddy whispered. After waiting a few minutes that seemed like hours, he let go with another string of goose talk that you would never believe came from a human throat, then reached over to touch my left arm. This meant they were going to be on our left. Had he touched me on my shoulder, they would have been in front of the pit and a touch lower on the back would have meant the geese would be on the right when we raised up to shoot.

Buddy whispered again, barely audible to me a foot from his mouth. "Setting their wings. Fifty yards. Thirty." I heard a faint rustle of air rushing through goose wings, growing louder, as I set myself to stand. A few drops of saltwater splashed over the top of the pit and trickled down the space between my hat and my collar. I supressed a shudder as the icy stuff reached the small of my back.

"Bust 'em!" Buddy hissed and we stood up. I pushed off the safety of my Winchester Model 12 three-inch magnum heavy duck gun and swung ahead of the big gander that was fifteen yards out, to my left. I pulled the trigger and his neck disappeared in a cloud of feathers.

Left: Author and pudelpointer, Fritz, wait beside a creek for ducks. The pudelpointer is listed as one of versatile breeds, but does well at retrieving. (Below) Pudelpointer, Winterhelles' Fritz, returns across the stream with duck downed on opposite bank. Requirement of a good retriever is that the dog goes where sent.

The air seemed full of geese; I picked out another as he flared to put on the brakes. He was almost still and I shot right at him, allowing no lead. The second goose crumpled and, beyond it, another folded a wing and scaled downward, struggling vainly to keep flying.

"Damn! Lined me," I mutter as I ejected the shell and put the third round into the struggling bird now fifty yards out. The shot didn't seem to do much good, and having learned the folly of shooting into crippled geese at long range on the water, I turned to drop one of the geese that had scattered in all directions, picking one that had flown into the strong wind coming off the mainland. This would make it easier to retrieve.

While I'd been shooting, Buddy had been wreaking havoc in goosedom also. He had four down and, climbing out of the pit, told me, "I'll get the downwind ones on this side first, then go after your cripple. Did you see the spinner? It and two others are coming down on your side."

I told him I'd seen the spinner — a bird with damaged wings that windmills as it attempts to fly, often managing to get a fair distance from the blind before hitting the water — and one other.

"The other was the first one I shot. It's toward the stake house from the other two," Buddy said, as he ran off through two feet of water at a speed impossible for someone who hadn't grown up in the area.

I climbed out and took off after the most distant goose on my side. I picked up my last one first, quickly slipping the loop of rope that hung from the belt of my Hodgman waders over its head. I saw another bearing down on me and tried to hurry to intercept it. As I picked up the heavy bird, it gave a sudden flop and the front edge of its wing caught me across the forearm, nearly causing me to drop my shotgun. Giving the big bird a flip around the shotgun barrel, I broke its neck and put it on the belt rope.

Spotting another, I started after it and ran into a tide rip in the sandbar that was nearly four feet deep. This slowed me down and I was pretty well out of wind by the time I got to the dead bird. I looked in vain for the fourth bird. Realizing it was useless to try to find the other bird that probably had been carried off the bar and into deep water, I looked to see where Buddy was. I spotted him pretty far out and headed for the pit which I could not have seen had it not been for the decoys around it.

I had almost reached the pit when I heard faint shouts and turned to see Buddy waving his gun over his head and

This black Labrador shows how to put up a pheasant for the gunner. This breed is often used to flush, retrieve.

pointing to the north. In that direction I saw a long line of geese heading my way. There was no way to make it to the pit, so I squatted in two-plus feet of water and waited. The birds came on flying low and fast. They had their eyes on our large spread of decoys and seemed bent on joining this apparent flock on the water. They were flying across the wind which was from the mainland to the west. In order to set down among the blocks they would have to circle to the east to land into the wind.

Sqatted there, watching them come, bits of spray hitting my face, my gun soaked with saltwater and the butt actually submerged, I thought again that we had to be really dedicated to waterfowling in order to put up with all this discomfort. The birds had the option of circling to the west and south to come into the wind to land; or they could choose to go far to the east and turn left into the wind. I was southwest of the decoys. If they went to the east I wouldn't get any shooting. If they went to the west they would come right overhead.

At about 150 yards, the leaders swung west and I scrooched down until the waves were perilously near the top of my waders. Keeping my face down as much as possible, I watched them come over. At ten yards, I stood up and took two of them, missing a third. It seemed only a second before they were gone, as they were on the downwind leg of their circle and simply speeded up. I took off after the two I had shot; in the thirty-mile wind, it wouldn't take long for them to be driven off the bar into deep water. Buddy shot twice and I turned to see a pair falling out of the flock as they passed over him.

I managed to retrieve the last two I'd shot and when I reached the pit, I was completely beat. I had run at least a half mile in two-feet-deep water. After a time, Buddy came in dragging six geese and collapsed onto the pit bench.

"Lost the cripple you edged. Got into the slough," he groaned as he started taking birds off his belt rope. "It's makin' up pretty rough. We'd best gather up and get out of here. It could be a two- or three-day low, and if the wind backs around to the north, you'll want to be on the beach for drum."

Now before anyone screams for the authorities, let me assure one and all that the described hunt was in the Good Old Days when such bag limits were quite legal and shooting such as we had was the norm rather than the exception. Someone is sure to say that the shooting of such numbers of waterfowl is the reason we don't have so many today. This simply isn't true. Waterfowl numbers stayed up until we started draining the pothole country where they bred. To-

Labrador retriever takes off with maximum effort to bring in a bird that has been brought down.

day there as many or more geese and ducks as the available nest and rearing areas will carry. This long-ago hunt was held on a sandbar four miles offshore in Pamlico Sound. The shooting there has not been so good the last few years, because the geese have been shortstopped by corn left unharvested in the Chesapeake Bay area. There are more waterfowl using the Chesapeake area than there is available food and a hard winter will bring disaster.

The preceding paragraphs may seem out of place in a dog book, but they should illustrate how much effort it is to retrieve game without the help of a dog. The next scene takes place a year later on the Eastern shore of the Chesapeake. There was no Bay Bridge then and we went across on the Oxford ferry. The blind was a brush stake house in what is called the Choptank. My friend, Eddie, picked me up at 4:30 a.m. I stowed my gear in his panel truck and, crowded in beside two big Chesapeake Bay retrievers, we soon reached the dock. We got into his thirty-foot Hooper Island boat which was towing an eighteen-foot rowboat loaded with decoys.

Reaching the blind, we hurriedly put out the decoys before Eddie ran the big boat some distance uptide and anchored it. Then we rowed back to the blind where the two dogs had been left, each chained securely to a stake. We pushed the rowboat under the stake house and threw bundles of saltmarsh grass over the part that still was exposed.

It started graying up in the east and we started hearing the whisper and sometimes the whistle of wings in the early light. A big flock of canvasbacks set down among the decoys, then a few bluebills pitched in. By shooting time, we had at least fifty ducks around us. I was puzzled then, as I am now; why can ducks and geese light and swim among wooden and plastic decoys without becoming alarmed or suspicious at what look like live birds from the air but are only imitations?

"It's shootin time. Try to get as many of them canvasbacks as you can," Eddie whispered. We stood up then and actually had to wave our hands and shout to get the birds to fly. We each took two dead and another fell out of the flock about a hundred yards out. The dogs had been watching with intense interest and were whining softly as Eddie released them. They made a beeline for the dead birds and each soon returned with a duck in its mouth. As soon as one of us took the bird, the dog headed out for another. In just a few moments all the dead ducks were in our hands except the one that had flown some distance before dropping. A wide board with slats nailed across it had been built for the dogs' use and they were brought into the blind. Putting one dog on the chain, Eddie reached into a gunny sack for a chunk of wood. Pushing the unchained dog into position to face where the remaining duck had fallen, he threw the piece of wood toward the dead bird and told the dog to fetch.

Of course, the chunk fell far short of the duck and when the swimming dog reached the chunk of wood, Eddie shouted, "Back!" The dog kept swimming in the same direction it had been going. When the dog started to pass to the right of the dead bird, Eddie shouted, "Hooouuup!" and waved his arm to his left. The dog turned, sighted the dead duck and headed back to the blind with it in his mouth.

Action continued like this for about an hour, then dropped off completely as the sun grew hot and the marshes behind us took on a drowsy warm aura. We lazed about in the blind for a while, drank some coffee and Eddie grumbled about the weather forecasters.

"Radio last night said there was wind and rain coming this morning. I don't know what we pay these guys for. The almanac does as well in predictin' weather," he said. We decided to stick it out for a couple hours more and lay down on piles of bundled swamp grass to sleep for awhile.

I was awakened by the bark of a dog and sat up to find Eddie also awakening. The sky had clouded over and there was a breeze from the southeast. "Looks like it's gonna be shootin this evenin'." Eddie ventured.

The wind rose briskly and the temperature dropped. We then fed and watered the dogs. By the time the dogs each had been released for a swim and stretch, the ducks were beginning to fly. We had a couple hours of good shooting and the dogs worked faultlessly, except when they got into a disagreement over a lone widgeon and literally tore it in half.

"That's one thing about Chessies, they're bullheaded and possessive. I'd best have one of them two on a chain if only one bird comes down," Eddie conceded as he chained the offending dogs to posts where they couldn't reach one another.

It started to rain and the wind really picked up. Ducks were everywhere and the dogs were hard-pressed to keep the downed birds gathered up. A flock of geese came over and we both emptied our guns with a thunderous barrage that brought one goose pinwheeling from the sky. We looked at each other and burst into gales of laughter. "Well, I have shot better." I ventured.

After we had settled down a bit, Eddie released one of the dogs that charged into the gray welter of falling water after the goose that was rapidly disappearing in the rippled water.

The dog disappeard completely and I became a bit concerned.

"He'll be okay. He knows where the shore is, if he can't make it back to the blind," Eddie assured me.

Presently we heard a bark and Eddie shouted, "Hyaaa ...heeah!" repeating this call every half minute or so until the dog emerged from the murk. Apparently the dog would drop the goose in the water for a second, bark, and then pick up the bird and swim, toward the sound of Eddie's voice. Soon the dog came up the walkway carrying the goose, delivered it to hand and flopped on the floor planks, tired and uncomfortable. It was growing colder and windier and I expressed concern that the dog must be wet and cold.

"He's as dry and comfortable as we are," Eddie said and

The gleam in this Labrador's eye seems to indicate the joy he takes in his work in bringing in a downed duck.

This Labrador has done an excellent job in flushing pheasants as this harvest shows.

motioned me over to look as he spread the outer layer of the dog's coat. The underfur and skin were completely dry. This is how I learned abut the waterproof coat of the Chessie.

The weather got worse and the shooting got better. We started getting more geese, but it was invariably a case of shoot quick and hope for the best. Visibility had shrunk to no more than seventy-five yards and the birds would suddenly materialize to be gone in a few seconds. The dogs were watching them fall and they marked them well. I don't think we lost more than a bird or two.

Without these two superbly trained dogs we would have lost half of the birds we dropped. I couldn't help thinking how much help these dogs would have been the year before in Pamlico Sound. I further determined to get a Chesapeake of my own and said as much to Eddie as we cruised up the inlet toward his dock that evening. Eddie hunted quail and grouse with me and my pointers and setters and was aware of the country in which I lived and hunted. He suggested that perhaps the big Chessie wouldn't be the best dog for my situation as they were pretty much a specialist breed. He added that, if he lived and hunted where I did, he

The golden retriever is another breed that has found great favor among serious hunters.

Golden retriever seems somewhat puzzled as to what is expected of him in this case.

The golden retriever has been found to be highly favored in the hunting fields today.

would have a Labrador or golden retriever as they were more adaptable and would be more useful in my situation.

It wasn't until after World War II that I finally got around to addressing the question of a retreiver again. There is a golden retriever and a pudelpointer lying here in the room where I'm typing this now. In addition to being an excellent retriever, the pudelpointer, Fritz, is a versatile dog.

We have pretty thoroughly covered the when, where and why one needs a retriever. The question of what breed to get is more difficult. There are many retriever breeds, each with its own characteristics, strengths and weaknesses.

The first two breeds we will look at are true American breeds, having been developed in this country. The Chesapeake Bay retriever is the descendant of two Newfoundlands that were on board an English ship that was wrecked on the coast of Maryland in the winter of 1807. These two dogs were mated with the local retrievers and the result was one of those lucky crossings that bring out the best

Golden retriver delivers a downed quail to the hand of the hunter. Breed's popularity is still growing.

traits of both of the original breeds. The pups out of this first crossing were found to be outstanding and ideally suited to the cold, icy conditions one encounters in the bay area in fall and winter. The coat of this breed is similar to the coat of muskrats and beavers in that it is almost completely waterproof. The coat is made up of a fairly short, hard outer or guard fur and a dense wooly underfur which contains an oil content that tends to repel water. These are exceedingly strong, heavily-built dogs that are naturally buoyant in spite of their mass. They are indefatigable swimmers, have excellent noses and boast good eyesight which enables them to mark the fall of a bird at great distance.

The Chesapeake Bay retriever is a very loyal dog, good with children of the family and a close circle of persons it sees often. With strange dogs, he is likely to fight, unless closely supervised, and will often get into a scrap with kennel mates. With strangers these retreivers are a bit touchy and one should get to know a Chessie pretty well while it is in the company of its master before trying to hunt the dog away from its owner. Several of the dog books I have note the Chessie as being of cheerful and affectionate temperament. I have hunted with several and, from personal experience, I would recommend caution in approaching a strange Chessie. I do not consider the above as a detriment, as I don't want my own dog to become too friendly with strangers. Friendly dogs get stolen too easily.

If you hunt large bodies of water — especially in windy, cold weather — the Chesapeake Bay retriever stands head and shoulders above any other breed you could choose. I do not think there is any other breed in the world that is the equal of the Chessie for hard work in cold weather and ice and snow. The Chessie is big, often weighing over eighty pounds when in hunting trim. If you hunt from a duckboat, you will find that when a big Chessie jumps off, it nearly upsets the boat and you will have to balance the weight of the dog if it climbs back aboard.

This retriever breed is strictly a water-retrieve specialist. They do not hunt on land or work as a flushing dog as do the other retriever breeds.

On the other hand, they can handle weather that will kill any of the other breeds and keep swimming all day without sign of fatigue. I have hunted other breeds in really cold weather. Some of them simply refused the water after the first immersion, others went reluctantly. My old pudelpointer, Fritz, will go eagerly into water with ice in it to make a retrieve and do it as often as I ask, but he then will lie down in the blind and shiver uncontrollably. It makes one ashamed to ask a dog to do something so obviously hard on it. So if you are looking for a straight retriever for tough hunting, get a Chesapeake Bay retriever.

Next in hardness are the Labrador retrievers. They boast a fairly heavy, water-resistant coat and can stand a lot of cold weather and water. In addition, most have the advantage of being a good flushing dog for anything from quail to rabbits and pheasants. Many consider the Lab to be the most intelligent of all the hunting breeds. These dogs are easy to train, eager to please and are strong, hard workers. After a few trips afield, a young Lab knows what game you are hunting and it soon will be working to flush

The well-bred retriever is patient, as illustrated below, while his hunters put out decoys for a day of shooting.

The steady nature of the Labrador is reflected in this dog's quiet pose. This breed's temperament has made it a favorite across the United States.

the game toward you without much training from anyone.

Labrador retrievers come in black, yellow and liver colors, but black is by far the preferred shading. The Lab has become one of the most popular dogs in America today, and deservedly so. With just a bit of training, it makes an excellent squirrel dog and most also are excellent watchdogs around the home. They have little odor and are excellent to keep in the house as a companion-watchdog.

Although the Labrador retriever is said to be native to Newfoundland, the dog we know today as the Labrador is largely American-bred. The early dogs that came from Newfoundland more closely resemble the flat-coated retriever and there are areas where this early strain of Lab is still present as the result of local breeding over the years.

Intense concentrative powers of the Chesapeake retriever, as illustrated, as he goes about business of bringing in a duck that has been shot from a blind.

The modern American-bred Labrador retriever is a short-coupled, solid muscular dog sometimes weighing as much as seventy-five pounds, but averaging around sixty pounds. Most have a blunt, thick nose and high forehead with a pronounced stop. The eyes are usually hazel, but occasionally chestnut with an intelligent, observant expression. The tail is covered with dense, short hair that sometimes divides as if parted at the bottom. The distinctive feature of the Labrador is a tail that is thick at the base and has a rounded appearance. This is known as an "otter tail." Show standards call for a tail that is as nearly straight as possible, but most Lab's tails have an upward curve.

Another American-bred retriever is the Boykin spaniel. This breed is the subject of considerable controversy as to origin. Different authorities have different theories as to the actual origin, but it is generally agreed that the Boykin is the result of crossing the cocker spaniel and the American water spaniel. This breed is quite similar to the American water spaniel, having a similar coat of curly or wavy hair, plus long pendulous ears covered with curly hair. The muzzle is longer than the water spaniel and the tail shorter, sometimes docked.

The Boykin is used throughout the swampy areas of the South as a waterfowl retriever and this breed seems to be able either to avoid or withstand the bite of the cottonmouth water moccasin which is the plague of water retrievers in the South.

Boykin spaniels are active hunters in the woods and fields for small game as well as being excellent land and water retrievers. They make excellent squirrel and rabbit dogs and sometimes are used for hunting raccoons and other night game, including bobcats. The Boykin has loyal following; everyone I have talked to who owns and hunts this breed is very enthusiastic about the dog.

According to the latest information I have, the American Kennel Club does not recognize the Boykin, main-

This Chesapeake Bay retriever does not seem impressed by the work he has done in retrieving the day's bag. This hunt took place on a Michigan river. The breed's physiology makes it an excellent worker around water.

taining that it is a strain of the American water spaniel, which they do recognize. My personal feeling is that there is a great difference between the two breeds with the addition of the cocker blood infusing a merry nature and joy into the Boykin that is not in evidence in the water spaniels I have seen.

Whenever I think of Boykin spaniels, my thoughts inevitably turn to a certain hunting camp on Barnegat in the days of great waterfowl shooting in that area. We were staying overnight in a primitive camp that consisted of a poorly constructed building made of driftwood and scrap lumber. The cabin was divided into two rooms: a kitchen with stove and table and a large bunkroom. The plumbing was totally primitive with a water bucket in the kitchen, the water reservoir on the Home Comfort woodstove for hot water and a "thunder mug" in a corner of the bunkroom.

As I remember, there were five of us: the owner of the camp who was associated with my father in the U.S. Postal

Chessie waits patiently for someone to take pheasant he has recovered. View shows coat that makes this breed impervious to cold, wet.

service; his brother-in-law; a guest of the owner, a rather portly, dignified gentleman who held some reknown as an outdoor writer; my father, and myself. There were a black Lab and a golden retriever in the dog boxes outside and a lively old Boykin named Lize that was the favorite of the owner and a really great retriever in her own right. Lize was allowed the run of the camp and had a pile of old feed sacks in which to bed beside the owner's bunk.

Most of us already were in bed and the only light was one kerosene lamp that had been left burning on a small table beside the alarm clock.

Remarking, "better now than in the morning," the outdoor writer proceeded to make use of the thunder mug. As he crouched there on the bucket, one of the big water rats that plague all such camps started across the floor. Lize spotted the rat and was after it in a flash. The terrified rat headed for the dark corner where the plumbing was, with Lize a jump behind. As the rat ran behind the bucket the dog dived for it and wedged herself between the wall and the bucket. The occupant of the bucket started shouting, "Whoah Lize...easy now...get out of here... dammit... yeeee..!" That was followed by a resounding crash as the bucket went over leaving the man, dog, rat and the contents of the bucket in a tangled, soggy mess in the corner.

Lize caught the rat and triumphantly shook it to death, adding somewhat to the general disarray of the bunkroom. A certain well-known writer took an unplanned swim in the frosty waters of a Barnegat tidal inlet and, being the newest kid on the block, I got the job of cleaning up the mess. I must say that the writer took it like the true gentleman he was. His strongest comment was, "Thank God, I wasn't wearing my hunting clothes."

The American water spaniel is another excellent retriever breed that deserves more widespread use than is presently the case. There are no exact records of this breed's origin, but the general belief is that the Irish water spaniel and the curly-coated retriever were the most prominent of its ancestors. This breed is most widely used in the Midwest where they are fairly popular. With a bit of publicity, this dog would become more popular, as it has a lot to offer the hunter. They work well as upland gun dogs of the springing type and as water retrievers. For the person who wants to use his gun dog as a watchdog and does not have space for a larger dog, this breed is an excellent choice. The American water spaniel will weigh thirty to forty pounds and that weight is all dog. It adapts well to outside kennels or makes a fine house dog that serves well as guardian and companion to the entire family.

The American water spaniel will flush all of the upland game birds as well as chase a rabbit around in a circle like a hound. It will even bark occasionally on the track so the gunner knows where it is. As stated previously, this breed deserves to be more popular.

The flat-coated retriever is a general purpose retriever

that was developed around 1800 by crosses between the Irish setter, Newfoundland, Labrador and curly-coated retriever. It once was much more popular than at present. One of the first breeds developed for use primarily as a retriever, it has been replaced largely by the modern Labrador and other allegedly more verstile breeds. This fine, easily-trained retriever is friendly, a good companion dog and will eagerly enter the thickest cover to make a retrieve. It will weigh about sixty-five pounds and usually is found in black and liver colors. The flat-coated retriever has a lot of good qualities and will serve well where a straight retriever is needed.

The golden retriever is another popular retriever in America today, ranking just behind the Labrador in registry. A solid, vigorous dog of about seventy pounds average weight, with a beautiful thick, water-resistant golden coat, the golden retriever attracts attention wherever it goes. It has a splendidly friendly disposition, is obedient, has a good nose and is an excellent retriever and hunter. These dogs are much liked as family companion dogs and, while not aggressive, are good watchdogs as long as they are not expected to serve as attack dogs.

I presently have a 9-year-old golden retriever in my house. Although he belongs to my daughter, he has been with us all of his nine years. As an example of the sensitivity of this breed, I just called to my wife, who is in another room, to ask, "How old is the Jerk?"

Hearing his name mentioned, the dog came from the kitchen and checked to see if he was wanted for some reason.

Actually the dog is named Joshua, but ever since he had a thing about going through doors as a puppy I have called him the "Jerk." He answers cheerfully to either name and is always ready for a trip afield or a swim in the river in front of the house.

We also have a 12-year-old pudelpointer in the house. The pudelpointer is much more aggressive and is unquestionably the boss, but in the event a car comes back the half mile of private road to the house, it is always the golden who barks first. In the event of a hostile act, it would be the pudelpointer that would attack viciously for the throat while the golden stood by and barked. It is all in the breeding. The golden retriever was bred as a small-game hunter and retriever. The pudelpointer was developed expressly to bring down a wounded roe deer and has a killer instinct that the golden does not. Both are fine companion dogs, but the pudelpointer must be watched when strangers first come into the house until he decides they are "peaceable."

The golden retriever is an excellent choice for the person who needs a hunter-retriever-companion dog. In the field it does not have quite as much snap and dash as the Labrador, but this is offset by a quiet, more relaxed personality. Most of the retriever breeds are fine family dogs and this is one of the main reasons they are so popular today.

If you are interested in a golden retriever for either field or companion dogs you should be sure to get one out of field-bred stock. Unfortunately, the show people have been mucking about with the golden. The breeding of dogs for show concentrates on coat and conformation and often produces dogs of silly, nervous temperament with little or no hunting instinct. The once excellent cocker spaniel and Irish setter breeds are excellent examples of how show breeding can ruin a strain for practical hunting use.

Retrievers form a large segment of the hunting breeds in this country at present and are fine dogs of many uses. There are many more retrieving breeds abroad, with only a few specimens found in the United States. Many are fine dogs but are too few in number to warrant discussion here.

He may not have been the finest retriever in history — although you'll get arguments on that — but King Buck was no doubt the best publicized and best known.

The dog died in 1962, just a few days before his fourteenth birthday. But during the years of his life, this famed black Labrador piled up a record of championships that have given him a permanent place in dogdom's Hall of Fame.

King Buck was owned by the late John M. Olin, then kingpin of the Winchester firearms empire and its parent organization, Olin Industries. There is no doubt that Olin loved the dog as though one of the family and today King Buck is buried at Nilo Farms near Alton, Illinois, his grave marked by a black cast iron statue in his likeness.

Yet the famed dog, which was pictured on the Federal Duck Stamp for the 1959-60 season, came from a relatively humble beginning. He was whelped in northwest Iowa on April 3, 1948, one of eight black Labrador pups.

They were by Timothy of Arden out of Alta of Branchory. The breeder, Ed Quinn of Storm Lake, Iowa, conducted the initial training for the entire litter, working them out several times a week in a spring-fed gravel pit near his home.

According to John Madson, who followed the life and development of King Buck as a then-employee of Nilo Farms, "The pups went for water as only young Labs can and did well in their early schooling. But, although all showed promise as gun dogs, none were considered outstanding at that point."

Records show that the entire litter had been sold by early fall, when each of the pups was approximately six months old. King Buck was bought by Bob Howard of Omaha, Nebraska, and was kept in a local kennel for several days. Although the pup — like the others in the litter — allegedly had been immunized before being shipped out of Iowa, it developed an acute case of distemper. Howard took the pup home and put it in a basket near the basement furnace, seeking to nurse it back to health.

During the month that followed, Howard was advised several times to give up and have the pup disposed of. The little Labrador, according to accounts, was so weak that it could not stand and even its owner did not understand how it was able to hold on to the tenuous thread of life.

Bob Howard's wife must be given much of the credit for the dog's eventual recovery. She tended him virtually around the clock, getting him to eat a diet of eggs. But it wasn't until the evening that Howard went into his basement and found the haggard, skinny pup on its feet, feebly wagging its tail that he knew recovery was in sight.

With the dog slowly recovering from the near-fatal disease, Bob Howard began to take him out for light exercise near his home. According to John Madsen, "The trainer had owned several dogs named Buck and liked the

King Buck, one of the all-time great Labrador retrievers, was featured on the 1959-60 Federal Duck Stamp. The painting was by noted wildlife artist Maynard Reese. King Buck's field trial wins set a record in his time.

yell of it, for it was an easily heard call name. Acting on the optimistic hunch that the convalescing puppy might someday rank high in his class, Howard named him King Buck. At the time, it was simply a hopeful idea. No one could know it was prophetic."

In fact, it didn't look as though the black Lab had much of a future. Even after he seemingly had recovered from distemper, the pup was not eating well, continuing to show ribs through his black coat. This prompted Bob Howard to take him to a veterinarian for a complete check. The vet's findings were less than welcome: He stated that the dog had a bad heart and certainly should never be run in the field. In addition, it was found that King Buck's feces contained blood and it was feared he had suffered some type of internal injury.

However, Howard continued to exercise the dog and found that he ran well. By the time King Buck was 18 months of age, he had gained weight and had developed a healthy appetite. All symptoms of ill health had disappeared.

The following fall Howard began serious training and King Buck experienced his first field hunting. Howard

King Buck is buried in the crypt beneath this statue of himself. He lived until March 28, 1962. The statue is at Illinois' Nilo Farms.

found that the dog was not a particularly good trailer when it came to finding crippled pheasants, but he was solid under the gun.

On one occasion, early in his training, Howard had shot a pheasant and started after it. He suddenly discovered the dog was not with him. King Buck was sitting there, watching, as though he was waiting for Howard to make the retrieve.

"Well, come on!" the trainer shouted at him. At the order, King Buck reacted immediately, charging in to scoop up the downed pheasant.

"He never held tight on field pheasants after that," Howard recalled years later, "But he always refused to break shot at field trials. He seemed to know when and where to hold steady."

Those who observed the young dog found that he was eager to learn and, once a lesson was learned, he made no mistakes. As a result, he won first place in the Missouri Valley Hunt Club's licensed field trial when only 18 months old.

With all of the fears and hopes that had been expended on the young dog during his illness and the training that followed, Bob Howard had come to believe King Buck had some special quality that he had found in few other dogs. There was a strange spark that each trial in which the dog participated seemed to fan to increasing brightness.

But Bob Howard came to accept the fact that he was not in a financial position to run King Buck in major field trials across the country in spite of the fact that he was becoming increasingly certain that the dog would go all the way to the top. With sadness, he agreed to sell King Buck to Byron Grunwald of Omaha. However, Howard would continue to handle the dog in trials.

The trainer had noted that King Buck still was not overly talented in marking dead birds, but seemed to make up for this seeming lack in other traits.

"He seemed to sense what his handler needed and wanted, and when he was given a line to a dead bird, Buck's course never wavered," according to John Madson. Before the dog was 2 years old, he had won a first, two second places and several thirds in field trials held in the Midwest.

John Olin, long a fancier of good gun dogs, had been watching King Buck at the various trials, noting his development and progress. Nilo Kennels had recently been added to Nilo Farms and Olin was seeking retrievers for his new kennels, specifically looking for dogs with traits that might prove good in a breeding program.

There is no admitted record as to how much John Olin paid for King Buck, but it is known that Byron Grunwald already had passed up several offers for the dog, thus it can be assumed that the price was more than respectable. Thus, in 1951, while King Buck was two months short of his third birthday, he was received at Nilo Kennels.

T.W. Pershall, a manager of the kennels, admitted later that he had serious doubts about King Buck. He had run checks on the other dogs that had come from the same litter and had found that none had shown any great amount of talent. Apparently Pershall had suggested to John Olin even before the purchase that this might not be the most wise of buys. True, the dog had good bloodlines, but Pershall feared the distemper bout and the heart problem reported earlier might have left permanent impairments to the dog's health. However, anyone who knew the late John Olin also knew he could be a stubborn man. He purchased King Buck over Pershall's voiced doubts.

With the decision made, Pershall set to work with the dog. At that time, he already had trained five national field trial champions and it had become obvious to his competitors in the training field that Pershall was a maker of champions. Thus, the trainer's know-how began to show in King Buck's further development.

In early 1951, King Buck won a first, two second places and a third in what were considered important field trials. A few months later, he took another first place, a third and a fourth, then completed ten of eleven series in the 1951 National Championship Stake, thus placing high among the nation's top retrievers.

Beginning slow in 1952, King Buck won a first and a third place during spring trials; during the autumn competitions, he won a first, second and fourth. As a result of these showings, he was in there again for November's national competition held that year at Weldon Spring, Missouri.

This event ran for three days with competition that was more than just stiff. As an example, of the thirty-two dogs that were entered, only one was dropped during the first six series of this toughest-of-all competitions.

Pershall, as the trainer, felt that King Buck handled himself well when it counted.

"He seemed to know when the competition was really rough," Pershall said later. "In those instances, he always came through. He couldn't be considered a big Labrador in size, but he showed great style. He was never excitable or flashy; instead, he tended to be quiet and well behaved. Whether working on land or in the water, he just went ahead with the job, showing steadiness all the way."

Those who were there that day still remember it and the fact that King Buck put on a real show at Weldon Spring. There was never an instance in which he didn't understand and obey every command sharply, adding to his laurels with perfect retrieves. After the first few series, it became obvious that this dog was in the lead and that there were none that could overtake him. As the final day ended, King Buck was honored as the top field trial retriever in the entire nation.

John Olin obviously appreciated the fact that he had a top-winning field trial dog, but as an avid duck hunter of long standing, he was equally interested in how well King Buck would do in a natural hunting situation without the controls of competition. As all too many of us know, a dog that does well in the field trial environent may not hack it when it comes to actual field work.

No sooner were the November trials ended that Olin and King Buck left for Stuttgart, Arkansas, often called the Duck Hunting Capital of the World. This area features what is called "green timber" duck hunting and is alive with mallards during the winter months. Several hunters were shooting from the same blind with Olin and King Buck handled the retrieving chores for all of them.

"He was one of the finest wild duck retrievers I've ever seen," John Olin said later. "In spite of his intense field trial training, he loved natural hunting. He used his head in the wilds just as he did in the field trials and he was beautiful to watch."

As an example of the comradeship that developed between dog and owner that day, King Buck was not relegated to a kennel for the night. He wasn't even forced to sleep on the floor of John Olin's hotel room. Instead, he spent the night on the foot of his owner's bed, according to Olin's own admissions.

T.W. Pershall continued to train King Buck, polishing his performance through that winter and the following spring. The Labrador took three first places in regional competition, then it was time to defend his title at his third National Field Trial Championship Stake.

During the first nine series of that 1953 contest, King Buck made perfect scores in spite of the fact that he was being pressed hard by a field of outstanding dogs. In the final series — the tenth — King Buck and another dog were so close in score that the judges called for an additional pair of series. When it was all over, King Buck had retained his national title for another year.

John Olin continued to enter the dog in the big field trials for the next four years, King Buck competing at full bore against dogs that were younger and with established champions. His success was phenomenal. As an example, in a single day in 1955, King Buck retired three challenge trophies simultaneously. Until then, these awards had been in circulation for forty-six years.

During the years of his competition on behalf of John Olin and Nilo Kennels, King Buck finished seventy-three series of a possible seventy-five; this was in seven consecutive National Championship Stakes. The only series he did not complete were the eleventh in the 1951 national competition and the twelfth series in 1957. Until that time, no other retriever in recorded history had been able to complete sixty-three consecutive series successfully in the National Championship Stake. There were countless other honors bestowed upon this dog which had begun as a sickly pup that was not expected to live!

The U.S. Fish and Wildlife Service decided that, for 1959, the design of the nation's duck stamp should feature a retriever at work. Noted wildlife artist Maynard Reese already had painted two duck stamps and selected King Buck as his subject. He arrived at Nilo Farms, paints in hand, and did a watercolor study of King Buck, a mallard in his mouth, while other ducks were visible in the background. This was the winning entry and became the first time in history that a dog appeared on any United States-issued stamp.

King Buck was growing white about the muzzle when he finally was retired, but he still continued to rule over Nilo Kennels until the day of his death. There were numerous offspring to carry on his bloodline, but somehow, none of his progeny ever measured up to the accomplishments of their sire.

When King Buck died on March 28, 1962, he was buried in a small crypt in front of the kennel entrance at Nilo Farms. The cast iron statue rests above his grave to remind others that, for all practical purposes, he still is king.

MODERN BREEDS & USES:

Flushing Game Depends More Upon Talent Than Specific Breeding

The springer spaniel is one of those breeds that doubles as a retriever as well as a dog that is used for flushing birds. Training has much to do with it.

WHENEVER WE think of flushing breeds, the spaniels come immediately to mind; this is as it should be. The spaniels, as noted earlier in this text, are the ancestors of almost all of today's field breeds. At present, the Labrador and golden retrievers are the most popular of the flushing breeds in common use today. These two breeds are properly called retrievers, but there is a lot of spaniel blood in them.

The most popular of the breed in America today is the cocker spaniel. It is deservedly popular, because in addition to field capabilities, it is a useful and handsome pet. The cocker has suffered to some extent from the attention of the show breeders, but in all fairness, the cocker has become the beautiful dog we have today due to the efforts of the show people.

Many of us have had cockers in our homes without ever realizing the field potential of the breed. They are too pretty to think of as hunting dogs, in the opinion of many. Pretty or not, the cocker is a hunter in his own right.

A fine springer and a good shotgun can lead to a good pheasant hunt in almost any part of the nation today.

The first cocker spaniel I had was a black female that was a pet for my daughter. She had a tendency to range out and jump game too far ahead of us for good shooting; for this reason, she was not used as much for a gun dog as she might have been or wanted to be. She was all heart and would plunge through the roughest brush and briar patches, leaving her coat matted with burrs and her ears torn by the thorns. This didn't make my daughter too happy, another reason the dog didn't get hunted much.

Doug Catlett pauses to give Ansil's Penny, his fine Brittany, a few minutes in the field during a hunting session.

Right: As a pheasant flushes, Penny breaks as hunter tries to get set for his shot.

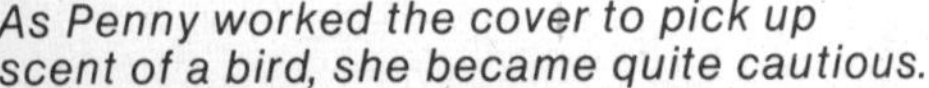

As Penny worked the cover to pick up scent of a bird, she became quite cautious.

The pheasant has started to run and Ansil's Penny makes a circle in an attempt to head the bird off for shooter.

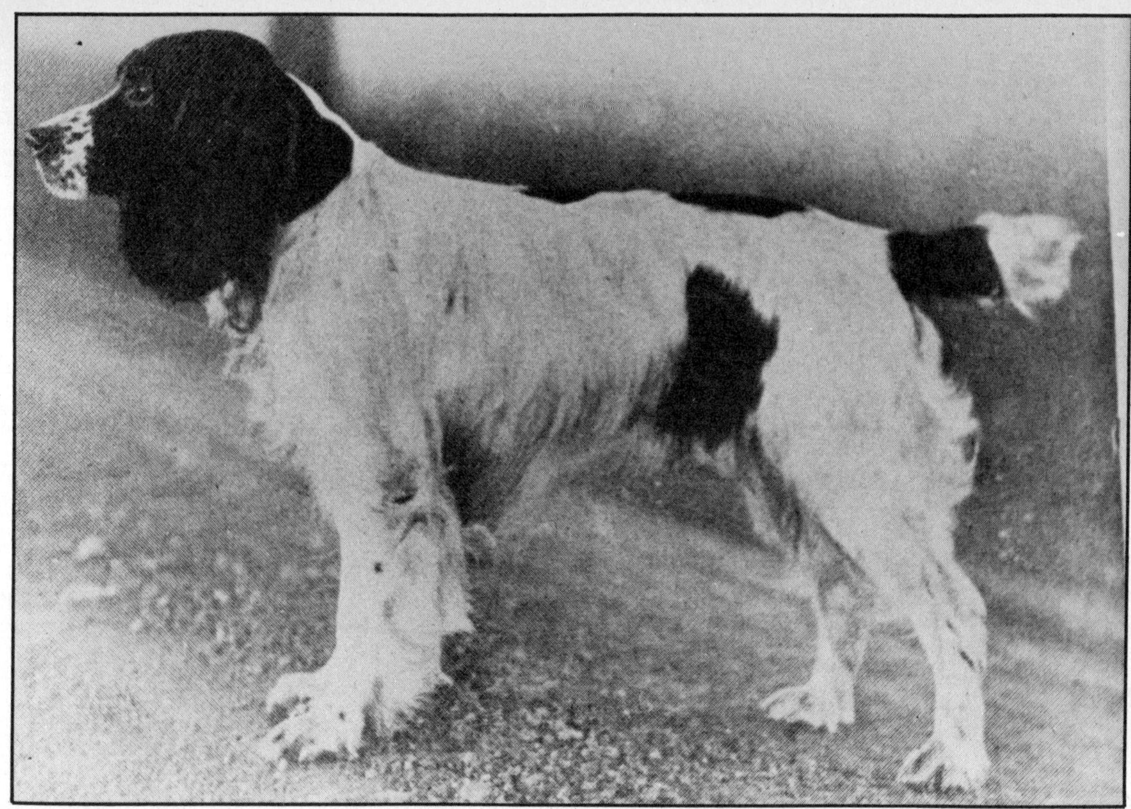

Tedwyns Trex, an all-time great champion, is undoubtedly the most famous of the field trial springers.

Other cockers with which I have worked afield have been splendid hunting dogs that left little to be desired in their performance. They were developed originally as flushing dogs for use on English woodcock and it is from this that they derive their name. They are the merriest of dogs, always ready for a romp or a trip afield. Excellent house dogs, they adapt well to cramped living quarters and get along nicely with only a daily walk in the park or even down a city street on leash. The cocker is better able to put up with such conditions than most breeds.

Standing as much as sixteen inches and weighing up to thirty-two pounds, the cocker spaniel is a lot more dog than is apparent at first glance. While not vicious by any measure, the cocker serves well in the role of companion and can be pugnacious when its domain is invaded by another dog or a stranger. They are really great with children. If anyone were to attempt to harm any child in a cocker's "family" he invariably would have to do it over the incapacitated body of the cocker. This dog will chase a ball happily or allow children to drag him around by the ears (although children should not be allowed to mistreat a dog simply because the dog will allow it) or roughhouse with older members of the family.

Cocker spaniels are excitable and emotional and should be handled with sensitivity and gentleness during training. They seem to know immediately when play stops and the boss gets serious. An act or motion that would not matter at all in play or roughhousing with a cocker, if done at a "serious" time, will cause emotional difficulty with many cockers. The breed is eager to please and the trainer has only to get across to the dog the idea of what action is desired to obtain obedience to the best of the dog's ability. With its long silky coat and heavy feathering, the cocker requires some grooming to maintain a decent appearance.

Clumber spaniels are effective in the field as gun dogs. They are large, heavy dogs weighing to 75 pounds.

This photo, taken in 1922, marked the first formal show of springer breed to be conducted in the U.S.

Back in the 1920s, when there were no limits on game birds, this spaniel had done a hard day's work in the field.

The field spaniels are quite similar to the English cocker in conformation, but have a longer body.

There are two cocker spaniel breeds: English and American. At the risk of offending some who quite likely know more about cockers than I, I'll say that there is little difference between the two breeds. The English cocker seems a bit more cobby of build, while the American variety seems to have a wavy coat that is mostly absent from its British cousin. Many colors are acceptable, but on solid-colored dogs, white is acceptable only on the chest. I think the prettiest colored ones are those with black and tan markings similar to those of the Gordon setter. There is much dissension as to the docking of the cocker's tail. American Kennel Club standards call for a docked tail on both the English and American cockers, but does not specify the length. Some so-called authorities insist that the English cocker's tail should be docked longer than the American cocker. I do not know why they consider this of such importance; perhaps it is much concern about nothing. It surely doesn't affect the dog, unless docked entirely too short.

Next in popularity among the spaniel breeds in this country is the springer spaniel. Formerly one of the most popular flushing breeds, the springer seemed to fade into obscurity for a time after the close of World War II. Returning soldiers brought back stories of the wonder dogs of Europe and the Continental breeds were in the ascendency for a lengthy period. Then many who had seized

upon the Continental breeds as the ultimate wonder dogs realized that these dogs had to be trained to become the all-purpose dogs they had expected.

Since the Continental breeds required so much training, those who didn't wish to spend so much time in this effort started looking around for something else. What they found was the springer. In addition to the springer's many excellent field qualities, the breed requires little space to train. They also are easy to train. This is mainly a matter of yard breaking, i.e., training them to come when called, "Hup!" This training command is peculiar to flushing and retrieving breeds, meaning to stop and sit immediately.

The worst problem encountered with the springer is that it usually tends to range too far out. This can be prevented largely by never allowing the young dog to range out far from the hunter and certainly never out of gun range. Thus, any birds or rabbits put up will be within gun range.

A bit of training to retrieve with a training dummy will complete the basic education of the springer. For more advanced training, the owner first should know what specialty he wants his dog to perform.

This springer, trained to retrieve with a training dummy, shows his versatility in the field by bringing in mallard.

Irish water spaniel, Chief Commanche, won honors as best of breed, other breeds at 1930 Los Angeles show.

The springer spaniel used in the field is a far different dog than the springer we see in the show benches. The show-bred springer with the long ears, heavy feathering and sloping back is just that: a show dog. The hunting breed of springer is much more lightly built and far more agile than the show strain. Like the cocker, the springer has a merry personality that makes it a real pleasure in hunting. He shares many other characteristics with the cocker and much of what has been mentioned here about the cocker applies to the springer.

A large number of the field springers presently found in this country are descended from dogs imported from Saighton Kennels in Anglesey, Wales. Strong Kennels, of Victoria, Texas, is currently the main importer of the Saighton dog. These dogs have pretty well taken over the springer field trials; Saighton's Sizzler won the national competition in 1971 and four more times since, as well as placing in the top slots eleven other times.

This field trial success is not entirely beneficial to the breed, however. As is usual with field trialers, these competitive owners and trainers seem to concentrate on speed and flashy performance. This tends to concentrate the breeding of the more radical dogs with an instability that may be expected from such dog's progeny.

Hunting springers — or any flushing breed — should hunt close in to the gunner, being dependent on the gun for all directions, swinging from side to side in front of the hunter in a pattern of fifteen to twenty yards on each side, then turning forward at the end of each sweep.

It is to be hoped that the hunting utility of the springer will be placed above the winning of field trials. At the present, the springer is at a point in its development that is almost ideal from the hunter's standpoint of gun dog use in the field.

In our ancestors' time, dogs earned their keep as can be seen by this hunter's score on prairie chickens, rabbits.

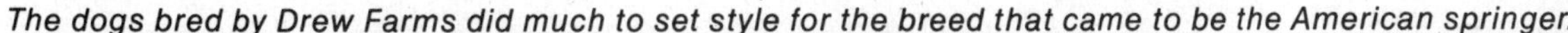

The dogs bred by Drew Farms did much to set style for the breed that came to be the American springer.

For the hunter who wants a gun dog and doesn't have the time or place to train it to the degree that the pointing breeds or some of the flushing breeds require, as well as those who do not particularly desire a pointing breed, the springer is an excellent choice. If you are interested in learning more about springers, go to a springer trial, where you will find no shortage of those eager to tell you all you want to learn about the breed. There were forty-eight springer trials in 1983, scattered all over the country with the center of activity in southern New England, Pennsylvania, New York and California. For information regarding field-bred springers, contact Mr. Roger Houk, 722 Division Street, Mukwonago, Wisconsin 53149.

Another popular spaniel is the Brittany which is thoroughly covered in the section concerning the pointing breeds. The Brittany is the only pointing spaniel that is recognized as a pointing breed. However, the clumber, the cocker and the springer often exhibit a tendency to pause before flushing birds and with a bit of encouragement some can be made into fairly dependable pointing dogs. This is considered rank heresy by springer field trial enthusiasts; pausing before the flush is considered a fault by springer judges. A springer is supposed to dash in and flush the bird, often jumping into the air after the bird; this characteristic of springing into the air after game is thought by some to have given rise to the name, "springer." As to the accuracy of this theory, I doubt we shall ever resolve this unless someone invents time travel.

Painting of a cocker spaniel, circa 1900, suggests the original heavy conformation not seen in today's dogs.

In Canada, the Beechgrove springer was quick to become popular as a strain. Photo is from 1930.

The clumber spaniel is few in numbers in the United States, but the breed's boosters are vociferous in their support. The clumber is the largest of the spaniels, standing sixteen to eighteen inches tall and weighing up to seventy pounds in the breed standard. Some of them weigh considerably more, however. The breed was developed by the Duke of Noailles and dogs were brought from France to England about the time of the French Revolution. In England, the Duke of Newcastle helped in establishment of the breed. White in shading, with some lemon markings allowed, the clumber is a distinctive dog with a large square-appearing head and large ears hanging well forward.

Having the playful, intelligent spaniel personality, these dogs make good companions as well as being a fine hunting species. The nobility that developed them used them for hunting in packs, but they are capable hunters for upland game, especially pheasant, when used singly. Like many spaniels, the clumber's diet must be watched as it tends to get fat. This condition is especially noticeable due to its size.

Author feels the fearful look in this dog's eye indicates it had been subjected to force-breaking.

The author contends that this is the type of conformation that judges look for in a top English springer.

Springer spaniels became popular in 1920s, as evidenced by the size of this training class of the period.

There also is a Welsh springer spaniel that is quite similar to the English and American springers. These dogs have just a bit longer neck than those of the other springer breeds and they display a strong tendency to wander too far from the hunter unless well trained and kept under close control while hunting.

The Sussex spaniel is another of the flushing breeds occasionally found in America. This is a strong, robust dog standing sixteen inches at the withers and weighing forty to forty-five pounds. The coat is a typical spaniel coat of a reddish-gold color similar to that of some golden retreivers. The Sussex spaniel is a good hunter, but barks almost continuously while hunting. Some people find this trait objectionable, probably one of the major reasons why the breed is not more popular. The Sussex spaniel was developed in the mid-1800s in Sussex, England; hence the name.

The field spaniel is one of the more popular breeds both in England and America. Like most of the spaniels, they are flushing dogs. There is considerable variance in weight in this breed, with the breed standard allowing from thirty-five to fifty pounds. Except for a longer body and larger size, the field spaniel is similar to the cocker and many persons have difficulty in distinguishing between the two breeds. They also share the same hunting characteristics and, at the risk of offending, I must say that I see no real difference between the two breeds other than size.

Other breeds that are used successfully as flushing dogs include the basenji, airedale, many of the harrier breeds, and the Norwegian elkhound.

The English cocker spaniel is a good game-getter and is larger than the American breed.

A Good Bark, Tenacity And A Good Eye Can Make A Squirrel Dog Of Even A Mongrel!

THE SQUIRREL dog is peculiarly North American. Squirrel hunting is an American sport, as there are not many squirrels hunted for sport in other countries. In England and Europe, the squirrel is considered a tree rat and looked on with about the same sentiment as we here in America show toward the Norwegian rat. The opinion of Europeans not withstanding, many Americans enjoy squirrel hunting. Some years ago, it was reported that more ammuntion was fired at squirrels in many states than at any other game. This includes the cottontail rabbit which many persons believe to be the most popular game animal.

Squirrel dogs are regional, however. In some areas, squirrel dogs are almost unknown while in seemingly similar areas nearly every hunter has a squirreler.

Many breeds are used as squirrel dogs, with even more mongrels used in squirreling insofar as numbers are concerned. The requirements for a good squirrel dog are fairly simple. The dog must have a good working nose, the ability to use its eyes to spot game and the desire to chase squirrels up a tree, then bark at them until the hunter arrives.

Species used as squirrel dogs seem to vary from one region to another. Throughout the Appalachians, the favored breed is the fice dog. Developed by the local residents, they neither need nor want any official recognition

Right: A pair of fat, healthy squirrels take their ease safely above the reach of a dog. (Below) This woodlot on a southern farm is area where squirrel dogs do well.

of their dogs as being purebred. They are interested in results, not papers.

The fice is a small dog weighing twenty-five pounds or less. They generally are black with brown markings, especially a brown spot above each eye. The belly may be brown or white with a brown edge around the white; there may be white on the chest and often the tail is feathered with a brown edge. Some of them look like miniature short-haired Gordon setters in their markings.

Feathering on the tail is not uncommon on short-haired dogs with the fice-type coat. The coat of the fice is not as short as the really short-haired breeds and is of fairly coarse, stiff hair that lies flat except for feathering on the rear of the legs and on the tail. This, incidentally, cannot be considered standard; it is simply a general description of the fice dogs bred for generations by the mountain people. The fice is a piece of Americana, as is the so-called yellow cur.

Normally, a squirrel will attempt to hide on the side of a tree away from hunter. Dog can attract its attention while the hunter moves into proper position for his shot.

The author prefers the challenge of hunting squirrels in his native West Virginia with a .36 caliber muzzleloader.

In the Blue Ridge country, the preferred squirrel dog is the yellow cur. This is a distinct breed — or perhaps it would be better to say strain — that has been developed over the years by the residents of the Blue Ridge mountains and the immediate surrounding area. Like the fice, the yellow cur is not an officially recognized breed, but this does not keep them from being really great dogs for the purpose for which they were developed.

The yellow cur is not as closely bred as the fice. There are wide variations between a yellow cur from the Virginia Blue Ridge, one from the Tennessee Blue Ridge or those found in the Great Smokies area. Any of these dogs probably should be considered mongrels, as they do not breed completely true to conformation. What they have in common is that they are medium in size, have extremely short hair, a slender build, a long slender tail covered with tight hair. The smooth, sleek coat on this slender dog reminds one somewhat of a greyhound in the line of the back.

The duties of a squirrel dog are pretty simple: to find and hold the attention of a squirrel, while the hunter comes up quietly and takes aim. The approved technique sounds, and is, simple, but there is a vast difference in the squirrel-finding and treeing ability of different dogs. The finest squirrel dog I ever hunted was the Norwegian elkhound, referred to in the early chapters of this book. I have hunted with some pretty famous squirrelers, but none of them even approached the ability of Lady.

Second in squirreling ability in my own experience was a yellow cur owned by a man named Whittington who lived in the Blue Ridge near Charlestown, West Virginia. This dog was named Sooner, and Whit always said the dog would sooner hunt squirrels than eat. I'm not qualified to comment on the pup's eating propensities, but I can guarantee Sooner could put a squirrel up a tree.

Bill Lunsford of near Raliegh, North Carolina, tells of a

Dogs such as this Fice-English shepherd cross develop into fine squirrel dogs when given the proper training. Extra length of the rear legs is common trait of Fice.

Moving around on the ground to get from one tree to another, squirrels leave scent trails dogs can pick up.

squirrel dog owned by an old hillbilly who rented the dog out to visiting hunters by the hour. This fice was supposed to be really good and there was never a renter who requested to have his money refunded. Quite a few hunters were said to have gotten a limit of squirrel in less than an hour, using this Rent-A-Dog.

It is not particularly difficult to train a squirrel dog. After the usual yard breaking, the dog should be taken along on a squirrel hunt and allowed to get its teeth into a few squirrels after they have been shot. This is usually all that is needed as squirrel dogs are born, not made. There seems to be something about squirreling that a dog either does pretty much on its own or doesn't do at all. The breed of dog is not important. What is important is the dog's ability to use its eyes to spot squirrels after it picks up the scent. Ideally, the dog goes off on short scouting sweeps of the woods until it picks up squirrel scent. After picking up the scent, the dog should follow the scent until it either sees the squirrel or follows the scent to a tree where the squirrel has gone up.

This is where the difference between a so-so squirreler and a top dog shows up. The really good dog will be able to tell if the squirrel has gone up recently and is still in the tree even though it can't see the squirrel. If the squirrel is still in the tree, the dog will start barking and continue until the hunter arrives. With the hunter on the spot, the dog should keep barking to distract the squirrel from noting the hunter's approach. With the squirrel interested in the dog, the hunter is able to get a good shot with a smallbore rifle, the only really sporting way to hunt squirrels.

There are good squirrel dogs of many breeds as well as mongrels that do a good job. Among the breeds that are best at squirreling are the Norwegian elkhound, yellow cur, fice, almost any of the spaniels, the labrador, golden, curly and flat-coated retrievers, Airedales, harriers, terriers, and even English shepherds and border collies. Hounds, with the exception of the Nordic breeds, do not do well as squirrel dogs, because they do not often use their eyes to spot the squirrels.

Dogs seem to have a certain disorienting effect on squirrels. At my farm home, we once had an English shepherd that would tree a squirrel some distance from any other trees, then sit and bark until the squirrel would come down and try to escape to another tree. The dog usually caught the squirrel.

When leaves are off the trees, shots must be taken at longer ranges. Author uses Model 52 Winchester for this type of hunting.

This golden retriever has done his share of squirrel hunting and indicates the position of hiding animal.

Chapter 6

A MATTER OF VERSATILITY

It's Still A Case Of Proper Training, If You Want A Dog That Does It All

As a segment of the versatility tests described in this chapter, feathers are removed from a bird to mark the start of drag trail for dog to take.

AT THE CLOSE of World War II, many American soldiers were stationed in Europe. Like healthy, active men anywhere, they soon began looking around for activities to fill their leisure time. Many had been hunters back home and they were soon hunting in Europe.

They found the European hunting customs to be considerably different from what they had been accustomed to at home. Whatever they hunted in Europe, they found that they must be accompanied by a *jaeger* hunter or gamekeeper. These jaegers invariably used a dog; in fact, dogs seemed to be used for every type of hunting. The Americans were familiar with hounds, pointing dogs, retrievers and flushing dogs, but they were not familiar with the concept of one dog performing all these duties. When an American hunter went out with the same jaeger and dog to hunt for different game, he would see the same dog trail and bring to bay a wounded deer, point and hold gamebirds for the hunter, retrieve those birds after they had been shot, trail and bring a rabbit (*hare* in Europe) around to the gun

The judges drag game to establish a track in the drag-tracking test that will determine the dog's talents.

like a hound. It is understandable that they came to think of these European dogs as "wonder dogs." Actually these dogs were *All Gebrauchshund,* which translates literally as an "all-purpose gun dog.'"

When the soldiers returned home, some went to great difficulty to bring one or more of these wonder dogs with them. They found that the dogs worked as well in the United States as they had in Europe. You could use one of these European-trained dogs as a waterfowl retriever in the morning in the duck marsh, as a pointing dog and retriever in the afternoon and have the dog chase a few bunnies in the evening. This was really a great change from the one-purpose dogs to which we had been accustomed to in this country and the fame of these dogs spread rapidly. Many outdoorsmen were particularly impressed with the big gray weimaraners, and fantastically high prices were offered and paid by breeders who had visions of making fortunes off the wonder dogs.

The crash came when those who had bred these Continental breeds started to hunt the puppies that had been whelped in the United States. They didn't perform any better than the familiar American pointers, setters, retrievers and hounds. All sorts of accusations were hurled around by disappointed breeders, who thought they had been cheated by those who had sold them their breeding stock. The imported dogs did all that they were expected to, but their pups just didn't have it. Finally, those who had imported these dogs started to *hear* what the European breeders had been telling them all along: These dogs were highly intelligent and capable performers, but a puppy is a blank slate on which the handler must impress what he wishes the dog to do by training it to do these things. European dog handlers were — and are — very demanding of their dogs performance, and would not accept anything less than the performance they desired. In order to obtain hunting rights, a jaeger had to demonstrate that his dog was well trained and capable of preventing game from being lost. In Europe, game is the property of the individual landowner and considered a valuable asset. Naturally, landowners would not permit hunters to use incompetent dogs that would permit valuable game to be lost. Game killed by the hunter in Europe is the property of the landowner and the hunter must make arrangements to buy the game from this owner. Thus, a system such as this produces dogs that are really game conservationists.

During the feudal days in Europe, the nobility kept great numbers of dogs, as hunting was one of their favorite sports. The privilege of hunting was reserved to these rich lords and, over the years, a strict set of rules as to what was considered "sporting" was developed. A large estate often

The handler brings in the shorthair and puts it down at the beginning of the track marked by bird's feathers.

had twenty to thirty persons whose duties were simply to train and care for the dogs. A different, highly specialized breed was developed for each type of hunting. Most of the specialist breeds we have today came from the development of these specific hunting breeds of that time. There have been improvements, but the basic types, such as hounds, retrievers, harriers, setters and pointers, were established here.

The rise of the so-called middle class and industrialization brought great change. Hunting no longer was exclusive to the wealthy landowners; anyone who had the wherewithal to afford to buy the needed hunting arms and accoutrements — and pay the landowner for the game — could hunt. Living in towns where there was no space available for large kennels, these people gave the needed impetus for the development of the all-purpose or versatile dog. Starting in the mid-1800s, there was a great effort to breed general-purpose dogs to fill this sudden need for a hunting dog that could be kept in a small space in the yard or home of the hunter, yet was trained to hunt all of the

The dog is released from its leash after the handler is certain that it is on the game track.

Author considers this German wirehaired pointer as being an excellent example of breed. Owner is Herman Heydlauf.

various kinds of game available. This required that a dog have a strong instinct to point, be a good performer in the water and swamplands, readily accept training and be strong and enduring to meet the various situations that would be encountered under such a variety of conditions in the hunt.

Working independently, many breeders developed strains that were similar. This was natural, as they were working toward similar goals using the same original breeds. Many breeds were developed and the less useful ones were replaced by the more capable until, today, we have several breeds boasting similar characteristics. These are what we term today as the versatile breeds.

The most common of these breeds are divided into three groups: the shorthaired group, the wirehaired group and the longhaired group. The shorthairs are made up of the German shorthaired pointer (GSP), the Vizsla (VI), and the weimaraner (WM). The wirehaired group includes the German roughhaired pointer (GRP), German wirehaired pointer (GWP), pudelpointer (PP), spinoni (SP), and the wirehaired pointing griffon (GR). The longhaired group is composed of the Brittany spaniel (BSP), German longhaired pointer (GLP), large Munsterlander pointer (LMP), and the small Munsterlander pointer (SMP).

By the time the average versatile breed owner came to realize that the desired traits were bred into a dog, but must be developed by training, the quality of those that had been imported from Europe had suffered badly from the indiscriminate breeding that had been conducted by those who had no knowledge of genetics. Others simply were not interested in maintaining the quality of a breed but were only interested in making a lot of fast bucks. To make matters worse, those who were truly interested in breeding for quality, and knew enough of genetics to do so, were handicapped by the fact that they had no standard against which to judge their dogs and little or no idea of just what they should expect from a good dog.

Fortunately, some Europeans came to the United States who knew what constituted a good versatile dog and how to test him. A few of these people decided to form a club to promote the testing of the versatile breeds and thus achieve the quality needed for good breeding programs. One per son who was instrumental in this campaign is Sigbot Winterhelt of Quartz Hill, California. John Kegel of Goodwood, Ontario; Dr. Edward D. Bailey of Puslinch, Ontario, and Don Smith of Simsbury, Connecticut, also were key men in the formation of the beginning versatile dog testing program in this country. There were others, of course, who

Top: Wirehair returned with duck used in the drag-track testing. (Inset) The dog comes in close in proper form. (Right) Dog delivers the bird to hand in performance that was flawless, won top score.

helped in the beginning of the versatile dog testing program.

Through the work of these dedicated men, the testing system was established and the versatile dogs came of age in America. One significant way in which the European system of dog testing differs from American field trials with which we are familiar is that the dogs are tested against a standard instead of being tested against one another, as we are accustomed to seeing.

I am often asked upon returning from a North American Versatile Hunting Dog test: "Who won?"

Well, the answer is everybody and nobody. The dogs are tested as to how well they meet the standard of performance which the NAVHDA system has established. In theory, every dog in a test could meet the requirements and thus every dog in the trial could be said to have won.

The elimination of competition — you don't have to beat the other dogs being tested — leads to a much more friendly and enjoyable atmosphere at a NAVHDA trial or test than at other competitive trials where only one dog can win

This weimaraner holds a solid point on bird as judge comes up.

Handler seems happy with the way her weimaraner holds point, while judge tries to flush bird at NAVHDA field test.

Fritz, a pudelpointer, locks on a bird in heavy brush. Note that coloration of breed blends into the background.

and everyone is jealously watching his neighbor. At a NAVHDA test, everyone is rooting for all the dogs to do well. This is certainly a welcome improvement in atmosphere at a trial.

The NAVHDA concept is to test each dog as fully and fairly as possible in respect to the abilities a versatile dog is expected to possess and to demonstrate that this dog has fully met the requirements of a versatile dog in whatever classification the dog is being tested. Dogs of less than sixteen months are tested in what are called natural ability tests. They are not expected to show any great amount of training other than simple yard-breaking commands. They are tested to determine their natural inherited hunting instincts such as waterlove, pointing instinct, (they need not point, only show the instinct to freeze up around birds), sensitivity to game and the desire to hunt.

The natural ability trial is a valuable tool in the evaluation of a young dog's ability and potential for future training and development. Some dogs do not possess the necessary natural ability to become really fine hunting dogs no matter how much time and effort is spent in training them. The time to find out how much training a dog is capable of accepting is when it is young instead of spending years trying to develop abilities that the dog did not possess in the first place.

The natural ability trial offers the chance to have the abilities of a young dog evaluated by a panel of expert judges who will not be influenced by "kennel blindness" or other extraneous influences. I have heard some persons make the statement that kennel blindness is not really a consequential factor. From long experience I know this to be wrong. It is almost impossible to remain completely objective about a dog which one has raised from a puppy and come to be fond of. We tend to make excuses for shortcomings in our own dogs that we would be quick to condemn in another person's dog.

The natural ability test is composed of the following elements: Use of nose, waterlove, tracking ability, pointing, search of grounds and search pattern, cooperation and desire to work.

Each of these tests is assigned an index number that reflects the relative importance as compared to the other tests. For example, use of nose carries an index number of 6. This is the highest index number accorded to any test. This means, in essence, that the manner in which a dog uses its nose and the sensitivity of the dog's nose is considered to be the most important single factor in its hunting ability. Without a good nose, a dog cannot ever become a topnotch hunting companion. The lowest index number is 2. This index is assigned to tracking and cooperation.

This German wirehaired pointer demonstrates intensity and a perfect pointing style during NAVHDA test in bird field.

Indexes of 4 and 5 are assigned to other phases of the testing in accord with the value placed upon the trait being tested.

Physical characteristics as well as temperament also are evaluated by the judges and it is recommended that the dog be tested for dysplasia. All things considered, I believe the natural ability test to be one of the most valuable assets for the owner of a young dog and I would strongly recommend to the owner of any young dog that he have the dog tested in the NAVHDA system. If you have a dog of one of the versatile breeds, I strongly recommend that you become a NAVHDA member and take advantage of the excellent program offered at far less than it would cost for even a month at a professional trainer's kennel. If the reader is the owner of one of the pointing breeds, it is still a good idea to have the dog evaluated under the NAVHDA system in the particular tests that apply to your favored breed.

In the case of a pointer for example, you might wish to have the dog evaluated for bird field, pointing, search, nose, gunshyness, cooperation, desire to work and physical attributes. You need not have the dog tested for waterlove and other abilities that would not apply to this particular breed for the use to which you wish to apply your dog. This can save a lot of training time spent on an inferior dog.

If you are not a NAVHDA member you will have to find a trial that is not filled up with dogs owned by NAVHDA members. As in any other organization, members come first. If you own a young gun dog, the entry fee for a NAVHDA test can be the best investment in dog lore you ever make.

The utility test is designed to test the proficiency of the dog in all types of hunting, covering all species of game for which it is likely to be used. A dog that qualifies as a NAVHDA utility dog is thoroughly trained and works efficiently. To qualify as a utility dog, the dog must have passed the field tests designed to demonstrate the dog's ability as an upland game dog and the waterwork sequence meant to test the animal's usefulness as a waterfowl dog.

In the search test, the dog is run for a period of at least half an hour in cover that is known to contain game. Such presence usually is assured by planting game birds before each dog is put down. The dog is accompanied by two proficient gunners, at least three judges and the dog's handler. The dog is expected to find the birds and point them until the handler and gunners and judges come up. The handler will flush the birds and the gunners will shoot the birds on the wing. The dog will be evaluated on how well it covered the grounds, the intensity and style of the point, whether or not it broke point when the birds flushed or at the shot, and

The handler steadies a German shorthair beside the blind before moving off to fire shots as part of behavior test.

This Brittany spaniel comes out of the water with a bird in its mouth during another segment of NAVHDA testing.

A gun is fired from opposite side of pond in an effort to distract a dog beside the blind. Note powder smoke.

on the search for and retrieval of the dead bird.

The pointing test is meant to determine the dog's desire and ability to point game. This test ends when the handler reaches the dog and the test passes on to the steadiness-on-game segment. The dog should remain steady to wing and shot and hold position until the handler sends it in to retrieve or gives the "Hie on" command in the event no game was killed. The next test covers the retrieval of a shot bird. The dog should be eager to find and retrieve the game that has been shot.

For the retrieve of dragged game test, two of the judges will place the game which has been selected by the handler on a rope between them and drag the game for at least a hundred yards in a pattern that leaves a "J" shaped trail and it is then hidden. The handler is allowed to designate whether he wishes to use either feathered game or furred game for this test.

The dog must not be allowed to witness the dragging of the game, although a few hanks of fur or feathers from the game are left at the beginning of the drag track. The dog is brought forward and put on the trail. The handler may accompany the dog for not over ten yards along the trail. The dog then should follow the track to the game and retrieve it without mauling or attempting to eat it. When the dog returns to his handler, it should hold the game until ordered to deliver it to hand, then do so willingly. One of the judges will have been hidden in such a position that behavior of the dog on finding the game is observed.

Water tests invariably are conducted in a swampy marshy area that includes an open pond that is deep enough to require the dog to swim. The first of these water tests involves the search for a duck. A pen-raised duck is rendered flightless by pulling the feathers from one wing or by taping one wing to the body. The duck then is taken about twenty yards from the edge of a pond or other body of water and, after a few feathers have been placed on the ground and the duck lightly brushed against the ground and weeds, it is released and allowed to run to the pond and swim away. All of the foregoing has been out of sight of both the dog and handler.

A shorthair is led through the slalom in walking-at-heel test.

When the duck has gone far enough, the dog is brought up and put on the trail of the duck. Although the dog is not required to retrieve the duck, it certainly does nothing to harm the dog's score in the event it does retrieve. Judges watch to evaluate the dog's efforts to locate and trail the duck.

The walking-at-heel test is conducted by leading the dog through a series of obstacles similar to a ski slalom run; the dog should follow the handler without undue tugging at the leash or tangling the leash in the obstacles. In another test, the dog is required to stay beside a blind while the handler goes out of sight and fires two shots. The dog should not move from the position in which it was placed by the handler.

When the handler returns to the blind, the test concerning behavior by the blind begins. Several shots are fired and a duck is thrown into the pond within sight of the dog. The dog must remain quietly beside the blind until the handler sends it in to retrieve the duck. When the handler sends the dog into the pond, this begins the retrieve-of-a-duck test which requires that the dog go to the dead duck, pick it up and retrieve it without undue delay, chewing or mauling.

Throughout both the field and water test, the dog's use of its nose, its stamina, desire to work, handling, obedience and cooperation are judged. The evaluation of all these tests are the basis for the judges' scores.

The main breeds seen today in **NAVHDA** trials in this country are the German wirehaired pointer, the German shorthaired pointer, the pudelpointer, Brittany spaniel, weimaraners, Visla and the wire-haired pointing griffon. Other breeds are used to a limited extent in North America. These include but are not limited to the German long-haired pointer, large Munsterlander, small Munsterlander and the Spinoni.

It is sometimes difficult to get the ideals and methods

The handler fires his gun, but the dog remains steadfast beside the blind despite the excitement.

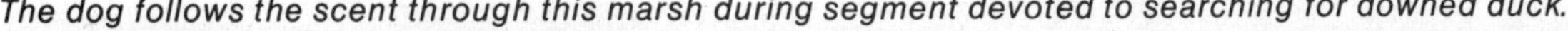

The dog follows the scent through this marsh during segment devoted to searching for downed duck.

used in the NAVHDA system across to those who are accustomed to working within the system of trials and training that constituted the only program in the United States before the advent of NAVHDA.

The first hurdle is to stop thinking of a NAVHDA field event as a "trial" and start thinking of it as a "test." NAVHDA members do not conduct field trials; they have field tests in which, as stated before, the dogs are tested against the standards set by the executive council. This takes a bit of getting used to, but will lead to much satisfaction once the dogowner has come to understand and accept this system.

Another point which must be understood is that the NAVHDA system of training and testing is not intended to replace or supplant any of the other dog trial and training systems now in use; the NAVHDA system is designed to

Dog has caught and is retrieving the duck in this part of test.

One of the dogs undergoing testing comes out of the water with a duck in its mouth at end of a long retrieve.

A gunner moves in on a pointing dog to flush and shoot the bird, while judges and handler watch for dog's reaction.

produce dogs of a type and capability previously unknown in this country.

The NAVHDA method of training is different in many respects from the training programs to which we have become accustomed. A large part of the yard-breaking is done on a bench where the dog has a tendency to be more tractable because it is up off the ground and out of its element. For those interested in this training program, I recommend you attend one of the tests held near where you live and to get a copy of the NAVHDA training book *The Training and Care of the Versatile Hunting Dog,* by Sigbot Winterhelt and Edward Bailey. Incidentally, both authors have donated all proceeds from this excellent training guide to NAVHDA to help promote versatile dogs in America.

Any hunting breed can benefit from the use of the training methods set forth in this book, as these guidelines are applicable to any breed one would wish to train to hunt upland birds, chase furred game as a hound or use as a flushing dog and retriever or a waterfowl dog. The training book may be had from Ros E. Scott, 10421 Rockville Rd., Indianapolis, IN 46234 at $6 each.

There currently are sixteen NAVHDA chapters. You may contact the nearest chapter secretary for further information:

Southern California, Davey Caven, 13258 Cypress Ave., Chino, CA 91710.

Northern California Chapter, Susan Swain, 941 Faris Dr., San Jose, CA 95111; Phone: 408-227-8107.

Palmetto Chapter, Sissy Girtman, 72 Smithson Dr., Oviedo, FL 32765; Phone: 305-365-4455.

Potomac Chapter, Bernice Carter, 14400 Willoughby Rd., Upper Marlboro, MD 20772; Phone: 301-627-4610.

Michigan Chapter, Sue Helser, 2738 Dover Dr., Troy, MI 48083; Phone: 313-689-1924.

Minnesota Chapter, Nancy Spaeth, 213 17th Ave., W.. Eveleth, MN 55734; Phone: 218-744-1772.

Southern Indiana Chapter, Nancy Foist, 1101 E. Kansas, Ft. Peck, MT 59223; Phone: 406-526-3441.

Big Sky Chapter, Jack Lulack, Box 748, Plains, MT 59859; Phone 406-826-3592.

Delaware Valley Chapter, Andy Lehner, RFD #1, Cedar Rd., Mickelton, NJ 14505; Phone: 609-478-6272.

Finger Lakes Chapter, Robert Brown, 5380 Russel Rd., Marion, NY 14505; Phone: 315-589-9484.

Pymatuning Chapter, Tom Chanda, 304 Ravenna Rd., Newton Falls, OH 44444; Phone: 216-872-0091.

Northeast Chapter, Dr. William Pacitti, 21 Linfield Cr., Lincoln, RI 02865; Phone: 401-724-9363.

Wisconsin Chapter, Kent Jensen, RT 1, Box 289A, Arena, WI 53053; Phone: 608-795-4486.

Grand River Chapter, Lisa Foster, RR #4, Bellwood, ON N0B 1J0; Phone 519-843-5428.

Ontario Chapter, Blair Smith, RR #2, Glansworth, ON N0L 1L0; Phone: 519-644-1910.

Toronto Chapter, Doris Morrison, Box 19, 3 Henry St., Keswick, ON L4P 2L5; Phone: 416-476-2917.

Should you write to any of these chapter secretaries, please enclose a stamped, self-addressed envelope.

Chapter 7

A LOOK AT FIELD TRIALS

The Author Has Jaundiced Views On The Nature Of Current Trial Policy

FIELD TRIALS have played a large and significant role in the development of the modern sporting dog. Most of the gun dog breeds seen in the field today owe a large part of their abilities to breeding programs that have been directed toward producing the type of dog desired to meet the conditions encountered in the trials.

The characteristics that judges look for in the dogs they place in these trials seem to change gradually during the years as conditions change; desirable traits are modified by conditions and other factors encountered by hunters in the use of their dogs in hunting. Judging changes follow slowly upon the changing conditions — there is generally dissatisfaction with the trial conditions and the type of dogs being placed before the judging catches up with the thinking of the majority of dog owners.

Such conditions exist now in the major trial circuits of the big running, professionally handled dogs. The trend for the last forty years has been toward ever-wider running dogs; thus the range and speed required to win a major field trial today is such that those dogs which are winning exhibit little that would be of interest to hunters. While a few of today's crop of field champions are usable as hunting dogs, the great majority have never had a bird killed over them since they became good prospects for the trial circuit; some of them have never had a bird killed over them in their entire lives.

This condition is not conducive to the production of good hunting dogs and there are many who protest the present state of our big trials, but those closely involved in this trial system resist any and all change in the standards of judging. They have good reason to resist such change, for if the judges suddenly start placing good, steady, sensible foot-hunting range dogs, the whole setup which has been so carefully nurtured during the years will fall apart. The breeders will find no market for dogs which run half a mile ahead of their handlers and professional handlers will find that much of their business has been lost as owners will be able to train and handle their own dogs. There is always more pleasure derived from running a dog you have trained yourself. Most breeders have only been trying to produce the dogs demanded by the big trail judges and are not to blame for the fact that the trial standard have moved away from anything even remotely resembling the more true hunting situation.

The blame, if we must place it, seems to rest with a large percentage of those who make a business of handling pointers and setters in field trials. Let me hasten to say that not all of these handlers are to blame. I have had some of the best of them tell me privately that they abhor the sort of dogs the judges are placing. The problem for these handlers is that, if they are to make a living from handling dogs, they have to train those dogs to win in the sort of trials they will be running in and under those judges who they know will be placing only the fastest and widest-running dogs. The conditions under which the big pointing dog trials are run are interesting in themselves.

Before the trial — usually the evening before, and often at a banquet sort of get-together — the names of all the dogs entered in the trial are put into a container, then drawn two at a time by some impartial party, often a child. The two dogs whose names are drawn together will be put down together as bracemates. This is an important step; a good bracemate can be of valuable help to a dog just as a poor one can make a good dog look bad.

The next morning, the trial starts with the dogs being run in the order in which they were drawn. The running order is of great importance also, as those dogs that are run early have better scenting conditions than dogs run in the middle of the day. When the trial is run on wild quail, as are most of the national championships, those dogs that get to run during the morning and evening feeding periods have much better chances of finding birds than those run during those

Field trial judge checks retrieved bird for teeth marks. Deep marks of the dog's teeth would tend to indicate a hard-mouthed dog. This would be considered a serious fault in a retriever and would lose points in scoring.

During beagle trials, dogs of this breed take the track, while handlers keep close watch on individual performances.

times when the birds are lying up for the midday rest.

The running of the trial is conducted under the supervision of the judges with the field marshal acting as the executor of the wishes of the judges. The first brace of dogs will be called out and, at the order of the judges, put down to hunt. The judges and field marshal, as well as the handlers and others who wish to watch the brace of dogs under judgment, are mounted on horses and they proceed at a rather fast gait under the direction of the judges and field marshal.

When any of the dogs finds game, the handler will call point and often hold his hat in the air to signify that the dog is pointing as the animals are often out of earshot of the judges and others. The judges arrive and instruct the handler to put up the birds. This usually is done with a flushing whip with which the handler strikes at the cover where the birds are thought to be. (The flushing whip also serves to remind the dog of what might happen if it chases the birds.)

When the bird or birds flush, the dog is expected to remain steady and not move until instructed to do so by the handler. Sometimes there are no birds flushed. This is termed an "unproductive" point. One unproductive point is usually not held against the dog, but more than one such point is definitely not in the dog's interest.

The judges try to take into consideration many factors regarding unproductive points. If, for example, a previous brace of dogs found a bird which was flushed from the spot where a dog has an unproductive in a later brace, the judges know that the dog was pointing the scent of the previously flushed birds and little if any account is paid to the unproductive point.

The handlers will try to keep their dog moving and will note where birds alight when they are flushed so they can direct their dogs into the area later in the trial should they pass close enough. Emphasis is on how far the dogs travel and how many birds they find in the time they are down.

Actually, I have seen dogs that covered a large amount of territory and found only one or two points scored high, while dogs that made repeated finds of many birds were not even considered seriously for placement. Dogs are judged on their ability to pick out distant birdy-looking cover and go immediately there. The thoroughness of their search, pattern and efficiency of their search, their response to handler's signals, as well as bird-handling ability is supposedly considered, but in some trials there is little evidence these traits received more than minor consideration.

When field trials first began in this country, they were meant to test one hunter's dog against another to determine who had the best hunting dog and to provide a reservoir of known top quality hunting dogs for breeding purposes. The judges were mounted, because it is impossible for a human being to follow many braces of dogs over a long and sometimes rapidly traveled course. Sometimes the handlers also were mounted as were some of those in the gallery primarily because some bird hunters hunted from horseback. Nearly everyone had a horse at the trial, since they had come there on horses, the most common way of travel at that time.

Gradually, during the years, there has been more and more emphasis on speed and range as qualities to be looked for in a trial type dog. Birds were shot over the dogs and retrieving was required as well as a tender mouth. Tender mouth means that the dog does not mangle or leave teeth marks in the birds when retrieving. This is a most important trait in gun dogs and should be thoroughly stressed as

A gunner prepares to shoot a duck for the water retrieval phase of judging, while dogs stand by, awaiting signal.

A wirehair retrieves shot pheasant in land retrieval phase of trial.

one of the desired qualities of a dog to which one wishes to breed. A hard-mouthed dog will ruin a lot of game and dogs displaying this trait should be faulted and certainly should not be bred.

Field trials prospered and grew into a great sport with an ever-increasing following. Time moved on, until we come to the time of the quail plantations. These quail plantations were huge southern estates whose main crop was quail for the hunting pleasure of the owner and his guests. They often had staffs of a hundred or more workers and produced cotton, corn, tobacco, barley, wheat and other small grain crops, but the main thrust and energies of the operation was the production of more and more quail; all other crops were simply by-products of the quail operation.

Naturally, it required a wealthy individual to be able to maintain thousands of acres with the necessary people to operate such an organization, but this was the time of the tycoons, moguls and ostentatious wealth. This sort of hunting brought the big running bird dogs into their own. Here was hunting where one could hunt all day from horseback without going over the same grounds and where the dog that ran the horizon and covered the most ground was the dog that produced the most hunting and birds.

When a hunt started out from the plantation house in the morning, there were several dogs in comfortable boxes on a spring wagon, plus at least two dog handler-trainers. Their job was to train the dogs and get them onto as many birds as they could find in the shortest possible time in order to produce the maximum shooting for the owner and his guests.

The owner of the plantation usually invited several friends or business associates to go along on a hunt. When the dogs found birds, the hunters would ride up, dismount and move in to shoot the birds as the covey rose.

Seldom was there any effort to hunt the singles. The hunters would simply go on to another covey as there were

The wirehair makes acceptable delivery to hand. This phase is important in trial judging.

enough coveys in the territory to allow this. Unfortunately, such a plentitude of coveys is not true of quail hunting in general, and we are training dogs to work in a situation which is not currently typical.

The above is a general outline of the conditions encountered in the era when the pattern for the major field trials was established. Over the intervening years, most of the big quail plantations have been turned to more lucrative endeavors and conditions encountered by John Doe Hunter have changed vastly. In the East, as late as the post-war 1940s, a bird hunter could reasonably expect to ask permission and hunt farms of several hundred acres. A bit of effort expended in farmer-hunter relations usually would turn up permission to hunt several adjoining farms of like acreage and the serious hunter could sally forth with his dogs and hunt an area of some thousand or more acres. Under these conditions, it was possible to use a far running dog to some advantage. At least the hunter could get by with only slight inconvenience caused by the dog running onto land which he did not have permission to hunt or by the dog coming close to a highway where it was likely to be endangered by traffic.

During the last thirty years this situation has changed, with big farms being broken up into smaller lots, houses being built in areas where there was formerly good bird hunting and no roads other than farm lanes. The last twenty years has seen an even more devastating blow dealt to the bird hunter in areas like the eastern panhandle of West Virginia where I live. The new interstate highway system has brought this and similar areas within a two-hour drive of metropolitan centers like Washington D.C. and this sudden accessability to urban areas has led to a great influx of moneyed professionals who offer big prices for the choicest farms.

Then there are the developers who buy three-hundred-acre farms and subdivide them into plots of five or ten acres and sell them off to city people as "ranchettes." This effectively removes these areas from the available hunting area as well as putting the land in the hands of persons who often are anti-hunting.

This, then, is the situation into which we bring the pointers and setters developed under the conditions of the major field trial circuit, where the dogs are encouraged to run to the horizon. In actual practice, a dog often may be limited to hunting small plots of land of twenty or thirty acres or even less.

There are literally hundreds of smaller pointing dog trials run under the auspices of the same organizations that hold the major circuit trials. The same rules apply in these trials and the main difference is that the grounds on which these trials are run usually are only a hundred acres or less; the course is generally a winding path over which the dogs pass a brace at a time on their way to a "bird field" in which there are several birds planted prior to the release of each brace of dogs.

This produces an even more artificial situation under which these dogs must run. The first couple braces of dogs over the course have some chance of finding wild birds at a location other than in the bird field. Succeeding braces are largely limited to those birds which have been introduced artificially into the bird field with their accompanying man scent and the trails left by the bird planters. I frequently have seen dogs that had been run in such situations seemingly look for the trails of the bird planters, then follow them to the planted birds. This is not a good situation, but bird dog clubs holding these trials have to make do with what they have to work with. Certainly no blame is to be attached to the local clubs sponsoring the trials, as there are only a few of the big quail-oriented plantations left and these are reserved for such big, nationally prominent trials as the Grand National Championship. There are many regional championships and dogs generally advance upward as their wins accrue. These trials have many devotees and many persons enjoy them. However, I feel the conditions are entirely too artificial to relate to the hunting ability of a dog inasmuch as there is no need for a dog to retrieve shot birds or demonstrate whether it is a soft or hard-mouthed retriever. Anyone interested in learning more

Still uncertain of the location of the duck it has been directed to retrieve by handler, wirehair takes to water.

about such trials should contact The American Field, 222 West Adams Street, Chicago, Illinois 60606 to obtain the address of the closest local club. The *American Field* magazine is the official journal of this type of trial.

In response to demands by dog-owning bird hunters for a trial system more truly representative of the conditions likely to be encountered in the hunting field today, several field trial organizations have come into being. These organizations feature foot-hunting, shoot-to-kill, retrieve-required field trials. Such trials are more truly representative of the conditions encountered by hunters in the field in the present day and should go far toward developing dogs more suited to the hunting conditions one might expect to encounter today while actually hunting.

Today's hunter often is restricted to small parcels of land that are surrounded by posted lands and highways. These highways represent a real hazard, as a dog interested in game is just not going to pay much attention to the fact that it is crossing a highway. The various state highway commissions do not help the situation by planting such growth as lespedeza and crown vetch in the median strips and along the berms of the highways. These plants produce seeds that attract quail and pheasants which, in turn, attract bird dogs.

By placing emphasis on foot-handling and shoot-to-retrieve, these new trial organizations should be able to breed a strain of dogs that will hunt closer to the gunner and be more biddable and easily handled. The two leading organizations of this type trial are the National Shoot to Retrieve Association and American Walking Field Trial Association. From a small beginning, these organizations have grown swiftly and seem to be meeting the demands of dog owners for a trial situation not too different from their daily hunting routine.

Retriever trials are conducted by an active group of dog people who are interested in promoting and improving the retrieving breeds. Trials are held in most all parts of the country and, if interested in the retrieving breeds, you should contact your breed club to find where the nearest retriever trial is being held.

You will find most retriever fans to be friendly people who will try to help you feel at home at your first trial and

The wirehair suddenly spots downed duck in the water and moves into high gear for retrieval during field trials.

A wounded pheasant runs from the handler during field trials. This can be an embarrassment to the gunner.

answer your questions about training and handling your own dog or if you have not yet gotten a retriever they will demonstrate the abilities and traits of the different breeds.

Retriever trials are conducted a bit differently than most other dog trials. The individual dogs are put through each trial or test separately, as in the NAVHDA testing system, but the dogs are scored against one another in evaluation of their performance. A retriever is expected to make several different types of retrieve, mark game down, make a blind retrieve in which the only clue the dog has as to location of game is recieved from the directions given by the handler.

A duck will be hidden in the brush on the opposite side of a stream or pond and the dog will be sent in to retrieve the game by hand and audible signals from the handler. The dog will have to follow an elaborate course strictly from the commands given by the handler which hopefully will lead the dog to the hidden duck. The dog also will be sent after a duck which has been thrown out into a body of water in sight of the dog while a gun is fired. In another test, a bird is hidden in brush or weeds and the dog sent in from the opposite side to recover the bird.

Different retriever clubs have different tests and to describe all of these tests fully would take more space than is available here. Some clubs have tests in which the dog must pass a dead bird in order to first retrieve a hidden bird farther out. The dog is faulted if it disturbs the bird it is supposed to pass.

There are many different types of retriever trials and the best way to learn about them is to attend one. Another way is to read a good book on the subject. One of the best books on retrievers I have been fortunate to have is: *Hunting Dogs Know-How* by Dave Duffey, published by Winches-

The dog handler moves in to catch the wounded pheasant, but a Brittany beats him to it for good retrieve move.

ter Press. Another good book pertaining entirely to retrievers is *Water Dogs* by Richard A. Wolters from E.P. Dutton & Co.

One of the leading retriever organizations is the North American Hunting Retriever Association (NAHRA) which was spark-plugged by Wolters. He has also written a large, well-illustrated book, *The Labrador Retriever.* Wolters can be reached at Box 67, Ossining, New York 10562.

The coonhound fanciers also have trials of several sorts. There are water races in which a coon is made to swim across a pond or river and placed in a tree on the opposite bank. The dogs are released and the first dog to cross the water and reach the tree is the winner.

There are also coonhound races in which the coon is put on a lead and taken on a meandering course across streams, through brush, over rock piles that hold little scent, around trees in such manner that it will appear to the dogs that the coon went up the tree, unless the dog is very careful. The path is made through fences and any other sort of obstacle which would delay or deceive the dogs, and finally the coon is made to climb a tree. The dogs are released on the track and the first dog reaching the tree where the coon is located wins.

In other less formal trials, a group of coonhunters will bring their best dogs and put them down on a good coon-hunting night in good coon country. Points are scored for the first strike of a coon track, the first dog to get the line straightened out, the first dog to pick up the track after a check and the first dog to tree where the coon is located.

Perhaps the simplest coonhound trial is one in which coonhide is dragged over the ground for a considerable distance, then is tied up in a tree before the dogs are put down on the track where the hide was dragged. Some dogs will not take such a drag trail.

If you would like to attend a coon dog trial, ask around the sporting goods stores in your area. If you contact some coonhunters in season, it usually is not too hard to wangle an invitation to go along on a hunt, but a word of warning: coonhunting is a tough sport which requires participants to be in top physical shape.

You will go into the woods at night and the dogs will be released. When they strike a coon, the hunters will follow in the general direction the dogs are traveling. When the dogs tree, the hunters will head for the spot. It makes no difference what sort of terrain they have to cross; whether mountains, streams, cliffs or laurel thickets. They will not wait for you. They have to get to the dogs before the coon leaves the tree. So, be prepared either to keep up or find your own way back to where the vehicles are parked.

With the recent increase in popularity of the breed, springer spaniel field trial clubs are being formed throughout the country. In the East, Pennsylvania, New Jersey and the New England states all have active springer trial clubs. The West Coast and Great Lakes areas now are becoming involved. Contact Roger Houk, Springers on the Line, 722 Division Street, Mukwonago, Wisconsin 53149 for information on springer trials.

With the upsurge in interest in field trials, there should be something to interest everyone seriously interested in sporting dogs. Another organization to contact for information regarding retriever trials is United Kennel Club, Hunting Retriever Operations, 100 E. Kilgore Road, Kalamazoo, Michigan 49001.

Note the dead duck in water among the decoys. Retriever must pick up the duck without undue disturbance to the decoys. (Below) Dog has picked up the dead duck and is returning, swimming strongly, to the hunter on shore.

The well-trained shorthair brings the duck to his handler during the water retrieve segment of the test.

Chapter 8

KENNELLING

One Should Know Where And How He Is Going To Keep His Dog Before He Gets It

KENNELLING YOUR dog is one of the most important facets of the relationship between you and your dog. Good living conditions give a dog a sense of belonging that can be achieved in no other way.

Dogs are a lot more intelligent than many people give them credit for: they are able to sense the regard — or lack of it — we have for them. This is largely reflected in the manner in which you house and feed them. This is especially true of the more sensitive breeds.

One does not require elaborate, expensive housing for his dogs, but where a dog is going to live is something you should plan *before* buying that good looking-pup you hope will develop into a fine hunting companion. Too often we have a chance to get a dog or pup that is just what we have been wanting without thinking what we are going to do with the dog or where we are going to put it; we purchase the pup and arrive home only to come face to face with the realization that we have no place to kennel the newest member of the household.

First, you must determine precisely what sort of relationship you are going to have with your dog. This is especially

This A-type hutch was found on a West Virginia farm and had been used from time to time to house both dogs and hogs. It is hardly ideal, but at least offered cover.

Author feels this is a nice doghouse that is well shaded in a location where the wind is broken. It also faces the morning sun. The only possible fault is that height allows body heat to rise.

true if this is your first dog. If you use makeshift housing for more than a few days, chances are you are going to be, at best, a mediocre dog owner and trainer.

I can tell a lot about a man from looking at his kennel, the manner in which it was constructed and the care and planning which went into it. A kennel must be more than just a simple doghouse. It must provide cool shade in summer and warmth and shelter from the elements when needed. If a doghouse fulfills these needs, the simplest type is adequate. Conversely, even the most elaborate and expensive kennel that does not meet these requirements is inadequate.

I've seen people spend hundreds of dollars to construct splendid kennels that are not nearly as functional as an old wooden barrel with boards nailed over half the ends to stop it from rolling. With a bit of bedding such as dry grass or hay thrown in and the whole thing placed in the shade under a tree with a pan of clean water nearby, a dog can be quite comfortable in such a home. Conversely, I've seen fancy dog houses sitting in the hot sun with no shade the dog can reach; these are pure torture for the hapless dog that is chained to them.

I have never believed in the practice of anthropomorphizing (the giving of human attitudes and emotions to animals), but in this instance, I can think of no more valid way to illustrate my point than to ask the person contemplating the acquisition or construction of housing for a dog: How would you like to live in it?

This should cause you to question what it would be like to live under the conditions that will be encountered in the structure you are about to force your dog to live in.

For example: It is a hot day in August at 2:30 p.m.; the sun is shining brightly and there is little, if any, breeze. What would it feel like to be on the end of the chain or enclosed within the fence around the doghouse you are contemplating? Think how good a spot of shade would feel, how nice to get out of the direct hot, burning rays of the sun.

Conversely, it is a cold morning in January, the mercury hovers around zero, the sun comes up bright and clear. How good it feels to be able to lie in the warming rays of the sun as they chase the chill of last night while we bask in the welcome heat.

Situation Three; It is a cold rainy fall day, the door to the usually comfortable kennel faces east; the wind and storms generally come from the west, but today the wind blows cold rain straight in the door of the kennel, keeping the occupant wet and miserable.

These are some of the conditions that may encountered in an ordinary dog box over a year's time. It seems almost too big an order to be covered by one dog box to successfully meet the challenge of all the above conditions and keep the dog comfortable under all these situations. But a simple modification can convert the inadequate classic Fido-type doghouse into a comfortable all-weather home for the dog.

The accompanying illustration shows what is quite likely the most satisfactory general purpose all-climate doghouse design ever worked out. The drawing shows a rather elaborate variation of this design which I use myself, as do the photos of several different views of my personal kennel. You can build this sort of box to suit your budget. If you

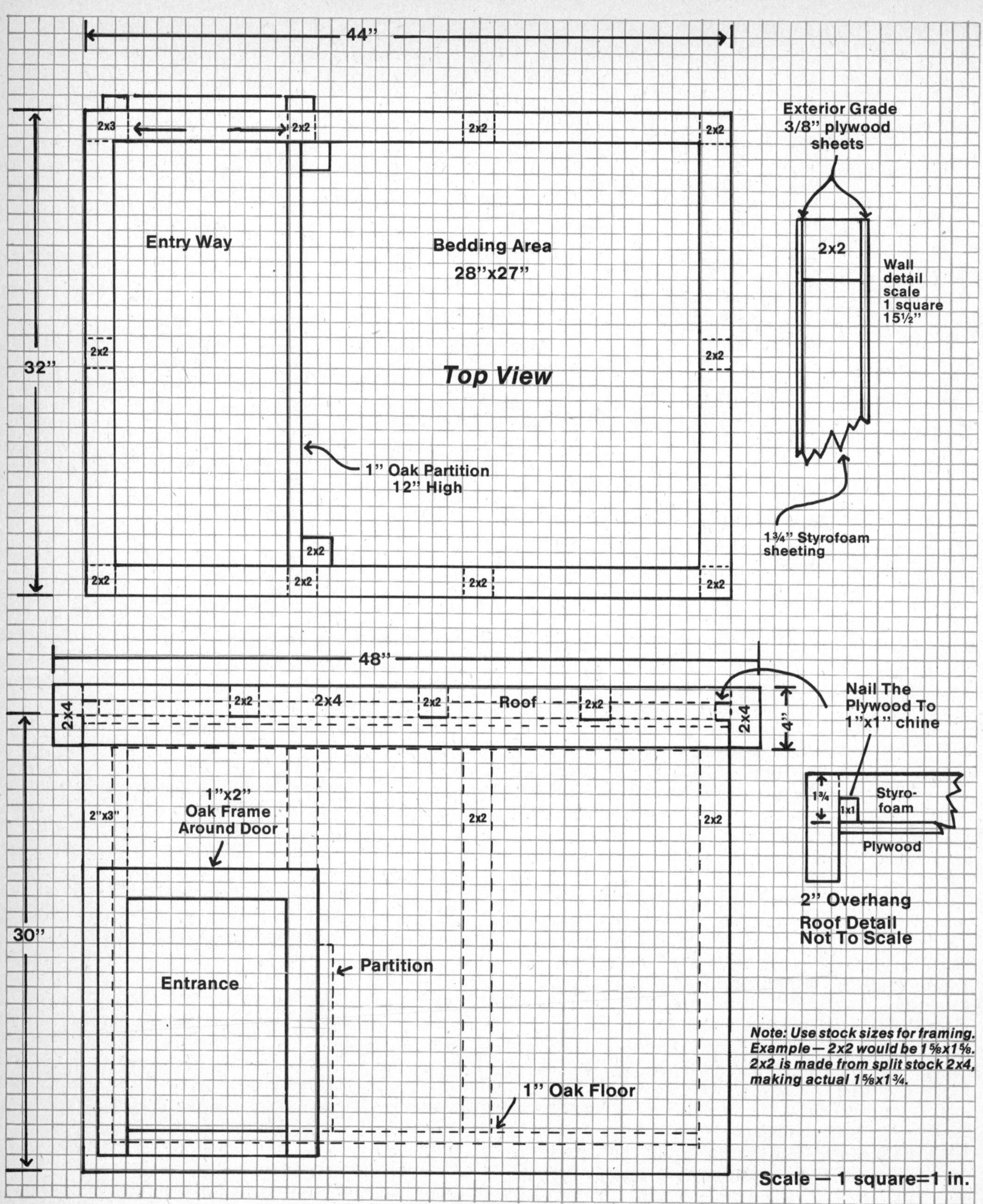
44"
2x3
2x2
2x2
2x2
Exterior Grade
3/8" plywood
sheets
Entry Way
Bedding Area
28"x27"
2x2
Wall
detail
scale
1 square
1 5½"
32"
2x2
2x2
Top View
1" Oak Partition
12" High
1¾" Styrofoam
sheeting
2x2
2x2
2x2
2x2
2x2
48"
2x4
2x2
2x4
2x2
Roof
2x2
2x4
4"
Nail The
Plywood To
1"x1" chine
1¾
1x1
Styro-
foam
Plywood
2"x3"
1"x2"
Oak Frame
Around Door
2x2
2x2
2" Overhang
Roof Detail
Not To Scale
30"
Entrance
Partition
Note: Use stock sizes for framing.
Example — 2x2 would be 1⅝x1⅝.
2x2 is made from split stock 2x4,
making actual 1⅝x1¾.
1" Oak Floor
Scale — 1 square=1 in.

DOGHOUSE

This drawing shows a good design for use with the larger breeds such as Pointers, setters, coonhounds, and foxhounds. For a smaller breed of dog the size can be reduced by 25% or to the dimensions which will suit your usage. Remember it is better to have a doghouse a bit too big rather than too small.

Be sure to insulate the floor as this is the hardest area to keep warm due to the oak flooring. This flooring is necessary because some dogs will scratch their way through the floor if it is made of softer wood. Heavy gauge aluminum flashing is used to cover the entire structure as this makes a waterproof covering which also reflects heat. The top should be fastened in place with ¼-inch bolts run into woodnuts on the inside of the inner walls. One each side is sufficient.

The removable top makes it easy to disinfect and clean the doghouse every six months or so as needed. Always remove all old bedding before adding new unless you are putting grass clippings over cedar shavings as noted elsewhere.

Although this drawing is a blueprint for the construction of an excellent home for your dog and a structure built exactly as is shown in this design will perform admirably (it is an exact copy of my own which are shown in the photos), this drawing is intended to act as a basic design from which you can build to your own ideas and available materials as best suits your needs.

already have one of the classic Fido boxes mentioned earlier, chances are you can modify it to meet the requirements of this design. The main advantage is that it provides a snug, draftfree sleeping and resting area into which the wind and rain cannot intrude to make the dog uncomfortable. The trick is in having the entrance at one side with a partition separating this entrance from the sleeping area. This partition also holds the bedding in place so it is not dragged out when the dog enters and leaves. This partition is a barrier against wind and rain as well.

I make no claim to originality with this design — this type of dog box has been around as long as I can remember. Many moons ago, some unsung genius came up with this design and thoughtful dog owners have been using it ever since; its efficiency is apparent.

An existing Fido-type box can be modified by closing the center entrance and cutting a hole to one side of the front for an entrance and adding the partition to make the entrance passageway. If the existing box is not wide enough for this approach, a simple addition to one side of the box and a hole cut in what was formerly one side of the box will allow an easy conversion. It is worth the effort to make the conversion, as the ordinary center entrance box without the partition is uncomfortable in windy cold weather and when the wind is blowing rain into the opening.

Some people use a curtain over the opening, but the results are poor at best, mainly because the curtains won't seal tight and dogs usually pull and chew at them until they come off.

There are patent doors on the market, but they seem to be more trouble than they are worth. I remember one such device which consisted of overlapping pieces of rubber. A friend bought one and after his dog got entangled in it several times, the dog refused to enter the kennel until its owner removed the offending closure.

With design of a good kennel determined, we should consider how we might use it best to make our dog as comfortable as we can. First, we must decide whether to chain the dog in the kennel area or to build an enclosure. An enclosure can be somewhat costly, but I find this extra cost overshadowed by the many advantages. An enclosure offers the dog protection from strays that may be rabid or carrying other diseases. It protects your dog from the growing menace of pit bulls and other killer dogs that are found in some areas where their owners turn them loose at night to gain fighting experience by killing their neighbors' dogs. A chained dog has no chance at all against such a vicious brute.

Dog fighting is an inhumane and degrading act which under no circumstances can ever possibly be considered a sport. Dog fighting is simply a gambling media whose practitioners are completely outside the law and have given up any right to consideration or decent treatment when they elect to enter into such a act. These are thoroughly nasty people. The only way to deal with them is to dispose of their brutes as quietly as possible.

The enclosed kennel will also protect female dogs that are in season from unwanted breedings and a good BB gun can keep unwanted suitors away from your home. Sting the unwanted visitors in the rear end, but never shoot even a BB toward the head where it may injure a dog's eye.

The enclosure allows a dog to move freely without having to drag a chain and to lie down without having to lie on a cold chain which may cause the collar to rub sore spots on the dog's neck.

This brings us to the strongest argument against chaining or tying a dog. Dogs that are chained up manage to hang themselves with amazing regularity. In spite of the most stringent safety measures, they manage to jump over, fall off of or wrap themselves around something which catches on the chain and strangles them.

A good swiveling tie-out chain and careful precautions will go far toward eliminating the chance of a dog hanging itself, but nothing can ever completely eliminate the possibility. Dog owners who have chained their dogs for a long period invariably have lost one or more dogs in this manner. Sometimes it is not possible to build a dog yard and we must chain the dog. In this event, every precaution should be taken to make certain there is nothing in which the dog can become entangled. Be certain the chain is of such length and placement that the dog cannot jump over anything such as a fence, the dog box or a shade arbor.

The chain should be of the type that has a stake driven flush into the ground with a swivel or ball on the end of the stake so the chain falls free at all times. There should be a swivel and snap fastening on the end where it attaches to the collar and the stake should be placed in such manner that the dog cannot get the chain wrapped around anything. There is no point in trying to tie a dog up with anything other than a chain as the dog will chew through anything else except a steel cable and a steel cable is even more dangerous than a chain. The stake must be located so that the dog can get into the kennel box, but not over it. The dog should be able to reach drinking water and shade.

Trees offer the best shade, but if you do not have a tree that is placed suitably, you can build an adequate shade arbor from boards or canvas placed in position so the dog can get into the shade cast by the arbor, but not over or around it. Clean water should be available at all times, unless the dog is being given medication that requires withholding water for a given period or another good reason the dog should not be allowed to drink. The water in a dog's pan should be replaced every day to keep down algae which is an excellent harbor for bacteria. Cleaning with hydrogen peroxide once a week in summer will keep the water sweet and clean. Once a month is sufficient in the cooler months. There must be shade in the hot part of the year and during cooler months, the dog should be able to lie in the sun to warm itself.

If possible, it is better to build a kennel and run for each individual dog. Never put two dogs together in a kennel run, no matter how well they seem to get along. They could get into a fight and the injured dog cannot get away when it is fenced in. This problem is avoided if there is one dog per run.

At present, I have only a two-run kennel. It is twenty-three years old and still in good condition. It has been in constant use for more than two decades, although often only one side is in use, as I like to keep my favorite dogs in the house. I built this kennel soon after I bought my present home on the bank of the Potomac River. First, I took some locust logs to the sawmill and had four posts sawed 6" x 6" x 9', six posts sawed 3" x 4" x 6' and some other lumber sawed 2" x 6" for the gates. I brought the lumber home and soaked the ends of the posts in Woodlife for about a week. I kept a garden sprayer filled with Woodlife and gave all the lumber a good spraying every other day for the same period. This gave me some lumber that is pretty near permanently rotproof.

The next step was to plant the 6 x 6-inch posts in the ground on the corners to form a 10 x 14-foot rectangle. Then I dug out on the uphill side and made forms on the low end to make a concrete slab 12 x 16 feet. This was reinforced with iron pipe and concrete reinforcing rod; and strap metal was placed around the corners outside the posts to reinforce the corners against breaking where the posts went through the concrete. Then I poured the forms full with a good rich concrete mix to a thickness of about five inches on the front end and whatever it took on the lower back end. As I remember, the job required about five yards of concrete. This was more than needed, but concrete was cheap in those days, delivered to the farm for about $12 per yard.

On a line even with the outside edges of the posts, and centered between them on all four sides, I inserted a piece of Inconel stainless steel one-eighth inch thick by two inches wide and about eight inches long with an L-shape bend on the bottom. I also placed one of these in the center of the slab. These were allowed to stick up about three inches out of the concrete.

When the concrete set up these pieces of steel were bolted with one-quarter-inch bolts through pre-drilled holes in the steel to the 3 x 4-inch posts placed to make the center frames. I kept these wooden center pieces about one-quarter inch up off the concrete so they would not be wet on the bottom and subjected to rot. This vertical frame was divided in the middle and top and bottom 2 x 4 boards were run around the enclosure to give a solid base to which to nail the #9 galvanized chain link fence. Pressure treated lumber was used for these pieces. The doors were made up by mortice jointing and the whole assembly has stood the test of time. It needs a coat of paint now, but it is in good-as-

Kennels such as this extensive structure at Remington Farms are ideal and the type often used by the professional dog training cadre. However, such a healthy investment is beyond most people's means.

This dog box apparently was fashioned from part of an old furnace. Metal does not make a good kennel, as it becomes overly hot in the sun, does not hold heat during winter.

new condition with the exception of some places where a pointer chewed up the wood and even some of the aluminum covering of the boxes.

The two dog boxes were set on locust 3 x 4-inch scantlings. The entranceways were bolted through the fence and the whole thing was roofed. The rear half of the run is roofed with fiberglass sheet, while the front half is covered with chain link fence. This makes a really dog-proof enclosure from both the inside and outside. The doors both have hasps on them into which a lock can be fitted. This is about as good as can be done in my opinion. This kennel is reasonably secure against theft of the dogs, absolutely impervious to would-be Romeos and good protection against rabid raccoon and other undesirables.

The green fiberglass over the rear portion of the runs gives pretty good shade, but a young hackberry tree which I planted between the two kennels gives splendid shade. The kennels face east and the tree is on the west side. This gives good shade from about 10 a.m. until sunset. On the south side, I allow tall weeds to grow and give good shade in the southern run along with the tree. In the event the dogs wish to lie in the sun, they have only to move to the front of the run and they have unobscured sunshine. The kennels are covered with aluminum sheeting which reflects much of the sun's heat. The kennel walls are double and filled with fiberglass to make a box that is cool and comfortable in summer, warm and snug in winter. With their removable roofs allowing easy cleaning and inspection of the bedding, these boxes are the ultimate in utility as well as being extremely comfortable for the dog.

There always has been considerable controversy over what type bedding to use for dog boxes. Cedar shavings will keep fleas off your dogs, but individuals claim they interfere with a dog's nose. I have never seen any evidence of this, but as token to this possibility, I put in new bedding in August and leave this bedding in all winter.

I make my own bedding by cutting a red cedar of about six-inch diameter into two-foot lengths, then run them over the wood planer with the blade set to take about a 1/64-inch cut so it makes soft, thin shavings. I put a wash tub under the planer to catch the shavings and soon have a fine aromatic tub full of bedding. At first, it smells very strong and may indeed interfere with a dog's sense of smell. However, by the time I am ready to hunt the dog, the odor has diminished to the point where it seems to do no harm.

For the coldest part of the winter, I put some grass clippings from the yard on top of the cedar shavings, as this seems to make an even warmer and softer bed. Simply save some of the cuttings when you mow your lawn and allow them to dry in the sun, then put them in a dry place and you will have all of the soft warm bedding you need. I personally put them on top of cedar shavings for both a soft bed and a flea deterrent.

There are other plants which will keep fleas off your dogs. I am told that eucalyptus leaves do a good job and I know that pennyroyal plants work well. Cedar is more simple for me, however. The area where I live has literally thousands of acres of abandoned farmlands growing up into scrub brush of which red cedar is a large component. In addition to keeping fleas off, red cedar leaves a pleasant scent on the dog.

In addition to the standard Fido-type dog house, there are other types of shelter. One of the most common is a wooden whiskey barrel with one end removed and boards nailed halfway up the open end to serve as a door and anti-roll device. Bedding is placed in the area below the boards and this makes a surprisingly good doghouse.

In using a wooden barrel, always be sure to drill a small hole about one-quarter-inch in diameter at the lowest point of the bottom to allow any water which gets into the barrel to drain. Never use a metal barrel or steel drum, as they are too hot in the sun and too cold in the winter, making an uncomfortable place for a dog.

Another commonly seen doghouse is a lean-to built against another building. If floored — and not built on the north side of a building — this makes satisfactory housing. A lean-to never should be built on the north side of a building, as the sun will never strike it and it will be cold in winter and damp and chilly in summer.

Still another type of easily built doghouse is the A-frame type which serves well if it is floored properly and has a tight rear closure to eliminate breezes which blow through and carry in rain and snow while carrying off the heat generated by the dog's body. The A-frame style can be adapted to the entranceway and divider-type kennel box shown in the drawing.

For ordinary size dogs an A-style can be built from three sides that are three feet wide and 3½ feet long. Cut the entrance hole at one side just far enough back from the edge to clear the frame and run the twelve-inch-high divider back even with the inside edge of the doorway the same as in the square type illustrated. The A-frame style is somewhat cheaper to build, as there are only three sides. For best results, the bottom, at least, should be insulated. Scrap styrofoam sandwiched between sheets of plywood makes excellent low-cost insulated panels. There are lots of other equally good designs for doghouses, so use your own ingenuity to come up with whatever suits you.

Around farms or other places where there are sheds or outbuildings, a bedding box often is placed inside a building to which the dog has access. But be careful, for this is the sort of place where a dog can easily hang itself if chained. This sort of housing usually is used in situations

On this hill country farm, dogs were chained under corner of this corn crib. In spite of the appearance, the author contends this is better kennelling than appearance shows. It offered cover, exposure to the sun, also protection.

wherein the dog is allowed to run free. Still another method is to shut the dog up in an unused stable or other enclosed space with a box of bedding. The possibilities are endless, depending on the situation and needs of the dog owner.

In the South, where houses often are built on posts set into the ground, the dogs often are quartered under the houses in bedding boxes or allowed to find their own bedding spots.

If you live near a road with heavy traffic, it is best to have your dog either in an enclosed area or chained to prevent the dog getting hit by vehicular traffic. If you are going to keep your dog outside, one of the above suggestions should meet your requirements.

A 1984 survey by a leading sporting dog magazine showed that over forty percent of the hunting dog owners keep their dogs in the home. I suspect that further investigation would reveal this figure is directly proportional to the owner's knowledge of and devotion to gun dogs. I cannot remember a time when there were no dogs in my home, my father's home, or my grandfather's home, and I have been assured there were both hounds and setters around the hearth in my great-grandfather's home.

They tell a story about one of my great-grandfather's hounds being shot in the front yard by damyankees; the dog growled at them while they were stealing horses.

A dog that lives in the home as a part of the ongoing daily activities is better trained and more knowledgeable than one kept in a kennel and allowed in the society of humans for only an hour or so a day. Further, a dog just released from a kennel is excited at being loose and its full attention is not on hunting; thus it's more likely to either bump or miss birds than a dog that is regularly accustomed to the daily society of its master. A good dog that is in close contact with you all the time seems to know just what you want it to do without any instructions from you; this is a powerful argument for keeping your best dogs in your home.

The most valid reason for not allowing dogs in the home is that someone in the family is allergic. Some owners reside in apartments where no dogs are allowed, while still others have spouses who become hysterical at the thought of a dog in an immaculate home.

One objection to dogs in the home is that they cause a smell in the home. I'll not deny this, even the cleanest dog has a "doggy" odor, but it is a smell that you will not notice after a week. As to visitors not liking the smell of dogs, I consider it my home and they are my dogs. Any person comng to my home is on my grounds, where my rules will apply.

The breed of a dog also has much to do with whether it should be kept in the home or in an outside kennel. Some breeds do not require as much human contact as do others. Pointers are a self-sufficient breed and I have never kept pointers in the house after they were about six months old. I firmly believe in raising all puppies you are going to keep and train yourself in the home. Setters, Labs, spaniels, elkhounds and beagles seem to do particularly well in the home and, if possible, they should be kept there. Beagles seem to do as well in an outside kennel, but they are pleasant little fellows to have around the house, so I include them with those to be kept in the home. The Labrador retriever above all breeds should be kept in the home. You can develop a rapport with a Lab that is uncanny to those who do not know this breed. This applies almost as strongly to the pudelpointer and wirehair, as these are breeds with which it is easy to develop a rapport.

Let me give an example: I can walk to the door and whistle for Fritz to follow me and we will go for a walk down the bank to the river with him scurrying around, investigating everything. Or, he will likely bring a stick for me to throw into the river for him to retrieve. We can go out into the field and he will run all over the place as if he just has to check out everything. On the other hand, if I pick up a gun as I go out, Fritz will fall in at heel and, as we reach the river, he will skulk along behind me as quietly as a cat, hoping for me to shoot a duck or goose. If we go into the field, he will begin his hunting search pattern, all without any instruction from me.

In essence, Fritz lives with me, is familiar with my wishes, knows my attitudes, and accoutrements, as well as what is expected of him. He knows that, if I am walking along the river carrying a gun, he should stay close and be quiet so as not to flush any ducks before I can get a shot. He has learned that, if I am not carrying a gun, there is no reason for him to remain at heel or be quiet, so he will do whatever he wants to except those things that are permanently forbidden. He knows he can probably cajole me into throwing a stick out into the river for him to seek out.

While he is out in the river retrieving a stick, I can hide another stick by throwing it a long distance into the weeds or brush when he cannot see me do it. When he returns with the stick he fetched from the river I will tell him, "Fetch," and point in the direction I threw the stick. Fritz will head out in the indicated direction and run an ever-widening, fan-shaped pattern until he finds the object for which he is searching. He will not be fooled into bringing back another object, since he recognizes the stick I have thrown by my scent and is not interested in anything else.

In the event that he should pass up the object he is seeking, I can put him back on the right course by calling him in. I then crouch down beside him, hold my hand in front of his nose in a line with the object of the search, then send him on again to search in the right location. In the event he does not go out far enough, I can send him out farther by holding my hand up and repeating the fetch command until he reaches the desired distance.

If he goes too far, I stop him by holding up two hands and waving them in a manner similar to the wave-off given an aircraft landing on a carrier when it is out of the slot. I continue this until the dog has reached the desired position.

Naturally, I gave Fritz the standard retrieving drill outlined in *The Training and Care of the Versatile Hunting Dog* by Winterhelt and Bailey, as well as some of the tricks of the trade learned from such master retriever trainers as Dave Duffey. However, much of what Fritz does is not the result of training, but is because he is in constant contact with me. Living in the house as he does, he has picked up the things I want him to do and does them, because he wants to please me. I am lucky in that I live at the end of a half-mile private drive and do not have to fear allowing the dogs out of the house on their own. Having a chance to move about outside on their own does much to give a dog seasoning and confidence.

An old barrel, partially covered with earth, was used as a one-time kennel on an abandoned West Virginia farm. It lacked architectural know-how, but served a purpose.

The learning process works two ways. Being in close contact with a dog living in your home also gives you a chance to learn much from and about the dog. Dogs are like people in that they have individual traits and characteristics. Breeding predisposes a dog toward certain traits and abilities, but we cannot be sure just what the individual dog will do, until we learn firsthand just what his reactions will be to a given situation.

Fritz becomes highly frustrated and determined when he is unable to find what he is sent to retrieve. I remember some years ago when we had continuing depredations from a raccoon that destroyed the sweet corn in our garden as fast as it ripened. After watching the garden for a few evenings with notable lack of success, I came to the conclusion that the masked raider was not making his depredations until after dark and the only way to catch him was to set a steel trap.

It was either late August or early September and I went down to the river in the evening with a couple of traps, some lure, bait and the other necessities. I was wearing a pair of shoulder-length rubber trapping gloves that I was careful to keep any human scent from so as not to leave human odor on the trap set.

I left Fritz in the house, as the last thing I needed was a dog running about where I was trying to set a trap, but someone opened the door and let Fritz out. He followed me down to the river and, to get him away from where I was setting a trap, I threw a stick for him away back into the brush. He went off to retrieve it and I didn't see him until I was ready to go to the house. He hadn't found the stick by the time I wanted to get him away from the area were I had set the trap, so I called him in sharply and took him to the house.

Above: Front view of the author's kennel shows center divider to separate dogs, double runs. He was careful to construct it so the front of the kennel faces morning sun. (Right) Paint is needed, but it is solid after 23 years.

The next morning when I came home from my night shift, the dog came out and went down to the river. I didn't give it any thought until I realized he had not come back. When I went down to look for him, he was still searching frantically in the area where I had thrown the stick the evening before. The weeds were broken down and the whole area showed evidence of much activity. Suddenly it hit me: Fritz could not find the stick I had thrown for him the previous evening and it was really getting to him. He could not find it, because it had no scent on it due to the trapping gloves I had been wearing. When he wasn't looking, I threw a small stick into the area and he soon found it and brought it in with an air of great accomplishment.

If I leave Fritz in the house and he gets out before I have returned, he will immediately pick up my trail and follow it to me. If my track ends at where one of the Volvos or the Jeep was parked, he is satisfied as he knows I often leave in the vehicles and he is not allowed to follow out the road.

In the event that my track does not lead to a vehicle parking place, Fritz always will follow my trail until he comes to me. Tracking is one of the stronger points of the pudelpointer and he demonstrates tracking ability to compare with the best of them. I have, on occasion, left him in the house with instructions that he be let out of the house at some later time. I then go about my business in the fields and yard, doing whatever it is that I have planned. Just before Fritz is due to be let out, I will hide in a place where I can observe his movements. On being allowed out of the house, he will pick up my track immediately and follow all of my meanderings to the point where he comes upon me. He will greet me, expecting a pat on the head which he usually answers with a "Whuff" sound made by a near sneezing action, then go about his business of "helping" me or just hang around to be near.

One day, while checking the deer, quail and turkey food patches, I made an inadvertent discovery about Fritz's actions. I had told my wife to let him out in half an hour, then became so engrossed that I forgot to hide before he was let out. I was in full view when he came past the chicken house and he made a beeline straight for me. This was not what I wanted, as I like to keep him sharp by making him track me. After he came up and greeted me, Fritz left me and went to where he had left my trail when he saw me and followed the trail through all of the different places where I had gone before I went into the soybean field where he found me. I suddenly realized that this dog wanted to know where I had been and what I had done after leaving the house.

There is still much to be learned about animal behavior and this is not the place to examine the motives, if any, of my dog. The point I wish to make is that, if Fritz did not have any of the reasons to which we normally attribute such behavior — a desire for food, or the companionship of his master — he must have made the trip around my tracks out of pure desire to know. No instinct was driving the dog to make this extra effort to see what I had been doing.

This is another advantage of living in close contact with your dog. Without such daily contact, I would not have observed this interesting aspect of the dog's behavior. In addition, keeping a dog in the home allows one to notice any small changes in the animal's behavior that might indicate the beginning of a health problem or other negative situation that might go unnoticed if there was only such contact as occurs with a dog confined to a kennel. Additionally, it is difficult to observe objectively an animal that is excited by your presence.

Any puppy you intend to keep for your own use should be brought up in the home. Yes, I know that this is asking for a lot of trouble: chewed legs on the tables and chairs,

Right: View is from northeast side of author's kennel. Note the trees for shade, tall weeds along south side. (Below) View from the rear shows placement of the dog boxes.

chewed broom handles, bar stools and whatever else the puppy can get at, but it is worth it. Such trouble can be minimized by confining the pup to one room, most likely the kitchen with its myriad of intoxicating smells and daily activities that will keep a young pup interested. This also will minimize the sense of loss of the mother and family group from which it has separated.

One mistake is to put a pup into a dark, damp basement. This is bad for the pup's health due to a lack of sunlight and it is bad psychologically from the sense of isolation it develops. In addition, being kept in an area of low light during its formative months seems to make a pup's sight unnaturally sensitive to bright light.

Placing a puppy of six or eight weeks age in a dark basement is almost guaranteed to produce a timid and shy dog, yet people continue to do it, simply because it is an easy answer to the question of where to put the puppy.

The question of where to keep the puppy during its first six months is one which should be discussed and an agreeable answer worked out before the puppy is purchased. This should include a thorough examination of the circumstances under which the dog will be kept, trained and utilized for hunting, field trials or whatever purpose you have in wanting a dog of the breed you are contemplating.

Each of us has a different home situation that will determine where we will keep the puppy. Many of those who have developed outstanding young dogs have raised them in their kitchens. This is a good choice, as the kitchen floor usually is of a material that is impervious to water and other stains; and puppies do make puddles for the first week or so, at least.

Some method of confining the pup to the room should be made. In my home, we use folding gates, although, in the past we have used 4 x 4-foot sheets of one-quarter-inch plywood set in front of the doors that lead to the rest of the house. As the pup gets older and stronger, it may be necessary to fasten one side of the plywood sheet to the door frame with hinges. This is not difficult and gives good results when coupled with a solid fastening of the other end of the plywood sheet. Use small-diameter screws and there will be no noticeable scars left when the pup reaches six months of age and the door is removed. The pup is either moved outside, given the run of the house, or limited to certain rooms only.

If you have trained the dog properly, within six months, you should be able to tell it "no" or "out" for the places in the house where it is not allowed and the dog will listen surprisingly well.

When you first bring the pup home, it will likely cry and yelp all night. This is an inconvenience, but should not be hard to understand and sympathize with; since it is a logical and understandable reaction, it deserves kindness and understanding. The pup has been a part of a family group consisting of its mother (dam) and littermates and has lived in a small confined space. This is all the pup has ever known and, when moved to a new and different area away from its mother and littermates, it misses the conditions under which it has spent its life to that point. It was not a gradual change to which the pup had a chance to become acclimated, but a sudden unexpected end to all the pup had known, followed by insertion into a completely strange situation where it is surrounded by strangers and unknown walls.

Do not be overly concerned by the new pup's yelps and whines, nor should you run to comfort it whenever it makes sounds of distress. By doing this, you would establish a bad precedent wherein the pup learns it need only make a few whines to get attention. Instead, simply make certain the pup is comfortable, has water and is fed at least four times a day until at least ten weeks old.

One thing you can do to help a puppy through the first few nights alone is to wind up a mechanical alarm clock, wrap it in a heavy towel and secure the wrappings with a

Author contends this is wrong way to kennel your dog. There is no shade and the wind can sweep across the barren hillside in winter, thus making these kennels miserable for the dogs. More thought should be given to their comfort.

needle and a few stitches so it will not become unwrapped and put the ticking clock into the puppy's sleeping box. We have an old Westclox that has been Best Buddy to a lot of pups. The ticking clock seems to make company for the pup.

The pup should have a sleeping box that it can recognize as its own. An easy way to do this is to use a cardboard box of about 12 x 18 inches; cut about halfway down the center of one side to leave a wall height of four inches or so. This low spot will make an easy entrance for the pup. A pile of old rags can be made into a nest and the puppy has an inexpensive, easily replaced bed.

Place a piece of newspaper on the floor of the room where the pup is being kept and, whenever you see it making a puddle, immediately pick it up and place it on the newspaper. With most pups, this will be all that is needed and within a few days the pup will be using the paper of its own accord.

In some instances, the pup may be a bit more stubborn and will require a light spanking with a rolled up newspaper when it is caught making a puddle in a place other than the newspaper it is supposed to use.

What you do when the pup starts making piles is dependent to a large extent on where you live; in some locations, it is easy to take the pup outside, but in other places, taking the pup outside involves going down a flight of stairs or a trip down a long hallway. Here at our home, Mockingbird Hollow, taking the pup out simply means picking it up and walking out the back door into the yard. We start this at the end of the first week the pup has been in the house. Whenever we see the pup start to make a pile, we pick it up and take it out into the yard. If after a week or so it is not going to the door and asking to go out when it needs to, we start spanking with a rolled newspaper. You will be surprised at how soon you will have a housebroken puppy. It is best not to try to do much training the first week until it has gotten over the separation from its dam and littermates and feels at home in its new surroundings.

Feeding your dog is another important aspect of kennelling. There are many excellent feeds on the market — and some poor ones. The old saying that "you get what you are willing to pay for" is not necessarily so when it comes to dog food. Some of the most expensive do not give results as good as the old standby brands; some of the more exotic brands are not even particularly good for your dog. The standard dry-type foods are the more practical and certainly less costly than the canned or other exotic packs. I have fed Purina brand for around forty years without complaint.

One of the things to watch in dog food is the protein content. A good dog food should have at least twenty-five percent *available* protein. Some dog foods list high percentages of protein, but that protein is not in a form that is available to the dog. For example, wheat flour has protein, but this form of protein is undetectable by a dog so is not available to the dog.

One of the best sources of protein that is available to dogs is corn meal. This meal is good for dogs, as it contains lots of available protein and has good fat and roughage content. If you want to take the time to make it up yourself,

Author's pudelpointer and golden retriever relax in his den, where this book was written. Some dog trainers are against keeping hunting dogs in the home, but the author feels it develops a good rapport that pays off later in the hunting field.

it is possible to make a fine dog food in the home. At one time I was in the business of raising and training beagle hounds and had as many as sixty beagles to care for at one time. The food bill for feed for this many dogs is somewhat stiff and mixing your own can effect an economy.

I operated a farm at the time and was raising a thousand or more bushels of corn each year. I had heard my grandfather speak of feeding cornbread to the dogs. I was working a dog for a vet at the time and he came up with an idea that proved to be a real winner. I ground shelled corn in an old burr mill and got cracklings from a slaughterhouse; I mixed the cracklings into cornmeal with a bit of Vimet vitamin supplement, making a batter which my wife baked in the woodstove oven in the kitchen into a fine cornbread which the dogs loved. They preferred this home-made food to any manufactured food I ever used. The dogs stayed in excellent condition off this mix and were fat and full of vigor.

For those who haven't been around butcherings, cracklings are the little pieces of brown fat left after animal fat has been fried out and rendered into lard and tallow in a press. Dogs love them and they are good for them. I was mixing fifteen percent cracklings into the corn meal.

Do not leave uneaten food in front of the dog. When the pup has eaten all it wants, any uneaten food should be removed. It need not be thrown away, if there is any worthwhile amount left. Just keep it cool and in good condition and perhaps mix a bit more fresh food into it for the next feeding. It will not take long for you to determine how much the pup will eat at a feeding and mix a suitable amount.

Chapter 9

THOUGHTS ON YARD-BREAKING

The Author's Techniques Encompass The Basics Of Teaching A Dog To Carry Out His Mission In Life

YOU HAVE had the new puppy for a few weeks and maybe it is using the newspaper to take care of its basic needs, or maybe it wants to go outside. But if it is not doing either of those, don't despair. Some pups learn faster than others. Some persons are better trainers than others, but all of us can get a puppy to do as we wish if we really keep at it. It requires time and patience, sometimes much patience and much time.

If you have never trained a dog, right now you can do much to determine what kind of trainer you are going to be and what results you get. The following is to some extent a cliche. But, it is also a truth and should be recognized as such. What is this pearl of wisdom? Just this:

If you view training your dog as a chore that you must suffer in order to have an animal that will be an efficient asset to your hunting activities and be socially acceptable when taking it afield in the company of friends, you probably are not going to achieve outstanding results.

On the other hand, if you are enthused at the prospect of working with the dog, really like the animal, and can view the training process as an enjoyable learning situation, there are possibilities for many rewarding experiences. For example, you will explore the possibilities of getting the dog to do what you want it to do and at the same time be engaging in an enjoyable hobby or sport in your spare time. You will be establishing a firm and lasting bond of trust that will cause the dog to become your buddy. The dog will desire to please you. You can achieve success in training your dog and have more real pleasure from the experience than from any other pastime. Dog training — like so many other worthwhile endeavors — is what you make it.

Owning a dog requires some planning before you even acquire the animal. First, you have to decide if you really want a dog. A dog will be around the entire year, not just during hunting season. Do you want a dog badly enough to train and care for it the entire year? Do you view owning a dog as a pleasurable experience which could mean you and the animal going for walks and romps in the fields at least once a week depending on weather and other factors?

If you answered postively, then you are the sort who should have one or more dogs. You should enjoy the pleasure of turning a "green" pup into a canine pal.

Few pleasures in this world are more satisfying than watching a dog you have trained perform flawlessly in hunting game. Conversely, it is discouraging to go afield with a half-trained, disobedient mutt that does everything wrong. This is especially true if some of your friends are along to witness the debacle. Some dogs, although well-bred, just do not have the ability to accept and retain training from one season to the next. Willingness and ability to accept training is known as "biddability." A dog eager to please and one that accepts traing is said to be a "biddable" dog. A dog that is highly biddable is highly valued.

Biddability factor is one of the things you will have to determine about your pup. It is sometimes difficult to tell a true lack of biddability because a spunky pup often has a natural stubbornness. The ideal dog should be spunky, but not to the point of being difficult to work with. Shy and timid pups do not make good hunting dogs. Dogs that are extremely timid are known as "soft" and are harder to train than a spunky pup. A "soft" dog, at the first sign of stern correction or punishment, becomes a quivering ball of fear groveling at your feet. Such a dog is worthless and cannot be trained due to a lack of aggressiveness and a tendency to immediately give up when meeting any difficulty.

The dog to look for is the one that can be spanked with a rolled newspaper, then bounce back into the spirit of things in half a minute or less. Such a dog has learned that what it was admonished for was wrong, but is not cowed by justly-earned punishment. Be it dogs, horses, or people, they all have to make mistakes and learn of the mistakes by experiencing a negative response.

A true lack of biddability usually is attributable to

stupidity and not too much time should be wasted on an ignorant dog. If you devote a quarter-hour or so of training daily to a spunky 3-month-old pup, it should be able to come when called, sit, and chase and retrieve a thrown training dummy with just a few weeks of instruction. The only things worth doing for a pup younger than 3 months are to train it to come when called and housebreak it.

Some individuals do try extensive training when their puppy is very young, but unless the animal shows unusual aptitude, you will do well to spend the first six weeks gaining the pup's confidence and trust. When it is time for serious training, you should make it obvious to the pup that playtime has ended. In the unlikely event that you are unable to make any progress with the pup during early training, it might be a good idea to have an experienced dog owner look at the animal and in a few sessions determine whether the dog shows promise of being trained extensively. This is especially true if it is your first effort at training.

Assuming you have a good pup at the age of about 3 months, start increasing the time period for making it remain where you tell it to stay. Take the dog by the collar and, holding up on its neck to prevent it from lying down, press its hind quarters gently but firmly into a sitting position. All of this should be done while repeating with a firm level of voice, "sit." After the dog is in a sitting position, hold it there a few minutes, repeating the word sit and repositioning the pup whenever it tries to move. Do not do this for more than fifteen minutes at a stretch while the pup is young.

After a short training period with the dog, end the sessions with a roughhouse romp or brisk walk. Always end a training period on a happy note that leaves the dog with pleasant memories of the session. Never conclude a lesson with anger. The dog will remember such anger and at the start of the next training session will display a negative attitude. Even when a session has gone poorly with nothing accomplished you will have to learn to "grin and bear it" without leaving the pup unhappy. This point cannot be stressed enough.

Everyone wants a finished hunting dog, no matter what the type of game, but it must be realized that such finishing does not just happen. It can be a long, involved process that has its beginnings in yard-breaking of a young pup.

Doc, the young puppy, and an old pudelpointer point a live quail from opposite sides. The pup was only three months old at the time of photo. (Below) The puppy gets wind of training dummy with scent on it, but the older dog is not fooled and tends to ignore the situation. Author has some definite thoughts on such scents.

Two months later, at five months, the puppy points dummy with quail scent on it. Older dog is mildly interested.

After the dog has learned to relax comfortably while sitting, start moving away from the animal as it remains in the sitting position. The time required to do this varies depending on the dog, so don't despair if it takes a lenghty period to accomplish. Continue to keep the training sessions to no more than fifteen minutes, but if you have the inclination, start conducting more than one daily lesson.

Soon the dog should sit in the spot where you placed it while you move ever farther away and even walk a complete circle around the pet. Whenever the dog moves, return it to the position where it was told to sit and verbally scold it. For a more difficult student, a few swats with a rolled newspaper are not amiss. When the dog will remain staunchly in place for ten minutes, move to a position thirty yards distance and pretend to be occuppied with something. The dog will eventually move, then you must make it return to the original spot at which it was told to sit. The command to sit should be given in a rough tone that shows your displeasure at the dog for having moved. If that is not sufficient to keep the dog from moving, out comes the newspaper for increasingly firm swats until the animal realizes it has got to stay where told to sit.

About this time, the dog is going to decide to run away from you. Perhaps you have been a bit overzealous, or it may be that the dog wants to learn if he can escape discipline.

There are several schools of thought as to what to do when this happens. Perhaps the best thing, if it's the first time the dog has disobeyed, is simply to wait a bit to see whether the dog will come back of its own accord. In the event the dog returns of its own volition, it should be reprimanded a little by scolding or otherwise expressing your displeasure at its behavior. Do not become angry and shout at the dog. That is simply going to compound an already deteriorating situation. Don't start chasing the dog unless you are sure you can catch it. In trying to catch it and failing, you teach the dog that it can get away from you by running.

It is probably good if the dog tries to run away from you when it is still small enough for you to catch it and reprimand it fairly severely. In all likelihood, such discipline will convince the dog that running away is impossible and you should not be troubled with the problem again. Disciplining a dog that runs away should not be a serious problem, if you use the training methods advocated in this book. There are as many training methods as there are persons who train dogs, but my own method is a combination of what I have learned from other trainers and gains made from the hard school of experience. Training is compounded by the fact that what is best for one dog may be no good for another. You have to suit the method of training to the dog.

Back in the days when there were many game birds in every cover, the favored method of training a dog was known as force breaking; and such training did not begin until the dog was a year old. Many more dogs ran away from force-break training than with the techniques commonly used now.

I am not an advocate of the radio-controlled shock collar, but it is the simpliest way to deal with a confirmed "bolter." A bolter dog is one that commonly runs away to escape training or supervision. The shock collar is made to order for such an animal and works this way: Just as the dog is relaxing out there at one hundred yards, feeling it has "put one over on you," and secure in the knowledge it can outrun you, hit the button to give the collar a good buzz. At the moment you push the button, call for the dog to come to you. Such a maneuver really shakes the bolter and soon it will know better than to run away. However, a shock collar should never be used with a 3-month-old pup unless the animal has some extremely bad habits or is very hard-headed. If the dog has been raised in the home, as I have recommended, and is properly "humanized" there should be little difficulty in getting the pup to do as you wish.

By humanizing, I mean that the puppy should have had daily contact with humans since opening its eyes. A few minutes playtime each day with a litter of puppies will prevent the dogs from becoming afraid of people. Such attention, will cause the pups to look forward to human contact.

The lack of human contact is one of the failings with puppies from the puppy mills, the large kennels owned by those whose only interest is to make a profit from the breeding of puppies. The practice of some kennel owners is to use dogs for breeding anything that is registered to anything else that's registered as the same breed without regard to the desired qualities. The dogs used in such breeding practices are known as brood bitches. Brood bitches often are the rejects that would not take training at professional training kennels and were sold at cheap prices. Such puppy mills are currently being investigated by Congress because of allegations that the mills fail to meet proper housing conditions and regulations of interstate shipment of unhealthy dogs as set forth by the United States Department of Agriculture.

Puppies bred and raised in such conditions have little contact with humans until sold. This causes the animals to be "man shy" to the extent that some never fully overcome the condition. Such man shyness can be avoided completely, however, by daily contact and handling of the pups when they are very small. Such handling causes the pups to accept the smell of humans. Puppies that are handled have instilled in them a basic foundation that causes them to accept contact with people as natural. It follows that a puppy with such an outlook is much easier to train and deal with.

The most critical period of humanizing a puppy is immediately after they have been weaned. When fed, the puppies should be petted and talked to. The puppies learn to recognize that man is a source for food as well as being involved in most of the events in their lives. Pups treated in such a manner will be much easier to train.

Previous to the sit-and-stay training you should have been using the "No" command with the pup in the house or kennel. When you say, "No," give the command as a short, sharp sound so that the dog will not confuse it with "Whoa" which should be given as a sort of long, drawn-out, "Whoooa." This is used as a command to stop the dog from whatever it is doing. If your dog is well trained to whoa, you will never have trouble with it chasing birds or going places you do not want it to go.

I have always used a rolled newspaper as a correction tool. One simply takes a newspaper, rolls it into a cylinder two inches in diameter, puts a few turns of masking tape around the end to be held and runs the tape halfway along the roll.

At five months, Doc brings in the dummy, taking care not to mouth it. Dummy is badly torn after two months' work.

The rolled newspaper is valuable. You can make one to use on a small pup with four or five pages of a newspaper. More pages should be used if the rolled newspaper is to be used on a larger dog. The rolled paper does not hurt the dogs. It is used for noise. The rather loud noise produced when a newspaper is used to swat a pup frightens the animal.

One authority on dogs contends that noise made by the rolled newspaper could cause a dog to become gun shy. I never found any evidence supporting such a claim nor have my many friends who use the newspaper method. I think it is probably the way in which the rolled newpaper is used that would make a dog become gun shy and not simply the noise.

To ensure that a young dog does not become gun shy, I shoot a pistol everytime I take him food for a period of a few weeks. In a few weeks, the dog will start to drool at the sound of a gun being fired. That is good training for a gun dog. The dog will look forward to the sound of gunfire and be excited and encouraged to hunt when hearing the sound.

Judgment should be used in introducing pups to gunfire. Most breeds of gun dogs seem to instinctively like the sound of gunfire and it excites them to more successful hunting efforts. The fact that a dog gets to retrieve and hold downed game in its mouth contributes much to the canine's attitude.

To receive maximum benefit with minimum damage when using a rolled newspaper, remember we are speaking of using it only occasionally in the training of a pup.

My training method is getting a dog to do what I want because it wants to please me. That goal requires some prerequisites. The only way to accomplish having a dog desire to please you is to treat it in such a way as to earn its complete trust. A young pup, when first brought home, must be treated with firm kindness. In time the pup will learn that as long as it reacts to our teaching it can rely on us for fair and kind treatment. Puppies, as well as dogs, must be subjected to discipline, but the younger animal must know why it is being disciplined. If the discipline is random and the dog is unable to associate with a given behavior, we will lose its trust. The young dog should be given ample time to learn to behave in the manner we desire.

I initiate a pup to the feeding time sound of gunfire gradually. That is because I want the dog to associate the sound of gunfire with pleasant things. I keep pups inside the house for at least three months and often longer. A pup accustomed to indoor temperatures could suffer severely if placed in an outside kennel during a cold winter. Two things that help determine whether to place a pup in an outside kennel at 3 months or 6 months of age are the breed of the dog and how many other dogs are in the house.

The procedure for familiarizing a pup with gunfire follows: As soon as a pup has "settled in" — a process that can take from two days to a week — I begin snapping a percussion cap on a muzzle-loading pistol in a room where the pup is not allowed. I do this just before putting food in the pup's dish. With each day I move closer to the pup before snapping the cap. At first, the dog will pay no attention to the noise but within a few days will begin associating the explosive sound with food. Reaction varies with each pup, but generally the animal will dash about and run to the spot where it is fed. The animal will be excited and show signs of anticipation. I never leave uneaten food with a pup. Therefore, the pup is hungry and anxious to eat at feeding time. If you do not have a muzzle-loading pistol you can use a modern arm with cartridges in which there is only a primer. Or you can use a blank starter pistol. A starter pistol is a bit loud. It might be best to close the door between the room occuppied by the puppy and the room in which you fire the starter pistol the first few times you use the tactic. Regardless of what you are using to fire, gradually move closer to the dog until you are shooting directly over it.

At seven months of age, author's pudelpointer, Fritz, holds a classic point on a quail visible in foreground.

When the dog has become thorougly familiar with the firing sound and shows only anticipation when hearing the sound, it is time to move to a louder gun. I graduate to a light blank load in a .38, which I make myself since I am a hand loader. A blank load is listed in most reloading manuals or you can use small charges of black powder held in place in the cartridge case with toilet paper wadding. Such loads should be fired into a tin can since the powder is likely to set the paper on fire. Black powder is corrosive, so the gun must be wiped out with oil each time it used and cleaned in soapy water at least once a week.

Now, just as before, gradually move the gun closer to the pup when you shoot until you are firing the weapon quite near the animal. When the pup has completely accepted the routine, it is time to take him into the open near feeding time and fire a shotgun while he is forty yards from you. This may cause the pup to come to you or to simply look for a feeding pan. The dog should then be fed.

If you follow this procedure, not one pup in a thousand will show signs of being gun shy. I realize not everyone can fire a shotgun in their backyard so you may have to adjust the training for whatever your situation requires. There is a rifle range on my property so it is no problem to fire a gun at any time.

Some people advocate taking the pup to a trap range and leading it behind the line while there is shooting going on. It can be rather difficult to subject a pup to such barrage, however, until it is used to having shotgun shells fired over it in a situation in which you and the dog have been the only ones in the field. Whatever kind of shell you are shooting over the dog, you must do the firing with safety. When using a muzzle loader with caps, be absolutely certain the gun is unloaded.

Muzzle loaders are often left with a charge in the barrel, but without the percussion cap in place. This is safe as long as someone who does not know that the gun is loaded does not snap a cap.

"No" is one of the most important commands your dog should understand. You should begin using the command as soon as the puppy is settled into your household. The command is used to get the dog to stop at once whatever it has been doing. When a dog hears "no" it should halt whatever it is doing without hesitation or delay. The command must be enforced with increasing strictness. By the time a dog is 6 months it should know full well that if it persists when told no, it will be punished immediately. "No" must be accepted by the dog as a no-nonsense command that demands instant obedience.

A gentle approach should be used when initiating the no command. For example, if the pup — as pups are so inclined to do — is trying to grab a dangling tablecloth, it should be told in a firm voice, "no." Obviously, if the pup is not familiar with the command, it will persist in trying to grab the tablecloth. When persistence exists, grasp the pup by the back of the neck and give it a gentle shake while again saying, "no." (Grasping a dog by the back of the neck is a dominant hold and the animal will recognize it as such.) The next time the pup grabs for a tablecloth give the dog a firm, but not too hard slap on the muzzle. The next time use a rolled newspaper. The severity of punishment should be increased gradually until the pup understands that "no" is a command that cannot be ignored.

Again, patience and persistence are basic. While some dogs will be more easy to train than others, nearly any pup can be trained if you keep it interested in the lessons. If a training session is kept short it will help in maintaining the interest of a dog. Whenever the animal shows signs of losing interest, either move move to another area of training, or discontinue the lesson for the time being. Another thing to avoid is feeding a dog just prior to a training session. Sessions are best held just before feeding time or even better, let the feeding time pass for an hour or so and you will really gain the animal's attention. Dogs are motivated by hunger to perk up and take an interest in their surroundings. In the natural wild state, dogs stir about and go hunt ing for food so the best time to train a domestic pup is when it is hungry and alert.

A dog should become thoroughly familiar with a command before it is introduced to another. It is not good to use several commands at one time as to do so will most likely result in thoroughly confusing the pup. The dog might become so confused that it won't do anything right because it doesn't comprehend what you want. To put a dog in such a position could interfere with further training until the confusion is forgotten. I have seen this happen and it is not the fault of the dog; it is the trainer's own doing.

When you first get a dog you should teach it to recognize its name and to come to you when called. There is an obivious necessity for this. In serious training, I like to use hand signals with all of the commands. This allows one to communicate with the dog at long distance, under noisy conditions such as when the dog might be near a roaring stream, or in the event that the animal becomes deaf in later years. The words "come" or "here" can be used as a come-in command. In fact, any word for any command can be used as long as you use the same word every time.

Command words should have a distinct sound unlike any of the other words used for commands. This is important as the dog must be able to differentiate the individual commands. Cadence and voice inflection are also important. Animals do not really understand the meaning of the words we use to tell them what we want them to do. Instead, they learn to associate the desired response with the sound and cadence of the word used to call for that response. I once hunted with a man who ordered his dog to stay by shouting, "Drop anchor." It worked like a charm, because my friend always used the same words and cadence when giving the command.

Choosing a working name for your dog is important. Some names of registry are plainly unsuitable for calling a dog in the field, so it is advisable to use a short nickname as a working command. The working name should be short and easy to enunciate. Joe, Doc, Jack, Bill, Fritz, Prep, Spot are good working names. The name should not sound like any of the commands you are going to use in the field. Moe would not be a good choice for a dog's name because it sounds too much like "no" and "whoa." Another thing to

Teaching dogs to work in close to the gunner can be one of the more frustrating chores, when they are excited.

A limit of bobwhite quail begins with the yard-breaking sequence, followed by further training on specific game.

consider in selecting a working name is how you are going to sound and feel when calling the dog's name in the field. The name should be one that is easy to shout if the dog is far from you. It is difficult to shout, for example, such commands as "Here Bucefhallis" or "Orion's Manor" or some equally complicated name. You get the idea. Make it easy on yourself and the dog. Once you start using a name for a dog stay with it to keep from confusing the animal.

From the beginning, make it a habit to pat yourself on the thigh when calling the dog in. The dog will associate such a motion with the command and in the event you cannot be heard, will still respond.

Whenever the dog responds correctly to a command it is important to display your pleasure. The dog is working to please you, so make it clear that it has done the right thing by giving it a pat and saying "Good dog!" A dog will cease to respond to training if not rewarded when doing the right thing. I cannot emphasize enough the importance of giving a dog approval when it responds correctly to a command. That is especially true when a young dog is in the housebreaking stage.

Once a dog does become familiar with a command and is accustomed to performing in response to the command, it is not necessary to make a fuss each time the right thing is accomplished. When a dog consistently performs correctly to a given command, the handler takes no particular note of it. However, when a dog suddenly makes an incorrect response to a command it has been doing correctly, it should always be reprimanded unless there is some extenuating circumstance.

Conversely, when a dog is in the process of learning, it should always be praised and rewarded when giving the correct response and only mildly reprimanded when responding incorrectly.

Severity of the reprimand should increase as the dog learns the meaning of the command. When you are sure the dog knows what is expected but deliberately disobeys, it is time to punish it a bit more severely. The severity of punishment is dependent entirely on on whether the animal is a "soft" or "hard-natured" dog.

Some trainers use dog candies as reward for correct reponses. There is nothing wrong with this. I have used it on occasion. The use of rewards such as candies are best used on dogs reluctant to please and may be an added incentive.

But there is a problem with the use of "goodies" as reward. First, it is necessary to always have a supply of goodies in your pocket. This is not always convenient. Everyone occasionally forgets the candies. Secondly, even the hardest dog candies will usually break when carried in a pocket and that can be quite messy.

Before using candies, consider whether you will continue the practice once the dog is trained. If you plan to discontinue the candies once the dog is trained, be prepared for a period when the animal is disappointed and often confused because it is expecting a reward for a job well done. A

Pointer is on the scent, being watched closely by handler, while shotgunner appears dubious about quail's location.

dog thus disappointed often will be balky.

After you have determinded which methods or rewards you are going to use for certain commands you will have to stick with it. In yard-breaking, for example, you have to proceed slowly and repeat each step until the dog has thoroughly learned the command. Then, and only then, can you proceed to the next step. In yard-breaking, you are setting the pattern of response and the relationship you will have with the dog for as long as you have the animal. It is extremely important to use much care and wise thought if you are to have a good relationship with the dog.

After the dog has been thoroughly trained to come without fail when called, proceed to the sit-and-stay exercises mentioned earlier. When the dog has fully learned the sit command, there is no question it is going to sit. And when you tell the dog to stay, you can walk away for half an hour and return confident the animal will be sitting where you left it.

Next comes the "whoa" command, or you can use the command, "hut." It is less likely to be confused with "no" if proper diction and cadence are not used in giving this command.

I personally prefer "whoa" as that is the command used by my father and grandfather. The command is reinforced by my farm background of working horses and from the time I was old enough to hold a barshare plow upright. It just seems natural for me to say "whoa," when I want something to stop.

Regardless of what you choose to use as a stop command, be ready to enforce it before giving it initially and many times thereafter. The dog must get the idea that when told to stop it should do so without hesitation regardless of how excited or interested in what is going on. Although the dog is in sight of or chasing game or is engaged in some equally exciting activity, when hearing the "stop" command, it must stop immediately and stand still until given further instruction. The dog's complete obedience to this one command is the secret of having a well-behaved, fully-trained animal. If you can stop a dog at anytime regardless of what it is doing, you have gained complete control whenever the animal is within hearing range.

I also like to use a hand signal with the stop command. The signal I use is both hands upraised toward the dog. If I am carrying a gun, I will hold it between my upraised hands. If the dog hears the command only as a distant noise, it will see the visual signal and still comply.

It is well and good to say a dog must instantly and dependably obey the stop command, but how does one make it happen? The answer is simple, yet requires much work with some dogs and surprisingly little with others of the same breed. The answer is repetition, making the dog stop on command so often and under such varying circumstances that it becomes an instinctive reflex.

To begin stop training seriously, you need a braided nylon rope about ten feet in length with a snap on one end and a wrist loop on the other end. I like to use rope of half-inch diameter as it is easier on the hands than rope of smaller thickness. With the dog on the end of the ten-foot lead and out in front of you, give the stop command you are going to use, then shut down tight on the rope and do not move forward. Naturally, this will force the dog to stop.

The dog probably will turn and come back toward you since it cannot continue away from you. Kindly, but firmly, take the dog back to the spot where you first gave the stop command and make it stay until telling it to move on. I use the command, "hie on," for this and anytime I wish the dog to move on. This command is used traditionally for pointing dogs. Some people use "go on" or other commands. Use a command to your liking, but always use the same command for the same desired response. This, along with repetition, will cause the dog to obey commands instinctively. And it avoids confusion. A basic of training animals is to always use the same command for the same desired result. This point cannot be overstressed.

There are no shortcuts or substitutes for commands; they must become so deeply ingrained in the dog that it is literally impossible for the animal not to follow a given command. In the event you cannot work the dog daily, put it on the lead and make it stop on command as frequently as possible. As the dog becomes more familiar with the command, become more firm in your response to disobedience.

If the dog resists the lead and tugs hard when you stop it, try using a slip collar that has a choking action as the dog pulls it tight; it becomes tighter as the animal pulls against it. The dog should soon learn that backing off from pulling against the lead eases the pressure around its neck.

Most dogs respond nicely to a a smooth choke collar and it should be all that is required for use on such dogs. But if a dog is stubborn and persists in pulling against a smooth choke collar, there are choke collars that have segments of teeth that will dig into the dog's neck when it pulls hard. There also are collars with spikes of varying degrees of sharpness on the inside of the collar. These can be used on dogs that seem determined to resist all training, or for dogs that persist in pulling so hard on the lead that they are difficult to hold. Never use a collar that is more harsh than needed to control the dog. There are notable differences as to how much force is needed until a dog becomes obedient. It is up to you to determine what collar to use.

After a few sessions of stop training, the dog should be familiar with what to do when given the command. If the dog persists in moving off the spot where it should remain, it becomes necessary to use even sterner correction procedures.

There is a story told about these parts of a man with a balky mule. The tale goes that this fellow hitched the mule to a wagon, then went to the wagon bed, picked up a club the size of a baseball bat, walked to the mule and hit it on the head with the club, knocking the animal to its knees. A bystander, concerned about the seemingly cruel treatment, protested.

The mule's owner explained that it was necessary to hit the mule to get its attention.

"Now that I have his attention, I can work the mule," the man explained. "If I didn't hit the mule on the head so I could work it, I would have to send it to the glue factory. I think it's better for the mule to do it this way."

I am not recommending anyone hit their dog on the head with a club, but it is necessary to use whatever means required to get the dog's attention so it can be trained.

After a few training sessions in which the dog has been told to stop, then forcibly dragged to the spot where it was stopped, it will learn to stop and remain at the place where you gave the command. Some dogs do this on the first training session with the use of only a slip collar. Let us hope your dog is one of these. If not, you will probably have to use the more harsh methods.

Concentrate on using this command until the dog has learned to be fully obedient to it. Once the dog is responding well to the stop command while on a leash, remove the lead and give the stop command when the animal is at about the same distance from you as when on the lead. Hopefully the animal will stop and remain in place. It is best to try this procedure the first few times in a small enclosed yard where you can catch the dog in case it decides to ignore your instructions.

When the dog is obeying the command off the lead as well as on the lead, gradually increase the distance between the two of your until reaching the limits of the enclosure.

Now comes the big test: take the dog into the field and, when it is about thirty yards away, give the stop command. If everything goes well, the dog will stop and remain where it is. If not, it's back to more training and as a last resort the use of a shock collar.

For those who think of the shock collar as a panacea, remember the collars have being used for only the last 20 or so years. Man has been training dogs for thousands of years.

If a dog tends to sneak off when first given the stop command when off the lead, it may help to use a twenty-foot lead and upset the animal a few times as it moves after being given the stop command. However, if you trained the dog carefully to stop on command before you start working it off the lead there usually is no problem. So much does depend on the dog and trainer that it is difficult to predict the reaction of the animal. The best we can do is state what will happen for the average dog handler.

Using the methods outlined here should enable you to get your dog to stop and stay on command if you really work at getting your animal to obey, but do not be afraid to try different things. If you think of something you believe will enable you to get better results, try it. But keep in mind that basics of animal training cannot be broken without creating problems that interfere with a training program.

Here are a few of the more basic rules:

1. Never reprimand a dog for failing to follow a command you are not sure it understood.

2. Always avoid allowing a training situation to deteriorate to the point that the dog would rather run away. You cannot chase and catch a mature dog, so it is better to keep the situation from getting to that point.

3. Try to anticipate a situation in which a dog might try to escape and take steps to thwart such behavior. Once a dog discovers it can avoid training by running away, you will have to take extraordinary measures to stop such action.

4. Keep training sessions as pleasant and exciting as possible. When a situation begins to sour and it looks as though the dog is going to become balky, cease training immediately. Take the dog for a walk in the fields or do something that will restore the dog's good feelings toward you.

Avoid putting a dog into a kennel when it is upset because of punishment or other unpleasantness it might associate with a bad training session. Keep the dog happy and anxious to please you unless you wish to train by force-breaking. This approach will be detailed elsewhere, but it is difficult and does not give results as good as those in which the dog works because it sincerely wishes to please the handler/trainer.

Many people believe the only way to train a dog is by force-breaking. These people include respected, experienced, successful trainers whose opinions are worthy of consideration. I believe that some dogs can be trained only by force-breaking. But as far as I am concerned, force-breaking is a last resort. Dogs that have been trained by force-breaking never exhibit spirit and joy in their work. Such attributes are a big part of the pleasurable experience of hunting with a good dog.

Force-breaking reminds me of Jack, a big hardheaded Irish setter that belonged to a friend. Jack was a confirmed bolter: whenever my friend used a hard bit on Jack, the dog would run to the top of a hill and sit there until he got good and ready to go back home.

The dog's owner ask if I had any ideas on how to cure the problem. My first response was that anything I might think of would probably be most unpleasant for Jack, since I have little use for hardheaded dogs. Most hardheaded dogs aren't worth the trouble they take to train.

However, Jack's owner was a friend and good sportsmen and had mountain land he allowed me to hunt on. Therefore, I made an exception in this case and agreed to observe a training session. Sure enough, as soon as Del started trying to get Jack to stay, the dog ran up a grassy slope, sat at the top and 'laughed.' Dogs can act in such a manner that it appears they are making sport out of making a fool of their trainers.

I asked whether Jack always ran off by the same route and Del said that was pretty much true.

Oklahoma's annual Grand National Quail Hunt brings dogs, gunners from far and wide to show their expertise. Actor Dale Robertson, second from right, rubs head.

I had a piece of gill net sixty feet long I had found at the beach after a storm. Del and I rigged the net between two saplings across the path Jack usually took up the hill. We bent the saplings to the ground and rigged them with figure-four triggers like snares. I ran a piece of monofilament fishing line from each trigger and got into position with the lines in my hands as Del took Jack from the kennel and began a training session. The net was flat on the ground, hidden from view.

After a time, Jack bolted up his usual track but, just before he arrived at the point where the net was hidden, I pulled the lines. The net jumped up in front of Jack and he ran into it almost full tilt becoming hopelessly entangled. Del, carrying a cardboard tube, ran to Jack and in the words of my friend, "Thumped the tar out of that mutt." We left the dog entangled in the net until he became frightened.

I left the net with Del in case he needed it again, but he gave it back to me a few months later saying Jack had not bolted after that initial experience.

I would like to say Jack became a fine bird dog, but the truth is he was too independent and hardheaded to amount to much. The dog would point a bird and retrieve it, but when you hunted with Jack you went where he wanted because he paid absolutely no attention to where you wanted him to hunt.

When your dog is dependably stopping and staying on command, it is time to teach it to assume and hold the "at heel" position.

It is important to have a dog trained to remain at heel if you are to truly enjoy hunting with the animal. The heel position is just behind and to the left of the handler. If you shoot left-handed, you might want to have the dog heel to your right so the animal will be on the side opposite the gun.

When a dog is at heel you don't have to worry about it running in places you don't want it to be, nor do you have to be concerned with it chasing cats, chickens or other farm animals. The heel position also keeps the dog from running in front of you when it is on the leash and entangling the leash in your legs.

The animal should have been trained to lead on a leash when it was still a very young pup. Such training is best accomplished by attaching the leash to the pup's collar and walking slowly along while the animal is on the lead. In all likelihood the puppy will fight the lead. It will drag its feet, lay down and try to resist the inexorable pull of the lead.

Inexorable — that's the key word. If you start with the pup on the lead when it is too small to pull very hard and simply walk at a slow pace, dragging the animal along when it resists the pull of the lead regardless of what antics it goes through in trying to get away from the pull, it will soon come to realize there is nothing it can do. The pup will stop fighting the lead when it learns it is easier to follow along than to be dragged.

For this phase of training use a grassy area free of stones or sharp objects so the pup won't be injured or cut. Start by making the first trip on the lead last five mintues and the second trip ten minutes. Soon the pup will follow the lead and often pull sharply and jerk when it wants to go faster or move to a position it cannot reach because of the lead. When the pup tugs on the lead, give a little jerk to set the animal back without hurting it. Gradually increase the intensity of the jerks until the pup finds that tugging at the lead simply causes a rather unpleasant pressure on the collar. The pup, by the third or fourth session, should be leading quite nicely.

Training the pup to walk at heel on the lead is done rather easily by repeating the word "heel" while holding the lead behind you in your left hand with the rope shortened so the dog cannot get past your legs. When you have done this often enough, the pup should know it is supposed to stay behind your leg. If it persists in trying to run ahead of your leg, put it on a lead long enough that you can hold the pup at your side and still have enough of the lead reach the ground in front of you. Use a rope or leather lead. If a leather lead is used, be sure there are no metal rings or rivets on the front end.

Swing the lead in a circle in front of your legs so that, if the pup attempts to get past your legs, it will be struck by the swinging lead. At first swing it gently, but if the pup persists in trying to get past your leg, swing harder so it will give the dog a sharp rap across the snoot as discouragement. Usually several training sessions will have the pup walking behind you nicely.

In the event your pup continues to be stubborn, cut a limber switch — I use peach or hickory — and carry it in your right hand while keeping the lead with the pup in your left hand. When the dog sticks its nose in front of your leg, give it a bit of a sharp rap across the nose with the switch. This soon will discourage even the most hardheaded pup from trying to run in front of you and it will soon be walking at heel on the lead. Whenever you rap the dog across the nose, repeat the heel command so the animal knows exactly why it is being punished. Persistence with this method will bring results.

With the pup walking properly at heel on the lead, it is time to train it to walk at heel without the lead. The easiest way to accomplish this is to gradually increase the length of lead allowed the dog while it is at heel. The dog should be trained to stay in the heel position regardless of how much slack it is allowed. If the pup starts to move away from you, take up the slack and give the lead a good jerk. As you pull the dog into proper position repeat the heel command at the same time. I begin to use a hand signal along with the word heel. This hand signal is made with a waving motion with the left hand beside the body just ahead of the left hip and moving the hand and arm to a position behind the left thigh. This motion clearly indicates to the dog where it should be and serves to remind the pup to stay in place or, if it has wandered, to get into position where it belongs when at heel.

When stalking, it is necessary for the dog to remain at heel so it won't flush or alarm game. For example, when I am walking the bank of a river in duck season, I want my dog at heel so I have a chance to sneak within shooting range before flushing the birds. A silent hand signal will put the dog at heel without alarming the ducks or whatever game I happen to be attempting to sneak up on.

The last of the yard-breaking commands is "down." This command means the dog must lie down and remain quiet whenever the order is given. If you have the dog broken to "stay," there should be little difficulty in teaching the command. Instead of saying "sit-stay," I tell the dog, "Down, you stay." This is taught by repeating the command while pressing the dog into a prone position. Pressure is put on the dog's withers instead of on the rump as in the sit command. Press down firmly on the withers or shoulders, if you will, and say, "Doowwn" in a sort of long, drawn-out command that is unlike the sound of any of the other commands you use. Some dogs will resist this pressure and you will have to pull their feet out in front of them while almost holding the animal down until it relaxes in the prone position. Once the dog has relaxed in the down position, the command, "Youuu stay," is given in a firm, nononsense voice and the animal is made to remain in this position, until it is evident it has accepted the position.

The down position is useful in many kinds of hunting. When the dog is to remain beside a blind or in the blind, one can use this position. It is also useful when transporting a dog in a vehicle if the animal is not inside a box. The down command can be used to keep a dog lying on a floor or seat of the vehicle. This position is also useful when flying game such as doves is seen approaching from a distance. You can put the dog in the down position and lie down beside it to hide from the approaching game.

Proper care of a dog during yard-breaking phase, is most important. Checking it for problems or injury after any session is only common sense as well as good for the dog.

The hand signal used with the down command is simply to point at the spot on the ground where you want the dog to lie down. If there is no reason for silence, I will use the verbal command as well. With my old dog, Fritz, I only have to point at the spot on the ground, look at the dog and he will lie down and stay until I release him with the command, "Come." This command is accompanied with a pat on my thigh, the same signal used to call the dog to me. I also can release the animal simply by using the hand signal. This is useful when stalking and it is necessary to move silently after having given the dog the down command.

All of these hand signals are extremely useful if the dog becomes deaf in its later years. Many top gun dogs whose owners hunt them hard and shoot a lot of game do become deaf in later years. Most hunters apparently never realize how badly they mistreat the ears of their shooting dogs. I think everyone who owns gun dogs and shoots over them should just once get down on their hands and knees and let someone shoot a couple of 12-gauge magnum loads over them in the manner we shoot over our dogs when they are on point.

My father had me do this when I was about 12. Dad was fussing about one of the dogs not responding well to the whistle after we had fired several shots over its head at a covey rise. The gun was not fired directly over my head and was fired upward at a rather high angle, but it still deafened me for fifteen or so minutes. We often fire guns within four or five feet of our dogs' heads and the sound is deafening. There is a heap more noise on the front end of a shotgun than that heard from the rear of the gun.

Yard-breaking of a young dog is perhaps the most significant and important part of training. It is the foundation upon which we will later build all the other responses that make up a finished shooting dog. So it behooves us to go carefully and give much thought to the proper establishment of this foundation.

It seems like a lot for a pup to learn, but if we take each command a step at a time and repeat it until the dog has truly learned it, all will be all right in the end.

Chapter 10

A PROPER START

Stopping Bad Habits Before They Start, Honing A Dog's Natural Instincts Accomplished This Demanding Chore

Author's dog, Fritz, is doing a good job of finding and holding birds at 8 months of age. (Right) Regardless of the breed, when dogs have been trained, they are eager to hunt.

GETTING THE young dog started properly by using a training method that will point the pup in the right direction and bring out those traits needed for the sort of hunting for which you intend to use the dog is paramount. While the pup is very young, its interests should be directed into channels that will intensify the desirable instincts that have been bred into the breed you have selected. If you have chosen well, the dog will have a predilection for the hunting activities you want to pursue. During the formative months for the young dog, our job is to use certain simple exercises that will intensify those instincts selectively bred into the pup.

In the case of a pointing breed, we will be encouraging the pup to point a quail skin on the end of a string tied to a pole. If raising a hound we should encourage it to use its nose to follow a trail. To get him to do this, drag some choice morsel of food along the ground, then put the pup down where it can find and follow the trail to the food; thus the pup learns early in life that desirable things can be found at the end of the scent trail.

A retriever pup should be encouraged to return a thrown training dummy to you and, as soon as it is returning the dummy with regularity, the dummy should be thrown into water. First use a puddle where the pup can wade to retrieve it, then into larger swimming-depth waters. The flushing breeds should be taken into the fields and thickets where every attempt should be made to lead the dog into contact with game. Later, before anything more than yard breaking is attempted, the flushing puppy should be allowed to catch a few wing-clipped birds of the species you intend to hunt with the dog. A versatile-breed puppy should have all of these experiences before it is twelve weeks old.

Woodland's Lord Hanschen, an 8-week-old pup, points quail wing dragged on a string. The pup is owned by Dan and Bernice Carter of Upper Marlboro, Md.

In addition to these experiences and learning encounters, the puppy should be encouraged to be interested in its surroundings and, simulations of the activities expected in later life should be brought into the play and humanization activities we engage in with the pup. This doesn't require any great expertise or extensive knowledge of dogs; rather it requires ordinary common sense.

When working with your pup, think of things you can do or situations you can bring about that will be natural for the pup to do. These activities should be similar to what you wish the pup to do when actually engaged in the sort of field work you will wish it to perform. A dog of any breed should be taught to follow your trail to find you. When you take a young puppy into the field and it becomes separated from you for the first time, it will probably whimper and whine when it realizes it is alone. Do not call out or go to the pup at the first sign of distress. Give it time to circle around and hope it will cross your trail and have sense enough to follow it. If the pup does follow your trail to find you, make a bit of fuss over the pup so it will associate a pleasant experience with following your trail. In addition to teaching the pup to be self-reliant, this will help train it to use its nose and

This 10-month-old pup has been tied out to learn that he must stay tied when necessary and to become accustomed to the fact that he cannot be allowed to roam freely. Note the barrel which offers shelter during this period.

This young dog has been allowed to catch a live duck in the field in an effort to build its hunting desire.

associate searching with sniffing something out.

All breeds should be taken afield at an early age, certainly no later than twelve weeks. Young dogs should be taken into thickets, tall grass, briar patches, mature timbered areas, across small brooks and into any other field situation they are likely to encounter in the hunting you plan for them. By allowing them to become familiar with areas and situations where you plan to hunt, you should not have problems later with the dog being distracted by the terrain or cover during serious training. This may not seem to be important, but you will be surprised at what can happen when a young dog encounters any unusual situation for the first time. I once had a young beagle put off from hunting for half a day because it encountered a herd of cattle that chased it. The terrified dog ran all the way back to the car and refused to hunt the rest of the day.

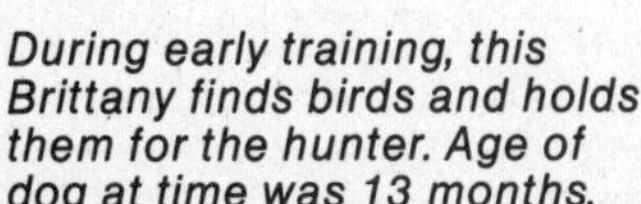

During early training, this Brittany finds birds and holds them for the hunter. Age of dog at time was 13 months.

When a dog has been introduced to hunting in proper fashion, flights such as this do not intimidate it. (Right) Bodo Winterhelt steadies a young Brittany held by Rudy Lorra as it points quail on string.

If you are going to be hunting in an area where the dog is likely to encounter cattle, you should familiarize the dog with cattle by taking it on a lead close to a barnyard. But carefully, as cattle will often chase a dog, especially one that shows signs of fear. A herd of cattle can corner a dog and kill it under certain circumstances. They also can harm you, if they became excited by your dog. It is well to remember that almost any herd, even dairy cattle, will chase a dog. The time to handle this problem is while the dog is young.

One of my hunting friends tells of a young setter he had spent the fall months training and had the pup hunting well on pheasants, finding and holding them like an old dog.

This friend set forth with great expectations, on opening day, to a covert he had not hunted all fall for it always had been a good ringneck producer. Shortly after entering this area, he shot and killed a pheasant that the dog retrieved beautifully. Soon the dog was on point again; up went several pheasants and the shooter dropped a nice rooster. The dog started off to retrieve, but came upon a small spring and tumbled down the steep bank into the water. He became frightened, returning to the owner, and would not leave his side for several hours. Finally, the dog was taken to the truck and moved to an area where he had trained as a pup. It was about a year-and-a-half before this dog could be made to cross even small streams.

This problem could have been avoided had the dog been introduced to such streams while still very young, when everything was a new experience. Of course, there was no way to foresee that the dog would fall in a stream and become frightened and, in my experience, the dog's reaction was unusual. However, I have learned never to be surprised by such strange happenings as this with dogs. Like people, they are unpredictable and it is difficult to anticipate what may frighten them. Thus, it is an excellent idea to consider such situations your dog will encounter in your hunting area.

Even in the city there will be park areas where you can

A young pudelpointer retrieves a dummy duck for the judges during natural ability trial segment.

take a beagle pup and let it get a snootful of rabbit scent. Sometimes the first encounter of a beagle with rabbit scent is dramatic; at other times, they seem to show no interest in rabbit scent. I have seen both reactions. I have had beagle pups walk into a freshly vacated rabbit squat and seem perfectly oblivious to the scent. In other instances, I have seen a beagle bristle up its hackles to growl and bark at the scent. Most of the many reactions fall between these two extremes.

If unable to get your pup into a spot where you know scent is present, the next option is to use the bottled prepared scents available from dog supply houses. I have mixed feelings about these scents. I do not feel they duplicate exactly the scent left by the animals they are supposed to represent in spite of advertised claims, although the odors may be similar. None of my dogs will point these scents, but they do show interest. In the absence of real game, these scents could be used to get the dog's interest in game scents aroused to the highest degree possible. This will make the transition to the real thing more easily accepted and will help get the idea of what it is all about across to the pup.

I have seen coonhounds follow and bay the trail left by a sack that has been impregnated with bottled raccoon scent and dragged along the ground. This shows that such scents are of definite value. A training dummy always should be treated with the artificial scent of the game for which we plan to use the dog. This will give the dog the idea that it is supposed to retrieve game that smells like the dummy. There sometimes is a problem when switching from manmade to natural scents, but it need not be if we take proper care in always keeping scent on the dummy.

If you live in an area where you can buy pen-raised game birds, it is a good idea to obtain a few and allow the bird-dog puppy to come into contact with them. The birds should be tied out to a stake or in some similar arrangement. The Pup should be on a lead for most of these encounters so you can control it.

During normal hunting season, there will be opportunities to save whole birds and freeze them in heavy plastic bags for use in training at a later time. There is no problem in keeping such game in the family food freezer if it is inside a sealed bag, then enclosed in another such bag to completely eliminate the possibility of leakage from game that should be left in unskinned natural condition. Some trainers pick up fresh, relatively undamaged road kills of the species they wish to train a dog to hunt.

I always skin a few quail, instead of using my regular method of plucking them, and freeze the skins and plumage with a ball of dried grass rolled up inside, the skin roughly sewn up over the ball of grass. This makes a nice training aid for bird dogs. The same thing can be done with various species of furred game. One important point is to always use grass or weeds instead of wadded newspaper, plastic or other artificial materials. Natural materials preclude an unnatural smell on the hide or skin. This stuffed skin can be put to many uses such as making drag trails.

There also is a use for the same sort of items made up from species you *don't* wish your dog to chase or point. This type of game is used to give the dog unpleasant experiences when it comes into contact with undesirable species. These experiences can range from scolding to light spankings or, with a stubborn dog, the use of a shock collar. It is easier to prevent bad habits from starting than to break the habit after it has become established. It is much easier to plant a few rabbit carcasses and let the young dog know your displeasure, than to try to catch and punish a dog that is supposed to be chasing coons, foxes or some other game. First, make certain the dog is pursuing something other than what it is supposed to be chasing; then you have to catch the dog in the act and punish it without discouraging the dog from chasing proper kinds of game.

Another good idea is to save deer feet and tails and make up a sort of dummy by tying the deer tail and a foot together with a strip of deer hide. This makes a neat scent bundle to hide out in the training area to teach the dog it is to have nothing to do with deer.

When deer are butchered, the entire leg is cut off just below the knee and it is this lower leg and foot we are calling deer feet. The hind legs have a gland that puts out a strong, durable scent and will last through several training sessions.

For those who train hounds to run deer, this also is a fine training tool. The hind leg with scent gland can be used to make long drag trails with plenty of scent for the dog to follow. If these hind legs with their scent glands are to be stored in your freezer, make sure you have them well sealed. I use three layers of heavy-duty garbage bags, each one closed with a tight twist and rubber band before it is put inside the next one. Wash your hands in peroxide after putting the feet in the first bag and before you touch the next bags. Deer musk is quite penetrating and of lingering persistence.

Last fall, I had two whole raccoons, four deer hides, six deer legs, several quail skins and a couple pheasant skins in our thirty-two cubic feet home freezer. My wife didn't fuss too much, because I was extremely careful to keep such items tightly sealed. Besides, after putting up with me for thirty-three years and helping train countless pups, she is accustomed to such dog/man shenanigans.

To get the young dog started right in hunting, try to minimize negative experiences with the game you wish it to hunt and give the dog every encouragement when it has any contact with the desired game, keeping it within reasonable boundaries of behavior. There is nothing wrong with a young pointing breed dog chasing birds. It shows that the dog is interested in the right sort of game and builds enthusiasm for searching for that game. The dog usually can be made to point by putting it on a long lead and bringing it into the game, then steadying the dog up to a pointing position.

Von Treffend's Caladen, 10-month-old pup owned by Ross Calaway of Bowie, Maryland, retrieves dummy in water.

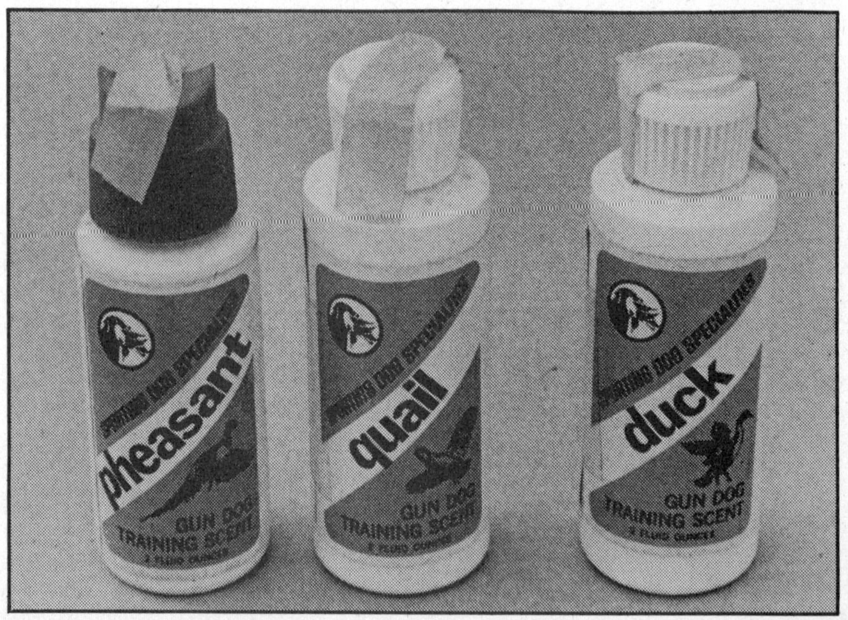

A variety of artificial game scents comprise an important tool for the trainer's kit, but author contends they do not replace the real thing.

Rabbit hunting is an important sport in some states such as North Carolina, where this event took place. However, if one is to hunt birds, the dog must be trained to concentrate on the winged game variety.

At one time pointers and setters were encouraged to run and chase gamebirds during their first year. One of the most popular bird dog training books of thirty years ago advocated this and recommended absolutely no training during the first year except for teaching the dog to come when called. Then, in the second fall hunting season of the dog's life, a crash course involving force-breaking was imposed on the dog. This method produced a lot of excellent dogs, but there were many more with a lackluster and spiritless mien, their performance mechanical and dull.

It would be catastrophic for the dog to show no interest in the desired game after having been given the scent and coming into contact with the live game and urged to take action. It is nice if your young dog points the first quail it encounters and this can be encouraged by the use of quail skins on a string at an early age, but if the dog chases the bird it still is showing interest; as long as the dog shows interest it has promise. If the dog is not interested after the steps outlined above, it's not advisable to spend too much added time on this dog. You can't give it desire. That desire to catch the game is the whole basis for a hunting dog's utility and these dogs must show keen interest in their game.

Hounds should be interested in trails and it is a good idea to get them familiar with the scent of the desired game while they are young. They can be helped greatly by putting them down with dogs that are running the specified game.

Retrievers should show the same interest and excitement as spaniels and other flushing breeds when they contact game. Actual retrieving can be taught by force-breaking, if the dog does not show proper interest. However, the dog that retrieves solely because it has been force-broken to do so will never give you the satisfaction or companionship of the dog that loves to hunt and work in the water.

Chapter 11

INTRODUCTION TO POINTING

Teaching Your Dog The Basics Slowly And Firmly Can Determine Its Future Value In The Field

CONCURRENT WITH the yard breaking, one should have been doing certain other things designed to bring out and strengthen the pointing instinct of the young pointer.

The basic exercise is the use of a teaser on the end of a long pole. A teaser is a quail skin, pheasant skin or quail or pheasant carcass that may have been frozen in a deep freeze, but still is in good, sweet-smelling condition when thawed. Tie the teaser to the end of a pole about twelve feet long with eight feet or so of heavy fishing line. I have found that the cane poles used by fishermen are light and ideal for this purpose.

The bird skin or carcass should be fastened tightly to the end of the line so that, should you inadvertently allow the dog to get hold of it, this teaser does not pull off easily. A freshly killed bird is best, followed by a recently thawed frozen one, a bird skin, or a bird wing in that order.

Take the pup out in the open and allow it to run for ten minutes or so to dissipate that first flush of energy and excitement at being loose, then get down to the serious business of training. When first let out of its kennel, the house or wherever you keep it, a dog should be allowed to run free for a short period; when first released, a dog is naturally interested in dashing about and checking out all the fresh scents in the area, at the same time, running off the excess energy it has accumulated while penned up. Until a dog has done this, you are not going to have its attention.

When the pup has finished his run, dangle the teaser on the end of the line in front of the dog. Naturally, the dog will try to catch it. Your problem is to keep the dog from catching it until its bred-in instinct to point takes over and the dog establishes a point. Once the dog establishes a point, encourage it and let it know it is doing the right thing. Once the young dog is pointing the teaser dependably, you will need an assistant to handle the teaser while you stand by to firm the dog up while it is pointing. This is done by gently pushing the dog toward the teaser while it is pointing. The dog will tend to resist this pressure, thus becoming more firmly established in its point. Get used to doing this, for it is the basic firming-up maneuver and you will do a lot of it during the training ahead.

The time required for a dog to learn to point the teaser can vary widely from one to another — and a few dogs never will point a teaser. I never have been able to determine to my own satisfaction just how much willingness to point a teaser affects the dog's later pointing and hunting ability. I doubt that it is much, since I've seen and owned dogs that would point virtually everything that moved as puppies, yet never became more than mediocre hunting dogs. They vary greatly in this early display of the pointing instinct and it can be exciting to see your young pup staunchly pointing English sparrows that come to pick over the crumbs around its food pan. We term such a puppy as being "birdy" and it usually will bring a premium price. Such a pup certainly is easier to get started pointing and would be suitable for the person who never has trained a pointing dog.

Again, pups that show such early promise are no guarantee of a fine hunting dog; this early display of instinct is merely an indication that the dog wants to point. Hunting desire and ability are an entirely different thing. I remember in particular a young English pointer that belonged to a neighbor some twenty years ago. He got the pup in the dead of winter and kept it in the house, giving it all the best. By the time the pup was nine weeks old, it was pointing a teaser and birds that were sitting in nearby bushes or sometimes just hopping around. The owner was quite proud of this display of promise. It was a good-looking pup out of a local bitch that I knew to be a good hunter. She had been bred to a field-trial winner that was also a good gun dog. If ever a pup seemed to have everything going for it, this one did. I expected this pup to make a fine showing when field-training season came around.

So I was quite surprised when the owner called about the first of October to tell me he was having problems with the dog. When I managed to get out with this fellow and his dog a few days later, it soon was obvious that the dog was sight pointing only. It didn't seem to connect the scent of quail with the birds it pointed by sight. I told the dog's owner — we will call him Al — what I suspected, but he didn't want to hear it, so I suggested that we take his dog where I had a recall pen set up and see what happened.

At the pen, I put a quail out in a weed patch and we brought the dog in from the downwind side so it had to smell the bird. The dog showed no excitement until the bird flushed in front

Taking Weimaraner gently in hand, trainer works it into position on a quail that is held in a harness fastened to a line on the end of a light pole.

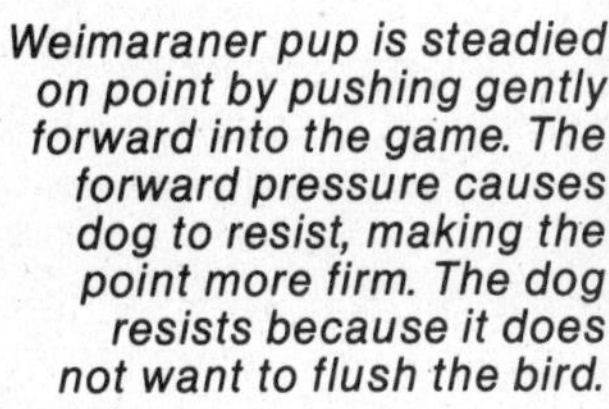

Weimaraner pup is steadied on point by pushing gently forward into the game. The forward pressure causes dog to resist, making the point more firm. The dog resists because it does not want to flush the bird.

With the dog established firmly on point, it should point the next game bird it encounters properly.

of it after being almost stepped on. The question was whether the dog had a poor nose and was not smelling the birds or it simply was not associating quail scent with the birds.

I have a method of testing a dog's nose that seems to work as well as anything I have ever heard of for this purpose. It is a simple test in which I put a piece of liver weighing about a quarter pound in a hot skillet and braise it a bit to bring out the scent. I have never encountered a dog that didn't get excited at the smell of braised liver. I put this braised liver out in the field and bring the dog toward it from the downwind side, taking careful note of how far the dog is from the liver while allowing for the strength or lack of wind. It is pretty easy to determine from what distance the dog can smell the liver and to thus make an objective evaluation of its nose. There was no problem with Al's dog so far as the nose was concerned. It picked up the liver scent from thirty yards out; after a few tentative steps, nose up testing the wind, it took off and devoured that liver like it was starving.

Having established that the dog had a good nose, we had to get it to point by scent. We tried all the usual ideas such as putting a quail on a release peg and bringing the dog in from downwind on a lead, then working up to where the dog could see the bird after having first smelled it for a period of time.

Al's dog would go on point the instant it spotted the bird, but simply wasn't interested in pointing scent. This became frustrating and highly discouraging. After a series of failures to get the dog to point scent, we finally got the young pup to make half-hearted scent points by allowing it to catch a few tethered quail on the ground. However, this particular dog never did approach the promise it had shown in its initial training.

But let's look at the other side of the coin; when my son was in high school, I gave him a well bred German shorthaired pointer pup out of what could have been advertised as the litter of the year. Both the sire and dam of this litter had done very well in NAVHDA tests and the bloodlines were impeccable. I looked forward to great things from this pup. We raised this dog in the home and it was thoroughly and dependably yard-broken by the age of six months.

This pup had never shown any desire to point a teaser — or anything else and it had shown no birdiness as a puppy. By the time this dog, which was named Gus, was a year old, I had serious doubts about it. Gus had been exposed to a lot of quail and pheasant hunting and had shown no interest whatever. He would try to catch a quail at the recall pen, but that was the extent of his activity except to pause and watch as we shot birds pointed by the other dogs.

I had just about given up on this dog and if it had not been my son's dog — and he liked the mutt — I would have gotten rid of it.

Late that year — I suppose it was at least the middle of January — my son, John, took Gus along with a friend and himself on a late season trip into a rough area that was partially cutover due to loggers with an old orchard along one side of the tract. The West Virginia quail season runs through the month of February and, late in the season, we often go afield to see what we can kick up in areas that are too rough for serious hunting. These are just casual outings with a gun in the hope that some sort of game — be it a rabbit, quail or

Winterhelle's Fritz, at 6 months of age, is let out to run off some of the joy of being a puppy before actual training session gets under way. Young dog should be allowed to run off this excess energy before any work.

Fritz, at 6 months, has been told to "Sit! You Stay" and is still doing so after half an hour. This pose is indicative of the slow, repetitious methods that get training results.

grouse — can be kicked up. We don't take a good bird dog along, because we never shoot rabbits over pointing dogs. This made an ideal situation to take Gus along simply for a run.

After beating the edge of the old orchard, the boys missed Gus and went in search of him when he didn't come to the whistle as he usually did. Gus was staunchly on point with a covey of quail in a brush pile. The boys dropped a couple of quail on the rise and Gus retrieved to hand like a champion. They marked the singles down and, after a suitable wait to allow the birds to exude fresh scent, took Gus in on them. Gus locked up like the championship-bred dog he was and after a bit of steadying up on his point, the two teenagers dropped a few more birds which he neatly retrieved. From then on Gus was a *bird* dog, in all that the statement implies.

There are many more dogs of pointing breeds that point birds than there are *bird* dogs. I have owned and hunted many dogs that did not earn the title of bird dog. To bear such an honor in our outfit, a dog has to do much more than just point and retrieve birds, any meat dog can do this. A true bird dog has that burning desire to find game that will keep it going all day in the roughest cover when game is scarce and conditions poor; it will stay on point for hours until either you find it in the thick cover that has hidden it or the birds it is holding grow restless and flush; it will display that intuition which allows the really good ones to hit all the hot spots while seeming to just drift through the cover in a search pattern that misses no bird hiding places. This seems a tall order, but the really good ones do it naturally.

I have come to believe there is no real sure-fire way to tell the good dogs from the mediocre until you have started them properly and found out first-hand just what the individual pup is going to become. This is why you will often find advertisements near the end of hunting season that will read something like this: "Nice 12-month-old English pointer, well started and pointing and retrieving nicely, no bad faults; guaranteed to get you birds if hunted in good cover."

In all likelihood, the advertised dog will do all that is claimed. If you are looking for a good meat dog most of these dogs are good buys as they can be bought for around $200. In many instances, this is less than the price of a six-week-old pup of good breeding. Certainly the asking price is less than the owner paid for all the shots, vets fees, and feed required to get the pup this far along.

Why is the owner selling this guaranteed paragon of doggy

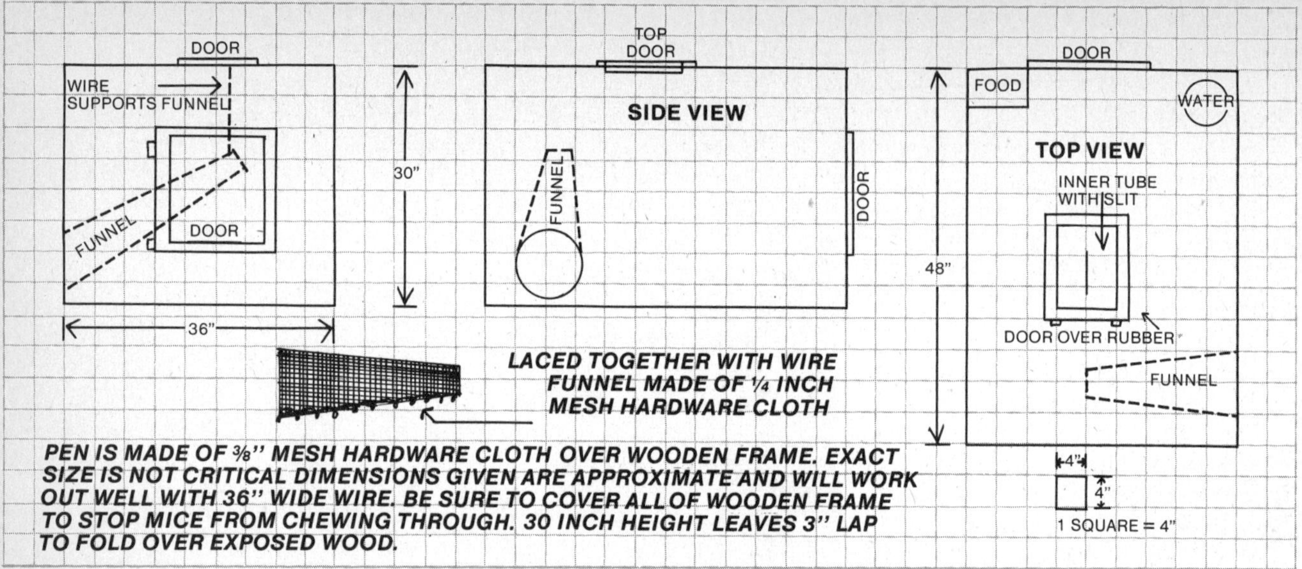

Author feels that a bird recall pen of the design illustrated is a must for the serious dog trainer.

virtue? Because he has gotten the pup well started and has seen what it will do afield; he knows it never will be more than a potlicker meat dog that will do a workmanlike job of finding and holding birds, but it doesn't have that spark of greatness that sets the really good ones aside from the average gun dog. Many hunters can do quite nicely without this extra spark, but some of us eagerly look for this little bit extra and must have it in our dogs to be really happy with them.

Dave Duffey, a top trainer, once told me that we have to raise and train a dozen dogs of good breeding to get one that is really great. I never have seen anything that would make me disagree with this observation. You can tilt the odds a bit in your favor by buying only the best bred puppies and, by best bred, I don't mean pups out of the big field-trial winners. I mean pups out of bloodlines that you know have been producing topnotch hunting dogs for many generations.

If you are lucky enough to find such a dog and get it started well enough to see that it has the makings of a really fine dog, proceed carefully. It only takes a couple of bad experiences at an early age to permanently take the edge of greatness off a fine prospective bird dog. Many of the better dogs are a bit "soft" in the puppy stage and must be handled carefully until a bit older and they develop more confidence. We have to get the pup pointing, because it is interested in the game and its pointing instinct makes it point. At the same time, the pup must be made to realize it must not bump birds, try to catch them or chase them. Put another way, the dog must point, because its breeding requires that it do so and because it wishes to please us by doing what we wish. The dog must be made to realize that bumping or chasing will bring punishment, yet it should not be afraid to find birds.

It is in this stage that some of the best prospects become "blinkers." A blinker is a dog that simply ignores birds, having received harsh punishment for bumping or other mistakes

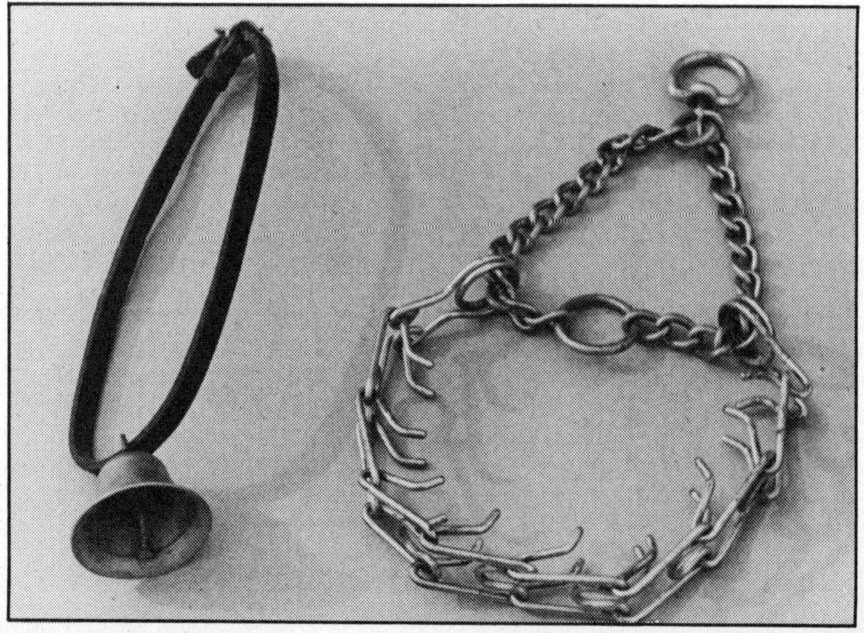

The bell is used to keep track of a dog in heavy cover, while spiked collar is used to enforce commands to a hard-headed dog that tends to pull on the leash or fails to stop when command is given by trainer.

made around birds. Gun-shy dogs often will become blinkers, because they come to associate pointing birds with the gunfire that frightens them. So it is imperative that we keep the experiences of a young dog when in contact with birds on the pleasant side to encourage its efforts and desire to find birds. Correct the dog's mistakes, but do it in such manner that the dog's enthusiasm is not dampened, but instead, is sharpened by the contact with the birds and the ensuing excitement.

Here is one of the training phases where you must make a judgment as to whether the dog's enthusiasm and hunting desire have been developed to the point where the dog is ready for serious correction of whatever faults it is showing when in contact with the birds.

The most common fault encountered with young dogs when they start to point is that they chase the birds when they flush. If you have done your *"Whoa"* training well, you will have little difficulty in stopping the dog should it break point to chase flushing birds.

If you are unable to stop the dog from chasing with the whoa command, then it's back to square one with more yard breaking on this command.

At this stage, when the young dog is just starting to point live birds, do not correct it harshly in the presence of birds, since the dog might mistakenly think the correction is for finding birds or pointing them.

It is easy to ruin a young dog at this point. If you don't have a recall pen or some other source of live quail and must hunt for wild ones, it is especially exasperating to hunt for hours to find birds, then have the dog mess up. There is a great temptation to start shouting at the dog. If you do, the next time the dog encounters birds, it may well remember the unpleasantness the last birds caused and decide to ignore them. This would mean you have made a blinker of your dog, big trouble that is possibly insurmountable.

Another fault commonly encountered is the young dog that will creep up on the birds after it has established a point. This too can be corrected easily if the dog whoas properly. If the dog won't obey the whoa command when it is on birds, the best thing for you to do is to call, "No! Bad Dog!" mildly and put the dog on a check cord before working it into the bird again. Make sure you approach from the downwind side, by this I mean that the dog should be working into the wind which has passed over the bird so it can smell the game from some distance away. When the dog picks up the scent it should work forward a short distance, then establish a point. It is your job to make the dog realize that, once it establishes a point, it must not move unless the bird moves off or you give the dog permission to relocate the bird. At this point, it is nice if you have a helper to flush the birds while you keep a firm grip on the check cord. If the dog tries to break and chase, you can put pressure on to stop him from chasing.

In the case of a hardheaded dog, make sure the animal has enough enthusiasm for pointing so as not to be discouraged by a bit of rough handling; when this stubborn dog breaks point, let the check line go until he comes to the end of it. You should have a couple of turns of the line wrapped around your hips. Just as the dog hits the end of the line throw your weight back against the line to bring the dog up with a hard jerk that will cause it to swap ends or flip in a hurry. This will come as an abrupt surprise to the dog and it should get the idea quickly that it is not supposed to break point and chase when the birds flush. Some of the hardheads will require several treatments

Training dummy, lead and collar from Buck Stop Lure Co. are made of heavy nylon webbing. This material is fast replacing leather for dog gear due to its durability.

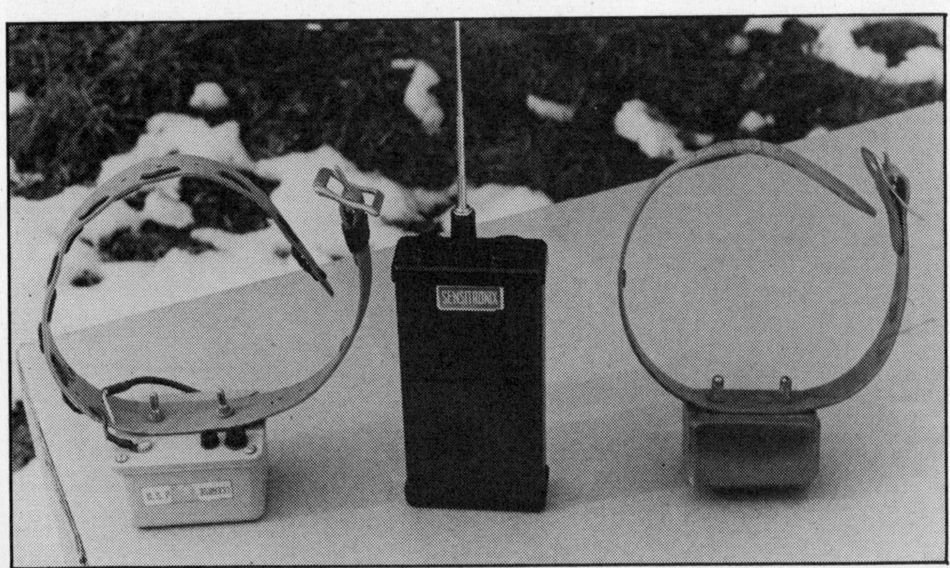

From left: Shock collar, unit for radio control of collar and a dummy collar that has a similar weight, configuration.

of this sort and may require even more strenuous measures, but this is dealt with in another chapter.

Mentioned earlier, the recall pen is one of the most valuable items in the dog trainer's bag of tools. The recall pen allows you to have your birds and use them, too. Basically, the recall pen is a cage made of chicken wire or hardware cloth with a funnel-shaped opening into the cage from the outside. Design is similar to that of a fish trap. This funnel-shaped opening allows a bird to get from the outside into the cage, but prevents the birds from getting out once they are inside the cage.

The recall pen works, because quail are gregarious or flocking birds. They crave the company of their own kind and will return almost invariably to where the rest of their group is penned up. It is best to have at least a dozen birds in the cage and twenty is even better. Take out only three or four birds at a time and plant them somewhere within a hundred yards or so where you can bring the dog in to come up and point them. After they have been flushed, you may mark them down and take the dog in on them one more time, but it is better to use several birds and work each bird only once each time you put it out to avoid chasing the bird too far from the recall pen.

By leaving most of the quail in the pen, you are establishing what amounts to a home covey. The birds in the pen will call and those outside will come to the calls of their fellows. The

Kate, author's Llewellin setter, was only 12 months old when she handled these two pheasants for John Wood. She was considered a finished dog at this early age. (Below) This is a small recall pen that can be used to keep quail in the training area and available for use.

quail soon will find the funnel opening and drop inside to join the rest of the covey. By the time you have used these birds several times, they will learn to get back to the pen in a hurry. You should not use the penned birds late in the evening, however, as quail will not travel after dark. A quail that is alone in darkness often does not make it through the night for one reason or another. You can mark the birds with a dye marker so you do not use the same quail every day. I did this for a while, but was unable to see any difference, whether I used the same birds every day or not. There will be some inevitable attrition as some of the birds will be caught by predators. Also, you will have to shoot a few for a young dog so it can get a chance to retrieve a bird. The dog must learn that the gun is what gets the birds so it can pick them up.

The quail in your recall pen must be watered and well cared for if they are to serve you well. If you use the right sort of feeders, they can be refilled once a week and will put feed down automatically for the birds from the hopper as it is used. There are waterers that can hold enough for several days. The less you have to move around in the area of the recall pen, the better it is for keeping the quail in a wild state.

A good recall pen setup has a dogproof and catproof fence in a thirty-foot square around the pen. I have found that four-foot-high hog-fence wire with three good solid posts to the side — corner posts with one in the center on each side for a total of eight posts — makes a fine enclosure.

The reason for this enclosure is to keep away from the pen dogs, cats, foxes and whatever else would try to catch quail. It will also keep your dogs from getting too close to the pen and bothering the birds. A gate is necessary for your own egress and this should also be made of the strong, tight hog wire. At today's prices, I would estimate $60 to build the recall pen and fenced enclosure if you cut your own posts. You can buy short pieces of hog fencing from most farm supply stores. Three strands of barbed wire should be run around the top about six inches apart and all of the fencing should be stretched tight for a neat job.

I use three-eighths-inch mesh hardware cloth for the recall cage itself. This mesh is fine enough to keep out snakes. I like a pen of about thirty inches high, three feet wide and four feet long. At one end, I put a door measuring about fifteen inches square. This door is made of the same hardware cloth with a light angle iron frame; the hardware cloth is laced to the frame with a wire to make sturdy enough to protect the quail from any marauders that might get inside the perimeter fence. I make brackets to hold the food and water holders, keeping them from being upset. In the center of the top, I cut out a ten-inch square door and fasten a piece of inner tube over this opening. The inner tube has a slit about five inches long in the center. This slit inner tube allows you to put your hand inside

This pair of hunters praise their pointer after it has has brought in a downed pheasant. Author advocates the stick-and-the-carrot method of training within reason. He feels a dog must be made to feel fully appreciated.

A well trained pointer moves in carefully on game bird. (Left) Hunter surveys his take of California quail, a tough species to take. He would not have scored as well for his meat pot without the aid of well trained dog.

the cage to catch a quail without having a door open through which the birds can escape. This inner-tube door is covered with a hardware cloth door of similar construction to the front opening to prevent any predator from gaining entry through this opening. I wire both doors shut in such manner that they cannot be opened by any varmints that might happen along.

The entrance funnel is made simply by lacing it together with wire. The sketch in this chapter shows how to go about making the pen. The outer end should be about eight inches in diameter, while the inner end should be no larger than three inches. This will allow a quail to slip through while keeping out most varmints. The outside end of the funnel should be about an inch above the bottom of the pen. The pen should be set on several 2x2 boards to allow the bird manure to fall through.

I make considerable effort to hide the pen, placing it in a honeysuckle thicket or some similar brush, then plant weeds and tall grass so the pen blends in with the natural appearance of the area. I have thrown small cedar trees around them and on the top, taking care to leave an opening at both the front and top doors. The pen I have now is so hidden by honeysuckle as to be almost invisible. When the wind is coming from the recall pen to the training area, your dog is going to smell the birds. The dog should be discouraged from visiting the area of the recall pen.

Using the recall pen, you should have an abundance of birds on which to work the dog. Daily, or as often as you can, work the dog into a bird that has been planted. To keep a bird from running away from where you put it down, tuck its head under its wing and turn it around several times to disorient it and place the quail gently on the ground with the head still under the wing. A bird that has been planted in this manner generally will remain close to the point where it was planted for a couple hours if not disturbed. This makes it easy to find the bird and work your dog into it on a long check line if you are having problems that require you do this.

It is an excellent idea to work even a finished dog occasionally on a planted bird while on a check line. It tends to remind the dog that you are the boss and it is hunting because you want it to.

While on a check line, a dog is conscious that you have complete control. Some hunters will take even their most experienced dogs out on a check line the first day of every training season. They subscribe, as I do, to the theory that it is better not to allow the dog to have the chance to make any mistakes or bad moves than it is to break bad habits after they have become established.

The recall pen with its convenient supply of reusable birds is helpful to anyone training bird dogs. If you can possibly find space for one you should have it. It need not be fancy, just practical.

Recovered grouse has the attention of this young English Setter. Grouse are difficult birds for gun dog to handle.

Chapter 12

FIELD WORK FOR POINTING BREEDS

With The Basics Behind, It Is Time To Move Your Dog On To More Complex Training

ONCE WE have established the pointing habit and instinct in the young dog to the degree that we can have reasonable expectations the dog will point birds with which it comes in contact, we are ready for extensive field work and training for the the experience needed to handle wild birds and to get the dog working in the manner in which we want it to perform under the gun.

Different people have varying ideas and expectations as to what they want in field performance of a shooting dog. It is up to you to train your dog to work in the manner that best meets with your requirements, but certain basics are common to most all dog owners; it is these that we will develop in this chapter.

We will assume you have a recall pen with a supply of birds or some other source of birds on which to work the dog. It is possible to train a dog solely on wild birds; in fact, it is highly desirable to do so, but given the conditions generally encountered today in the field, it is not practical to plan on training your dog on wild birds exclusively. It will be necessary, however, that some wild birds be available as the dog nears completion of its training.

Basically, field training is simply more of what was described in the last chapter, with the addition of increasingly difficult situations into which you bring the dog; in this sequence, we try to simulate conditions that will be encountered while actually hunting.

To accomplish this, bring the dog into contact with the birds by more devious methods and, when the dog points, take your time in getting to it. Another excellent trick is to approach the pointing dog from a frontal position, so it will seem you are going to step on the bird. This usually will make the dog very nervous and it just might jump the birds. Be prepared to catch the dog immediately if this occurs and administer proper punishment. At this point in training, the dog should know it is not supposed to jump or flush birds; when it does so it is misbehaving and should be treated so. Be vigilant to ensure that the dog is not jumping birds secretly. Some dogs will not jump or chase birds, when they know that you can see them, but when they are out of sight, they seem to take great glee in flushing and chasing every bird they can find. This is a difficult situation to handle and requires some ingenuity.

In the days before the invention of the shock collar, the most common and practical method of dealing with the out-of-sight bird flusher required the assistance of a helper who would hide near where a bird had been planted. When the dog came upon and flushed the bird, the helper would jump out and chastise the dog. To use this technique, it is necessary for the helper to remain hidden downwind from the approach of the dog, for a dog can find one by scent as well as by sight or sound. This may seem an unnecessary warning, but I have seen people forget this fact, then wonder why they could not catch the dog in the flushing act. This method works well, but is time consuming and has been supplanted largely by the radio-controlled shock collar, which requires much less time and effort.

In using a shock collar to break this habit, it is only necessary for the helper to hide at a point where he can see the spot where the bird is planted and observe through binoculars whether the dog flushes the bird, then zap the offender in the event it does. During this phase of the dog's training, it should wear a dummy collar all the time, the operative collar being put on the dog before each training session. It is best if someone else remains out of the dog's sight most of the time and carries the transmitter; dogs do become aware of the purpose of the transmitter and show only their best behavior when you are carrying it, then act up when they know you do not have the mechanism with you.

If you are able to have the dog shocked by signaling a helper who is invisible to the dog, it gets the message across in a big way. I do not advocate frequent or indiscriminate use of the shock collar, but, when properly used, this item can be one of the most effective tools in the trainer's bag of tricks.

When carrying the transmitter, I generally try to wear a jacket with a big enough pocket to hide the unit and draw it out only if I plan to use it. For this approach, it is a good idea to buy a couple of spare antennae, as they do not hold up too long when constantly collapsed and extended every time the transmitter is used. It is not much of a job to replace the antenna and can be done in a few minutes.

The Sensitronics transmitter I use now measures 1-3/16 x 3 x 6 inches, with the antenna in the telescoped position. The shell pockets in most hunting coats and shell vests will accommodate a transmitter of this size.

If you run into a hard-headed dog that requires frequent use of the shock collar, it is not long before the dog knows what is coming when it sees you pull out the transmitter. Just the sight of the transmitter often is all that is required to put the dog on its good behavior. I do not like to see a dog shocked so often it recognizes the transmitter, but in some few instances, the shock collar is the only thing that has saved a hard-headed dog from having been put down; there is not much place for the untrainable dog.

After the dog is performing well at finding and pointing birds, it is time to shoot a few birds and get the dog to retrieve them. The dog should require little training to retrieve birds; like pointing and field search, this is one of the desirable traits that, hopefully, have been bred into the dog. Retrieving should be instinctive, with only a little prompting and training in good manners and delivery needed to have a top field dog. It is well to get the dog retrieving naturally and out of desire to please you, in addition to the dog's natural instinct to retrieve.

Retrieving, like "whoa," "stay" and "down," is a command that must be reinforced by force training, so the dog knows that it must retrieve on command without fail. My own method requires a pulley fastened around a pole or some other anchor point. A rope is run through the pulley and back to the dog, which should be standing beside the trainer about ten yards from the pulley. The dummy should be placed beside the pulley and the dog ordered to "fetch." In the event that the dog goes willingly to the dummy and retrieves it as it should, it is necessary to put some distasteful but harmless substance on the dummy so the dog does not wish to pick it up.

Yes, I know it seems silly to mess up the dog's good behavior when it is doing as it should, but we have to get the dog to refuse the retrieve so we can force train the retrieve.

When the dog refuses to make the retrieve, we then pull the dog up to the dummy using the line and pulley arrangement. This leaves no doubt for the dog that it is going to do its best to make the retrieve, whether it wants to or not. It should not be too difficult to make the dog go to the dummy under any circumstances. My own dog, Doc, did not take kindly to the idea of being forced to approach and pick up the dummy, even though, had he had been loose, he would have made the retrieve without fuss or bother. Force breaking

A pigeon tied to a release pin can be used in training a dog. Birds are inexpensive, but, author has discovered, can cause later training problems if too plentiful.

The mating ritual of game birds, author feels, is something special, since it is increasing the population to be hunted.

a dog to retrieve reinforces the natural retrieving instinct and creates a sure-fire retriever.

Much the same procedure is followed in making the dog steady to wing and shot. If the dog tries to creep up on the birds, come down pretty hard on it. We are past the stage in training where the dog is coaxed to perform. While being careful not to destroy the natural desire to please and encouraging enjoyment of the hunt, we must make the dog realize its obedience is not a voluntary act, but a mandatory performance which it must carry out flawlessly. This is the ideal for which we aim our training efforts. Unfortunately, nothing is actually perfect, so we do our best.

It is also necessary to make the dog become more careful and stylish in its pointing and approach to birds. Most young dogs will try to point too close to birds. They usually have been trained on pen-raised birds and, when they try to get as close to wild birds as they have been getting to the pen-raised variety, they flush the wild ones. Good breeding and sense usually will cause a dog to correct its own error and start staying back from wild birds. Some dogs will not learn this on their own and must be force trained to stay back far enough not to flush birds. The distance a dog has to stay from birds varies greatly with the species, weather conditions and cover in which the birds are located. Woodcock in good cover will lie so tight that you often will touch one with your foot before it will move. I have shot woodcock that my dog pointed, then flushed at my command, taken a step forward and flushed another woodcock from under my feet.

At the opposite end of the scale, chukars often flush twenty yards ahead of a dog and only the most careful canine will be able to get these wily speedsters to hold to be pointed. The bobwhite quail is supposed to be the ideal bird for the pointing dog, but I have seen them so wild on certain days that they would flush out of range from even the most cautious dog. I have had woodcock flush out one end of a clearing as the dog entered the opposite end. There seem to be certain days that, for some reason, the birds are skittish and wild for no apparent cause.

Ringneck pheasants are almost invariably hard for a dog to hold, yet I have had them crawl into brush and sit so tight that they could literally be picked up by hand.

Ruffed grouse are the trickiest of all. There is no way to know how these sly tricksters are going to behave. I have seen them flush forty yards ahead of the dog and I have had them hold tight like quail. Observation has shown that grouse seem to hold better if they are aware of the dog while it is still some distance away and they have time to find a hiding place to their liking. For this reason, I have a bell attached to my dogs' collars while hunting grouse.

Some dogs seem able to divine just how close they dare get to a bird, while others display no idea whatever as to how to handle a particular bird under the existing conditions. Really great bird dogs have an instinctive knowledge of bird handling and there is nothing one can do to instill this ability to handle birds under varying conditions. It is one of those instincts dogs either are born with or never have. All one can do is to teach the dog to be cautious at all times in approaching birds. It is better to be overcautious than to flush the birds. If a dog doesn't have that extra sixth sense that enables it to know instinctively how to handle most birds, the best thing for me is to sell the dog before I become really attached to it. I complete its training and sell it as a gun dog to someone who is not quite so demanding in performance; I am honest enough to tell the prospective buyer that I'm selling the dog because it bumps a few more birds than suits me. I take the customer out and let him see

Once your dog has learned to hold steady when coming upon game, you must shoot some birds over it. This helps dog to realize fully that its best chance of getting to pick up a bird is by pointing and holding it well for gunner.

the dog work. After having seen the dog handle a few birds, the buyer almost invariably gets a look in his eyes that tells me he thinks I am nuts.

If we consider the performance of most of the half-trained dogs we see in the fields these days, this buyer still is getting a good deal. The average gun dog owner has neither the time nor inclination to train his dog to the degree of performance I want. I get as much pleasure from watching the flawless performance of a well trained dog as in hunting the game the dogs are trained to pursue.

Extra bird sense is not always a blessing. The major problem encountered in finishing Fritz, my old pudelpointer, was that he possessed extra bird sense to the extreme. I ran him in two trials to qualify as a NAVHDA utility dog, one in Maine and the other in Virginia. The birds available were not too well flighted and Fritz, sensing this, just picked up the birds and retrieved them as though they were cripples. With this failure to point, he received a zero score in pointing. After all, it is rather difficult to tell the judges: "Yeah, but he would have pointed if the birds..." It was frustrating to know what was going on and be unable to do anything about it. Some of the judges knew what was going on also, but you score a dog on what it does in the trial, not what you know it can do.

At a trial held at Fort A.P. Hill, Fritz qualified as a NAVHDA utility dog; the birds were good, strong flyers and Fritz made no attempt to retrieve them until they had been shot and he was sent in to retrieve them after a good, solid point.

At this stage in your dog's training, it is time to start working on the search pattern. The search pattern is important. To a large extent it will determine the success your dog has in finding birds.

There is considerable variation and disagreement among trial judges as to what constitutes a good search pattern. The disagreement is largely over the extent to which natural cover and terrain should influence the pattern laid down by the dog, as it covers the area to be hunted. In theory, a perfect search pattern would be for the dog to swing back and forth across in front of the handler in a perfectly even series of sweeps. The dog should always turn forward at the end of the sweep so as not to turn back and cover ground it already has passed. The width of the sweeps — distance traveled on each side of the handler — is varied according to the type cover and scenting conditions, as well as the size of the area being hunted.

As a rough rule of thumb for gun dogs, in open, short cover, the sweeps might extend as much as a hundred yards on each side of the handler. In dense, thick cover, sweeps might be only ten to twenty yards on each side. The dog should adjust the search pattern to suit the conditions and the game.

Another factor involves the size of the area being hunted under any given situation. If hunting a field that is sixty yards wide and the cover is open enough to see the dog the full width of the field, it would be natural for the handler to go down the center of the field and the dog to make sweeps thirty yards on each side. In the event the field has dense, thick cover, where the dog can be seen only a short distance, it is proper to work the field in two passes with the dog searching fifteen yards on each side of the handler.

Most likely there is cover that is a lot more "birdy" looking in certain sections of the field. The natural instincts of a good bird dog should cause it to seek out the best cover and hunt hardest there. By "best" I mean cover that seems most likely — by reason of terrain, location or vegetation — to hold birds.

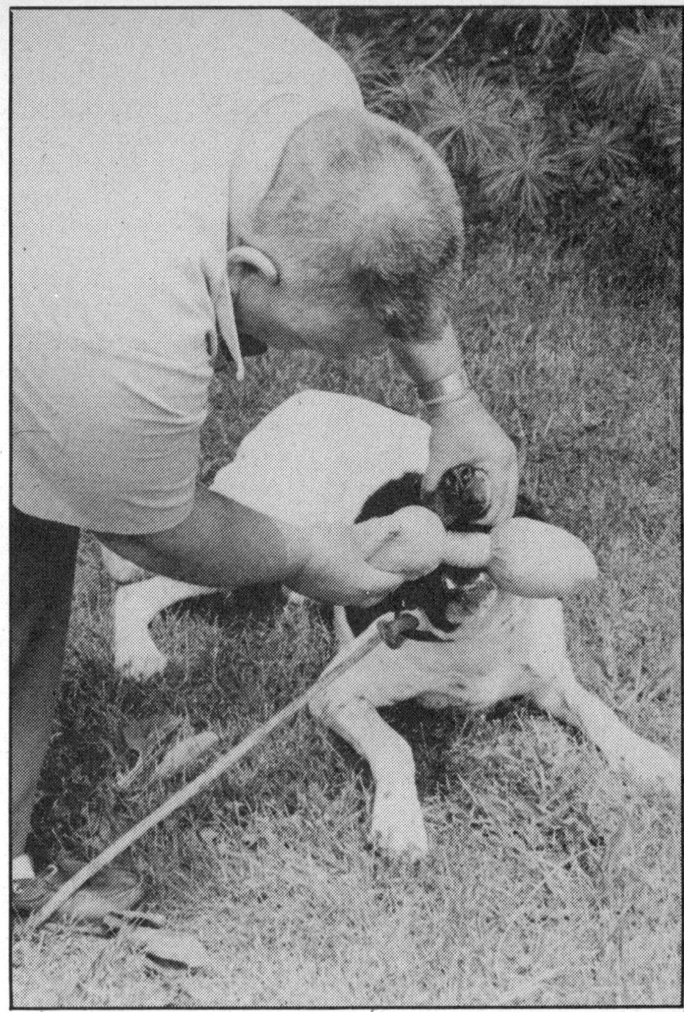

In early training, pressing the upper lips against its teeth will cause the dog to open its mouth so that the scented dummy can be placed in its mouth for learning.

Bird dog men often disagree as to how the dog should work the cover. Certain men hold the opinion that, regardless of cover, the dog should work the regular pattern of sweeping back and forth across in front of the handler or gunner. This opinion is especially prevalent among certain American Kennel Club field trial judges. Even though the rule book states, in effect, that the dog should search likely looking cover, as soon as the dog leaves the regular pattern of search, some judges start cutting points.

You can help your dog in learning how to spot the most birdy places by taking the dog directly to these places as soon as you start to hunt a covert. Be careful, however, to avoid giving the dog the impression that it need only hunt the best looking places. We should train the dog to make a proper search pattern in the field by working the dog on a long lead and making sure it always turns forward and keeps its sweeps fairly even to each side. It does no good to have the dog make a long sweep toward a side that has open cover if the other side is composed of thickets that require you to work the area in two or more sweeps to cover it. Dogs will tend to reach a bit on the open side and this should be controlled by calling the dog in when it starts to work out too far from you.

One of the best ways to control the dog in the field is to use the European-type whistle. This is a device that has a clear, high-pitched whistle on one end and a police-type whistle with a pith ball on the other end. Usually carved from chamois horn, some are fine objects of art made in Germany many years ago. I have a real beauty that was given to me by Rudy Lorra; very old, it is one of my most prized possessions. There still are some of these chamois horn whistles available from Germany at a premium price, but there is no reason to despair, as a quite serviceable whistle of plastic is available from Thomas Scott, 10421 Rockville Road, Indianapolis, IN 46234. Scott has a nice catalog of hard-to-find dog items at sensible prices. To the best of my knowledge, this is the only source of supply in the United States for some of the NAVHDA items such as Jaeger leads.

Use these specialized whistles carefully and judiciously. Indiscriminate blowing will ruin any hope of getting your dog to work properly to the whistle. The exact signals you use with your dog can best be determined by yourself, but the signal function you assign to one of the ends must always be the same and the dog must be made to accept that the whistle is a signal to be obeyed.

Start by using the whistle in the yard along with hand and voice signals. I use the end with the burr in it as a stop and come in signal. One blast on the burr end means stop and whoa. The single blast is accompanied by my right hand being held above my head. Two blasts, with my right hand held up and waved back and forth means come in. Work with the dog, using these two signals and the training methods given in earlier chapters, until you can depend on the dog obeying the whistle signals. Gradually increase the distance, until the dog is responding nicely to the whistle at two hundred yards or more. This distance factor is the reason for the whistle signals. Dogs have much higher-pitched hearing than humans and the human voice is well toward the lower frequencies the dog is capable of hearing. The whistle seems to be in the center of the canine hearing range and a dog can hear it at incredible distances when young, before its hearing has been ruined by shooting over it. Be sure you do not mistake your dog's not wanting to hear the whistle for actually not hearing it.

The clear end of the whistle gives a high-pitched, far-reaching sound which I use for controlling the dog's direction. One blast on this end means turn right and two blasts means turn left. This point is gotten across to the dog by working it on a lead and blowing the whistle to indicate a turn, then promptly turning in that direction.

Find a fairly large field and walk through it with the dog on the lead. Blow one blast on the whistle and sharply turn

This is the proper way to hold the dummy in the dog's mouth. Pressure applied upward against the bottom of the dog's tongue should keep the dog from dropping the dummy. Teaching the dog this facet of work can take some time.

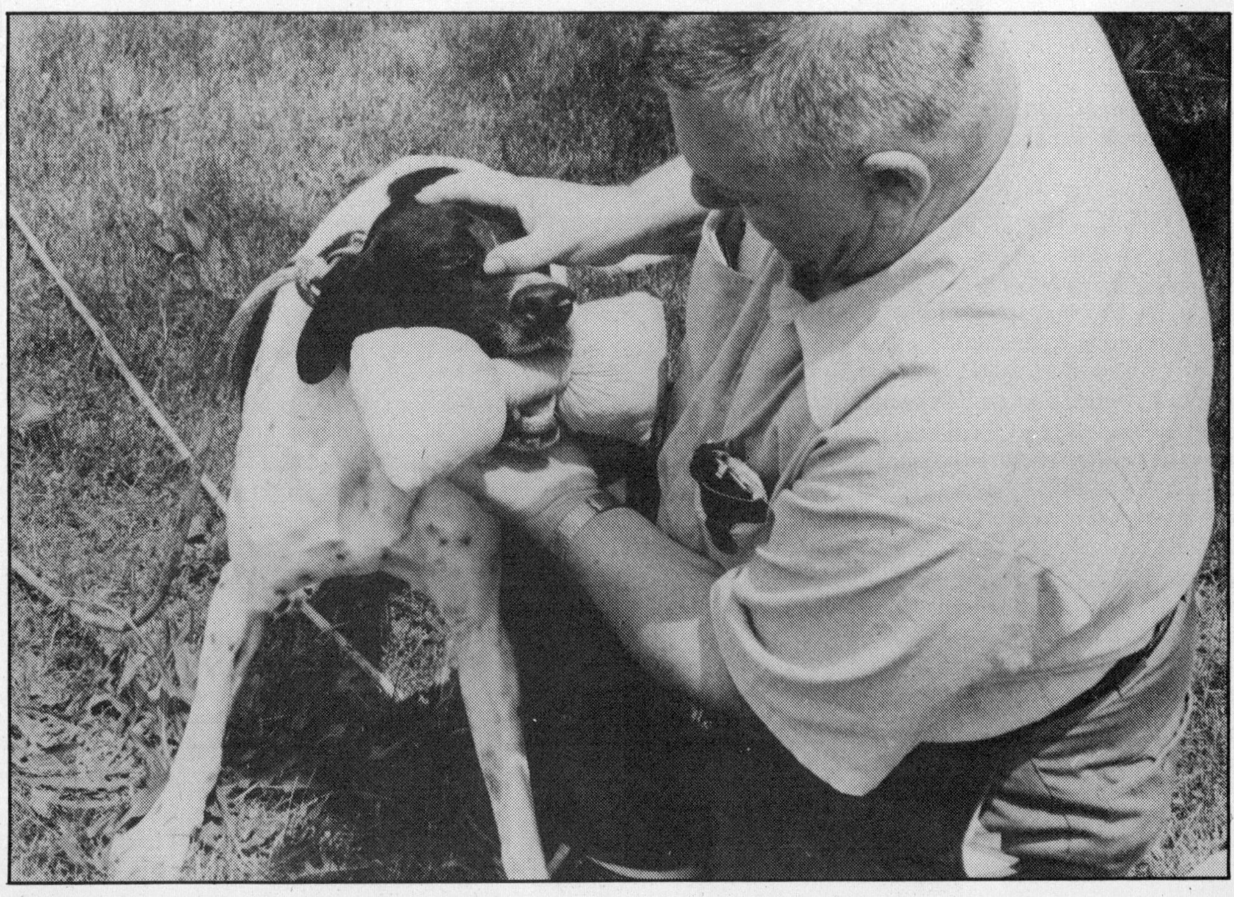

Well broken to retrieve, this young pointer takes a dim view of being forced to make retrieve of this game dummy.

Still battling the rope, the pointer is drawn toward the training dummy by means of rope and pulley arrangement that is described in the text.

to the right. After going in this direction for a bit, blow two blasts on the clear end and turn to the left.

Occasionally blow a sharp blast on the burr end and make the dog stop and sit until you allow it to move on. Let the dog reach out the entire length of the lead, which should be at least twenty feet in length; blow two blasts on the burr end and make the dog come in to you. Soon you will have the dog working back and forth across the field at the whistle signal, also stopping and returning on command.

It is a pretty good feeling to stand at the end of a large field and send your dog to any part of that field by whistle commands. When working the dog at a distance, I make sure I am in a position where the dog can see me, then I will wave my right hand with a gesture to the right when I blow one clear blast; using my left hand, I gesture to the left when I blow two blasts for a move to the left. These movements help keep the dog from getting mixed up on the directions.

When you have the dog working well to the whistle signals, plant a few birds in some of the birdiest looking cover, then put the dog down and direct it to the birds by whistle signals. The dog soon awaits these signals that send it into cover where it can find birds with eagerness. The dog never should be allowed to become dependent upon the signals to find birds. To avert this possibility, it sometimes is necessary to allow the dog to go into a field and hunt it without interference.

You can depend upon the dog to see just how much it can get away with while being directed by whistle signals. It will try you to the limit of your patience until you chastise it or use the shock collar. This is normal and is the dog's way of establishing the boundaries. Once these boundaries are determined, it will require only an occasional jog of the dog's memory to keep it performing. If you let the dog get away with disobedience, you are in for a tussle, since the dog has established a pattern that will have to be broken up.

Take the dog out and shoot a few birds over it when it is pointing them and make sure it does not hard-mouth the birds. Your dog is now mostly trained and should be hunted at least a part of a season before any further training is undertaken. Too much added training will cause the dog to go stale and lose interest, unless it is allowed to work on wild birds with the excitement of the hunt to kindle interest.

In this phase, you may have a problem with the dog hard-mouthing the birds it retrieves. This is the result of overexcitement, unless the dog is really hard-mouthed or a bird eater. You should have learned earlier whether the dog was a bird eater and not spent the time to get it this far along. In the event your dog is a bit hard-mouthed, the old trick of putting nails sharpened on both ends inside the bird is the best method I know of breaking this habit.

If your dog performs as outlined here, you have it pretty

well trained. This is a dog you can take afield in the best of company and feel reasonably confident it is not going to embarrass you; be assured it now is trained better than eighty percent of the gun dogs you will encounter anywhere.

You may elect to stop training at this point. Your dog will bring you much pleasure and will do the job in the field, but keep close watch to be sure it doesn't develop any bad habits. A small bad habit that is allowed to pass will soon turn into a whole batch of bad habits and your dog will not be the one you trained. Catch that creeping as the birds flush at once and it will not turn into bird chasing.

Some years ago, we owned a large piece of mountain ground made up of old farms and orchards abandoned when the tractor and other big modern equipment made operating small horse-powered hill farms uneconomical.

I had cut out a stand of prime hardwoods along the edge of an old orchard where there were a few old apple trees still bearing fruit. In the late afternoon feeding period, I could count on finding at least one grouse feeding on the dropped apples. The road I had bulldozed to get the timber out ran west of the old apple trees and it was possible to walk quietly along this road and observe any grouse that were feeding.

The grouse-shooting season had not opened yet and J.M. Hawk and I were using the area for training our dogs. Hawk had a young dog that was flushing a good many grouse, so I slipped ahead up the timber road and got into position to watch the dog's handling of the grouse.

Three grouse were within an area of fifty feet or so and, as the dog burst upon the scene, they flushed wild and went over the ridge. The dog had made a fairly quiet approach and I could not really fault anything the dog had done. It seemed that these grouse were flushing wild without any particular reason.

The next evening it was my turn to work my dog into the birds. I often used a bell to keep track of my dog in thick cover and there was a bell on the dog this evening. Hawk did not use a bell. I wanted to see the reaction of my dog to these wild birds and asked Hawk to bring my dog in after I had gotten into position.

There were only two birds that evening. Pretty soon, I heard the approach of the dog's bell and the grouse scurried around and found hiding places well before the dog came into the clearing. The dog scented one of the birds and pointed it. The grouse held well and we went in and flushed the birds.

Hawk chided me about my dog getting a lucky break in having an evening when the birds weren't wild. I wasn't so sure. I had seen the grouse raise their heads and listen to the sound of the approaching bell. It seemed almost as though they had hidden in preparation for the dog's arrival. With the unbelled dog, they had been startled by its sudden arrival and flushed. I suggested to Hawk that we put a bell on his dog and try it the next evening. He agreed, to shut me up.

The next evening, there again were three birds and they scurried around and found hiding places just as they had with my dog. We repeated the experiment — belled and unbelled — and concluded that the grouse hearing the bell in the distance tended to find hiding places and prepare for the dog. When there was no warning of the dog's approach, they were startled into flushing.

Left: Realizing he cannot escape from the rope, the dog begins to take an interest in the scented dummy and (above) picks it up.

Chapter 13

FINISHING THE POINTER

The Author Contends There Is No Reason For The Woods And Fields To Be Full Of Half-Trained Dogs!

FOR THE purposes of this chapter, let's assume that *pointer* refers to all of the pointing breeds. It is much simpler to use the word, *pointer* — which is the name of a particular breed, but still describes the field function of all the pointing breeds — rather than to specifically identify individual breeds each time we refer to a dog that points game.

The term, "finishing," means putting the final polish on a dog's training for that dog to meet the requirements of the owner. Different persons will have widely varying expectations of performance for the same breed. Our purpose is to describe some of the possibilities for the finished pointer and to demonstrate some methods that can be used to obtain the desired performance of the dogs under varying field conditions and requirements.

The so-called average shooting dog usually is expected to: Search available cover diligently to find the majority of game birds present in the area; spend the greater portion of search time in cover most likely to hold game; accept and obey hand, voice and whistle signals regarding the direction and distance of search.

This same dog is expected to establish point when game is located and hold that point until the hunter-handler comes up and flushes the game; remain steady to the flush of the game and subsequent shooting, if any; mark the fall of all game, if possible, and find and retrieve all game shot, when sent to retrieve.

Our hypothetical average dog must pursue and catch any crippled game, even though this requires considerable tracking and chasing; accept signals that will help in finding the downed game, and retrieve all recovered birds to hand without chewing or otherwise damaging the game. The dog should resume search for fresh game when sent on without pottering about the area of former kills after that game has been disposed of. The finished dog should return to the handler when called unless it is on point.

There is an old saying among bird dog men that a dog that can be called off point "ain't worth its salt." If a dog on point cannot be found by the handler within half an hour or so, it is normal for the dog to leave without flushing the birds.

From here on, reactions of individual dogs are as different as their natures. Perhaps the most common reaction is for the dog to return to the hunter and continue to hunt. Some other dogs will come to the handler and bark for the handler to follow them. Many dogs seemingly reason this out without training. The dog, having gotten the attention of the hunter, will return to the place where it left the game and attempt to reestablish the point. Most likely the birds will have moved, but it is quite likely that the dog will relocate them and put them to the gun. Still other dogs will remain on point for indefinite periods of time.

Assuming that the birds or birds would hold, an unlikely, but sometimes occurring situation, my dog, Kate, would not leave a woodcock point until dark, even if she had established this point in the midafternoon. I have found her after she had been missing for hours, lying down, but still holding her bird. On quail and pheasant, she would hold for an hour or so, then come hunting for me. Grouse, she would hold for somewhat longer periods. These traits are highly variable with individual dogs, but are an indication of what you should expect from your well-finished dog.

My own requirements for a canine hunting companion are somewhat different from those of the average gun dog owner. I like my dogs to flush the birds after I have gotten into shooting position and am ready. At this point, I give the command, "Get em!" and my dog will jump into the center of the covey or, in the case of a single, right onto the bird if possible. Such behavior is considered a cardinal sin by many dog men, they maintain that a dog allowed to flush birds will soon be flushing every bird it finds. To a large extent, they are right. It requires a great amount of hard training and control of the dog to be able to do this, but I consider the result worth the extra training.

By having the dog put up the game on my command, I am in a good shooting position, instead of being off balance or tangled in thick brush or weeds, while the birds fly away. Having a solid shooting stance and the chance to pick a position from which I can easily swing my gun barrels — plus knowing when the birds are going to flush instead of stumbling around, trying to kick them up — enables me to shoot much better. Any extra work I have to do to train the dogs to perform in this manner is repaid in extra shooting and in the satisfaction from watching my dogs perform as

It sometimes is difficult to find water near hunting cover. This pointer takes advantage of a water tank.

A hunter moves in on his solidly pointing shorthair. There is no need to hurry to get to this finished dog.

they should to enhance my pleasure in the hunt.

Such performance does require extra effort and training and I generally do not attempt to get this until the second year of gunning over a dog. The first requirement for a dog to flush on command, then hold to wing and shot is that the dog be completely trained to the "whoa" command. If a dog is absolutely obedient to "whoa," it is no great problem to have it flush the birds, then stop and hold position at the flush.

I accomplish this by having the dog stand in place about eight feet from a training dummy after it has been inspired by repetitious training to retrieve the dummy until it is anxious to retrieve any dummy lying in front of it. This is accomplished by putting the dog on "stay," then tossing the dummy eight or ten feet in front of it.

If the dog has been properly trained, tossing the dummy in front of it will create the desire to retrieve. This desire should prove intense in a good dog and should be intensified by the trainer getting down on hands and knees and seeming to derive great pleasure from playing with and tossing the dummy about in front of the dog. This will drive the dog almost wild with desire to get the dummy and it may break and grab the dummy. In this event, the trainer should place the dog back in the position from which it broke and let the dog know his displeasure in no uncertain terms.

With the dog at a peak of desire to retrieve, give the command, "Get 'em!" and let the dog pick up the dummy. As soon as the dog has the dummy, give the "whoa" command and make the dog freeze where it grabbed the dummy. Repeat this general sequence with variations until the dog will jump on any dummy lying near it on command.

Now we are ready for the flushing act on birds. Instead of a dummy, place a quail or whatever bird you use for training in the training area and allow the dog to come up on it and establish point. Make the dog hold the point for five minutes or so, then give the "get 'em" command. Hopefully, if you are lucky and have good rapport, the dog will jump in and try to catch the bird. Be ready to stop the dog with the whoa command, as it *must* not be allowed to chase the bird. If not certain you can make the dog stop on command, take the dog in to point the bird on a check line; if it does not halt on command, stop it by upsetting it when it hits the end of the check line.

It may be that the dog becomes so thoroughly conditioned to hold a point that it will not break point when told. This is a sign of strong pointing instinct and conditioning and is not an undesirable trait, merely inconvenient at this point of training.

What we have here is a confrontation between the dog's pointing instinct and training and a new circumstantial situation that has suddenly confronted the dog. The dog's reaction depends on instincts, training and its ability to adapt to a new situation. A dog that will not break point to flush upon command usually can be made to do so by allowing it to hold point until it starts to lose some of its intensity and starts to flag a bit. ("Flag" means that the dog starts to loosen up and to wag its tail a bit while on point. This usually is a sign that the birds have moved away from it.)

When the dog starts to flag, throw a dummy near the bird, but not so hard or near as to cause the bird to flush, then tell the dog to "get 'em." The dog should move in to pick up the dummy and thus cause the birds to flush.

Now comes a ticklish situation: The dog will probably expect to be reprimanded when the birds flush, as it has been conditioned to expect a reprimand when birds flush. The trick is to teach the dog that it is right to flush birds on command, but at no other time. It requires knowledge of the individual dog's psychology and working rapport as developed when the dog lives in the house with you. Having daily contact with you for long periods of time, it learns to read your moods and desires instinctively.

I don't say that, to have a dog accept the advanced training required to flush on command, you must keep the dog in the house. But it does help build the understanding between man and dog for such advanced training to be successful. If there is such contact between handler and dog, both come to trust each other fully.

Many good dogs simply cannot be trained to this degree without endless daily work, just as a few dogs accept advanced training with little extra effort on the part of the trainer. Like people, some dogs are smarter and easier to work with than others. This brings us back to learning early in the dog's training just how much it will accept and selling it as a plain gun dog if it won't measure up to your requirements.

The finished pointer also should follow hand and whistle signals readily and be under control at all times, adjusting its range to cover and visibility conditions. A dog learns this from the way you either send it on or call it back under varying conditions. Eventually, it should range instinctively to where you want it to run. Persistent training will teach the dog to turn in the direction you wish from whistle signals and you can augment this with the hand signals discussed earlier.

In retriever training, the dog should be taught to take a line toward game it did not see fall as will be explained in the chapter on training retrievers. It also should display good manners such as bringing retrieved game to hand in a proper manner. A well trained retriever should circle behind the handler and deliver the game gently into the hand rather than dashing straight up to the handler and dropping the bird on the ground or shoving a bloody bird against your leg. Most dogs require slight additional training to keep them handling and behaving properly, instead of the slapdash performance so many dog owners accept. To train a dog to deliver nicely to hand, it must be made to circle to the rear by telling it to "heel," as it approaches with the bird in its mouth. This should cause the dog to come up behind the handler on the left side. When it comes up in the correct manner, the handler should make the dog stand, holding the bird for a few seconds, then take the bird from the dog's mouth with the command, "Out" or "Give." Should the dog drop the bird on the ground before it has made proper delivery, make the dog pick up the bird again and carry it until it makes proper delivery. When it has been made to heel and bring the bird in to the left rear side of the handler numerous times, the dog will learn to make the proper approach when retrieving and it no longer will be necessary to give the heel command.

One reason we see so many dogs with only minimal training in the field today is that their owners, more interested in getting a limit of birds, allow the dog to get by with a sloppy performance rather than correcting it where and when poor performance occurs. Once a dog has been allowed to get by with poor performance, it can be depended upon to try to get by with such substandard tricks until thoroughly corrected.

What these handlers fail to realize is that an hour or so spent working with the dog would assure them of far more

These two pointers show good form even though one has been caught in an awkward position atop the log, when it points to honor the point of the other big pointer.

It can be difficult for one pointer to keep four hunters going, but this big pointer seems to have managed the problem with great aplomb. The take of pheasants is an indication of good training, stamina in a finished dog.

game than they will get with a misbehaving mutt. If time is spent in training and conditioning the dog during the training season, which generally precedes hunting, there should be little reason to take time out from hunting to obtain minimal gun dog performance.

Many gun dog owners fail in training their dogs to heel dependably. There are many situations where it is very convenient to call in your dog and have it remain at heel. A hunt may take us near farm buildings or along the edge of posted lands; in either situation, the best procedure is to have the dog at heel until the area of risk is safely behind. The gun dog should be trained so it can be put at heel with the reasonable expectance that it will stay there. This is accomplished by the methods for training a dog to remain at heel and occasionally putting the dog through the heeling procedure and routine. Many of us expect that, once a dog has been successfully trained to perform a given act, no further attention need be paid to that routine. This is not correct. To keep a dog performing well, it must be put through all of the actions it has been trained to carry out with regularity to keep it performing smartly.

When taking even the best trained dog into a situation where it is likely to be placed under severe stress it is best to use a leash. I prefer the Jaeger-style lead that goes around the shoulder of the handler and leaves both hands free to carry your gun, open gates, etc. When the dog is taken off the lead the end is snapped onto a keeper ring, thus the lead remains available for instant use.

Even the best trained dog can be enticed to break away from the heel position. My longtime hunting companion, Marv Hawk, demanded absolute obedience and never hunted with an unruly dog, unless it was a young pup being trained. Fully confident in his feisty little setter, Snap, Hawk had put the dog to heel while walking through the farmstead. They came upon an old hen with a brood of chicks and, filled with the courage, the hen ran up and flopped Snap with her wings. This was too much for the hapless dog and he promptly disposed of the hen and chicks. Suitable reparations were made for the deceased chicken family and that was the last time Marv Hawk went through a farmyard with a dog not on a lead.

I learned the same lesson under somewhat similar circumstances on a farm where I had hunting permission; not finding anyone at the house, I took my big slab-sided blue Belton Laverack setter, Old Doc, out of the cage and put him at heel to head for a field of ragweed that fairly shouted quail. I heard the sounds of axe and crosscut saw and soon came upon the whole family cutting firewood.

A yappy little fox terrier-type that gun dog people call "insects" was with them and it made a great fuss as I cautioned Doc to hold at heel. The insect dog, apparently mistaking Doc's discipline for cowardice, grabbed Doc by the hock. That did it!

Doc whirled, snarled, there was the sound of crunching bones and I was in a spot! There I stood, surrounded by a farmer, his wife, their three sons and two daughters with a very dead family dog. I can think of many situations in which I'd rather be. These were West Virginia hill folks who were not overfriendly with strangers. I had hunted their place once the previous fall with a friend who knew them well and had been invited to come back as much a matter of courtesy as anything else.

These proud people would accept no money for their dog, but the farmer having heard my friend speak of my black and tan hounds did allow that it would be nice to have a nice black and tan pup next spring. He got his pup, but I was never invited to hunt that place again.

The entire episode was my fault. I should have put my dog on the Jaeger lead at first sight of the little terrier.

A finished dog shows proper behavior in a vehicle. I believe strongly in keeping a dog where it cannot possibly interfere with the driver, either in a crate or behind a partition that separates the dog from the driver. The dog should be trained to jump into the vehicle and get into a dog box or wherever it is to be transported.

I use the command, "Kennel," when I want my dogs to enter a vehicle, cage or pen. After using this command repeatedly when putting the dog into a box or even when

Shorthair shows the result of good training in circling to rear of the gunner to make proper delivery approach.

you wish it to go into the house, it soon learns it should get into whatever entrance is in front of it when this command is given.

For those who insist on transporting their dogs in the vehicle sitting on the seat beside them, it is necessary that the dog be trained to sit still and not climb all over the vehicle. Let the dog know there is one place it may sit and that it must stay there until told to get out of the vehicle. If the dog moves to another position, it should be reprimanded and replaced in its spot assigned. The severity of the reprimand should increase until the dog learns to stay put.

There will be other things you will wish your finished pointer to do. Remember that much of dog training is simple repetition of the action you wish, until the dog does them as a natural reaction to the command. With common sense, you can train a dog to do most anything within reason.

A dog learns one lesson at a time, but you cannot allow it to forget the other things you have taught it while you work on a new action. Make a dog go through every one of its learned responses at every training session, if possible. Naturally, you cannot have the dog retrieve a dead duck from the river, unless you are at a river and have a dead duck, so set up your training routine in such a manner as to keep all your dogs' routines fresh and active.

The experienced dog trainer does not assume his dog is hunting just because it is out in the field and out of sight. In fact, the dog should not be out of sight long. The well trained dog maintains contact with the hunter-handler at all times. If a young dog disappears for a period of time, it may be hunting or it may be doing something else, so call the dog in to check on what it is doing.

While fishing one late fall on the Potomac River, I watched several deer come down to the water to drink as I sat in my boat offshore. The deer, suddenly frightened, hurried off into the woods. I watched a Brittany spaniel come down the hill, following the trail of the deer. The dog followed the deer out of my sight over the hill.

Later, I asked a friend to whom I thought the dog belonged if he had been hunting that area at the time I saw the dog following deer. He had been hunting that particular cover for woodcock, but had been unsuccessful as the dog kept disappearing for lengthy periods.

I had recognized the dog, because this owner had come to me for advice on how to break the deer chasing problem. We had used the shock collar treatment since the dog lived in the house and he didn't want to tie a smelly set of deer scent glands onto it while it was in the home. Apparently

Setter shows a good search pattern indicative of a finished dog, as it quarters back and forth in front of the hunters in search of game.

A well trained wirehair comes in from a long retrieve.

what happened was that the dog had simply stopped barking on deer trails and had been smart enough to keep its deer chasing at a distance from the hunter. This time the dog was put on a chain and smelly deer scent glands tied tight to its collar until it learned its lesson. To the best of our knowledge, it is now deer proof.

Insofar as the individual owner is concerned, when the dog meets the standards of performance set by that owner, it is a finsihed dog. This will not hold true should the dog be entered in certain invitational gun dog trials where a dog must meet what some trainers consider a ridiculously high standard of behavior. My own personal feeling is that too many of us are satisfied with minimal performances on the part of our shooting dogs. Many people feel that, if a dog will point and hold a bird for a few minutes, search cover in some sort of pattern, remain somewhere in the vicinity of the hunter and eventually come in when called, they have a great shooting dog.

Some owners of minimal performing dogs will say theirs cannot accept the training to become good finished dogs. Some dogs can accept more training than others, but almost any of them can become at least reasonably well trained shooting dogs if time is taken to train them to a better standard of performance. As an example, look at the awesome amount of training that a seeing eye dog must accept for daily performance of its duties and, keeping this in mind, think of the simple requirements for a reasonably well finished shooting dog.

To enumerate these requirements, the shooting dog should be willing to stop dependably on the "whoa" command, stay in a given place without undue fidgeting about when told to "stay," and work the area it is hunting in a good search pattern. It should turn in either direction or increase or decrease its range according to whistle, voice or hand signals, establish and hold a good solid point until the birds are put up by the handler or, in the case of running birds, hold position until told to relocate.

The finished dog can handle tricky running birds with reasonable intelligence, be steady to flush and shot, hold position until sent to retrieve and, when sent to retrieve, search in a diligent manner until the game is found or it becomes obvious there is no game. This dog must retrieve the game without chewing or hard mouthing, deliver the game to hand in a well mannered fashion, enter and leave a vehicle or kennel on command, remain reasonably still in a vehicle when told to stay, and walk at heel when ordered to do so without trying to edge away from the handler.

I consider these the minimal requirements for a shooting dog, but no more than two dogs out of ten that one encounters in the field today meet these requirements. This matter of poorly trained dogs frightens me. The average sportsman can be turned off by the ill-trained, misbehaving mutts he sees and will come to believe that all shooting dogs are like this. He may decide he does not wish to own a dog without ever having watched a good shooting dog at work.

Chapter 14

TRAINING THE RETRIEVER

Well-trained retrievers lie quietly as their owners wait for cars to be unloaded from pheasant hunters' ferry. (Photo courtesy Ontario Department of Lakes & Forests)

New Thoughts And New Signals Are Needed For This Canine Pursuit

Baron Gunn starts off on a long retrieve in the land retrieve test.

SO HERE you are with a fine new retriever pup you have been saving to buy. He's just 7 weeks old and you want to teach him a few things. Well, contrary to what some retriever trainers say, you can go start training the pup in the fundamental yard breaking program just as outlined for pointing breeds. There is no reason to wait until the pup is a year old. While retrievers seem to do a bit better if started more slowly than the pointing breeds, you should start teaching him the first fundamentals of good behavior. Commands such as "whoa," "sit," "stay," "come," "no," and "down" may be taught in the same manner as with the other breeds discussed.

Retrievers are slower to develop than the pointing breeds, which is all the more reason to work on yard breaking as early as possible so you can proceed to the actual retriever training. It is important not to be too harsh with these dogs so as not to destroy their natural desire to retrieve anything thrown out in front of them. It is especially important with the retrieving breeds that you do nothing to destroy the natural desire to please you and that you do everything possible to intensify that bred-in desire to retrieve. These desires are important, for when the dog is way out on the other side of a partly frozen marsh or the far side of a river and you have no boat, there is little you can do to enforce your order to "fetch" or "get back," the commands commonly used. It makes little difference which terms are used so long as you use the same words consistently. When the dog is way out there, you are depending solely on its desire to retrieve which should have been reinforced by training.

With retrievers, there is a more abrupt delineation between yard breaking and serious field training. When you shift from the yard breaking phase, you should make it very plain to the dog that now is business time and you will brook no fooling around. Start by standing in front of the dog when you throw the dummy to prevent the dog from chasing after it before it is commanded to retrieve.

If you plan to run the dog in organized field trials, start using the dog's name as the command to fetch. In other words, throw out the dummy and make the dog wait until you are ready for it to retrieve the dummy, then call the dog's name as the command to retrieve the dummy. Never name a retriever Jack, as it sounds too much like the command, "Back."

There are a few tools that are important in training a retriever. The first and most important need is a suitable pond, lake, creek or river. We can do a lot of the training in the early stages in our yard, but for the advanced stages, a fairly large body of water is necessary. For many, finding suitable water can be a problem, but don't make the mistake of training your retriever only on a small pond or, when the dog is confronted later by a sizeable mass of water, it may be frightened by it. You need a body of water at least a hundred yards long and seventy-five yards wide. The river in front of my house is about a half-mile wide and this is none too big.

There are problems with large bodies of water that you

must consider. On most large rivers, there are motor boats with sadistic drivers who would enjoy running over the dog and chopping it up with the prop. Another problem is that if the retriever crosses a river to emerge on the far side, you have a possibility of the dog being stolen by someone who knows he can be long gone before you can get across the river. To handle the problem of the motor boaters, I take along a high-powered rifle. When one of them heads for my dog, I pick up the rifle and the sight of an armed man discourages them.

Needed for retriever training are various kinds of choke collar, short and long leads, a good whistle and the various training dummies. Sometimes a dog will start to play with or chew on a dummy. Most retriever trainers cry, "Ah, Ah, Ah!" to discourage retrievers from such undesirable actions. This command is used where pointing dog people would say, "No!" There are many other commands used by retriever people that are different from those used in pointer work. Another of these commands is "Leave it." This is used when the dog picks up something it should not. Retrievers should be force trained to hold onto dummies or birds they are retrieving. The command used for this is "Fetch." Place the dummy in the dog's mouth and, while making the dog hold onto the dummy, give the command, "Fetch!" Make this a part of the daily lesson routine.

There are many ways of introducing the young dog to water. My own method is to get the dog excited and anxious to retrieve the dummy, then throw it into the edge of the shallow part of the water. As the dog becomes accustomed to going into the water, I increase the distance from shore until the dog is in swimming depth. Since retrievers swim naturally, they often make the transition to swimming so easily they never seem to notice it. Some dogs can be a bit difficult to get into the water and for these, I will go

Above, Baron Gunn is returning with the duck, after finding it in distant woods. Below, he circles around owner Andy Lehner and deposits duck in his hand for another perfect score.

swimming and try to coax the dog to come to me. If this does not work after several tries, I won't spend much more time. A retriever without a basic love of water is pretty worthless, unless you intend to use it only on upland game. In this case, the dog should never be bred as we do not need retrievers that won't go in the water.

Once the retriever is working well in the water, it is time to get him started with feathered game. Place a freshly killed duck in his mouth, using the fetch command to make him hold it. Stay beside him to ensure he doesn't chew or damage the bird. A proper start should assure that this dog will not become hard mouthed.

After the dog has held the bird for a while, walk about fifty yards, then call the dog to you using the fetch command at the same time to make sure it brings the duck. Do this at least eight times before ending this training session. Always keep training sessions short as to prevent them from becoming tedious for the dog and causing loss of interest, but later the same day, throw the duck out and have the dog retrieve it from land several times until the dog seems to be familiar with retrieving the duck the same as it has the dummy.

The next day, take the dog, with both the dummy and the duck, to the water where you work the dog. Throw the dummy out for the dog to retrieve several times, then throw the duck out into the water and send the dog to retrieve it. The dog should make the retrieve routinely, as if it were the dummy. If it does so, make a big fuss with a lot of pats and "good dog" encouragement.

Have the dog retrieve the duck several more times from the water and try to get the idea across that this is what the dog is meant to do.

Training a retriever to respond to hand signals is a bit different than training for pointing breeds. For one thing, it is necessary that the retriever respond more accurately when given a line to follow to find game it has not marked down. The retriever must depend on you for directions to find the area where the game fell so it can use its nose after reaching the proper vicinity. I use multiple whistle blasts to indicate the direction of turn, but this is not used generally in retriever trials. Instead, most trainers use multiple whistle blasts to hurry the retriever in once it has picked up the dummy or game. Generally, one whistle blast is used to get the attention of the dog, then the direction of movement is given by movement of the hand and arm as discussed in field handling of pointing breeds.

I have found it more satisfactory to put the retriever on the sit-stay command, then stand in front of the dog and throw the dummy to either the right or left. I use the right hand to throw to the right, my left hand to throw to the left. I blow one loud blast on the whistle and call the dog's name to send it to retrieve the dummy. Several such training

Andy Lehner fires in water retrieve test as "Lehner's Baron Gunn" awaits the command to fetch, which will send him after the downed duck. Note the alert stance!

Baron Gunn takes off into the water as he's sent to retrieve the duck.

sessions should have the dog turning to either side to retrieve the dummy, depending upon which arm you used to throw the dummy.

The next step is to hide the dummy when the dog is not watching. It is best to approach the place you intend to hide the dummy from the side so you can be sure the dog will not follow your tracks to the dummy. The dummy should be about thirty yards from the dog for these first tries.

Take the dog to the position from which you wish him to make the retrieves, then back off from the dog about fifty yards. Blow a blast on your whistle and call the dog's name to send it to retrieve, while you make a throwing motion with your arm on the side toward which the dummy has been placed. It should appear to the dog that you have thrown the dummy toward that side and the dog should move off and search in the proper direction. I keep the dummies scented with artificial duck scent, as this helps the dog find them and offers encouragement during those first few blind retrieves. As the dog becomes proficient in such retrieves, increase the distance of the dummy from the dog until the dog is working comfortably out to a hundred yards or more.

After the dog has mastered the right and left turns, repeat the same sequence, using an overhead throw with the dummy and the command, "Get back!" to send the dog to retrieve in a direction away from you. To clarify the position of the dog, yourself and the direction of retrieve, think of a clock face with the dog at the pivot position of the hands and yourself at six o'clock. This would put twelve o'clock directly in front of you and behind the dog. Right would be at three o'clock and left would be at nine o'clock.

When the dog is working well to all the signals, start mixing them up by placing the dummy at say 4:30. Signal the dog to make a right line, then as the dog starts to pass the dummy, stop him with a "Whoa!" Then, facing the dog directly, wave your hand to the right, thus directing him to turn in the direction which will bring him directly to the dummy.

If you have done your work correctly, the dog will soon learn that following your hand signals will bring it to the dummy or downed game. At this point you have a dog that should be a good hunting retriever.

Put the dog through most all of the trained responses such as sit, come, heel, whoa and stay periodically so it does not get rusty on these learned responses while you are concentrating on the hand direction signals. There is a tendency on the part of trainers to neglect those parts of a dog's training that it seems to have mastered, spending all of the time on teaching new accomplishments.

The next thing a hunting retriever needs to learn is working from a blind. In a shore blind, the dog generally sits in front of a hole through which it can mark the fall of game or, in some instances, the dog may sit beside the blind. Sitting beside the blind or the hunter has a disadvantage in that the dog can see only to one side and cannot mark game that falls where the dog's view is obstructed. This results in many more blind retrieves than would be necessary if the dog has a field of view from which it can mark the fall of game in all directions.

Perhaps I should verify that we are using the word, blind, for two meanings. In one context, a blind is a structure intended to hide the gunner and his dog. A blind retrieve is one in which the dog did not see the game fall and is dependent upon the gunner to direct it.

When possible, the dog should be directly in front of the hunter near his feet. In this position, the dog is behind the muzzle blast, yet in a position from which it can mark the fall of game in all directions. Some offshore blinds are built on stakes or pilings that have been driven into the bottom and the blind can be anywhere from five to twenty five feet above the water at low tide. Such heights can cause some difficulty in getting a dog in and out of the blind to make a retrieve. The most common entrance is a dogplank fashioned from two or more planks with small slats nailed crosswise every foot or so in order to give the dog traction. In the northern latitudes such as Maine or Canada, this is a pretty long and heavy plank and some arrangement must be made to raise and lower it with the rise and fall of the tide and to keep it out of rough water during storms or high seas.

The lower end should run at least a foot beneath the surface and have the edges rounded so the dog will not be hurt by sharp edges when it swims onto the plank. The plank should be at least twenty inches wide, although I have seen them that were no more than six. Such a narrow plank is dangerous to the dog The dog should be stationed directly in front of a hole leading to the plank and from which it has good visibility for marking the fall of game.

In training the dog to use such a setup, it is easiest to

Baron Gunn has a hot chase when the duck displays sharp reluctance to playing the game!

If you were wondering about Baron Gunn, he got his duck and is returning with it here!

build a land blind with a hole in the center large enough for the dog to pass through easily. One can toss the dummy through the hole and immediately order the dog to retrieve the dummy. With the dog passing through the hole and returning through it with the dummy, the dog becomes accustomed to using such entrances.

When you go into an offshore blind for the first time with a young dog, lead the dog carefully through the hole, as well as down and up the plank several times, to allow the dog to get the feel of the plank and learn to use it. An old dog that has been in many different blinds generally understands the use of such entranceways, but still should be shown through it once.

The shooting retriever also must learn to deal with crippled birds. A large duck or a goose can give a dog quite a fight in the water if not too badly wounded. The elbow of a goose's wing can deliver a hard blow and a small retriever has its work laid out in retrieving a big goose with a broken wing or other minor wound.

It does not take a giant Canada goose to make a young retriever game shy. A young dog coming suddenly into contact with a pugnacious old drake or gander may be overwhelmed by the spunky bird's attack. The best way to handle this problem is to work the dog with small birds such as pigeons first to allow the retriever time to gain experience in handling live game before sending it in on a full grown and pugnacious duck or goose.

Get the dog used to working around and through decoys without becoming entangled in the anchor ropes. Should he try to retrieve the decoys, come down on him with the "leave it" command in a positive, no-nonsense tone.

Your retriever will travel often in small boats, so get him used to the idea; he should be trained to lie down and remain still in the boat. A dog must enter and leave a small boat over the stern or bow. If the dog goes over the side of a small duck boat, he could upset the boat.

Many of us use canoes for hunting waterfowl on small lakes and marshes. To get a large heavy retriever in and out of a canoe, use a sixteen-inch ramp made of three eighths-inch plywood with thin strips of wood nailed crosswise about six inches apart. I fasten this ramp to the front seat thwart on each side of the canoe. Suspended from an eyebolt at the bow, it will enable your dog to climb into and out of the canoe. Do not let the dog jump into the water from a canoe as there is too great a chance of upsetting. Make the dog enter and leave over the bow ramp by training it to do so in warm weather, when you can get into the water to help.

The dog can be trained to make multiple retrieves in the event more than one bird is killed on the same fly-over. If the dog sees all of the birds fall, there is a likelihood it will retrieve one bird and go for the others without any instruction other than being sent back to retrieve. In the event the dog did not see the other bird or birds fall, it can be sent for them, if you have done your job right in training it to make blind retrieves. You can direct the dog to the area where the birds fell just as you directed blind retrieves in the training yard and water, using hand signals.

Circling to deliver his duck by the book, the "Black Baron" got perfect scores from the judges.

It sometimes is necessary for a dog to chase down wounded game in various types of cover and water situations. A lightly wounded duck in a soft-bottom marsh is a real challenge and I have watched a dog try to catch a duck for as long as an hour in such places.

Conditions vary with different types of hunting. I have seen retrievers work many different kinds of terrain from the salt marshes of Maine and New Jersey to the mud bars of Chesapeake Bay; from the seashore breakers of Bodie Island on the Outer Banks to blinds on sandbars several miles offshore in Pamlico Sound, and from the sandbar blind on the Potomac in my own front yard. Each of these places requires a different behavior and approach from the dog. When working offshore bars and the ocean surf, be watchful that the dog does not get carried out to sea or dashed onto the beach by heavy waves; they can literally smash the strongest dogs. In Southern marshes, there is an ever-present danger of snakebite and you must be vigilant for the first signs that the dog has been bitten. In rivers, make sure the retriever will not be swept away by swift waters or rapids. In cold weather, have some sort of heavy cover to throw over light-coated dogs. Heavy-coated dogs such as the Chessie and lab can make out on their own regardless of the temperature.

A back Lab and his handler at Winchester's Nilo Farms hunting preserve.

Brittany spaniels can make excellent water retrievers if the water is not too cold.

Chapter 15

TRAINING THE VERSATILE DOG

Here, the judges are putting down a clip-winged pheasant.

TRAINING A dog to work in the manner of the European gun dog is somewhat demanding of both the trainer and the dog, but the results are worth the added effort. A dog that has been trained to meet the standards set up for versatility or multipurpose is far more useful in the hunting field than one that has been trained by the far less demanding methods commonly in use throughout the United States prior to introduction of these methods.

Thanks to the efforts of Sigbot "Bodo" Winterhelt, Dr. Edward D. Bailey, John Kegel, George Adolph, Rudy Lorra and a few others, the European methods of training to produce a dog of greater utility are available to anyone who wishes to take the time and effort to use them.

While these methods of training were not exactly top secret prior to their introduction in North America, they certainly were not widely known and were used only by a few European trainers. The results produced are so far superior to the product of other training methods that they have given rise to the Superdog myths discussed in Chapter 6.

Most of the training methods outlined in these pages are based upon these European methods to which I was in-

Off he goes: That bird is in a hurry!

This Old World System Can Make Your Dog A Better Hunter And A Hard Working Companion

The handler puts the pup down in the natural ability tracking test.

After being released, the pup in the photo on previous page blasts off on the trail of the fleeing pheasant.

troduced by Winterhelt and Dr. Bailey during a demonstration in 1970. Although I had been training and writing about dogs most all of my life, I immediately recognized the superiority of these methods and adapted them to my own training methods for all breeds of shooting dogs.

There is a common misconception that these methods are only for use in training versatile dogs, especially those dogs intended to be run in NAVHDA trials. On the contrary, such training is useful for any shooting dog.

The methods described for training the pointing breeds are primarily versatile dog training methods, as are those for training the retriever; certain modifications have been made, however, to meet the standards set forth in retriever trials. It is not difficult to continue the training of your young dog as a versatile dog by extension of the yard breaking and field handling methods described in earlier chapters.

The most important of all the training steps is the training the dog to "Whoa." All other training is dependent on this single step. If your pup won't halt on command, there is no point going further in its training until it will do so. My method of training pointing and retrieving breeds is based upon a solid training to stop on command.

An innovation introduced by Winterhelt is the training table. Basically a table strong enough to support any shooting dog, it is about eight feet long by two feet wide and two feet high. A ramp at either end allows the dog to walk up and down, when coming onto and leaving the table. Most NAVHDA members and many others use such tables for training their dogs. Recently, there has been a move away from the table by some trainers and some never adopted this training aid.

The table accomplishes two main objectives. First, the dog is out of its element when it is up on the table, thus it is more amenable to training than when on the ground where it feels more secure. Second, the table allows the trainer to work with the dog on an eye-to-eye level without having to stoop to a position that can quickly become tiresome.

All of the yard breaking commands are started on the table and progress from there to the ground in the versatile training method. These training procedures are detailed in the yard breaking chapter.

The dog is first made to whoa on the table, then the training proceeds to the ground. Concurrently, the dog is trained to hold a training dummy in its mouth, using the methods previously detailed. When the dog halts dependably at close range on the ground and carries a light dummy for lengthy periods of time without dropping it, we can proceed to the more advanced work of putting the dog through these steps on a long lead. When the dog works dependably on the leash, we can proceed to working the animal without a leash at increasing distances. This continues until we have the dog stopping on command and carrying the dummy at distances of a hundred yards or more.

When the dog has learned to obey well at these greater distances, we are ready to increase the time periods. You should be able to put your dog on whoa or sit-and-stay, then leave it unattended for periods of increasing length until the dog will sit where ordered for half an hour or more. This is accomplished by gradually moving farther and farther away, until one is giving the command to stay from thirty yards away from the dog. One then should move out of the dog's sight for gradually increasing periods of time.

In the final stages of this training phase, I put the dog on the stay command in the yard, then go into the house for half an hour to read, type or carry out whatever project is under way. At the end of this time, I return to the dog. Finding it in the same position in which it was left, I praise it extensively. In the event the dog has moved, it is "bad dog" and back to the kennel to be followed by a shorter session the following day. Since I usually raise and keep my personal shooting dogs in the house, it becomes punishment for them to be banished to the kennel.

In the event a dog misbehaves, it is put into the kennel for several hours while I will bring one of the other dogs out of the house and romp with it in the yard, making much over it, then taking it into the house by calling it noisily. It is surprising how well and how fast a dog will shape up under these circumstances. I do not take this action until I am certain the dog knows it has misbehaved in moving from the spot where it was put on "stay."

Having brought the dog to the point that I can depend on it to remain on the spot where it was halted and told to stay for lengthy periods, I then start making it hold light training dummies for up to ten minutes. I do not like to make a dog hold a dummy for longer periods as it prevents a dog from panting, the only method it has of cooling its body heat; there is no point in causing the dog unnecessary distress. When the dog is handling light training dummies for ten minutes or so, introduce heavier dummies for shorter periods of time. Do not make a dog hold a heavy dummy too long. If you will try holding a proportionately heavy weight

Triumphant after turning in a perfect performance, the pup leaps in front of handler after delivering bird.

steady for long periods yourself, you will see why.

Satisfied with this progress, begin throwing the dummies out for short distances, making the dog wait for a time before being sent to retrieve it. The weight of the dummy should be increased as the dog becomes more proficient.

The next step is to start throwing the dummy into the water as outlined in a previous chapter, sending the dog to retrieve it. Make the dog wait for the signal to retrieve the dummy before it is allowed to go into the water and be sure the dog does not fidget about on the shore while waiting to be sent in on the retrieve. This can prevent no end of problems in making the dog wait quietly by the blind in later stages of training. It is much easier to prevent a dog from starting a bad habit than it is to break it of one that has been allowed to become established. At the risk of sounding like a broken record, it is totally important to make the dog remain steady beside the water until sent in to retrieve, as it will later be required to remain beside the blind while you are out of sight, shooting.

It will prove difficult to make some dogs hold the dummy for an extended period of time. Some have an inherent bias against holding anything in their mouths for any reason. This difficulty occurs in dogs from even the best-bred litters, without regard to the retrieving desire. I recall one dog in particular that was an excellent and eager retriever of game, but from puppyhood it had an aversion to training dummies. The owner tried many different types and it seemed to make no difference to this Brittany; a training dummy was still a training dummy. The eventual solution was to use pigeons in place of dummies, but the dog still displayed dislike for carrying anything in its mouth. Usually, however, the versatile breeds demonstrate willingness to pick up almost anything that they are asked to carry.

Getting back to basics, the dummy should be placed on the training table or the ground in front of the dog and the dog trained to pick up the dummy on the command, "Fetch." This usually is not difficult, but in the event the dog does not pick up the dummy willingly, force the dummy on the dog when it is made to open its mouth by pressing the lips against the teeth. When the dummy is placed in the dog's mouth in such fashion, the command, "Fetch," is voiced

The judge is putting down a duck for waterfowl portion of the utility trial.

Judges examine dog for any signs of physical defects or shortcomings.

and the dog made to hold the dummy until the command, "Out," is given.

If the dog persists in dropping the dummy, a strap can be fastened beneath the dog's chin to hold the dummy in place behind the lower canine teeth; in such manner, the dog cannot get the dummy out of its mouth.

Regardless of the method used, the dog must be made to hold the dummy until released by your command and it also must pick up the dummy from the table or ground on the fetch command. The point at which you switch from the dog taking the dummy from your hand to having it pick up the dummy from the ground is the moment in which you can encounter difficulty.

I've found that the easiest way to accomplish this is to toss the dummy shorter and shorter distances in front of the dog and have it retrieve the dummy. Soon you will be simply dropping the dummy in front of the dog and telling it to fetch. At this point, the dog simply picks up the dummy and hands it to you. It is just a short step to laying the dummy on the ground and telling the dog to fetch. Again, the dog should pick it up and place it in your hand.

Some trainers have difficulty in getting dogs to pick up the dummy. Perhaps I've been lucky, but this has been no problem for me. It may have to do with my method of starting the puppy out in retrieving by throwing the dummy out on land for it to retrieve as a sort of game in the dog's early training. The pup becomes accustomed to picking up the dummy and does so without problems. The method described for getting the pup to pick up the dummy and hand it to me — along with the rope and pulley method of force breaking — has produced sure-fire retrievers for me.

Some trainers recommend that the dummy not be thrown, but should be hand-carried to the point from which the dog is to retrieve it. And there are times that the dummy must be hidden so that the dog must hunt for it, as outlined in the chapter on training retrievers.

After the dog has mastered the retrieve completely, move on to the tracking training. This has many useful applications in a shooting dog as well as helping in two of the tests a versatile dog is required to pass. In testing natural ability, a dog is required to track a live bird, usually a pheasant that has had some wing feathers removed so it

NAVHDA members awaiting news of the judges' decision at the ability testing event.

cannot fly. The dog is put down on the track where there are a few feathers which have been removed from the bird. The long leash is allowed to slip gradually through the handler's hands, as the dog picks up the track and moves off. A thirty-foot flat leash can be slipped around the dog's collar and allowed to pay out by sliding under the collar until the end is reached. Be sure the dog is really on the line before allowing the dog to slip off the leash. The natural-ability dog is not required to retrieve the pheasant, but it certainly does no harm to its score, if it does. The primary test, however, is for the young dog to show it can and will follow the track of the bird.

In the utility trial, the dog is put down by the same long leash method on the drag track of a dead bird or game animal and is required to follow the track to the end — usually at least two hundred yards — and return with the game. The dog is judged on how well it followed the track and its carry of the game, as well as manners displayed on delivery to hand. In training, I drag a dead game bird and hide it around the training area, then have the dog retrieve the game by tracking. Familiarize the dog thoroughly with this drag tracking techniques, as we are likely to take the dog's ability to track for granted and lose points in a trial on this test.

Another test for which the versatile dog must be trained is the search for a duck. Abilities learned for this test are highly beneficial to any dog used as a waterfowl retriever. For this training, one needs a marshy area bordering a pond, as well as a live domestic duck.

First show the duck to the dog, then take the duck to a point near the bank of the pond; the more marshy this area, the better. Remove the primary flight feathers from one wing — as well some of the soft feathers from the belly. Put the softer feathers on the ground, then the duck itself should be rubbed gently on the ground to ensure there is plenty of scent at this spot. When released, the duck should

The winners! These dogs qualified in the natural ability trial. Wood's wife Ivy holds Fritz, second from right.

head for the water; if it does not, herd it into the pond and chase it out of sight. During all this, the dog should be positioned so it cannot see the duck being released.

Bring in the dog and put down at the point where the duck was released as indicated by the feathers on the ground. Keep the dog on the leash, until it has picked up the duck's trail, then release it. In tests, the dog is not required to retrieve the duck, but it must show that it can follow the trail through the brush and reeds and into the water. Many well trained dogs do retrieve the duck after a chase and this usually insures a top score.

The dog should be taught to point and remain steady to the flush, using the methods outlined in Chapter 12. Search pattern training should follow the methods found in Chapter 13. Most dogs will instinctively honor another's point, but in the event your dog does not, it should be trained to do so by bringing it in behind a dog on point and ordering it to "Whoa."

The versatile dog is trained to obey the command, "down," by instantly dropping and lying still, regardless of the circumstances. This command should be learned during yard breaking. It is accomplished by giving the command, then pressing down on the dog's neck and shoulders, while pulling its legs forward and out from beneath it, while repeating the command in a firm voice.

If the dog tries to rise, it should be pushed down with increasing firmness, until it decides it is easier to remain where it was "downed." When the dog tries to get up after having been commanded "down," it should be whacked with a switch. It is a good idea to have the dog on the leash should it decide to run away during this training phase.

The same methods used to train the dog to "stay" are applicable to the "down" command and it may be necessary to resort to a shock collar when the dog is at a distance. I have had good results, however, by making eye contact with the dog and pointing at the place where I wish it to lie down. One long blast on the burr end of the whistle is the signal for down and this should always be accompanied by the verbal command for down, while waving the hand from side to side over your head. This command is useful to keep from spooking incoming game and to hide the dog when hunting furred or big game.

The versatile dog should flush on command and the methods outlined in Chapter 13 I've found satisfactory. If your dog is doing all of the above, you have a finished versatile dog ready to run in a utility trial and I suggest you do so. Those interested in versatile dogs can join the NAVHDA organization by sending $20 to Bruno Bortolin, 15 Krafty Court, Hamilton, Ontario, Canada L9C 6R7. I also recommend the NAVHDA training book *Training and Care of the Versatile Hunting Dog* by Sigbot Winterhelt and Edward D. Bailey. All funds from the sale of this book go to NAVHDA, the authors having donated proceeds to the club. Price of the book is $6.

If you join NAVHDA, ask for the location of the nearest chapter and contact them. Chapters all have training sessions at which experienced dog trainers can give you hands-on help with your dog. The organization conducts several training clinics each year at which you can work your dog under the eyes of expert trainers.

The only cost would be for quail which are sold for use in training. With lectures and demonstrations by master trainers and judges, the program is meant to help train member's dogs.

Chapter 16

A MATTER OF PHILOSOPHY

Choose The Training Method That Fits Your Own Personality And That Of Your Dog

There are nearly as many kinds of dogs as there are kinds of people and that only includes the hunting types of dogs. Training methods must be tailored to the individual dog, as well as to the type of hunting for which used.

THERE ARE as many training philosophies as there are dog trainers, but these approaches seem to fall into general types, so we need discuss only the general schools of thought in training a shooting dog to fulfill our needs.

One thing to remember is that different individuals have differing needs and requirements where their hunting dogs are concerned. The man who is going to hunt rabbits in the mountains where there are snowshoe rabbits or varying hares, as they are more properly known, needs a bigger, faster and stronger running hound than the fellow who is going out in the meadow to shoot cottontails. The man who is hunting the mountains may try a good beagle and decide that beagles are worthless, while the fellow hunting in the meadows may be ready to swear by the beagle. The fellow in the mountains needs a Walker or one of the other larger hound breeds, while the cottontail hunter can do nicely with his beagles unless he happens to come across one of those old mountain rabbits. For those who hunt both the mountains and the meadows, the basset hound may be the answer, if it is trained properly.

That leads us to three different ideas regarding the ideal dog for the job. We might overhear an argument between the beagle and basset man in which the latter insists the dog should be trained to run the rabbits as fast as they can cover the ground, while the beagle fancier feels the fast running dog chases all of the rabbits into holes by charging them too hard.

Coon hunters have been arguing over silent trailers and open trailing dogs for a long time, but there doesn't seem to be any solution in sight; preference comes down to whether the coons are being hunted for sport or profit. There's little doubt that the silent dog will get more coons, since it usually comes upon them suddenly and pushes them up the nearest tree without any warning; the open trailer gives them plenty of warning and time to find a den, but the sounds offer more pleasure to the hunters, as they listen to the dog run.

German longhaired pointer is a breed rarely seen in U.S.

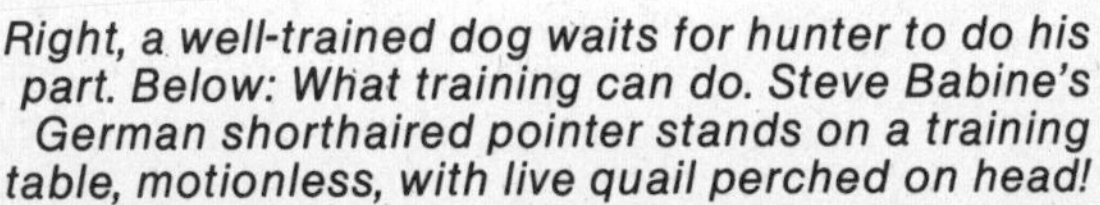

Right, a well-trained dog waits for hunter to do his part. Below: What training can do. Steve Babine's German shorthaired pointer stands on a training table, motionless, with live quail perched on head!

Applying bird scent to pigeons for use in training class.

Desire to hunt and bird sense combine to make up the "birdiness" of a dog. They are developed to a high degree to intensify the pointing instincts.

Gunners are selected for safety-consciousness and for shooting skills. Dog at rear is being led away, while the other dog in the brace will retrieve the shot bird.

But the big battles are in training methods for shooting dogs. There was a time when the only game in town was the JASA method. Those initials stand for J.A. Sanchez Antunano, a popular trainer who authored a widely used book on bird dog training. He advocated no training until the dog was at least a year old. Then came a crash course of intense education that was imposed on the hapless dog with use of heavy spike collars and force training of all sorts. It seemed as if Antunano's aim was to leave the dog in shock and dazed to the point that it went along with the training through lack of any other course.

This method got results to a point, but I feel that it also destroyed many excellent dogs that were a bit spunky or on the sensitive side.

There is another method wherein the dog is not trained until it is a year old, then is trained only by coaxing it to do what the trainer wants, rewarding it when it does so. My own observation has been that this method produces a lot of highly unpredictable dogs that can't be depended upon to do anything, unless they happen to want to perform at the time.

Then there is a method in which the dog is not started until it is a year or more old, training based upon trying to get the dog to do what is wanted by a combination of coaxing and force breaking. This method leaves a lot to be desired, as such dogs are too old to accept this sort of training completely.

Some trainers advocate an early beginning at ten weeks or so, using only a force-breaking routine. This method turns out some pretty good dogs too, but I feel that it ruins a lot of the best ones.

The method I use and favor is to start a pup at the earliest possible age and make most of the training into a romp with the dog, getting it to do what I wish, because it wishes to please me. After I have the dog pretty well trained, I reinforce the training with mild force breaking which allows me to end up with a dependable dog that is not afraid of me and which can still be depended upon to turn in a good showing when we are afield for game birds.

By keeping the dog in the home and having daily contact with it, I develop a rapport that creates mutual understanding and enables me to get the dog to perform well. Not everyone will wish to use this method and other systems may work better for others. This method suits me, though, and produces the results I want.

There are many other training methods, but most are combinations of one or more of the methods outlined, with personal additions by individual trainers.

General quality of this rig shows owner's deep interest.

Bird dogs are run in braces on fifty feet of check line, starting on whistle.

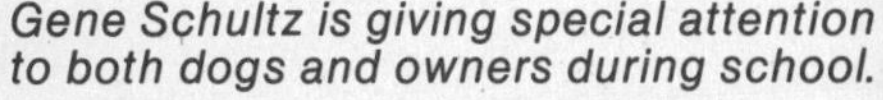

Gene Schultz is giving special attention to both dogs and owners during school.

Chapter 17

WHEN TO CALL THE VET

Some Illnesses You Can Treat Yourself, Others Require Attention Of An Expert. Knowing The Difference Is Wisdom

THERE ARE plenty of minor health problems that can be treated by the individual dog owner and a great deal of this should be done simply as a matter of maintenance. Worming, for example, should be done on a regular basis and there are a number of preparations that do the job well and don't necessarily need to be administered by a veterinarian.

I know a number of hound men who run dogs on wild boar, mountain lion and bear who carry first aid kits with them and should a dog be cut or mauled, the dog men can suture such injuries on the spot. If the cut is serious enough, the dog undoubtedly is taken to a vet, when the owner can get it to civilization, but the emergency repair work has been done.

The wisdom, of course, is in knowing when you should forget the home remedies and get your dog to the vet for treatment.

CANINE PARVOVIRUS

Perhaps the most wide-spread problem of the current age is a relatively new disease designated as *canine parovirus.* Most dog owners are familiar with it, but I've found that few really are aware of what causes it or the effects, unless they've had dogs affected by this disease.

Canine parvovirus — usually initialled as CPV — reached what amounted to epidemic proportions in 1978. It has been brought under control, but that doesn't mean it has been eradicated.

CPV is caused by a tiny virus that is similar to that which causes a disease in cats known as *feline panleukopenia.* Scientists differ in their opinions as to how the disease got started in this country; however, the dominant theory leans toward the idea that this is a mutation of some other closely related virus.

As nearly as these scientists have been able to determine, the highly contagious virus is transmitted by the fecal matter of infected dogs. It has been discovered that as many as one billion particles of infectious virus can be found in only one gram of fecal matter from an infected dog. Complicating the problem is the fact that the virus is airborne, thus it can spread with startling rapidity.

Once the virus is inhaled by a dog, the disease quickly causes an infection in the lymph tissue of the pharynx. From there, it tends to travel through the entire blood stream, affecting other tissues and organs in its passage.

It has been found that the incubation period for canine parvovirus ranges from two to twenty-one days, depending primarily upon the age and health of the infected dog. The virus tends to multiply quickly in growing tissue, making puppies the more likely victims. However, dogs that have weak immune systems or those that are in poor health also tend to be highly susceptible.

Veterinarians reports that usual symptoms of CPV are poor appetite, a high fever of short duration, dehydration, vomiting, watery or bloody diarrhea and generally listless behavior. Bloody diarrhea usually occurs in the last stages of this disease and inevitably is accompanied by a foul odor.

Vets report that treatment of CPV can require what is termed as "massive support" and usually requires hospitalization of the infected dog. This, of course, can be expensive and the results of the treatment are never guaranteed. Some dogs appear to recover fully in a short time, but this is not usually the case. There also have been numerous instances of seemingly recovered dogs dying of heart failure shortly after being released from treatment.

The answer, vets say, is prevention, which is both easy and relatively inexpensive. A vaccination program may differ from one veterinarian to another, but most suggest

These Southern deer hunters who use hounds save injury or death for their dogs by painting names on their bodies. This prevents the dogs from being shot as stray deer chasers and thus avoids gun shot treatment by veterinarians.

that adult dogs should be vaccinated every six months for the optimum in protection. The vaccination of puppies should begin when they are eight weeks of age, if their mother is current in her own vaccination program. During those initial two weeks of life, the puppies rely upon the bitch's milk for temporary immunity.

After the initial vaccinations at the eight-week mark, some vets recommend that the treatment be repeated at two-week intervals up to sixteen weeks. At the end of that four months, a booster shot also is recommended by many vets.

In instances where there is no record of the mother being vaccinated against CPV, it is recommended that the puppies receive their first shots at six weeks of age, continuing on the two-week schedule through the sixteenth week.

If this sounds like a lot of visits to the vet and a resultingly high bill, take heart. It's not quite that bad. At present, there are several CPV vaccines which are available at pet stores on an across-the-counter basis. Most of these preventive kits include a syringe for giving the shots and the sales clerk should be able to instruct one on how the shots should be administered.

For those who have owned dogs over a period of time, the following piece of advice is gilding the proverbial lily, but it needs repeating for those with less experience:

It is important that the dog owner maintain a record of his dog's various shots. First, if there is no shot record, there is no proof of vaccination. Secondly, if you do not maintain a record, it becomes a bit difficult to remember when the next shot may be due. This, incidentally, involves other shots than those for canine parvovirus.

Should you purchase a dog from a kennel or even a private party, you should ask for copies of the dog's shot records, then make an effort to keep them up to date. If the dog you want to purchase has no shot record, it would be a good idea to have a vet do a health check on the animal before you put down a lot of money and gamble on its future.

Equally important as preventive measures against CPV are isolation and disinfection. When you are hunting with others who may have dogs, it is a bit ridiculous to say you should keep your dog away from them, if they are not vaccinated, but an effort should be made to keep your own canine away from the fecal matter of those that might not

Beagles or any other type of hound that is used to hunt deer should be in excellent health for such endeavors.

be properly immunized. Again, inhalation of the fecal product of an infected dog is the most common type of transmission.

Some veterinarians contend that fleas and flies may also be contributing factors in spreading the CPV virus. They say that fleas from a dog that is infected can transmit the disease directly to another dog's blood stream.

Vets recommend that, should you have a dog die of CPV, you should wait no less than three months before you bring another dog — vaccinated or not — into the environs inhabited by the old dog. One should disinfect these surroundings with a solution of bleach and this should even be used to treat the deceased dog's leash, collar, bedding, food and water bowls and anything else that can be cleaned. A better move is to destroy all of the old dog equipment and start over anew. Incidentally, this applies to all infectious diseases.

One also needs to eliminate fleas before bringing a new dog into these environs. Since one pair of fleas can produce six million offspring every three weeks, this can become something of a monumental task. In fact, total eradication is virtually impossible, but you can get rid of the vast majority with preparations now available at pet stores and in super markets.

A further effort involves the use of anti-flea shampoos and dips and the use of flea collars. One also should wash and spray the dog's bedding and surrounding areas periodically. Flea sprays or aerosol bombs should be used, then there should be a follow-up in two weeks to kill the fleas that have hatched from eggs.

Sprays and dusts can be used to kill fleas and their eggs in areas around your kennel as well. Be sure, however, that the commercial preparations you use are of the proper strength. Those concocted for adult dogs may be too strong to use around puppies, so read the labels carefully and be sure to use them in the manner prescribed by the manufacturer's directions.

Oddly, certain plants tend to deter fleas. In the West, for example, the leaves of the eucalyptus tree often are placed under the blanket or pad in a dog's bed. If you aren't in an area where this particular type of tree grows, try cedar shavings. They work in much the same manner. A castile soap with a eucalyptus oil base can be used to bathe your dog and to wash its bedding for good results.

Bobcat hunting with dogs is a tough business; it won't hurt to have your dog checked by a vet before the season.

A dog's coat can tell the experienced handler much about its condition and health. If it's rough, dog may have problem.

Other serious health problems can result from an infestation of this tiny parasite. There are many known cases of dogs dying of anemia due to severe flea infestation. I can't imagine a man who is a serious dog owner allowing this to happen, but it does.

According to vets, fleas cause a severe loss of blood and iron as they prey upon the dog — or any other small animal. Because of this loss of iron, the blood is not replaced rapidly enough and there also results a loss of protein in the dog's circulatory system. Such a loss of circulating blood serum protein allows the lungs to fill with fluid; this can lead to respiratory failure. Vets suggest that, in addition to ridding the animal of fleas, the dog so affected should be fed either raw ground beef or raw liver as a diet supplement until he recovers his weight and energy.

Fleas, incidentally, also can cause dry skin, loss of fur, hot spots, infections and sores, allergies and even tape worms. If you suspect any of these, it's best to consult a vet.

As for flies, these can land on infected feces and thus spread CPV, often carrying the infectious virus to a dog's food. Keeping fecal matter cleaned up and the area hosed down is one way of defending against this possibility. The dog's food and water bowls should be disinfected periodically by using one part of ordinary household bleach to ten parts of water; allow the bowls to soak for a time before rinsing them well.

DISTEMPER

For many centuries distemper was the greatest killer of dogs and I have lost favorite dogs to this dread disease. Every few years, a wave of distemper seemed to pass through the country; taking with it many of our best dogs.

Early canine distemper vaccines were unreliable for one reason or another. Some veterinarians claimed this type of distemper vaccine was permanent, while others recommended annual vaccinations. I can remember losing an entire litter of pups out of my field champion beagle. I had followed the recommendations of the vet to the letter. His instructions were to rely on the bitch's immunization until the pups were six weeks old, then bring them in for their shots. Only a few days after receiving the shots, the puppies started showing nasal discharges, one of the first symptoms of canine distemper. Soon the other symptoms — watering eyes, weakness, loss of appetite, bloody feces and diarrhea — followed and all six pups were dead within a week. Once a dog contracts distemper, the disease is almost always fatal. Recovery is less than one out of twenty with surviving dogs having severe after-effects such as loss of nose.

The canine distemper vaccines of today are much more reliable than those of twenty years ago, but still not completely so. Usually, distemper vaccine is given annually in combination with vaccines for two other dog diseases; canine hepatitis, and leptospirosis. These combined shots are known as DHL (distemper, hepatitis, leptospirosis). Any good dog owner will have his dogs given DHL shots each year. The usual fee in my part of the country is $10 for the DHL shot. This, along with the parvovirus shot, can be given in one visit to your vet.

HEARTWORM

The other major danger to our dogs (against which we can protect them by medication) is heartworm. The heartworm is a small worm that lives in the blood vessels of the dog and tends to concentrate in the heart-lung area.

Heartworm is spread by mosquitos. A mosquito will carry heartworm from an infected animal to a healthy one just as is the case with malaria in man. The danger from heartworms is that they can gather in the heart and interfere with or even stop the action of the heart valves, usually with fatal result.

Medications are available to prevent heartworms, but they should never be used without first having a vet check a blood sample to determine whether the dog already is infested. Should an infested dog be given heartworm medication, the worms will be killed, their bodies moving to the area of the heart to cause blockage of the circulatory system and death.

Pups such as these — or any other hunting breed — should receive proper inoculations at an early age. Such a precaution can stave off many later problems.

Rabies has been a dread disease for centuries and can still be found among dogs, cats and wild animals over the globe.

After determining that your dog is free from heartworm, a daily dose of an approved medication will prevent heartworms. There are several such medications on the market. I use *Filarbits* which is convenient in that it is made in pill form and is administered as dog candies. Dogs like them and they gobble them up without any fuss. Filarbits can be purchased from your vet at modest cost.

Formerly, heartworm was confined to the southern section of the United States. But within the last fifteen years — primarily due to the greater movement of dogs from one part of the country to another through field trials, traveling owners, et cetera, — heartworm now is found in all of our lower forty-eight states and much of southern Canada. There is great concern among biologists that a heartworm-infested dog will get into Canada's northern mosquito-infested areas and bring heartworm infestation to the wolves which have no resistance to this parasite and might easily be wiped out completely.

RABIES

Rabies is a disease that seemingly has existed for almost as long as man has had dogs. That may be a fact of life, but another fact that dog owners find frightening is the report from the Center for Disease Control in Atlanta, Georgia, that states that the incidence of rabies has increased dramatically over the last three years. Previously, the center reports, the incidence of rabies had been declining over a twenty-year period. The current increase brings incidence of the disease to levels experienced in 1954. While rabies has increased in all species, cats have shown the largest increase, with incidence up nearly two hundred percent in the last four years. However, it should be pointed out that all warm-blooded animals — including man — are susceptible to rabies infection.

The usually fatal disorder is described as an acute disease of the central nervous system that is caused by a virus; in this country, it has been propagated largely in domestic dogs as well as wild carnivorous animals such as the coyote, the fox, the skunk and even the seemingly friendly raccoon. The disease also has been known to be carried by bats in some environments in this country.

The peoples of such ancient civilizations as Rome, Egypt and Greece tended to credit rabies to evil spirits, since the disease turned normally docile animals into vicious creatures that ultimately died of paralysis. Ancient records show that Aristotle recognized rabies in man as being caused by the bite of a dog. He recommended cauterization of bites by rabid dogs but there is no record to show that his remedy was particularly effective.

As early as 1804, European scientists had determined that rabies — or hydrophobia, as it was sometimes termed in man — was transmitted from an affected dog to a normal dog. As a result, measures were taken in Norway, Sweden and Denmark to destroy all stray dogs and to quarantine those that had owners. By 1826, these countries were said to be free of rabies but it was a temporary respite. As the disease again showed itself, it was theorized that domestic dogs were infected by wild animals.

The rabies virus usually is present in the salivary glands of a rabid animal, thus the bite of an infected animal introduces the virus into a fresh wound. The virus then becomes established in the central nervous system, following nerve tissues from the wound to the brain. The disease usually takes from four to six weeks to appear, but the incubation period has been known to take as long as eight months. Thus, in the early stages a rabid animal may appear to be healthy and even friendly, yet will bite without provocation.

Rabies in dogs usually is classified as furious rabies or dumb rabies; determination depends upon the actions of the dog. In the furious type, the excitation phase is lengthy, while the latter variation tends to leave the canine paralyzed early in its infection. To add to the problem, sudden death without obvious signs of illness is not especially uncommon, according to veterinarians.

Dogs that incur the excited type of rabies usually die within three days, while there are many instances of dogs suffering from the paralytic variety recovering. While the ancients tended to equate rabies with periods of summer and called them "dog days," scientists contend that there is no seasonal incidence.

Most people are familiar with Louis Pasteur's treatment of rabies in humans and its effective though painful successes. In 1889, two European researchers developed a serum whereby animals could be immunized. However, control of rabies in dogs has been most effective through strict quarantine regulations except in those areas where the disease is known to be present in wild animal populations. For example, rabies has been kept out of Great Britain, Denmark, Norway, Sweden, Australia and Hawaii by lengthy quarantine of imported dogs. Hawaii has been particularly dedicated to this effort, since the islands hold large populations of the mongoose, which was imported from India many decades ago to depopulate rat infestations. It long has been feared that, should a rabid dog be introduced to the islands, the mongoose ultimately would become diseased. This naturally vicious creature then would create havoc among domestic animals and man!

In spite of these efforts, there have been dogs that developed rabies in these countries during quarantine. In Great Britian, one dog and possibly more developed the disease some eight months after being put into quarantine.

Scientists contend that the vaccination of dogs, combined with the collection and destruction of ownerless canines, will do much to reduce the incidence of rabies. Until recently, a single-dose vaccination with a Semple-type vaccine was used to immunize dogs. Most veterinarians recommended a yearly booster shot for dogs — and cats — with this type of vaccine.

More recently, Fort Dodge Laboratories of Fort Dodge, Iowa, has come up with a new and improved Trimune rabies vaccine that is claimed to provide three years of immunity for both dogs and cats. This is a killed-virus, murine origin vaccine that is available only to practicing veterinarians and must be administered by them.

"Safety of the improved vaccine has been demonstrated through the successful immunization of pregnant dogs," according to Dr. William E. Ryan of Fort Dodge Laboratories. "No untoward reactions were noted in the pregnant females or in their unborn puppies."

Trimune is available to your vet in ten-dose vials or in packages of twenty-five single-dose syringes. Dr. Ryan recommends that the vaccine be administered in both dogs and cats at three months of age "using aseptic techniques. Those animals vaccinated at less than three months of age should be revaccinated at one year of age. Repeat the dosage every three years or as required by local ordinance."

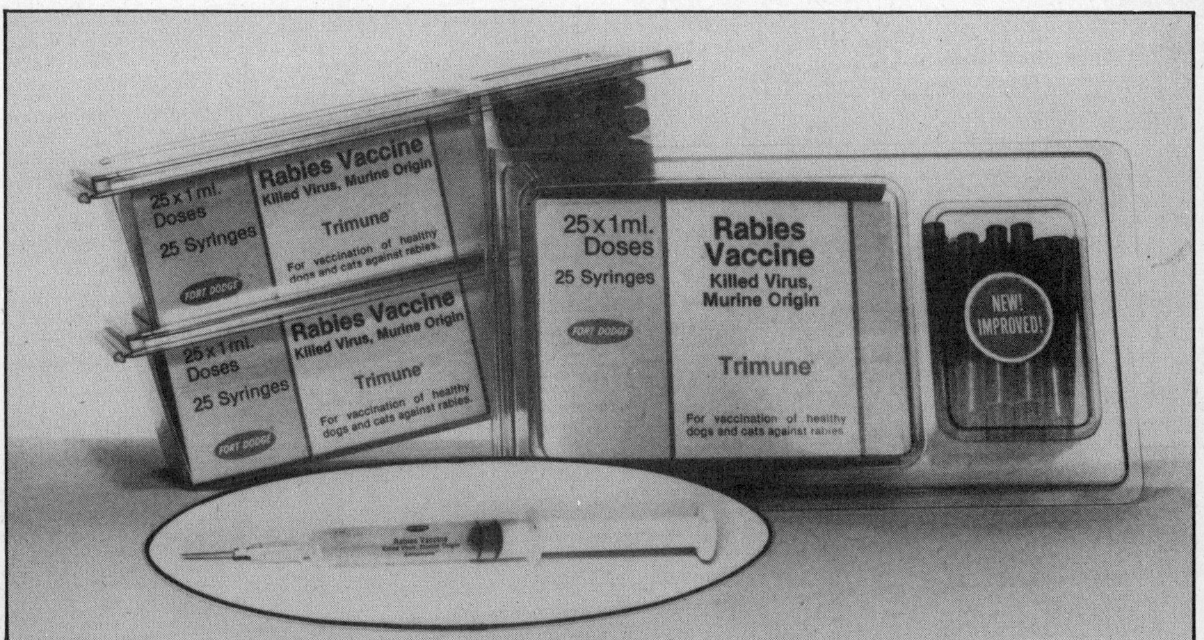

There are numerous brands of rabies vaccine available. Fort Dodge Laboratories supplies one of the best to vets.

NORTHERN COPPERHEAD SNAKE
(Agkistrodon contortrix mokeson)

BLACK-TAILED RATTLESNAKE (Northern)
(Crotalus molossus molossus)

SNAKE BITE

According to Knowles, Snyder, Glenn and Straight, authors of "Bites of Venomous Snakes," more than 100,000 animal deaths are attributed each year to snake bite world-wide. In the United States alone, it is estimated that 15,000 domestic animals are bitten each year. Surveys conducted by these and other veterinary scientists illustrate that a majority of these animals die unless treated properly. The principal victims are dogs, but fatalities also occur in horses and cattle, especially if they are bitten about the head or neck.

These statistics probably are believable for sporting dog owners, since every state in this country is inhabited by at least one species of poisonous snake and many areas have several species.

With the exception of the coral snake, virtually all of the poisonous snakes of this country are of the pit viper type. This group includes the cottonmouth moccasin, the highland moccasin, the copperhead and some thirty-two species of rattlesnakes.

"Pit vipers are characterized by a deep 'pit' located between the eye and nostril, and by their elliptical pupils in contrast to the round pupils of nonpoisonous snakes," according to Dr. William Ryan of Fort Dodge Laboratories. Members of the pit viper family invariably have two well-developed fangs that are connected to venom sacs situated on either side of the snake's jaw. "Rattlesnakes almost always have rattles on the ends of their tails, but rattles can be lost through trauma and one species — *Crotalus catalinensis* — found only on Isla Catalana off the coast of Baja California does not have rattles," Dr. Ryan verifies.

Of the various North American species, Ryan and other scientists tend to consider the bites of the large rattlesnakes and the cottonmouth moccasin as more dangerous than

DUSKY PYGMY RATTLESNAKE
(Sistrurus miliarius barbouri)

EASTERN MASSASAUGA RATTLESNAKE
(Sistrurus catenatus catenatus)

ARIZONA BLACK RATTLESNAKE
(Crotalus viridis cerberns)

SIDEWINDER OR HORNED RATTLESNAKE
(Crotalus cerastes cercobombus)

those of the copperhead and the so-called pygmy rattlesnakes.

"Few dogs or other small animals, left untreated, will survive the bite of a large eastern diamondback or the western diamondback," Ryan contends. "The pugnacious eastern diamondback, which may grow to a length of six feet, is probably the most dangerous snake in the United States."

Another highly poisonous snake found in limited geographic areas of the United States — primarily the deserts of the Southwest and, for some unexplained reason, Florida — is the coral snake. Being of the elapine group, the poison of this snake acts in a different way, affecting the central nervous system. However, the coral snake is sluggish and seldom aggressive, thus accounting for less than one percent of the bites inflicted on either humans or animals in this country.

In a Florida survey, a graduating increase in snakebite incidence was found to begin in March and reach a peak during August and September. This seasonal correlation seems to coincide with the habits of snakes since they usually hibernate during the cold months. However, in warmer climates, such as those of the South and the Southwest, snakebite does occur in every month of the year, according to reports from physicians and veterinarians.

Oddly, in at least one instance, a four-foot rattlesnake was found crawling across a snowdrift, when such creatures are supposed to be tucked away for their winter hibernation.

A group of outdoor writers, some thirty in number, had set up a makeshift range near Cimarron, New Mexico, several years ago so they could zero in their hunting rifles before going after mule deer. This was in December. They had fired several dozen shots, when one of them discovered the rattlesnake — sluggish and slow-moving —

EASTERN COTTONMOUTH OR WATER MOCCASIN
(Agkistrodon piscivorus piscivorus)

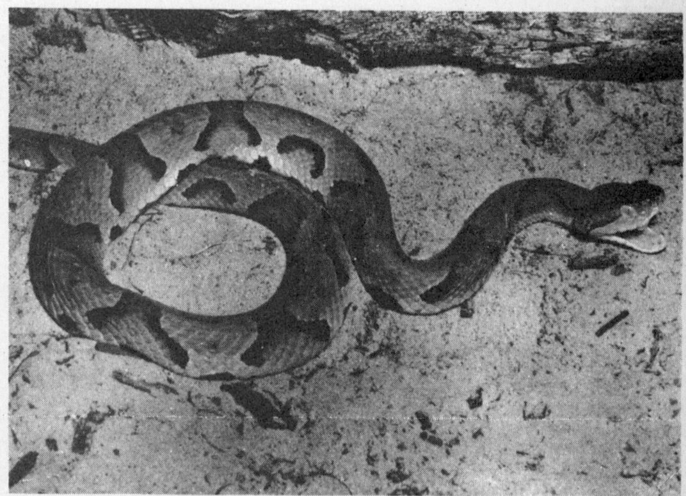

SOUTHERN COPPERHEAD SNAKE
(Agkistrodon contortrix contortrix)

CANEBRAKE RATTLESNAKE
(Crotalus horridus atricaudatus)

MOHAVE RATTLESNAKE
(Crotalus scutulatus scutulatus)

slithering across the snowdrift toward the shooters. It was theorized that the collective reverberations of the gunfire had aroused the western diamondback from his hibernations and brought him out to find out what all the noise was about.

Various factors determine the severity of the bite from a poisonous snake. Among these are the size and species of the snake; the age, weight and general condition of the animal that has been bitten; the location and nature of the bite, and the toxicity of the poison from the specific species of snake.

"Envenomation always is more serious in small animals, as the ratio of units of body weight is greater," Dr. Ryan states.

As for the manner in which the venom does its damage, snake venoms have been found to be comprised primarily of proteins; their toxicity, however, is attributed to proteolytic enzymes, phosphitdases and neurotoxins. The poisons also contain what are called "spreading factors" that include hyaluronidase.

It has been found that the proteolytic enzymes tend to destroy capillary vessels and local tissue, while the phosphatidases act upon the circulation and the heart, causing hemolysis, an action whereby the hemoglobin is separated from the red blood cells. With this, histamine is released into the body and the neurotoxins poison the nerve tissues. This can lead to motor or respiratory paralysis or both.

Scientific investigation shows that snake venom invariably is spread through the lymph system. Although the fangs of a large rattlesnake may measure as much as an inch in length, the venom usually is deposited in the tissues just under the skin, rarely penetrating as deep as the muscle areas.

The animal — or human — that has been bitten by a

GREEN ROCK RATTLESNAKE
(Crotalus lepidus klauber)

RED DIAMOND RATTLESNAKE
(Crotalus ruber ruber)

PRAIRIE RATTLESNAKE
(Crotalus viridus viridus)

TIMBER RATTLESNAKE (YELLOW)
(Crotalus horridus horridus)

poisonous snake may suffer from shock. This usually is caused by the loss of blood through the break-down of its components as outlined above and the liberation of histamine, which causes the dilatation and increased permeability of blood vessels. If sufficient venom has been deposited, there may be further problems with the heart, liver, brain, kidneys and even the intestines. The body's coagulation system can be altered to such a degree that bleeding is prolonged and coagulation becomes difficult. The wound resulting from snake bite can produce further complications, since it becomes an excellent medium for bacterial growth. Gangrene, infection and tissue slough can become serious problems.

In the case of dogs — and particularly hunting dogs — bites from poisonous snakes usually occur on the head, neck, shoulders or forelegs. The venom causes immediate heavy local pain, edema and discoloration around the fang wound. These particular symptoms, incidentally, are not evident in the case of nonpoisonous bites.

Experience has shown that an animal that has been bitten usually will exhibit excessive thirst and other accepted signs of shock. If the envenomation is severe, the dog may lapse into unconsciousness, with or without convulsions. The amount of swelling and other signs of the dog's system may vary from light to severe; this depends largely upon the amount and toxicity of the injected venom. Incidentally, one may expect one or two fang punctures, but as many as four sometimes may be found. This does not mean necessarily that the dog has been struck twice. Instead, it usually is an indication that the snake has been growing new fangs and that all four were operational.

For dogs that have been bitten by pit vipers, there are several first aid steps that should be taken according to Dr. Ryan.

WESTERN DIAMONDBACK RATTLESNAKE
(Crotalus atrox)

EASTERN DIAMONDBACK RATTLESNAKE
(Crotalus adamanteus)

Many dogs have developed a fear of snakes, but others are bitten because of curiosity.

1. Immobilize the dog as much as possible, avoiding excitement and exertion on its part.

2. If possible, kill the snake so positive identification can be made by your vet. It does not need to be said that one should not endanger his own being while making this effort.

3. If the bite is on the leg, apply a tourniquet. If loose enough that you can insert a finger under it easily, it can be left in place for as much as two hours.

4. Cleanse the skin area of the bite and incise the fang marks with a single straight cut through the skin. Do not make a cross incision. That technique may be good for old movies, but it doesn't help your cause.

5. Use mechanical suction to remove some of the venom. Chances are you won't get it all, so don't try to play hero by sucking the venom out with your mouth, unless you perhaps would like to find yourself comatose beside your dog.

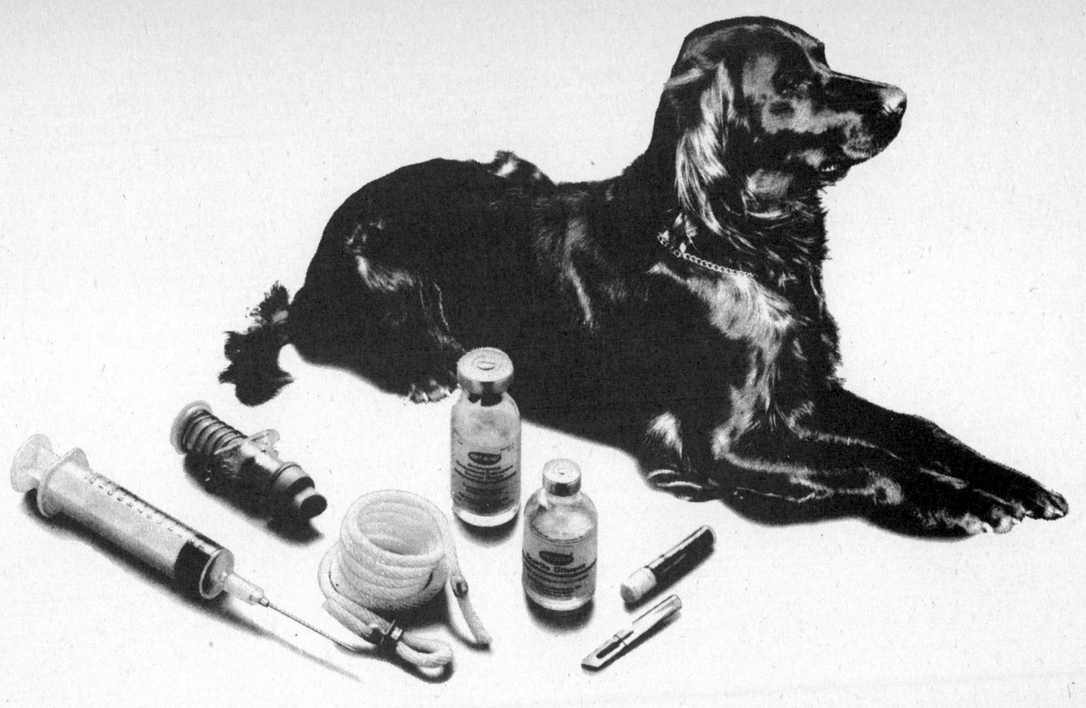

Fort Dodge Laboratories offers an anti-venom kit that can be obtained from veterinarians for use in the field.

6. Rest the dog's legs on a level with the heart; do not raise or lower them.

7. If your dog is not allergic, this is the time to administer an anti-venom serum such as Fort Dodge's Antivenin. Do not inject it around the snake bite, but administer it intramuscularly.

8. About all you can do after that is get your dog to a veterinarian or an animal hospital as soon as possible.

The Antivenin/Polyvalent marketed by Fort Dodge Laboratories can hardly be considered new, since it was licensed by the U.S. Department of Agriculture in 1976. The product is identical with the antivenom used to treat human snake bite victims. It is restricted to use by, or on order by, licensed veterinarians, but you usually can get your vet to give you enough that you can include it in your dog first aid kit. If you have to use it yourself on a dog bitten in the field, follow the directions to the letter.

Antivenin, incidentally, is processed from the serum of horses immunized with the venom of eastern and western diamondbacks, Central and South American rattlesnakes and the South American fer-de-lance. When injected intravenously, it tends to neutralize the venom present in the dog's bloodstream.

All you have read here, of course, has to do with what happens if your dog should be bitten by any member of the pit viper family.

Snakes tend to den up in specific areas and to stay pretty much in that area unless disturbed. Thus, to learn to avoid them, one first must learn where they might be. If you're planning on hunting your dog in an unfamiliar area, take

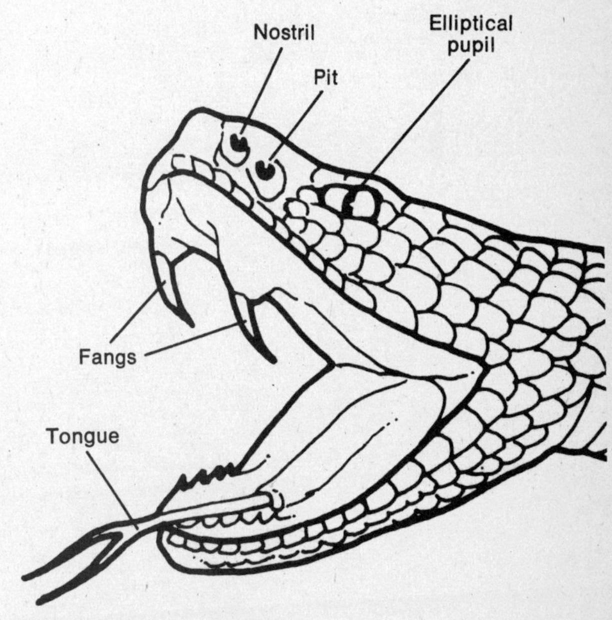

Most of the poisonous snakes found in this country are classed as pit vipers because of the visible pit found behind the reptile's nostril. Note identifications above.

time out to check with the locals. They usually know the areas to avoid. It's also a good idea to do some scouting on your own to determine the terrain and see firsthand what looks like rattlesnake habitat.

There also are some common sense approaches. For example, if there has been recent high water, rattlesnakes usually will tend to seek the higher ground surrounding swamps and flooded areas so don't let your dog get too close to the water. At the other extreme, in southern climes where they thrive, cottonmouth moccasins often crowd banks of creeks and streams during drought or low-water periods. If your dog ventures into such water to slake his thirst, he can find himself in serious trouble.

Dogs tend to be like people in many respects: some are naturally curious, others couldn't care less. Some will point a rattlesnake, while other dogs tend to give them a wide berth. But even curious dogs can be trained to stay away from snakes of all types with a bit of patience.

Some hunters and trainers use an electric collar to train their dogs against snakes. They usually start out by getting the dog close to a snake that is held in a cage. Then, when the dog shows curiosity and gets too close, it is shocked to show that this is something to be avoided, because it hurts! A few such shocks tend to make a believer out of most dogs.

Incidentally, there is at least one professional in the business of training dogs against snakes. This is Steve Starr of Starr Taxidermy at 5438 Schertz Road, San Antonio, Texas 78233. He has defanged rattlesnakes that he uses in electric collar training. The last I knew, he was getting $35 for enough sessions to teach your dog that a rattler is not a toy!

I have mentioned administering medicines both by injection and orally by the dog owner. There are many medications which the owner can use and it is well to know how to give them. Giving pills to a dog that does not want them can be a battle. There are certain things you can do to help win this battle.

When administering pills to a reluctant dog, the following procedure is effective: First, get behind the dog and

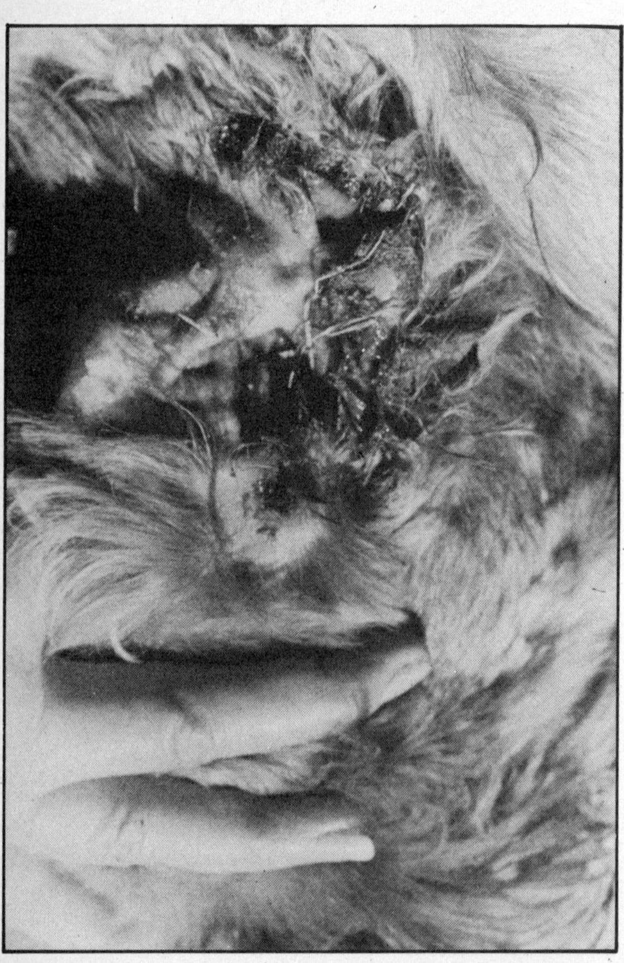

This dog's ear is badly infected. Note heavy discharge, grass and other foreign matter that have been imbedded. Such infections can be treated orally with medicines.

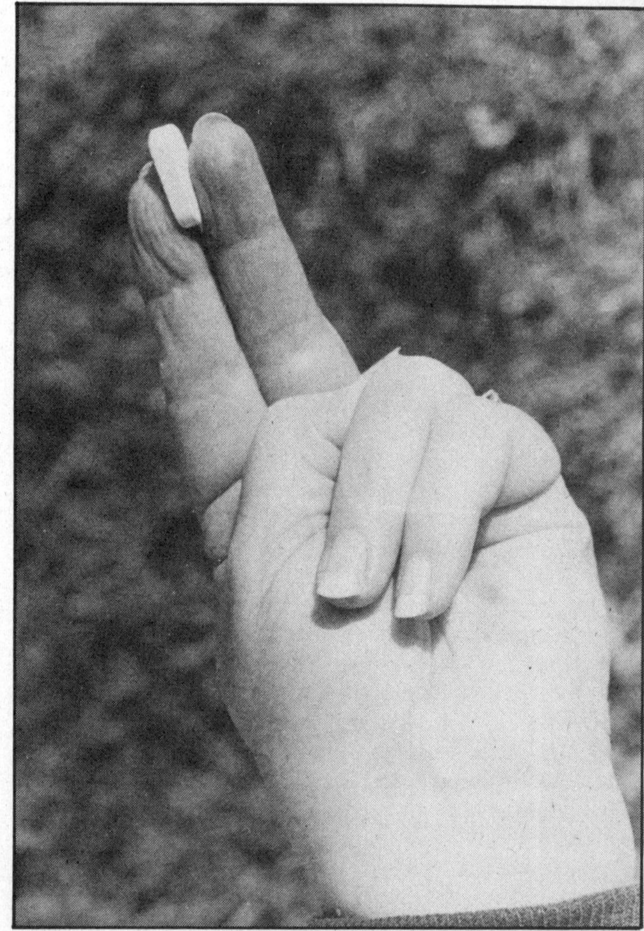

This photo illustrates the proper method for holding a pill that is to be inserted in the throat of any dog. It's easier than trying to use the thumb, forefinger.

make it sit. Squat behind the dog with one knee on each side of it, then grasp the dog by the muzzle and open its mouth. The mouth can be opened by pressing the lips against the side teeth with one hand over the top of the muzzle. In the other hand, you should have the pill between the tips of the index and forefinger.

When the dog's mouth is forced open, quickly insert the fingers with the pill deep into the dog's throat and, withdrawing the hand quickly, close the dog's mouth. Then, still holding the dog's mouth closed, stroke the throat gently. This will cause the dog to swallow. In inserting the hand with the pills into the dog's mouth, keep the thumb tucked into the bottom of the palm so it will not interfere with easy insertion of the pill. Do not try to hold the pill between the thumb and forefinger, as this will prevent the deep insertion of the pill and the bulk of the thumb will likely cause the dog to choke. Your knees on each side of the dog allows you to keep a firm hold on the dog so it cannot pull away from your hands on its muzzle.

There are three types of injections given with the needle. A subcutaneous injection is given by gently pinching the skin between the fingers in a convenient location such as the back or haunch, then inserting the needle into the place where you have raised the skin away from the muscle tissue and depressing the plunger. The needle should not be inserted into the muscle tissue, but between the skin and the muscle.

Intramuscular injections are given by inserting a needle into the muscle issue about half an inch on small dogs, deeper on larger dogs. The haunch is the preferred place for this type, but any fairly large section of muscle is acceptable. Never insert a needle into the abdomen, as it is possible to go through the thin wall of the abdomen and enter the intestine. This can lead to serious complications.

In an intravenous injection, the needle is inserted directly into a blood vessel, usually the vein at the "wrist" in the front leg. *I do not recommend the intravenous injection be done by the amatuer except in an emergency.* There are two reasons for this: First, any dog sick enough to need intra-

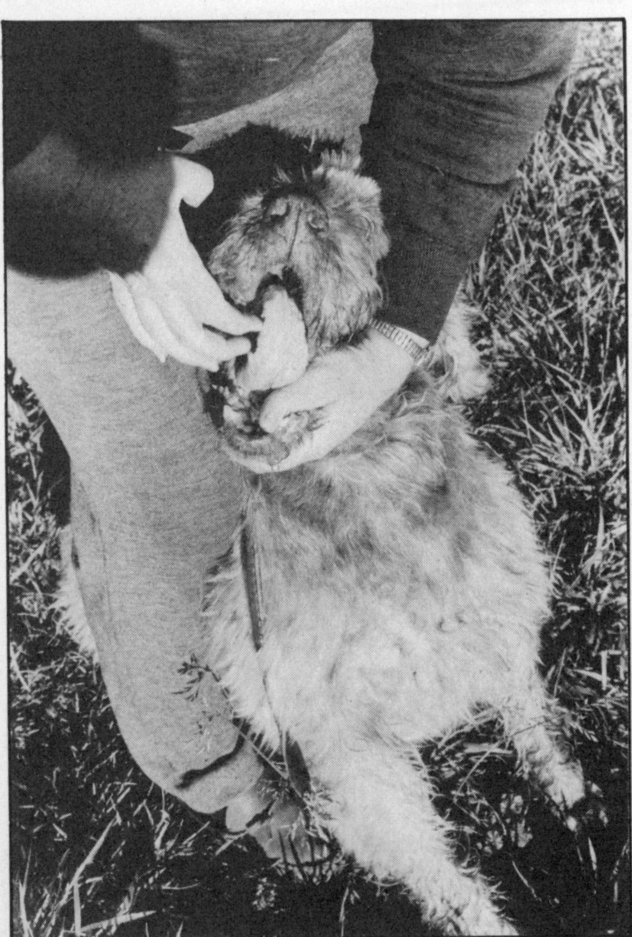

With dog's mouth open, lips are rolled over the lower teeth. This assures dog won't bite in struggle against medication. Note that dog is held firmly between legs.

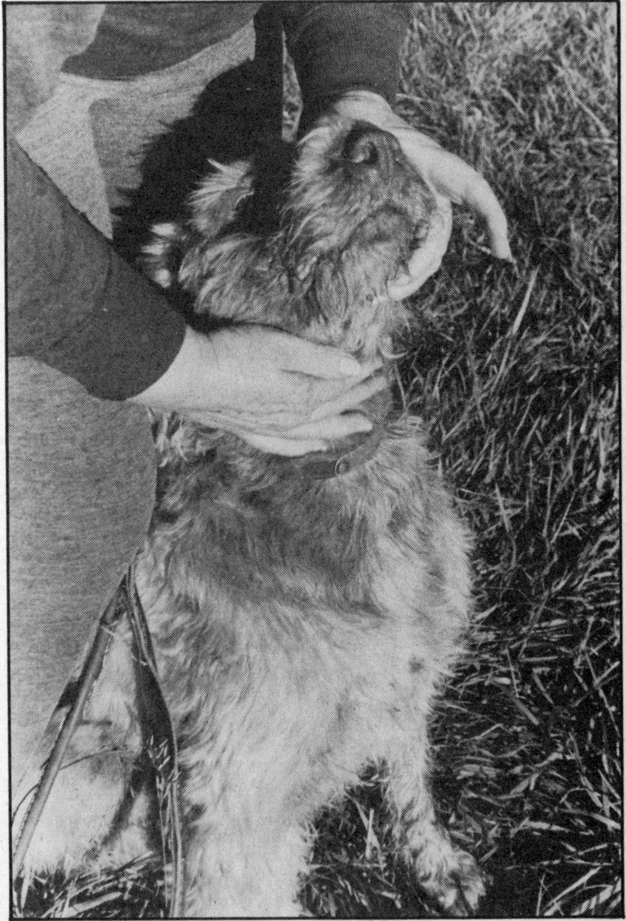

After administering capsules, hold the dog's mouth closed and stroke the throat. This causes the dog to swallow the medication which has been placed in throat.

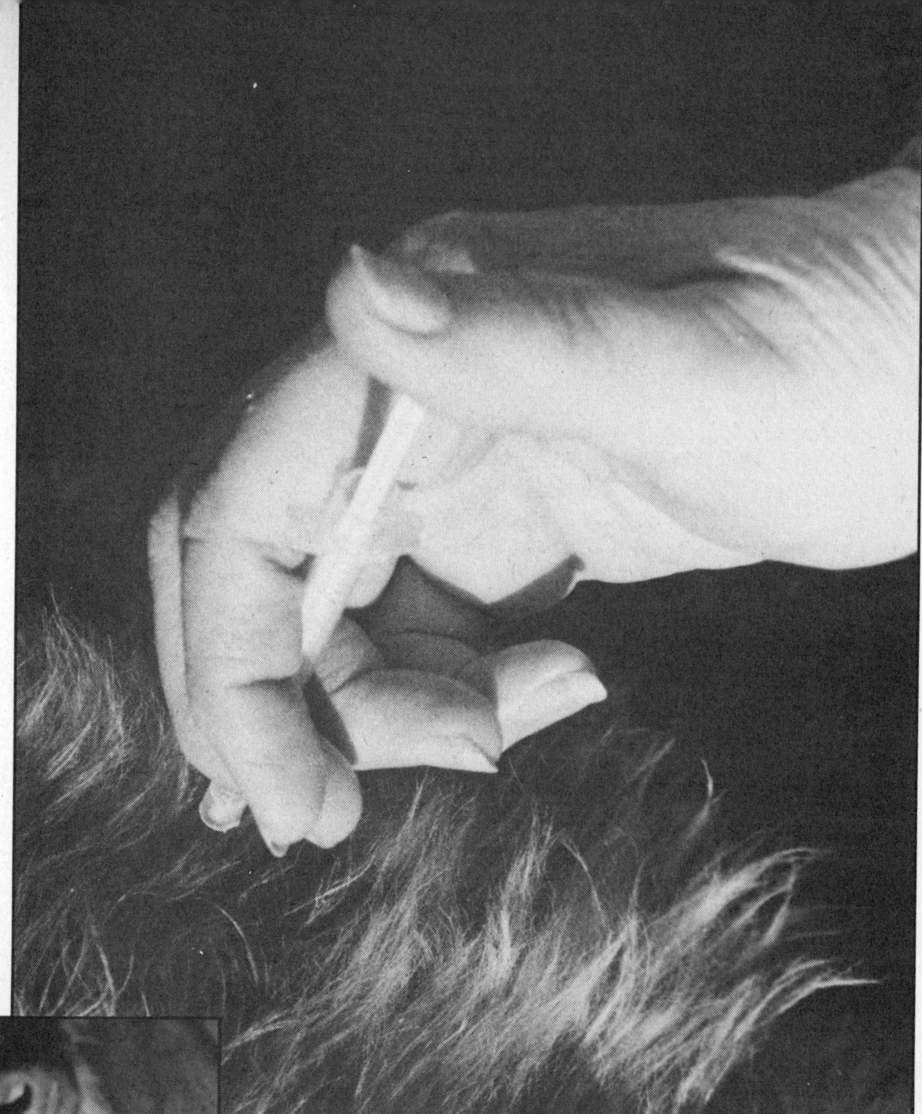

Below: The dog's mouth can be opened by pressing lips against the teeth. (Right) Injections should be intramuscular. This one is made into the backstrap.

venous injection is in need of a veterinarian. Secondly, the types of medication given intravenously are not the sort of stuff the layman should be administering, as improper dosage can kill your dog.

In using a syringe, it is important that all air be removed from the syringe and needle before making an injection. Any air injected into the body can cause trouble for many reasons. The most dangerous is that air can get into the bloodstream and cause a blockage of the heart or stop the flow of blood into a limb or vital organ.

Relative to the mechanics of the use of the syringe, I do not advocate the widespread use of such do-it-yourself and save-money kits. Next to you, your dog's best friend is his vet. A dog should be seen by a vet at least once a year. I usually manage to get all of the immunizations (parvovirus, DHL and rabies) done in one half-hour visit to the vet. In addition to the immunizations, he checks the general health of the dog and tells me of anything out of the ordinary that he finds. In addition, I generally take a feces sample along so he can check for worms and other parasites. I consider the thirty or so dollars this costs a good investment in my dog's health and thus in my pleasure in owning a dog I know to be healthy.

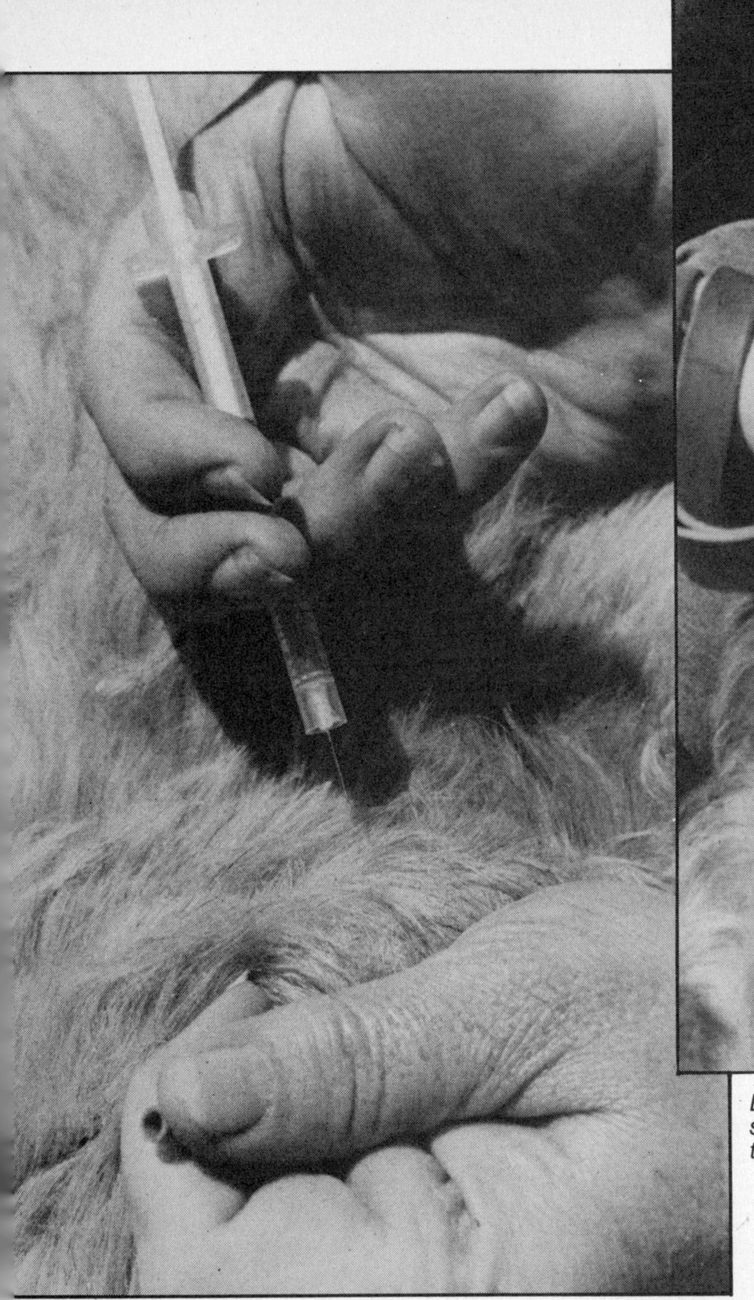

Both of these photos illustrate the proper approach to subcutaneous injection. Note that the skin is raised, the needle inserted beneath skin, not into the muscle.

If you are raising a litter of puppies, it might be justifiable to go the do-it-yourself route which will save some money. When you sell the pups, you should recommend that the new owner get the permanent shots from a vet and have the dog checked thoroughly.

These kits usually consist of a vial containing the vaccine with a rubber cap and the syringe. In filling the syringe, insert the needle through the rubber cap and into the vaccine. Draw the proper dosage into the syringe which will be marked in cubic centimeters. Holding the needle straight up so the air is on top, depress the plunger until a tiny drop of the vaccine appears at the end of the needle. This shows tha all of the air has been removed from the syringe and needle. Now insert the needle to give the injection as recommended by the instructions that come with the vaccine. These vaccination kits have expiration dates on them, so certain to check that date to determine that the kit is still within the recommended shelf life.

Unlike people, dogs do not fear the needle and usually do not even flinch when it enters. Be sure to follow the instructions which comes with the vaccine in all respects. The layman often does not understand, but there is usually a good reason for such instructions.

Dispose of used syringes properly by physically destroying them, putting the remains in a closed container and throwing the container into the garbage bag. Above all, do not let them lie around where children can get them.

When should you call a vet? When your dog is sick or injured, when it is time for the annual checkup and immunizations and when your dog *needs* to be seen by a vet.

German shepherds are among the breeds that are subject to dysplasia. A dog of advanced years cannot stand on its hind legs without suffering deep pain.

Chapter 18

A PROBLEM OF BREEDING

Science Is Searching Endlessly For Cures For Hip Dysplasia In Dogs, But The Real Problem Is Heredity

HIP DYSPLASIA in dogs has been a continuing problem that probably grew out of breeding programs wherein other traits were considered so desirable that this hereditary fault either was ignored or overlooked.

Canine hip dysplasia is essentially a condition in which the ball and socket is deformed at birth or fails to develop normally as the dog grows. In the worst cases, there is no socket in the hip and the ball on the end of the thigh bone is not set in a permanent position and, being held in place only by the muscles, oscillates freely. In such cases, the dog can stand only for short periods of time — until the muscles tire — if the condition is present in both hips. There may be wide variation in the hips on the same dog with one side being badly displastic, the other normal. In less severe cases, there is a poor fit between the ball and socket and this changes gradually as the dog grows, often resulting in pain and the slowly increased crippling of the dog.

According to Professor George Lust of the Cornell Research Laboratory for Disease of Dogs in Ithaca, New York, "The hereditary basis of the disease has been emphasized extensively. It is a developmental deformity, since abnormalities in hip joints have not been detected at birth, but appear later in the life of dogs at risk."

Studies at the Cornell University research lab have suggested a number of events that precipitate hip dysplasia in dog breeds or contribute to the severe nature of the disease. Other facets of the disease are under continuing investigation. For example, Cornell studies show that the disease is found usually in larger dogs. With these canines, the abnormality is manifested primarily in the hip joints, thus individual dogs with unilateral hip dysplasia are not uncommon.

Those unfamiliar with the disease may ask why hip dysplasia is considered such a problem. In addition to causing arthritic pain in the joints, the disease eventually restricts the functional capacity of the dog. Thus, many a high-priced dog becomes incapacitated at an early age. Even more frightening to the shooting fraternity that hunts over dogs is the fact that the disease is widespread among the sporting and working breeds. For this reason, studies have been going on at numerous universities and through the Morris Animal Foundation for several decades. Understanding and, hopefully, controlling of this debilitating disease is sought by dog owners, breeders and veterinarians throughout the sporting world.

One of the first efforts to phase out the disease was among dog breeders. For a number of years, they have been attempting to eliminate hip dysplasia among sporting dog populations through their own selective breeding programs. The practice in this doctrine has been to breed only those dogs that have been found to have normal hip joints.

This effort has been successful only to a point and progress has been slow, according to those who have participated in the selective breeding program. Some admit, as suggested earlier, that some breeders have failed to stick to a rigid program, but the fact is that evidence of the disease is not always seen in young dogs even with the aid of radiographic examinations.

Research has shown that canine hip dysplasia is a disease which dates back several thousand years from evidence found in a series of bone finds at various early habitations.

Radiographic examination is the method used in most instances of diagnosis for dysplasia. At the Cornell facility, for example, a standard pelvic radiograph of the dog

The Labrador retriever is another breed that has been found to suffer from a high incidence of hip dysplasia. A selective breeding program seems to be the only answer.

under examination is taken with the subject animal in the extended ventro-dorsal position. Taken while the dog is anesthetized, scientists report that the results are about ninety-five percent accurate when the dog is two years old.

However, according to George Lust of the Cornell staff, "The variability of this diagnostic method and its degree of sensitivity should be considered in interpretations. It is important to recognize that the radiographic procedure is not an absolute standard and inherently has errors due to lack of sensitivity — it may predict in favor of normal hip joints — and requires some subjective interpretation by the radiologist. Evaluation of borderline cases are particularly susceptible to error and might influence conclusions adversely.

"Greater accuracy and sensitivity in the diagnosis of hip dyplasia may be achieved by employing pathological examination in conjuction with radiography," according to the Cornell University findings. "For example, in a long term study of canine hip dysplasia about twenty-five percent of the dogs had degenerative hip joint lesions at necropsy, although by standard pelvic radiographic evaluation, the status of their hip joints was normal. Although pathological examination of joints is a more conclusive indicator of hip joint disease, it negates the benefits of external radiographic evaluation."

Scientists both in this country and abroad are seeking new procedures for diagnosing disease of the hip joint in spite of the fact that these joints may appear normal on the radiograph. It is felt that such procedures, once properly established, can be of major help in selecting breeding stock.

Cornell scientists also say that "better methods are required for the diagnosis of the disease in younger animals where the characteristic features of hip dysplasia may not be seen by the radiographic technique."

A rather recent science called scintigraphy is being used in conjunction with other diagnostic means. This technique requires that a radioisotope be injected into the hip joint in conjunction with the standard radiograph of the area. According to some scientific types, it is felt that a great deal more research is needed to fully evaluate the usefulness of the development, but is felt by some that valuable information on the origin and development of the degenerative joint disease can be gathered with this technique.

"For example, its use may resolve the conflict of whether joint laxity or a tissue metabolic-defect is the initial discernable abnormality," states one scientist. At the time of the experiments, analysis of accessible body fluids had not been "productive in identifying either the presence of normal or dysplastic hip joints."

There is little doubt that the main cause for dysplasia is heredity, although there are some environmental influences. In view of the former findings, selective breeding appears to be the obvious answer and there are those who recommend a broad program of progeny testing.

In the progeny test approach, pelvic radiographs are made of many offspring, thus gaining insight into the breeding value of the parents. It is generally agreed that progress of a genetic nature is slow but shows positive results. The greatest problem, according to George Lust, lies in the plan's limitations, "for the breeding of dogs is not conducted in the same manner as the breeding of livestock." For example, artificial insemination, utilizing frozen semen, appears to be somewhat impractical.

"Such a technique would facilitate the distribution of a prospective sire's semen to many dams in different environments needed for progeny tests, as well as to preserve semen of a proven dog," the Cornell laboratory spokesman contends.

Hip dysplasia in dogs is a polygenic trait. In other words it is transmitted by inheritance with no apparent pattern. This tells us that the only way to eliminate the disease is by breeding only dogs with sound hips. This will cause an increase of pups with sound hips. It will be a long and difficult process as we have been breeding this trait into dogs for thousands of years and cannot expect to breed it out overnight.

Action photo of an older German shepherd shows that he favors his rear quarters in movement. This dog suffers hip dysplasia.

"The length of time required to prove a sire's breeding value adds to the difficulty in making this method practical for dog breeders, since offspring used in progeny tests should reach the age of two years for valid radiographic evaluation of pelvic phenotype with regard to hip dysplasia.

"A substantial portion of a dog's prime breeding life will be lost while the test is in progress. The relatively small population of each breed and wide distribution of that population also hinder the application of the progeny test."

The added problem lies in the fact that serious breeders tend to select breeding stock for hunting and retrieving abilities, conformation, temperament, intelligence, size, ad infinitum. Most don't think too much about the hip dysplasia problem in relationship to these other facets of salability. Thus, hip problems may be retained in the bloodline, while the breeder is attempting to combine the other wanted traits.

The Orthopedic Foundation for animals has evaluated many thousands of dogs of almost a hundred different breeds. The first 25,000 X rays were analyzed and showed the following:

Breed	Number evaluated	Percent dysplastic
English setter	203	30.5
English springer spaniel	437	28.1
Chesapeake Bay retriever	199	25.6
Golden retriever	2200	25.2
Gordon setter	111	24.3
Brittany spaniel	508	21.1
Weimaraner	714	17.2
Irish setter	969	16.4
Labrador retriever	3022	14.9
Wirehaired pointing Griffon	129	10.1

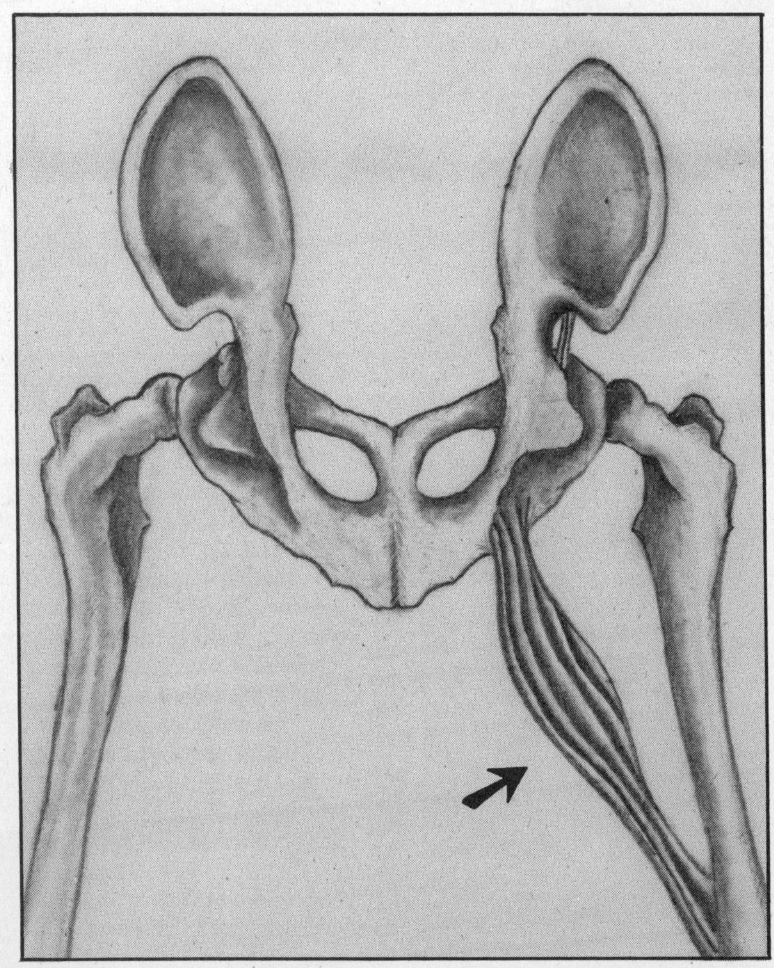

Surgical exeriments have shown some promise in remedying hip displacia. For this, the pectineus muscle is cut from insertion on the dog's pelvis. This tends to correct the luxating force on femur only if the muscle is contracted, veterinarians say.

This would seem to confirm that certain breeds — probably due to heritability — tend to be more prone to hip dysplasia than others For example scientists have found that the German shepherd has a high incidence of the disease. Outdoor writer Roger Combs, who also raises German shepherds for the seeing-eye dog program, contends that all of this specific breed have the disease; how pronounced it becomes and at what age is dependent largely upon bloodlines.

Another breed that suffers from hip dysplasia to the extreme, according to some investigators, is the Labrador retriever.

"In order to understand and to select effectively against a genetic characteristic like hip dysplasia, one must know its mode of inheritance, Lust states. "Although some basic information is available, it is evident that researchers and breeders alike face a complex problem in dealing with this disease.

"Progeny testing, while theoretically sound, has a number of operational impediments. It is evident that environmental factors actually do play a prominent role in the expression of the disease. By utilizing genetic selection programs in conjunction with defined environmental manipulations, more rapid progress might be realized for eventual elimination of the condition from the dog population."

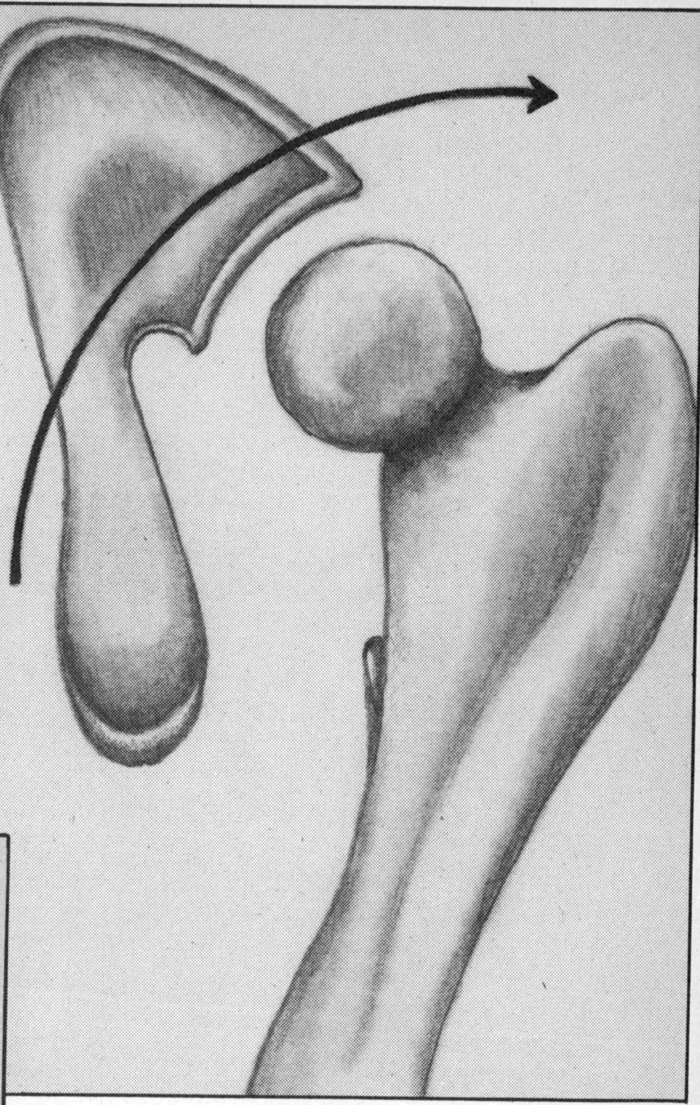

Triple osteotomy of pelvis allows full coverage of the femur by acetabulum, It corrects distribution of hip forces.

Artist's concept shows means by which femoral head and acetabulum have been replaced by plastic/steel prostheses.

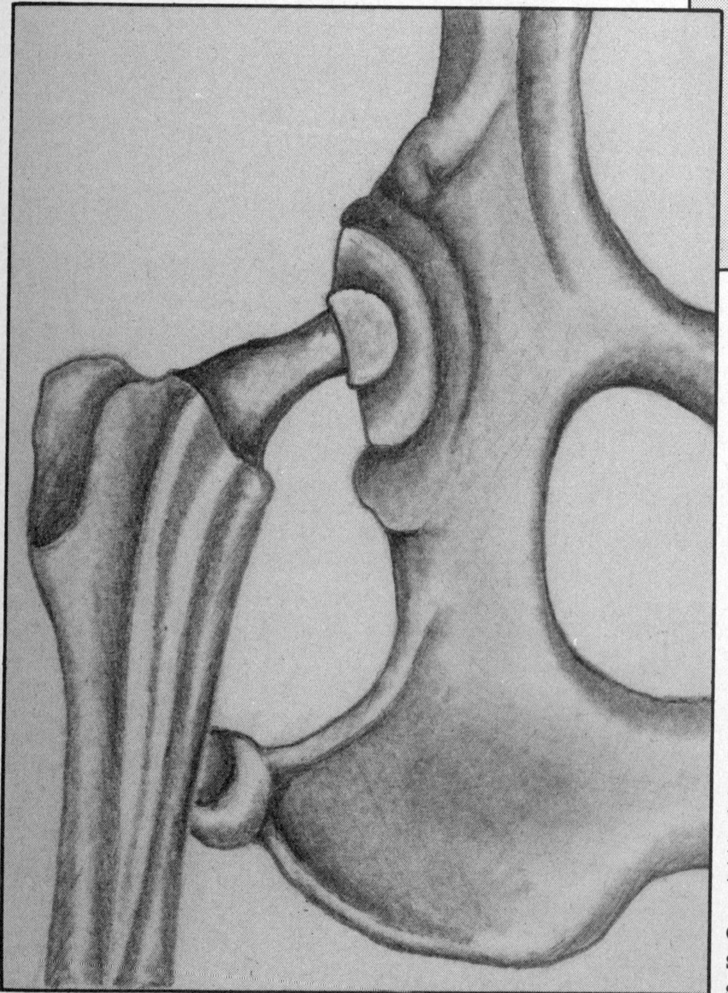

Regarding the relationship between environment and the disease, indications that hip dysplasia development could be prevented in dogs at risk was found in a study involving Labrador retrievers.

In this particular study, it was learned that pups from parents with dysplasia born through cesarean delivery, deprived of colostrum intake, then raised at a reduced growth rate had a low rate of hip dysplasia when they reached adulthood.

At the other extreme, pups born under normal conditions and reared in the usual fashion suffered a high incidence of hip displasia by the time they reached full maturity.

Experimentations have shown that young pups that have fast weight gains often are subject to dysplasia, while those that are fed a diet that holds back rapid weight increases may suffer the disease, but the problem appears later in the dog's life cycle and usually is less severe.

Scientists at the Cornell Research Laboratory for Diseases of Dogs conducted studies wherein pups from the same litter of Labrador retrievers were placed in two groups shortly after birth; in this instance, both parent dogs were known to suffer from hip dysplasia.

One control group was fed restricted amounts of a balanced and nutritional diet, bottle-feeding taking place for the first five weeks. These dogs were maintained on this special diet for twelve weeks before being returned to the normal level of dietary intake.

Results of that particular experiment showed that, of the dogs consuming normal amounts of food from time of birth, ninety percent of them suffered from hip dysplasia by the time they were six months of age.

At the other extreme, of the group that had been fed the restricted diet, approximately seventy-five percent of them showed no signs of hip dysplasia when they had reached the age of ten months.

In another environmental study, it was observed that dogs confined to small areas during the early part of their growth were less likely to develop the disease than those that were not confined in the same manner. But to cast doubt on that particular hope, an almost identical study of dogs from another litter showed that the differences in exercise made little if any difference in disease incidence. Over the years, any number of other possibilities have been investigated with little positive results. Such studies have included the use of live-virus vaccines, investigation of trauma or physical stress, the introduction of supplemental vitamins and minerals, even the presence of fever in the pups during the teething period.

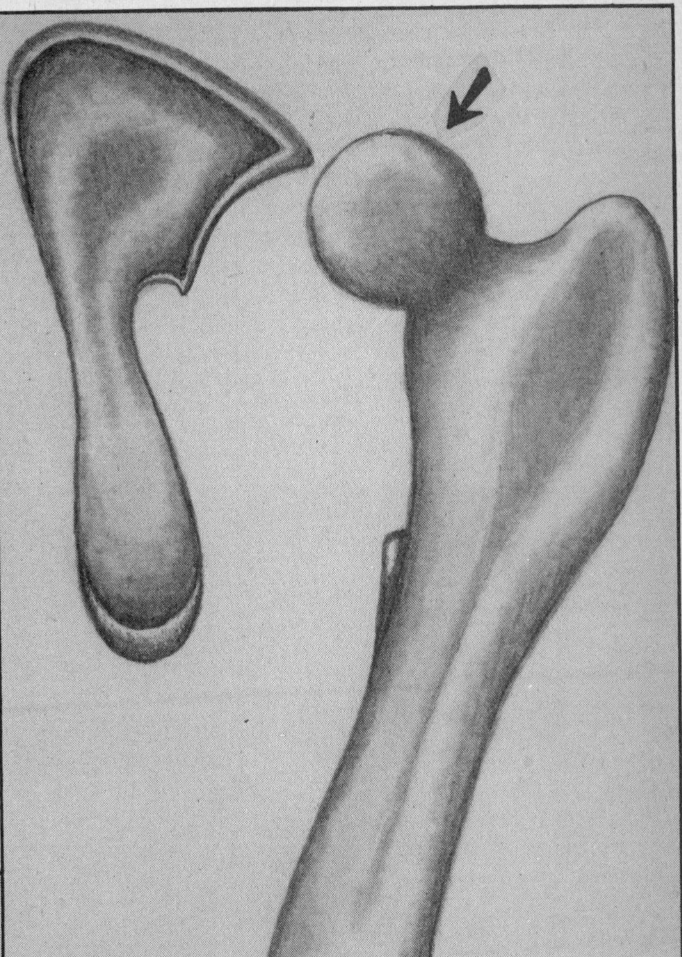

With femoral head impingement on the acetabulum, the cartilage of the femoral head becomes denuded. This results in an improper distribution of forces on hip.

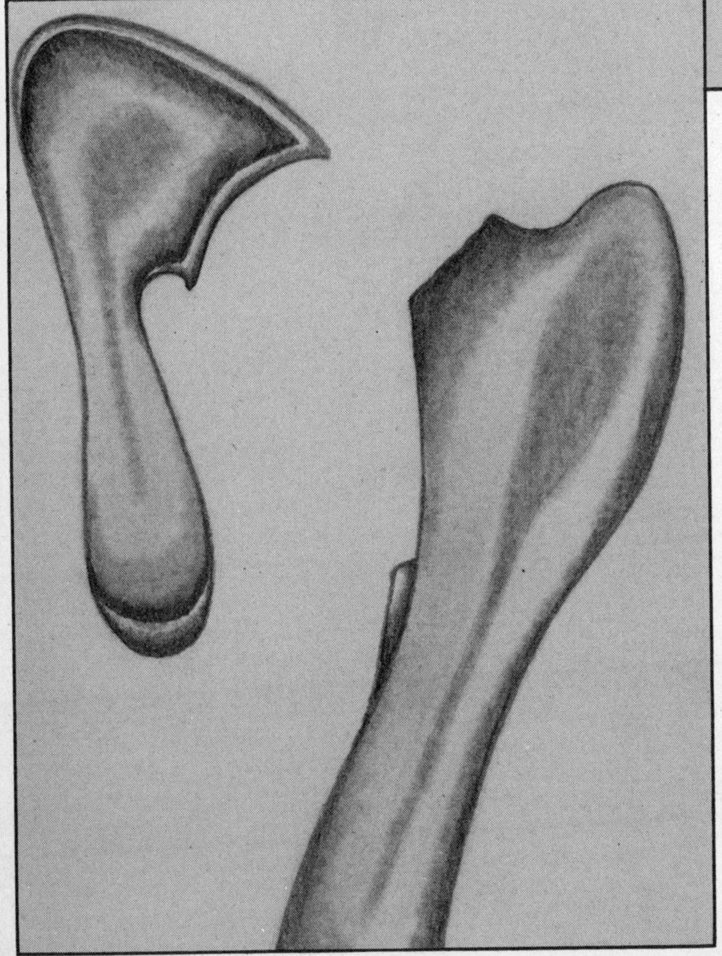

In a technique known as femoral arthroplasty, femoral head is removed to prevent pain. Muscle supports animal.

Studies are continuing at several universities in this country and in Canada as a means of determining what factors might create hip dysplasia, but the interrelation of genes appears to be the closest to an answer.

During the 1950s, many breeders refused to admit the existence of dysplasia in their breeds. The first breed club to take positive action to combat dysplasia was the Golden Retriever Club of America. This breed club organized a dysplasia control program in 1960. They soon offered certificates attesting that Golden retrievers that had been X-rayed and the hips judged to be sound by a panel of radiologists were free of hip dysplasia. This soon was expanded into a central agency which would serve to certify good hips in all breeds.

This effort was the beginning of the Orthopedic Foundation for Animals (OFA), and the Dysplasia Control Registry. These operations have been run by the University of Missouri School of Veterinary Medicine, which has done a splendid job of dysplasia certification. If you wish to have dogs that you plan to breed certified by OFA, you must submit an application for OFA certification together with an X-ray of the dog's hips made by a veterinarian who is familiar with OFA rules and procedures. These should be sent to the Orthopedic Foundation for Animals, Inc., 817 Virginia Avenue, Columbia, MO 65201.

The best cure for hip dysplasia, of course, is prevention and the Orthopedic Foundation for Animals has been doing its part by X-raying 2-year-old dogs, as suggested earlier. Those with "clear hips" are certified as non-dysplastic and breeders are being urged to use only these dogs for perpetuating the breeds.

Nonetheless, veterinarians have introduced several surgical techniques that are meant to provide free and relatively painless activity in the joints of these dogs.

For many years, relief of arthritic pain in movement was provided by means of a surgical technique called femoral arthroplasty. Following surgery and recovery, the dog becomes dependent upon his muscles and scar tissue to support the weight of his body. For small dogs, this is no particular problem. However, with larger dogs the weight is too much for the muscles to support. For the average hunting dog, the operation would tend to limit his usefulness in the field.

Another surgical technique is called pectineal myotomy. This involves the process of cutting the pectineus muscle from its attachment on the pelvis. This procedure has largely replaced the arthroplasty technique in recent years, but has shown only varying degrees of success, according to Barclay Slocum, DVM, who operates the Slocum Clinic.

"The procedure definitely is not the panacea it was once

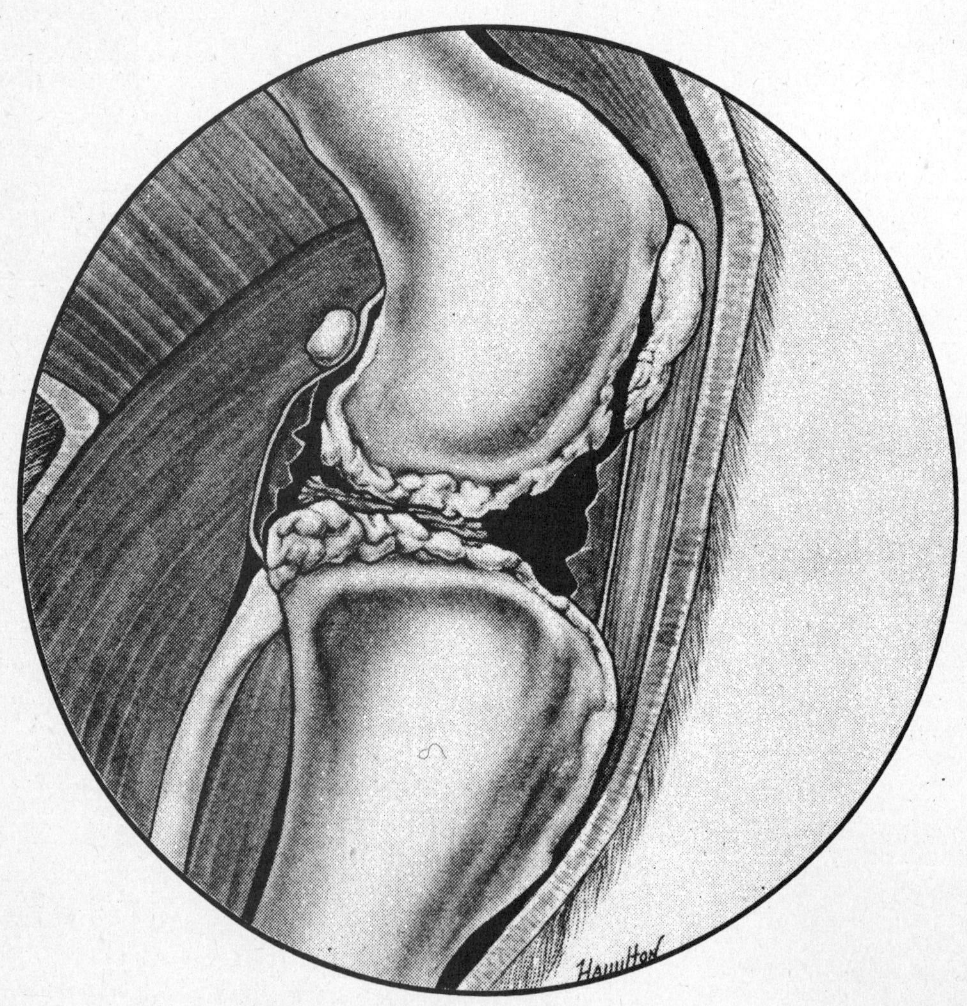

This artist's drawing of the affected joint in a dog's leg shows the growth of calcium which can create pain. It can be relieved, but there is no cure.

thought to be," Dr. Slocum says, "but it does serve a purpose. If a pectineus muscle is contracted, joint stress is exaggerated, causing the hip to luxate." (Luxation is described by Webster as a "dislocation.")

"In these cases, cutting the pectineus muscle removes those stresses, allowing the hip to remain in its socket. If the muscle is not contracted, removing the pectineus has no effect."

In 1979, another technique described as pelvic osteotomy was introduced among veterinarians. This surgery requires that the pelvis be rotated to cover the femoral section of the hip. According to Dr. Slocum, "the shallow acetabulum is rotated to cover the head of the femur and evenly distribute the forces exerted on the hip."

Dr. Slocum and others feel this particular surgery technique has shown outstanding results. "Dogs that have been crippled with pain before surgery are, in six months, running, jumping and playing with normal function."

Should there be damage to the hip and if damage to the cartilage has progressed too far, there now is a total hip replacement procedure available. In this particular surgical operation the acetaulum is replaced by a femoral head of stainless steel in a plastic socket.. When these foreign prosthetics are cemented in place, the dog usually can resume normal activity. The drawback, as with the other methods of treament, lies in the fact that the operation is expensive.

Perhaps less serious, but nonetheless debilitating, is

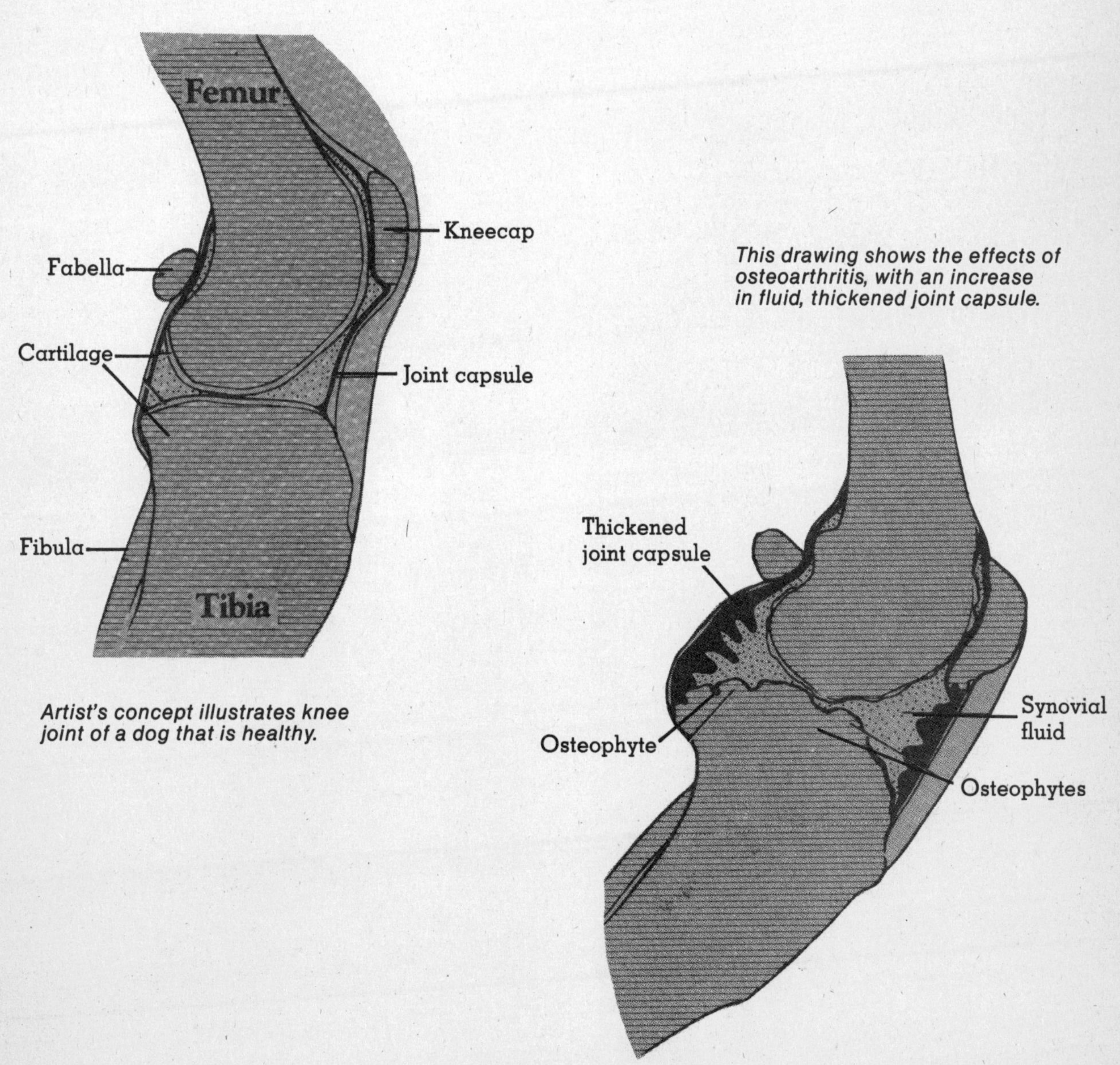

Artist's concept illustrates knee joint of a dog that is healthy.

This drawing shows the effects of osteoarthritis, with an increase in fluid, thickened joint capsule.

osteoarthritis, known more commonly simply as arthritis. A major cause of infirmity in both humans and animals, the disease is quite common among larger breeds of dogs, although all of the breeds can be affected.

Osteoarthritis, a degenerative joint disease, is the most common affliction of dogs. According to the James A. Baker Institute for Animal Health, it can "Occur as a result of trauma, in association with malformations in the region of a joint, or as part of the aging process. Although osteoarthritis occurs most often in the elderly, it can occur in dogs at any age.

"The progress of the disease is similar in most dogs. The articular cartilage that covers the ends of bones is affected early. The normally smooth and elastic tissue becomes rough and is worn away, exposing the underlying bone. The ligaments and joint capsule become stretched and even muscles in the region of the joint are weakened. Opposing bones move against one another unnaturally, causing inflammation, deformation and further injury. Movement is impaired and painful."

As with human beings, osteoarthritis in dogs can affect a single or many joints, but the large weight-bearing joints such as the shoulder, hip, stifle and elbow are those veterinarians find affected most often.

"Joint disease that results from trama or infection is not inherited," according to Dr. George Lust, a professor of physiological chemistry. "Other cases do have a strong genetic association. Osteoarthritis is often observed in litter mates and in the offspring of affected parents. Not all dogs in a line are equally affected; environment and nutrition probably influence the expression of the disease."

However, it is recommended by scientists studying the problem that dogs not be bred, if they have severe osteoarthritis that is not a result of injury or infection.

The Baker Institute of Animal Health reports that "injuries or malformations that cause joints to become unstable or alter their weight-bearing function favor the development of osteoarthritis. Hip dysplasia is the most frequent predisposing condition in dogs. Other causes of osteoarthritis include abnormal knee cap placement and unfused bones in the elbow joint. Separation of the articular cartilage from the underlying bone is another cause. This condition — called osteochondrosis — occurs in the shoulder, elbow, stifle and hock joints and is ob-

This X-ray from the James A. Baker Institute of Animal Health shows the joint structure of an unaffected dog.

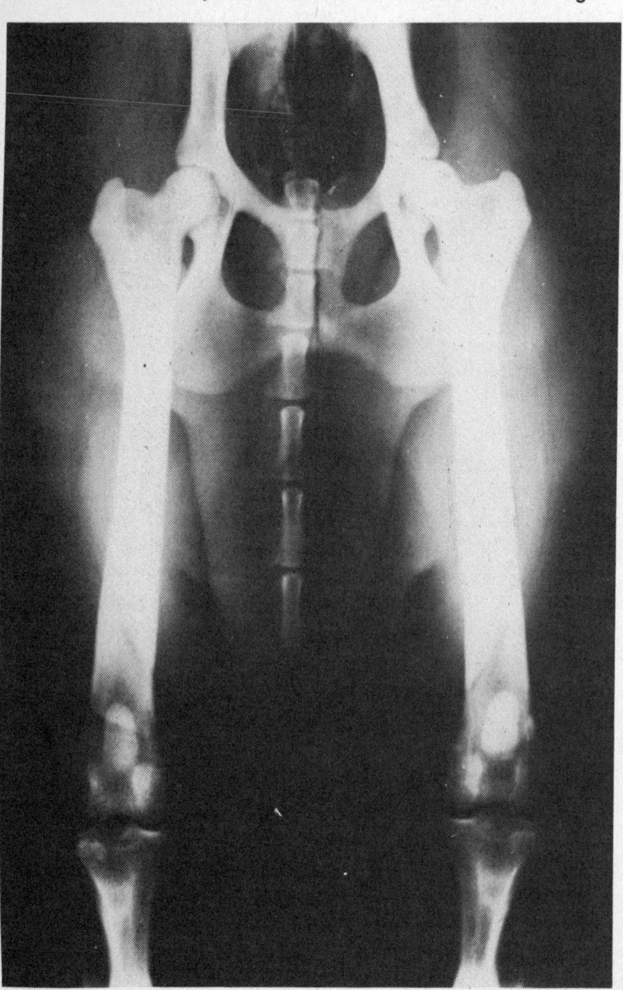

This X-ray from the same source at Cornell University is of large dog that is suffering with hip dysplasia.

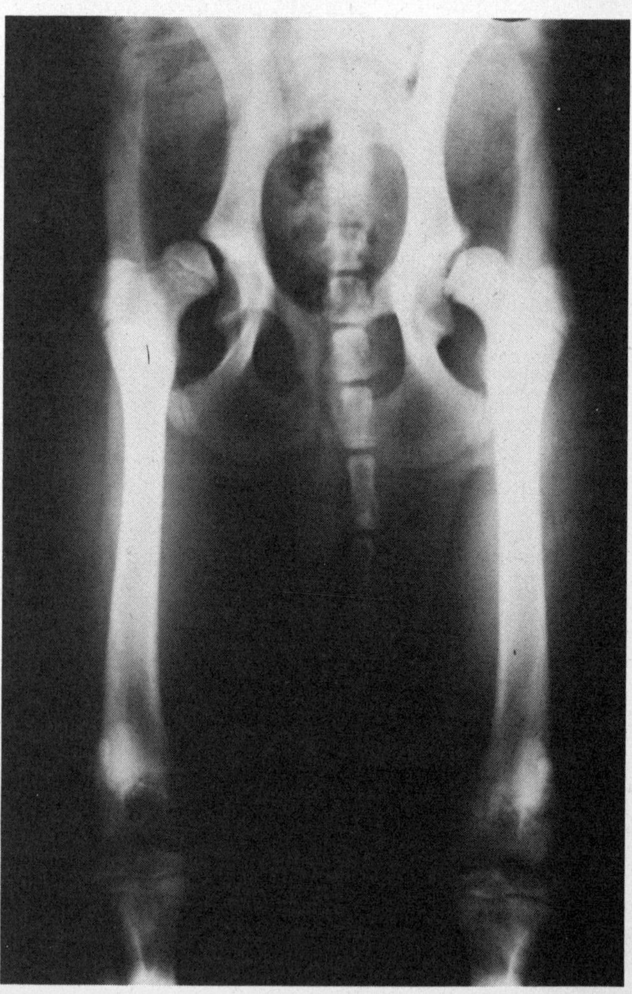

served most frequently in rapidly growing dogs. Less common causes of osteoarthritis are aseptic necrosis of the femoral head — also called Legg-Calve-Perthe's disease — and improper healing of fractures with misalignment of the bones near a joint."

The obvious question, of course, is how can the dog owner or breeder determine that his dog is suffering from osteoarthritis. One of the early signs concerns a dog's reluctance to jump, perform tricks, go on extended walks, run or to hunt.

"While standing, dogs put less weight on an affected limb," according to researchers at the Baker Institute. "Other signs become evident as the disease progresses. The dog may limp or appear stiff. It may have difficulty rising from a lying or sitting position. It may whine or snap when the affected joint is manipulated. Intense activity such as running may cause pain and reveal disease in an apparently normal animal. The pain often is made worse by cold or a sudden change in the weather."

Confirmation of osteoarthritis requires X-ray examination of the affected area of the dog's body by a qualified veterinarian. The evidence that should be shown in an X-ray negative will include mineral deposits in the soft tissues surrounding the affected joint, thickening of the joint capsule, new bone formation of an abnormal nature at the edge of the dog's joint, any changes in density or thickness of the bones and any narrowing of the joint space. The last usually is the signal for a loss of cartilage.

Artist's drawing illustrates the manner in which the femoral head should fit properly into adjoining socket.

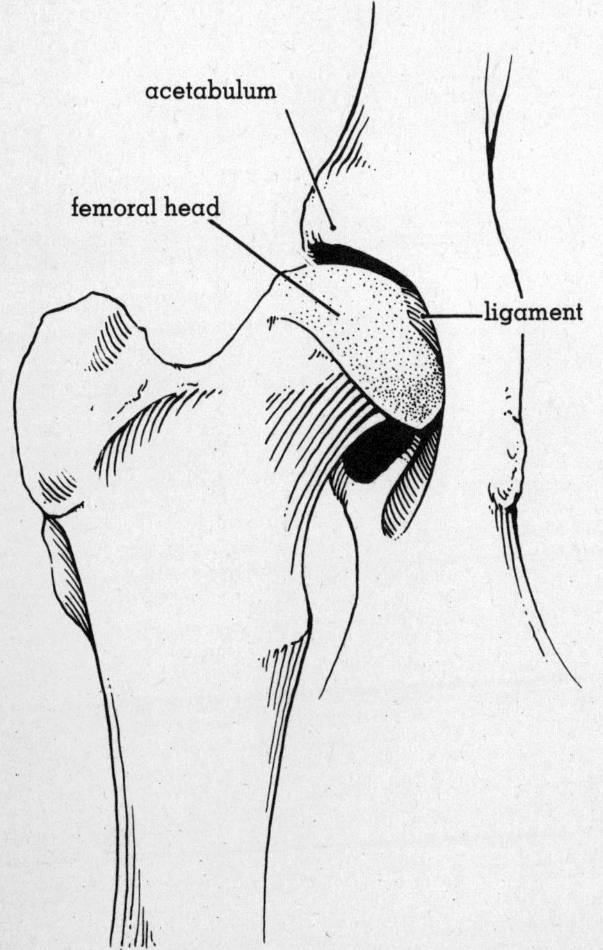

Veterinarians say that examination of the actual joint fluid can offer more information, since those joints free of disease should carry only a small amount of a clear, viscous fluid. In the event there is an increased amount of fluid or it tends to show discoloration, there is a strong possibility of disease. The same possibility is likely if the fluid shows white blood cells or discarded tissue. Further chemical tests of the fluid can offer additional information and narrow the problem.

The question of how the disease should be treated is something else again. There are measures that can afford relief. For example, walking and swimming for short periods of time tend to keep the dog's muscles limber and to promote lubrication and nutrition for the affected joints. Equally important is proper rest, as excessive use — as in hunting — can aggravate pain in a diseased joint and even create further damage to the affected area.

A spokesman for the Baker Institute adds that "anti-inflammatory drugs also relieve the pain. Buffered aspirin with food usually is well tolerated. Indomethacin — an antiarthritic drug frequently used in humans — should not be used in dogs, because it invariably causes severe gastric ulcers. Other anti-inflammatory drugs are available, but they usually are more expensive and may be no more effective than aspirin. A veterinarian should be consulted for dosages."

Corticosteroids, such as the well known cortisone, have been used in advanced osteoarthritis cases, but only when prescribed by a vet. It has been found that, while cortisone is potent as an anti-inflammatory agent and will relieve pain, it also tends to accelerate the disease. Scientists have found that corticosteroids tend to alter the composition and strucure of the tissues in the joints, making them weaker. Also, with the pain relieved temporarily, the affected dog tends to become more active; in turn, this aggravates his condition. While medications may make a dog suffering from arthritis somewhat more comfortable, they do not arrest the degeneration. Diet supplements such as vitamins have shown little worth in restoring joint function or arresting the degenerative process.

Most vets recommend warm packs to ease pain for the dog stricken with chronic osteoarthritis. These dogs, they say, should be kept warm and dry, which automatically reduces their worth as hunting dogs. Pain resulting from a recent injury can be eased by applying crushed ice in a plastic bag to the affected joint. The resultant transfer of cold will reduce inflammation and bring a degree of relief.

Surgery, as suggested earlier, can correct the abnormal growth and often relieve pain. However, once the degeneration has begun, the disease in the joint cannot be stopped; it can only be slowed. Vets agree that surgical procedures are impractical in many cases. While you may have had Old Spot for years and consider him a member of the family, there are times when it is more kind to the dog simply to have the vet remove him quietly and painlessly from his world of discomfort.

Chapter 19

FEEDING & NUTRITION

A Lot Of Expertise Goes Into Keeping Your Dog On A Healthy Diet

Author's pointer, Big Jim, points a covey of quail. His ribs show, but the old dog is not undernourished. Instead, he is in top hunting condition after daily work for three months.

FEEDING your dog properly can mean the difference between a healthy, active, vital and alert hunting companion and a lethargic, listless mutt that is too lazy to get out of its own way.

The saying, "A lean hound for a long chase," is true, but that leanness must be arrived at through exercise and the proper amount of good food containing the proper balances of basic nutrients.

A month or so before hunting season, hunting dog owners begin cutting the rations of their dogs and running them occasionally to start conditioning for the coming season. This is a case of too little-too late. To get the dog down to good running weight will require a near starvation diet that can weaken the dog physically and make it susceptible to disease and debilitation. A month may possibly be long enough to get a young dog into good hunting condition by daily strenuous exercise of rapidly increasing intensity. In the case of an older dog, there is no hope, if it has been allowed to become obese and lazy. The older dog is subject to heart problems, if suddenly called upon to put forth great physical effort when out of condition.

Begin the training period with gradually increasing intensity accompanied by a mildly reduced diet of a high protein, low fat nature. It is even better to keep your dog in top shape all year by occasional exercise accompanied by a moderate diet of reliable dog food.

There are dog foods on the market today that are not really good for your dog. In dog food, as with everything else, we get what we pay for. The label of a dog food bag should indicate much of the protein content available to the dogs, but we must depend on the reputation of the manufacturers since a food might list twenty-five percent protein, but only ten percent of that protein is in a form that a dog can digest. It is only the available protein that is of value.

There's an old saying that, if you want an expert job done, you go to an expert. When it comes to nutrition, you do the same; you find an expert.

I contacted Jane Popham, technical writer for the Purina Pet Nutrition and Care Research Division, who supplied data and put me in touch with a host of experts.

Nutrition research for dogs was begun in June, 1926, nearly sixty years ago at the Purina Pet Care Center. This is a part of the 1585-acre Purina Research Farm, located at Gray Summit, Missouri. In the years since, more than 25,000 dogs have been used in the center's nutritional research program and more than 1000 puppies are born there each year for use in nutritional studies. I found that, when the studies are complete, the pups not kept as replacement breeders or on lifetime studies are sold, primarily to Purina employees. At any given time, there are more than eight hundred dogs of all ages at the Pet Care Center. These are purebreds ranging in size from miniature poodles and schnauzers to Labrador retrievers, German shepherds and even St. Bernards.

These dogs are used in tests to prove the worth of a product before it is introduced to the dog-owning public. Five different tests must be passed: palatability, digestion, reproduction, growth and maintenances.

PALATABILITY

Palatability studies utilize an appropriate testing procedure to determine the food that is most acceptable to the dog. This is critical because a dog must eat the product in order to obtain the necessary nutrition. Palatability of the food is influenced by the formula, ingredient quality and the mouth feel of the particle.

Formula, or the kinds and relative amounts of the ingredients used, determines the taste of the finished product. Dogs generally prefer foods high in fat and low in fiber. They like flavors such as onion and garlic.

Ingredient quality influences the flavor and aroma of the finished product. The dog's nose and taste buds are quite sensitive. Generally speaking, a formula using low-quality, overcooked or scorched, spoiled or severely rancid ingredients does not give the most desirable taste to the dog and may cause reduced intake or complete rejection of the food.

Although many dog owners may not be aware of this fact, mouth feel is important in determining the relative palatability of the food. Mouth feel is influenced by the texture, density, size, shape and other physical properties of the particles. For example, a dry dog food that turns very mushy and soft when water is added is not as palatable for the average dog as a dry food that retains a crunchy texture when moisture is added. Mouth feel is one of the reasons dry pet foods come in a variety of shapes.

Color does not affect a dog's taste preference. Artificial color is added to a dog food product primarily to give and maintain a consistent product appearance for the benefit of the pet owner.

At the Purina Pet Care Center, nearly 300 adult dogs of different breeds are used to determine food preferences. Each dog is fed individually and offered a choice of two diets in the same size bowls. Each bowl contains more food than the dog will eat; otherwise, the dog will consume all the preferred diet and still be hungry enough to eat a portion of the less-preferred food. The only measurement taken is the amount of each food consumed, with no observation made on which food is sniffed and/or eaten first. The size and length of this experiment is designed to yield statistically significant results. The bowls of food are switched each day to make certain that the dog is not a "position eater." (Some dogs eat from only the right- or left-hand bowl without regard to the kinds of foods offered.)

A new product or a product that has been significantly modified to improve palatability is not only initially tested several times but is also subject to a storage test for at least nine months. Palatability tests are conducted initially and after three-, six-, and nine-months storage to make certain that the flavor or formula modification has not changed. During this time, observations are made not only on palatability, but also on product appearance and package condition.

Food consumption figures gathered from the palatability tests are put on a computer, calculated and sent to pet nutritionists for interpretation and summary.

Palatability improvements require, at the very least, one year of study before production plants implement a change.

DIGESTION STUDIES

Digestion studies measure droppings volume and condition to determine the utilizable percentage of certain nutrients in the food. These studies are done on new products, any major modification in a current product and on new ingredients being considered for use.

The condition and volume of droppings are important factors to single-dog owners who clean up after their dogs. It is important that the droppings be in firm condition and that the volume be as small as possible. Besides being difficult to clean up, many dog owners believe that soft droppings with high volume indicate that the food is not as digestible and that the nutrients are not being properly utilized by the dog. This is not necessarily true, but the belief persists.

In addition to determining droppings condition and volume, the actual digestibility or utilization of protein, energy and certain vitamins and minerals is determined. Both quantity and quality of nutrients in a dog food are equally important. For example, a dog food that contains 21 percent protein with 85 percent digestibility would be equally as good as a diet containing 23 percent protein with a 77.6 percent digestibility.

REPRODUCTION STUDIES

To be declared a complete and balanced diet for all

stages of a dog's life, a Purina dog food must pass two kinds of tests — reproduction and growth. The purpose of reproduction or breeding studies is to determine if the dog food has the correct amount and balance of nutrients dogs need during the period of gestation and lactation.

In reproduction studies, two similar groups of brood bitches are used. Each group, those fed the control diet and those fed the test diet, are the same breeds and similar in age and whelping experience. The control diet is a product such as Purina® Dog Chow® brand dog food or Purina® brand Hi Pro Dog Meal that has been fed to hundreds of brood bitches at the Purina Dog Care Center and which gives normal reproductive performance.

All dogs are housed under the same conditions, eat from the same size bowl, are fed at the same time and receive the same care and medication. Pen size, the amount of available exercise and all management factors are the same except for the food in the bowl.

The test starts prior to the time the females are bred. From that time until the puppies are weaned, they eat only the test or control diet plus water. No vitamins, minerals, meat or other supplements are added.

During a reproduction study, a number of observations are made and recorded. These include:

- Daily food intake of each bitch and/or pups.
- Body weight of the brood bitches at regular intervals.
- Body weight of the pups at birth and every week thereafter until weaning (six weeks of age).
- Number and sex of pups born and weaned.
- Veterinarian examination of the bitch and pups.
- Any unusual factor.
- Blood chemistry profiles.

Since all brood bitches do not come in heat at the same time, this test requires 12 to 18 months to complete. The test ends when all litters are weaned at six weeks of age. For a test diet to be successful, the performance results from the dogs on this diet must be equal to or better than the control food. If the performance is not as good, the test diet is reevaluated in an effort to determine what may have occurred.

GROWTH TEST

The purpose of this test is to determine whether the food will support normal pup growth after weaning.

For a growth study, litters of puppies are taken from the test diet lot of the reproduction study and divided as equally as possible by sex and weight into two lots. One lot is fed a control diet of known performance, and the other lot eats the same test diet as fed during reproduction studies. This test starts immediately after the puppies are weaned and lasts a minimum of ten weeks. Because their growth period is longer, growth tests for large breeds may last 25 weeks.

During the test period, the following observations are recorded: body weight, body lengths, food intake, veterinarian examination, blood chemistry profiles and any unusual conditions. X-rays may be used for checking bone and teeth development. In some studies, urine analysis is conducted.

As in the reproduction study, puppies on the test diet must perform as well as or better than their littermates on the control diet. If the results from both the reproduction and growth studies are positive, the food can be labeled complete and balanced nutritionally for all phases of a dog's life.

Excessive calcium can cause incorrect leg structure such as that illustrated. This cow-hocked stance is found in the St. Bernard and other large-dog breeds.

MAINTENANCE TESTS

The purpose of a maintenance study is to determine if the food will maintain normal body condition and weight on adult dogs. Adult dogs with normal activity do not require as high a level, per pound of body weight, of protein, energy, vitamins and other nutrients as does a growing puppy or pregnant and lactating bitch. Consequently, if a diet is designed solely for maintenance, the nutrient level can be lower.

Maintenance test dogs are fed the test diet only, plus water, for a minimum testing period of 26 weeks. No other supplements are used. During the test period, food intake, body weight, body condition and blood chemistry patterns are checked.

At the end of the test, individual dogs must have maintained their original body condition, had no significant variation in body weight and show no other abnormal factor that may be due to diet. If this test is successful, the food can be labeled complete and balanced for maintenance of the adult dog. This means that the product is not recommended for feeding the growing pup or pregnant and lactating bitch. Dog food labels should include this information.

Any new or modified Purina dog food which has a different nutritional profile or contains new and different ingredients than a current Purina dog food on the market has to prove itself through the palatability, digestion, reproduction and growth studies. For a new product, it can require up to two years from initial concept until it is ready to go to market.

Pet food labels give basic information as to the product name, manufacturer's or seller's name and address, ingredient content, nutrient guaranteed analysis, feeding information, net weight, and many times, other interesting information about the product.

The guaranteed analysis and list of ingredients are required on all pet food labels. These lists are based on regulations established by the Association of American Feed Control Officials (AAFCO) that have been adopted by the states. The label format and copy must comply with these regulations. Enforcement of composition and labeling is the duty of feed control officials in each state. Specific nutrient guarantees required on labels of all pet foods are: crude protein (minimum amount); crude fat (minimum amount); crude fiber (maximum amount), and moisture (maximum amount). The reason for the word "crude" is that the minimum and maximum amounts shown are determined by laboratory assay and not by feeding tests conducted with dogs or cats. Additional nutrient guarantees can be listed if the manufacturer desires.

The ingredient listing on labels is in descending order of predominance, by weight. Publishing this data becomes the manufacturer's guarantee that the product has the nutrient assay and ingredient contents declared on the label.

While the laboratory assay indicates the nutritional values in the diet, these values may not be readily available to the pet. The palatability, digestibility and nutritional performance of a dog food can be determined only by research conducted by the manufacturer in accordance with recognized testing procedures such as those established by AAFCO.

Two types of additives are included in pet foods: those that are nutritional and those that add some other benefits to the food. Nutritional additives include vitamin supplements such as A, D-3, E and B-complex; essential minerals such as calcium, phosphorus, salt and iron; and amino acids such as lysine. These are added to supplement and/or provide nutrients in addition to those provided by the primary ingredients. Among non-nutritive additives are BHA, BHT or tocopherols which are added at extremely low levels to help prevent fat rancidity.

Although pets are unable to distinguish color, their owners can. Because ingredient color can be influenced by moisture content and many other factors, it is sometimes difficult to achieve color uniformity without the use of color additives. Artificial color is used in some pet foods to give the product a more desirable and consistent appearance and to differentiate between flavors in the same product. Artificial colors used in pet foods are approved by the Food and Drug Administration.

Instructions concerning the amount to feed dogs should be included on the label. Products which are complete and balanced for more than one life stage should have appropriate feeding instructions. These instructions are a "rule of thumb" or a starting point as the actual feeding amount will depend upon the pet's age, activity, environment and body metabolism. Feeding levels are best determined by observing the pet's body condition and adjusting the amount accordingly.

Dog owners learn little about the relative values offered by two similar products with identical guarantee and ingredient labels. The actual ability of the pet food to meet the pet's nutritional needs may not be indicated. This ability depends upon the testing of the product on a large number of pets conducted by the manufacturer during research and development in accordance with recognized testing procedures such as those established by AAFCO; the quality of the ingredients and the manufacturing process. Two diets with the same formula may be processed differently, so one diet produces a superior food while the other is completely unsatisfactory. Overheating or overcooking frequently damage nutrients so they become unavailable or perform poorly in the diet.

The reputation of the manufacturer is perhaps the best assurance that the right quality assurance standards are maintained.

The best way to evaluate product performance is through statements on the label. For example, the Purina Hi-Pro brand dog food label defines the purpose of this diet: to provide higher levels of protein and energy for the more active or hardworking dogs. This product is also suitable for dogs with normal activity. The label should include whether or not the product provides complete and balanced nutrition for all life stages, just for a particular life stage (such as maintenance of the adult pet) or if it is just a snack.

Sometimes pet food labels can cause confusion as the dog owner questions the differences among products called beef flavor, beef dinner, beef or a hundred percent beef (or fish, liver, etc.). When a flavor designation is made, such as "beef flavor," the words "beef" and "flavor" must be in the same size, color and type of lettering. The source of the beef flavor must be shown in the ingredient listing. This could be "beef" or "beef and bone meal" or other similar beef source ingredients.

Maintaining a dog's condition is important when it is not being worked. Most good commercial dog foods carry instructions on the label to determine proper feeding.

If the product name includes the words "beef dinner," "beef dish," or words of similar meaning, there must be at least ten percent beef in the product and the source must be shown on the ingredient listing.

When the product name includes only the word "beef," such as X Brand Beef Dog Food, this means the product contains at least seventy percent beef and the word beef would be first on the ingredient list. If the name is X Brand Fish, Liver and Chicken Cat Food, the product must contain at least seventy percent of all three of these ingredients with equally as much or more fish than liver or chicken and equally as much or more liver than chicken. This product can also be formulated for complete and balanced nutrition.

All or one hundred percent beef means that the ingredient is the total content of the product. The hundred percent or "all" does not permit the addition of nutrients other than water for processing and trace amounts of preservatives and condiments. Such products cannot be formulated to be a complete and balanced diet.

Pet food labels do provide the pet owner with a great deal of information. However, labels do not tell everything one might want to know about various pet foods. It is still necessary to rely on the manufacturer's testing, research and overall reputation to ensure that the pet food is of high quality and provides complete and balanced nutrition. This information does not appear on the label. The reputation of the manufacturer is perhaps the best assurance that the research behind the product proves its nutritional merit and that rigid quality assurance standards are maintained. The best way to evaluate product performance is through statements on the label such as "complete and balanced nutrition." If pet owners have questions about the food that are not answered on the label, they should write to the manufacturer or distributor.

Protein is found in every living thing, and is an essential component of all body tissues. About sixty percent of the dry matter in a dog's body is protein.

A protein molecule is like a chain made of amino acid "links." There are 23 different amino acids. The way they are arranged determines the nature of the protein. Ten amino acids are considered "essential" to dogs, since the dog's system cannot manufacture them in large enough quantities to maintain body functions. Like a chain, a protein source is only as good as its weakest link. That is, an absence or deficiency of even one essential amino acid will prevent the utilization of all others.

Most people know that meat, milk and eggs are excellent sources of protein, but plants also contain valuable amino acids. Plant proteins, when combined with animal proteins or other plant proteins, can give the proper amino acid balance for every life stage of the dog.

When looking at the protein levels of different dog foods, the digestibility should be considered, as this is the true measure of the availability to the dog. As the digestibility is not listed on the package, the manufacturer's reputation is important. Two diets may have the same protein level listed, but different levels of digestibility.

Also, if you are comparing different types of pet foods, they should be put on the same moisture level for accurate comparison. For example, a canned diet (which contains about seventy-five percent moisture) with a protein level of seven percent converts to twenty-eight percent protein on a dry moisture basis. The formula for determining this is: percent protein ÷ percent dry matter = dry matter protein.

The requirements for dietary protein differ during the various life stages. Higher levels are needed during stressful conditions, such as growth, pregnancy, lactation and hard work. The normal dog's system can adjust to a wide range of protein levels above the minimum requirement. When the diet contains more protein than is needed for the maintenance of body functions, the excess protein can be used for energy.

If a dog develops a specific health problem, particularly with the kidneys, a veterinarian may recommend a low protein diet as a part of the therapeutic program. No research has shown that protein levels in complete and balanced rations would cause health problems. In a study by Dr. K.C. Bovee, the effects were evaluated of diets with 19, 27 and 56 percent protein (on a dry matter basis). In thirteen months, the dogs on that study showed no adverse effects on a high protein diet.

According to Dr. Richard M. Kealy, Ph D., minerals have several functions in the body. Certain minerals such as iron and copper are important in blood formation. Calcium, phosphorus and magnesium are necessary for rig-

Poor bone structure to the point of a deformity can result if dog suffers a calcium deficiency as a pup.

idity of bones and teeth. Sodium, potassium and chloride are required for fluid balance in the body. Other minerals serve as catalysts for chemical reactions within the body. Dr. Kealy is Purina's manager of pet nutrition and care research.

Calcium and phosphorus are minerals which must be considered together, since they interact with one another. Their primary function is as structural components of bones and teeth.

Three considerations ensure a proper balance of these minerals in the diet:

Calcium should always exceed phosphorus, the ratio being in the range of 1.2 to 2 parts calcium to one part phosphorus.

Research at the Ralston Purina Pet Care Center has indicated that calcium in excess of two percent in the diet depressed the growth of pups and reduced the digestibility of food fed to adult dogs. Excessive levels of calcium also increased the degree of bone structural incorrectness in pups.

Calcium or calcium and phosphorus deficiency can result in rickets, characterized by bending of the bones, accompanied by pain. Feeding a diet containing adequate quantities of calcium and phosphorus can alleviate the situation.

A source of Vitamin D is necessary to regulate the absorption of calcium and phosphorus and to ensure that the minerals are deposited in the bones and teeth.

Calcium and phosphorus should be in an available form. Meat and bone meal, steamed bone meal, dicalcium phosphate and defluorinated phosphate are all excellent sources of both.

Magnesium is a minor structural component of bone and is also involved in many enzymatic reations in the body. Magnesium deficiency almost never occurs in nature, since most foodstuffs contain more than adequate levels; but when it does occur it can cause weakness in dogs' tendons and ligaments.

Manganese sulfate is a good source of manganese, a deficiency of which has not been identified as a problem nutrient in dogs' diets. Manganese is required at low levels for a number of body reactions, including bone maintenance, metabolism and enzyme production.

Iron is required as a structural component of red blood cells, It is a component of hemoglobin, which is required to transport oxygen in the blood. Symptoms of iron deficiency include pale gums and generalized weakness. A suspected deficiency should be diagnosed by a veterinarian who can check the blood hemoglobin content. Usually less than ten percent of oral iron is absorbed. This dictates the use of highly available sources of iron in dog food diets. Ferrous sulfate and ferrous fumarate are excellent sources of iron for the dog.

Copper is also necessary for hemoglobin formation. The deficiency results in anemia. In cases where iron is deficient, copper deficiency intensifies the anemia. Copper sulfate is an excellent source of copper.

Zinc is needed for normal skin and hair health. It is also involved in enzymatic reactions in the body. A zinc deficiency results in growth depression and skin lesions. This deficiency is intensified in high-calcium diets. A zinc deficiency can best be avoided by feeding a nutritionally complete and balanced diet. Zinc oxide is a good source of the element.

Iodine is required for the synthesis of thyroid hormone and is part of the thyroid hormone structure. Deficiency is marked by enlargement of the thyroid gland (goiter). Good-quality dog foods contain adequate amounts of iodine to meet the dog's requirements during all stages of the life cycle. Although the iodine content of plants varies with soil iodine content, plant products frequently are below the dietary requirement. The additional iodine needed in dog foods is provided by iodized salt.

Sodium, potassium and chloride are minerals that are involved in body fluid balance. Together, they maintain osmotic pressure, control acid-base balance, influence absorption and control water balance in the body. Deficiency symptoms are general in nature and may include decreased appetite, fatigue and depression. Sodium and chloride are provided by table salt. Potassium is distributed throughout most foodstuffs and is frequently highest in protein-rich foods.

Selenium, like Vitamin E, plays an important role as a physiologic antioxidant, protecting cells from the harmful effects of oxidation. Selenium deficiency is unusual in dogs, since there is a low requirement for this nutrient; but when it exists it can contribute to skeletal and cardiac myopathy (a disorder of muscle tissues). Brewers dried yeast is a good source of selenium.

When a good-quality, nutritionally complete and balanced dog food, produced by a reputable company, is fed, supplementing a normal dog's diet with minerals is not necessary. Be certain that the dog food label states that the food is nutritionally complete and balanced so that all the minerals, vitamins, protein and other nutrients dogs are known to need will be incorporated in the product in the proper balance.

The dog food label will also tell you if the diet is for a particular life stage such as adult maintenance or growth for puppies, or if it is formulated as complete and balanced for all life stages. In addition to a good-quality nutritionally complete dog food, a constant supply of fresh drinking water in a clean bowl is all that is necessary to provide the nutrition a dog needs.

Carbohydrate is an extremely important nutrient in the dog diet because it is an economical source of food energy essential for life functions. Through proper ingredient processing, dogs are able to utilize carbohydrates at an efficiency level of 80 percent and above. In reviewing the basics of food carbohydrates and their utilization in dogs, Dr. Kealy defines some technical terms:

Glucose — The basic unit of carbohydrates which is utilized for energy production by the body.
Monosaccharide — The simplest form of sugar. Glucose is a monosaccharide.
Disaccharide — A sugar in which two monosaccharides are combined. Sucrose is a disaccharide.
Sucrose — A disaccharide which yields two units of glucose when digested.
Starch — Long chains of glucose molecules having a linkage which can be broken down into glucose by digestion.
Cellulose — Long chains of glucose molecules having a

linkage which cannot be broken down efficiently to glucose units by digestion.

Glycogen — Long, branched chains of glucose units which are stored in the animal body.

Cereal starches of the types used in pet foods (Table 1) are made up of long chains of glucose units. These starches convert to maltose (a disaccharide) and then to single units of glucose which can be readily utilized by the body.

Table 1. Typical Sources of Carboyhdrates in Dog Foods

Corn	Corn gluten meal	Dried skim milk
Oats	Corn gluten feed	Dried whey
Wheat	Oatmeal	
Barley	Wheat middlings	
	Wheat germ meal	

Most sugars are also utilized efficiently by the body. The most common sugar source is the disaccharide sucrose which can be converted to two units of glucose by the body. This charateristic is also true of the disacchardies maltose and lactose. Lactose is the predominant sugar in milk. The lactose digestion rate is somewhat slow, and there is also a certain amount of breed-to-breed variability in the ability to break down lactose.

Glycogen is found in animal tissue foodstuffs. Although the quantity is low (below five percent), it is readily utilized by dogs.

Because of the unique linkage between glucose units, cellulose cannot be broken down efficiently by the carnivorous animal. Cellulose makes up part of the fiber which provides bulk to the diet. Dietary fiber is of value for stool formation and normal bowel function.

The conversion of carbohydrates to glucose varies depending on the type of carboydrate (Tabel 2). The enzyme amylase breaks starch down into maltose units. These units, in turn, require maltase to yield the basic glucose units.

Table 2. Enzymatic Reaction in the Small Intestine of Dogs

Foodstuff	Enzyme	End Product
Starch	Amylase	Maltose
Maltose (from starch)		
Maltase	Glucose	Sucrose
Sucrase	Glucose	Lactose
Lactase	Glucose	

Glucose itself is readily absorbed and utilized by the body and serves as a rapid source of energy for the dog. However, if the dog does not require glucose for energy at any particular moment, it is stored as glycogen in the liver and muscles. During periods of fasting, stress or accelerated muscle activity, glycogen is released and used for energy by the body. When muscle glycogen is used to provide energy for work, it must draw on the liver glycogen storage to replace that lost in the muscle.

The ability of the liver to store glucose as glycogen is limited to approximately 15 percent of the liver (by weight). When carbohydrate intake exceeds the current need of the body for glycogen storage or energy production, glucose is transformed into fat.

Two clinical problems are associated with carbohydrate utilization by the dog: diabetes and hypoglycemia. Glucose utilization by the body's cells is dependent upon insulin, which is produced by the pancreas. Diabetes occurs when there is a lack of insulin and the body cannot utilize available glucose. Diabetes is a serious disease, and a veterinarian should be consulted concerning the various approaches used to control this problem.

Hypoglycemia results when the blood glucose level becomes so low that the body is unable to function and the dog may go into shock. Feeding glucose will alleviate the condition temporarily. The condition occurs in small puppies or the underconditioned hardworking dog. Treatment for this condition should be under the supervision of a veterinarian.

Carbohydrate makes up twenty to fifty percent of semimoist and dry dog foods. These products generally contain 1300 to 1850 digestible calories of energy per pound. Cereal grains provide an economical, yet highly available source of energy for dog foods, provided the carbohydrate is rendered available by careful heat processing. The reputation of the manufacturer is the best assurance of this kind of processing.

"Fat is frequently a maligned ingredient because of its connotation of poor health in humans. However, fat transports fat solubles into the body and is a beneficial part of the diet of animals, provided its use in not abused." Dr. Kealy contends.

There are three basic fat categories:

Triglycerides represent the type of fat that most people relate to: the typical fat seen in meats. Triglycerides are complex, consisting of even smaller components — one molecule of glycerol and three molecules of fatty acids combined to form a triglyceride.

Phospholipids are similar to triglycerides but combine a water soluble molecule with phosphorus in place of one of the fatty acid molecules. Phospholipids are structural compoments of various tissues in the body and are especially prevalent in skin.

Cholesterol is a molecule in itself that is primarily synthesized by the body. Some is usually provided in the diet, depending on the foodstuffs. Dietary cholesterol supplies the structure for many hormones in the body. Cholesterol is of little clinical significance to the dog, due to the low incidence of canine arteriosclerosis.

DIETARY FAT

Although dogs do not have a specific requirement for dietary fat, they do require dietary linoleic acid, a fatty acid which is a component of many fats. The dog also requires arachidonic and linoleic acids but is capable of synthesizing these from linoleic acid. A diet should contain at least one percent linoleic acid (dry moisture basis) to meet the dog's requirements. The National Research Council recommends a minimum of five percent dietary fat, on a dry moisture basis, even though there is no documentation for a specific fat requirement. If the dietary fat intake is high, it can reduce total food intake; thus the rest of the nutrients must be at a high level as well to prevent a dietary deficiency.

The balance of fatty acids in the diet will markedly influence the resuting balance of fatty acids in body fat over a period of time, an example of "you are what you eat." When unsaturated fats such as corn or soybean oil are fed, a deposition of soft (oily) fat having a similar fatty acid to that of the diet will result. Also, the dietary Vitamin E requirement becomes elevated when the more reactive polyunsaturated fatty acids are elevated in the diet. Vitamin E retards fat breakdown in the body.

DIETARY FAT AND OBESITY

Fat can influence obesity in the dog, because dogs like the taste of fat and it is a source of concentrated calories as this comparison shows:

Nutrient	Kilocalories Provided per gram
Protein	4
Carbohydrate	4
Fat	9

Fat provides 2¼ times the calories provided by protein and carbohydrate.

Dogs eat primarily to meet their daily caloric needs, which is an imperfect system because it is influenced by many factors, such as metabolic rate, haircoat cover, daily activity plus environmental temperature.

If the system were perfect, there would be no thin or fat dogs. Obesity occurs primarily because of the inadequacies of the food consumption/calorie relationships. The factors listed above influence the caloric needs of dogs. As a result, caloric requirements are only guidelines for the intelligent feeding of dogs and should be adjusted to help maintain normal body condition.

Ralston Purina research has demonstrated that a dog will lose weight by reducing caloric intake twenty percent from these daily caloric requirements:

Breed Category	Weight Range (lb.)	Dig. Calories required per lb. body weight	Dig. Calories reduced 20%
Miniature Dogs	3-20	40	32
Medium Dogs	21-75	28	22
Large & Giant Dogs	76-200	24	19

Before any significant reduction is made in calories, the dog should be checked by a veterinarian. If a dog fails to respond to the twenty percent calorie reduction, more severe food restriction should be under the supervision of a veterinarian.

Dietary fat has been the target of a great deal of controversy in the public press, with implications being made that fat in the diet is related to some health problems. However, such problems usually result only from excessive dietary fat. Any nutrient in excess is capable of being detrimental. When fat is balanced in the diet, it can help maintain good health in any species.

Dog owners frequently ask about adding supplements to commercially prepared pet foods. This supplementation is usually not needed, because the major pet food manufacturers incorporate into their products — whether they are dry, soft-moist, soft-dry or canned diets — all the protein, vitamins, minerals and other nutrients pets are known to need. The diet may be for a particular life state such as adult maintenance or growth for puppies or it may be formulated as complete and balanced for all life stages. Look for a statement of this kind on the pet food label.

When a complete and balanced diet is fed to normal dogs of any breed, no additional supplementation in the form of vitamins, minerals, meat or other additives is needed. A constant supply of fresh drinking water in a clean bowl is all that is necessary besides the complete and balanced commercial diet.

There are only two times when supplementation may be necessary. These are:

1. To correct a specific deficiency due to the pet's inability to utilize the normal level of a particular nutrient.

2. To stimulate feed intake particularly during periods of hard work or heavy lactation. This includes hard-working dogs such a bird dogs or sled dogs as well as dogs that have large litters and, therefore, require a high level of milk production. For both of these factors, a high level of food intake is needed.

If a dry diet is fed, feed it moistened and, if the food intake is still not sufficient to maintain normal body weight, the addition of ten to twenty percent meat or meat by-products to the diet will normally increase food acceptance and food intake. This level of supplementation will not affect the nutritional balance of the commercial diet.

While certain nutrients are reduced during processing and shelf storage, the manufacturer who produces good quality commercial diets adds a higher level to maintain a "safety margin" of essential nutrients in product formulation. This compensates for any loss during processing and storage and also provides the "safety margin" needed for those owners who dilute the complete and balanced diet with a small amount of table scraps or meat. Although there are slightly higher levels of certain nutrients in the diet, these levels are not high enough to create any type of nutrient toxicity. This "safety margin," or nutrient balance, can be destroyed by over-supplementation or by improper supplementation.

COMMON SUPPLEMENTS AND RISKS

Raw Eggs: Eggs contain an excellent source of protein and normally pets like them. However, repeatedly adding raw eggs to a pet's diet can cause a deficiency of the vitamin biotin. Raw egg whites contain an enzyme which ties up the biotin. Symptoms of biotin deficiency include dermatitis, loss of hair and poor growth.

Cod Liver Oil/Wheat Germ Oil: These oils are normally considered good sources of vitamins D and E. The addition of excessive cod liver oil can supply more vitamin D than the pet requires, particularly if a pet is receiving a complete and balanced diet. Excessive supplementation

This 3-year-old dog is in good condition, as maintenance diet has been adopted. He will lose some weight when worked in field.

of vitamin D over a long period can result in soft tissue calcification and skeletal disorders.

If cod liver oil or wheat germ oil is in the process of turning rancid, certain fat-soluble vitamins are destroyed which can create a vitamin deficiency. Both vitamins D and E are added in sufficient amounts to good quality commercial pet foods to meet the needs of normal, healthy cats and dogs. These vitamins are added in a stable form and can withstand long-term storage.

Supplemental Minerals: Some pet owners and breeders feel that additional calcium, and possibly other minerals, should be added to the diets of pregnant and nursing females and growing puppies. They feel that during these life stages, a pet needs more of these particular minerals. It is true that more minerals are needed at these times, but these minerals are normally obtained through increased consumption of a good quality complete and balanced commercial diet.

Most commercial pet foods contain proper levels of calcium, phosphorus and vitamin D for normal bone and tooth development. If the level is not adequate or if the ratio of calcium and phosphorus is not correct, rickets and other bone abnormalities can result.

Supplemental Vitamins: Good quality nutritionally complete commercial pet foods contain levels of vitamins which are adequate to meet the particular life stage or stages of the pet. Excessive supplementation of certain vitamins can create toxicity symptoms. This is particularly true with vitamin A. A dog owner who is already feeding a complete and balanced diet and is adding liver and a high level of a supplemental vitamin A source could cause not only poor growth and abnormal eye conditions, but also impair reproductive performance.

Meat or Meat By-Products: Meat in itself is not a complete and balanced diet. A dog or cat cannot live on a diet consisting of extremely high levels of meat or meat by-products unless certain vitamins, minerals, and other nutrients have been balanced. The only time supplementation of meat is recommended is when pets are very active (such as working dogs) or have an extra-large litter and need additional food intake to provide sufficient milk production and maintain normal body condition.

Table scraps: The addition of table scraps to a dog's diet should be limited. A small amount of table scraps, five to ten percent, can be added for variety and flavor. Although this adds extra calories, normally it will not upset the nutritional balance of commercial diets. Care should be taken to avoid adding poultry, chops or other types of bones that can splinter and cause injury to the intestinal system.

A dog is less likely to become a finicky eater if fed on a constant diet of a nutritionally balanced commercial food. Supplementing with excessive meat or table scraps can create a "problem" eater which may cause problems for the owner. Many pets accustomed to variety in their diet will demand to continue a diet with variety. Just because a pet prefers a particular food is no sign that the product provides a nutritionally complete and balanced diet.

Milk: Although there is some variation among individual dogs, normally the adult is not capable of digesting and utilizing large amounts of milk in its diet. Although milk is a nutritious food, the consumption of a high level can cause diarrhea.

Prior to weaning, many puppies are fed a mixture of milk, baby cereal, vitamins, eggs, meat or other similar ingredients. This type of diet is both expensive and time-consuming to prepare. Most important, it may not be nutritionally complete and balanced.

Puppies can begin nibbling solid food at three to four weeks of age and should be allowed continuous access to it. A complete and balanced commercial dry food that is moistened with water is recommended. Such a diet is nutritious, gets the pre-weaned pet to eating correctly and facilitates weaning. The amount of water added to the food can gradually be decreased, and the product fed dry, if desired, when the pups are twelve to sixteen weeks old. Your veterinarian should recommend types and amounts of supplements given to pets who require special dietary management.

Even though complete and balanced commercial dog foods make it easy to give a dog the nutrition it needs during every stage of life, the nutritional requirements of dogs do vary greatly over the course of their lives.

Normal, healthy dogs that are not pregnant, nursing, or working hard have relatively low nutritional requirements. For example, adult dogs on a maintenance diet have a lower energy requirement than growing puppies, and can tend to become obese if overfed on a high energy diet. A good quality commercial diet, that is complete and balanced for all life stages, will supply proper nutrition for normal dogs of any age.

Some commercial diets are especially designed to meet the needs of adult dogs. As an example, Purina Fit & Trim brand contains less fat, fewer calories, and a lower level of protein for adult dogs who are not pregnant, nursing or working hard.

In general, feed the normally active adult dog a good-quality complete and balanced diet according to these guidelines:

Don't add vitamins, minerals or other supplemental nutrients.

Feed once a day. If the dog is very large, you may want

to feed twice a day. If obesity is not a problem, you can leave the dry food available to the dog at all times.

It is not necessary to vary the dog's diet.

Feed intake will vary from day to day, and from dog to dog. If the dog maintains good body condition, has normal stamina, and appears to be in good health, he is getting the right amount of nutrition.

If you have a question concerning your dog's proper weight, check with your veterinarian.

Many factors can influence the amount of food a dog needs. They include:

Breed size: Small-breed dogs (less than 20 pounds) need about 30 percent more calories, pound for pound, than do dogs in the 20 to 75 pound range. Large-breed dogs (over 75 pounds) need about 15 percent fewer calories per pound of body weight than those in the 20 to 75 pound range.

Outside temperature: Dogs that spend most of their time outdoors during cold winter weather need additional food. Long-term Purina research studies show that dogs consume about 30 percent more calories during December through February than during June through August.

As a general rule, dogs need about 7.5 percent fewer calories with each ten degree rise in temperature. Like people, dogs are individuals, with individual food requirements. Even when all other factors are the same, two dogs of the same size, age and activity may need different amounts of food simply because they have different metabolism rates.

FEEDING PUPPIES

In most cases, feeding your dog is easy. You should give your dog all it cares to eat of a complete and balanced commercial diet. If the dog seems to be gaining too much weight, reduce its food intake. If the dog seems too thin, and there are no health problems, encourage it to eat more.

Fresh water in a clean bowl should be available to puppies at all times.

Even though complete and balanced commercial dog foods make it easy to give dogs the nutrition they need during every stage of life, the nutritional requirements of dogs do vary.

Some commercial diets, however, are formulated to help meet a special nutritional need. For example, Purina® Puppy Chow® brand puppy food contains higher levels of protein, iron and other ingredients in a highly palatable combination of ingredients that help puppies get all the food they need for growth.

Most puppies are ready to be weaned when they are six weeks old. If they have started to eat solid foods from their mother's dish at three to four weeks of age, it's not unusual for puppies to begin to wean themselves at about four to five weeks of age.

For the first few weeks after they are weaned, the puppies' food should be fed moistened to encourage adequate food intake. You can gradually decrease the amount of water added to the food beginning when the pups are about 12 weeks old.

During the first few months after they are weaned, puppies require about twice the amount of nutrients per pound of body weight as when they are adults. Young puppies should be fed at least three times a day until the puppies' food requirements, per pound of body weight, begin to level off as the puppies mature. You can reduce their feeding schedule to twice a day when they are four or five months old, and to once a day when they are eight or nine months old. (For some large and giant breeds, which continue to grow up to two years, you may continue to feed twice a day throughout their life.)

If puppies are fed a complete and balanced diet, they do not need supplemental vitamins, minerals, or meat. In a study of Labrador retriever pups at the Purina Pet Care Center, researchers determined the effect of adding a vitamin supplement to Purina Puppy Chow. The pups were studied form the time they were weaned until they were one year old. The results are given in Table 3.

Table 3

Avg. Weight Gain, lbs.	Puppy Chow	Puppy Chow (plus Vitamins)
Males	76.4	75.1
Females	65.0	66.5
Avg Length Gain, ins.		
Males	22.0	22.7
Females	20.4	20.0

No difference in the measurable growth factor or general body condition was observed between the two groups of puppies.

Other studies at the Pet Care Center and studies by other researchers have suggested that over-supplementation can be detrimental to proper development as Table 2 illustrates. This study of the effects of calcium and phosphorus supplementation show that high levels of minerals in the diet could slow, or even stop growth.

Table 4

	Ration 1	Ration 2
Amt. of Calcium	2.3%*	4.34%
Amt. of Phosphorus	2.04%*	3.85%
Weight gain, lbs.	4.9	-0.3
Length gain, ins.	4.8	1.2

*Subsequent research has shown that even these levels are somewhat higher than the desired amount.

These studies began with eight-week puppies and ran for five weeks. They indicate why a veterinarian should decide if individual puppies require supplementation.

FEEDING FOR REPRODUCTION

Good nutrition is important during pregnancy. Developing pups depend on the mother's diet for essential nutrients, while the female needs to maintain good body condition to be prepared for the stress of nursing. During the female's pregnancy and while she is nursing, be sure to feed a diet that is complete and balanced for all life stage.

Surprisingly, the nutrient requirements of the female during the first six or seven weeks of pregnancy are not much higher than for maintenance. During the last two to three weeks of pregnancy, food intake should be increased 20-25 percent.

Unless a female has a tendency to put on too much weight during pregnancy, she can be given all the food she wants to eat. If she seems to be losing weight, it may be helpful to add water to her food according to package directions. This will make the food taste better and she will probably eat more. It is neither necessary nor advisable to add any other supplement to a complete and balanced diet during the gestation period.

Milk production is one of the most nutritionally demanding stages of a dog's life. A complete and balanced commercial diet will supply the nutrition the female needs during this stressful time, but you may need to ensure that she eats all the food she needs. Add water to the mother's food and feed her at least twice a day. Moistening the food will encourage her to eat more and make it easier for the puppies to nibble from their mother's pan.

If, after the food is moistened, the mother is still not eating enough to maintain good body condition and milk production, ten to fifteen percent meat can be added to the diet. A limited amount of meat will improve the palatability of the diet, which results in increased food intake, without altering the nutritional balance of the diet.

The demands of nursing increase as the pups grow. By the end of the fourth week of nursing, the female and her pups may consume more than three times as much food as during her maintenance period.

The weaning process can be difficult if the mammary glands continue to produce milk at a high rate when the puppies are about to be weaned. Possible serious complications can develop.

Restrict the mother's food during the first few days of weaning. This will help limit her milk production. (While restricting the mother's food, it is especially important to give her all the fresh water she wants.) On the day you plan to wean the pups, don't give the mother any food. On the next day, feed her one-fourth the amount she ate before she was bred. On the third day, feed her one-half her maintenance level. On the fourth day, feed her three-fourths, and feed the full maintenance amount on the fith day. From the time the puppies are weaned until the next breeding, feed the female to maintain good body condition, without obesity.

If the litter is quite large, the female may be thin when the puppies are weaned. In that case, the female should be given extra food after the fifth day of weaning until her normal body condition returns.

With a complete and balanced diet, there is no need to supplement it. In fact, vitamin and mineral supplements can be harmful to a dog on a nutritionally complete ration.

FEEDING THE HARDWORKING DOG

In most cases, feeding your dog is easy. You should give your dog all it cares to eat of a complete and balanced commercial diet. If the dog seems to be gaining too much weight, reduce its food intake. If the dog seems too thin, and there are no health problems, encourage it to eat more. Fresh water in a clean bowl should be available to the dog at all times.

Complete and balanced commercial dog foods make it easy to give dogs the nutrition they need during every stage of life, even though the nutritional requirements of dogs do vary.

The hardworking dog uses a large amount of energy which must be supplied by a good-quality, nutritious food. While it is important to give such dogs all the food they need, they should not be maintained in an overweight condition. Ordinarily, the dog will obtain all the nutrition needed if fed once a day. However, if the dog seems thin but otherwise in good health, twice-a-day feeding of a moistened commercial diet should help the active dog eat more and maintain the desired body condition. Feeding the food moistened will help increase food intake. Digestive problems can develop if the dog is fed immediately before or immediately after a period of hard work. Immediately after working, a dog should be allowed to drink cool (not cold) water and rest for a period of time.

A diet intended only for maintenance dogs is not suitable for hardworking dogs. Some commercial dog foods are especially designed for the working dog. Purina Hi-Pro dog meal, for example, contains higher levels of protein and enery, all in a dense, highly palatable particle that helps the dog eat enough food to meet its higher nutritional requirements.

With a complete and balanced diet, it is usually not necessary to supplement. Vitamin and mineral supplements can be harmful to a normal dog that is eating a nutritionally complete ration. Vitamin and mineral supplements should be given only in unusual situtations and then under the direction of a veterinarian.

If the dog is extremely active, particularly in cold weather, supplementation with meat or a small amount of fat can help a dog meet its energy requirements. These supplements will provide additional calories and will make the food taste better to the dog which helps increase total food intake.

If animal fat is added to the food, we recommend a level of no more than two or three percent, or approximately one tablespoon of fat for each four to five cups of dry food. Supplemental meat can make up as much as twenty percent of the dog's ration (by volume) without affecting the nutritional balance of the food, if other supplements are not added. Your veterinarian can determine whether your dog is in good condition, and can recommend the right feeding and exercise program to help maintain your dog's good health.